MEDIEVAL DUBLIN XVII

This volume is dedicated
by the Friends of Medieval Dublin
to the memory of

Eileen Reilly

BA (NUI), MSc (Sheff.), PhD (Dubl.)
(1970–2018)

Medieval Dublin XVII

Seán Duffy

EDITOR

FOUR COURTS PRESS

Typeset in 10.5 pt on 12.5 pt Ehrhardt by
Carrigboy Typesetting Services for
FOUR COURTS PRESS LTD
7 Malpas Street, Dublin 8, Ireland
www.fourcourtspress.ie
and in North America for
FOUR COURTS PRESS
c/o IPG, 814 N Franklin St, Chicago, IL 60622.

A catalogue record for this title is available
from the British Library.

ISBN 978–1–84682–730–3 hbk
ISBN 978–1–84682–731–0 pbk

This book is published with the active support of
Dublin City Council/Comhairle Chathair Átha Cliath.

Printed in England
by TJ International, Padstow, Cornwall.

Contents

Abbreviations

AClon	*The annals of Clonmacnoise, being the annals of Ireland from the earliest period to* AD *1408 translated into English* AD *1627 by Conell Mageoghagan*, ed. D. Murphy (Dublin, 1896)
AFM	*Annala rioghachta Eireann: annals of the kingdom of Ireland by the Four Masters, from the earliest period to the year 1616*, ed. J. O'Donovan, 7 vols (Dublin, 1851)
AH	*Analecta Hibernica, including the report of the Irish Manuscripts Commission* (IMC, Dublin 1930–)
AI	*The annals of Inisfallen (MS Rawlinson B. 503)*, ed. S. Mac Airt (DIAS, Dublin, 1951)
ALCé	*The annals of Loch Cé: a chronicle of Irish affairs from* AD *1014 to* AD *1590*, ed. W.M. Hennessy, 2 vols (RS, London, 1871; repr. IMC, Dublin, 1939)
ATig	'Annals of Tigernach', ed. W. Stokes in *Revue Celtique*, 16 (1895) 374–419; 17 (1896) 6–33, 119–263, 337–420; 18 (1897) 9–59, 150–97, 267–303; reprinted in two vols (Felinfach, 1993).
AU	*Annala Uladh ('Annals of Ulster'), otherwise Annala Senait ('Annals of Senat'): a chronicle of Irish affairs* AD *431 to* AD *1540*, ed. W.M. Hennessey and B. MacCarthy, 4 vols (Dublin, 1887–1901); *The annals of Ulster (to* AD *1131)*, ed. S. Mac Airt and G. Mac Niocaill (Dublin, 1983)
Bateson, *Customs*	Mary Bateson, *Borough customs*, 2 vols, Selden Society (London, 1904–6)
BL	British Library, London
CARD	J.T. Gilbert (ed.), *Calendar of ancient records of Dublin*, 19 vols (Dublin, 1889–1944)
CCD	*Calendar of Christ Church deeds*, ed. M.J. McEnery and Raymond Refaussé (Dublin, 2001)
CCR	*Calendar of the close rolls* [...], *1272–[1509]*, 47 vols (PRO, London, 1892–1963)
CDI	*Calendar of documents relating to Ireland, 1171–1307*, ed. H.S. Sweetman and G.F. Handcock, 5 vols (PRO, London, 1875–86)
CGG	*Cogadh Gaedhil re Gallaibh*, ed. and trans. James Henthorn Todd (London, 1867)
CIRCLE	Peter Crooks (ed.), *A calendar of Irish Chancery Letters, c.1244–1509* (available at http://chancery.tcd.ie/)

Civil Survey	*The Civil Survey,* AD *1654–56*, ed. R.C. Simington, 10 vols (Dublin, 1931–61)
CJRI	*Calendar of the justiciary rolls of Ireland*, ed. James Mills et al., 3 vols (Dublin, 1905–56)
Clarke et al. (eds), *Ireland and Scandinavia*	H.B. Clarke, Máire Ní Mhaonaigh and Raghnall Ó Floinn (eds), *Ireland and Scandinavia in the early Viking Age* (Dublin, 1998)
Clarke, *Dublin, Pt 1* (IHTA)	H.B. Clarke (ed.), *Dublin Part I, to 1610*, IHTA, no. 11 (RIA, Dublin, 2002)
CPL	*Calendar of entries in the papal registers relating to Great Britain and Ireland: papal letters* (London, 1893–)
CPR	*Calendar of the patent rolls* [...], *1232*–[*1509*], 53 vols (PRO, London, 1911)
CPR Ire., Hen. VIII–Eliz.	*Calendar of the patent and close rolls of chancery in Ireland, Henry VIII to 18th Elizabeth*, ed. J. Morrin (Dublin, 1862)
CS	*Chronicum Scotorum*, ed. W.M. Hennessy (London, 1866).
CStM	*Chartularies of Saint Mary's abbey, Dublin*, ed. J.T. Gilbert, 2 vols (RS, London, 1884–6)
DGMR	Philomena Connolly and Geoffrey Martin (eds), *Dublin Guild Merchant Roll* (Dublin, 1992)
DHR	*Dublin Historical Record*
DIB	*Dictionary of Irish biography*, ed. J. McGuire and J. Quinn, 9 vols (Cambridge, 2009)
Extents Ir. mon. possessions	*Extents of Irish monastic possessions, 1540–1541* [...], ed. N.B. White (IMC, Dublin, 1943)
FAI	Joan Newlon Radner (ed.), *Fragmentary annals of Ireland* (Dublin, 1978)
Gilbert (ed.), *Hist. & mun. docs*	J.T. Gilbert (ed.), *Historic and municipal documents of Ireland,* AD *1172–1320, from the archives of the city of Dublin* (RS, London, 1870)
Griffith (ed.), *Cal. inquisitions*	Margaret C. Griffith (ed.), *Calendar of inquisitions formerly in the office of the chief remembrance of the exchequer prepared from the MSS of the Irish Record Commission* (IMC, Dublin, 1991)
Hogan, *Onomasticon*	Edmond Hogan (ed.), *Onomasticon Goedelicum: locorum et tribuum Hiberniae et Scotiae. An index, with identifications, to the Gaelic names of places and tribes* (Dublin, 1910)
IAS	[missing]
IHS	*Irish Historical Studies*
IHTA	Irish Historic Towns Atlas (RIA, Dublin, 1986–)
IMC	*Coimisiún Láimhscríbhinní na hÉireann* (The Irish Manuscripts Commission)

JRSAI	*Journal of the Royal Society of Antiquaries of Ireland*
Mac Niocaill, *Buirgéisí*	Gearóid Mac Niocaill, *Na Burgéisí, XII–XV aois*, 2 vols (Dublin, 1964)
MGH Script. rer. Germ.	*Monumenta Germaniae Historica: Scriptores rerum Germanicarum* (Hanover, etc., 1841–)
MGH SS	*Monumenta Germaniae Historica: Scriptores* (Hanover, etc., 1826–)
NAI	National Archives of Ireland
NLI	National Library of Ireland, Dublin
O'Brien, *Corpus geneal. Hib.*	M.A. O'Brien (ed.), *Corpus genealogiarum Hiberniae* (Dublin, 1962)
PRIA	*Proceedings of the Royal Irish Academy*
Reg. Alen	*A calendar of Archbishop Alen's register,* c.*1172–1534*, ed. C. McNeill (RSAI, Dublin, 1950)
Reg. All Hallows	*Registrum prioratus Omnium Sanctorum juxta Dublin*, ed. R. Butler (IAS, Dublin, 1845)
Reg. St John	*Register of the Hospital of S. John the Baptist without the New Gate, Dublin*, ed. Eric St John Brooks (IMC, Dublin, 1936)
Reg. St Thomas	*Register of the abbey of St Thomas, Dublin*, ed. J.T. Gilbert (London, 1889)
Rep. DKPRI	*Reports of the deputy keeper of the public records in Ireland* (Dublin, 1869–)
RIA	Royal Irish Academy
RLC	*Rotuli litterarum clausarum, 1204–24* [*etc.*], ed. T.D. Hardy, 2 vols (London, 1833–44)
TNA	The National Archives of the United Kingdom [including former PRO], Kew

Contributors

GILL BOAZMAN holds a PhD in archaeology from University College Cork.

SHEILA DOOLEY holds degrees in history and archaeology from University College Dublin and Maynooth University and currently works with Tandem Design, Belfast.

PAUL DRYBURGH is principal record specialist at the National Archives, Kew.

ÁINE FOLEY holds a PhD in medieval history from Trinity College Dublin.

PHYLLIS GAFFNEY is formerly a senior lecturer in French at University College Dublin.

MÁIRE GEANEY holds a PhD in archaeology from University College Cork.

ANTOINE GIACOMETTI is a project manager with Archaeology Plan, Dublin.

RUTH JOHNSON is the Dublin City Archaeologist.

RANDOLPH JONES is an independent scholar, based in England, who has an interest in medieval Ireland.

THERESA O'BYRNE holds a PhD in medieval studies from the University of Notre Dame and currently teaches at the Delbarton School in Morristown, NJ.

DAGMAR Ó RIAIN-RAEDEL is a historian and author formerly of the School of History at University College Cork.

YOLANDE DE PONTFARCY SEXTON is formerly a senior lecturer in French at University College Dublin.

LINZI SIMPSON is an archaeological consultant and project manager.

Editor's preface

This is the seventeenth volume in a series of publications arising from a symposium organized by the Friends of Medieval Dublin and held annually in May in Trinity College Dublin. The volume, besides freshly commissioned material, contains the published text of papers delivered at the Medieval Dublin Symposium held on Saturday 21 May 2016 before a capacity audience of members of the public, academics and students. The 'Friends', and the editor in particular, are grateful to the Department of History at Trinity for the financial support that makes it possible to run the symposia as an event entirely free of charge to the general public.

The 'Friends' is a wholly not-for-profit organization that exists primarily to foster interest in Dublin's wonderful medieval heritage. In addition to the annual Symposium and this resultant volume, we organize free walking tours of the medieval city conducted by volunteer members of our group, a free lunchtime lecture-series which has been taking place for many years now in the excellent Wood Quay Venue, and we have a website which contains notices of our activities, news items, an archive of our past events, and important educational aids such as an ongoing bibliography of medieval Dublin (see www.fmd.ie).

It has only proved possible to publish this seventeenth volume in the *Medieval Dublin* series because of the ongoing commitment to the project by Dublin City Council. The unseen hand behind this collaboration is that of the City Heritage Officer, Charles Duggan, whose support the editor greatly appreciates. Likewise, the series, and all the activities of the Friends of Medieval Dublin, benefit hugely from the input and encouragement of the City Archaeologist, Dr Ruth Johnson, and it is a privilege to include in this volume her description of an extraordinary new resource that she has spearheaded, the County Dublin Archaeology GIS, which contains previously hard to access unpublished archaeological 'grey literature' and information generated through the 3267 archaeological investigations conducted under licence in Co. Dublin prior to and including the year 2012. Available at the Heritage Council's excellent site www.heritagemaps.ie, this new resource provides electronic access to copies of all the available archaeological reports for diving, excavation, and geophysical survey to 2012. Along with metadata, it includes copies of the National Museum of Ireland's topographical files for the county, links to the *Excavations* bulletin summaries at www.excavations.ie and a number of historic and synthetic maps provided by the Royal Irish Academy's Irish Historic Towns Atlas.

The entire *Medieval Dublin* series has been published by Four Courts Press for whose collaboration and commitment the Friends of Medieval Dublin remain most grateful. With regard to the current volume, the editor would like to thank Martin Fanning for the patience he has shown and the attention to detail which has characterized his work on the papers below.

Please fell free to contact the editor (sduffy@tcd.ie) if you have work meriting publication relating to any aspect of the story of Dublin or its geographical and cultural hinterland from its earliest origins to the emergence of the early modern city, in particular, the results of unpublished archaeological investigations.

SEÁN DUFFY
Chairman
Friends of Medieval Dublin

Dr Eileen Reilly

(15 May 1970–27 July 2018)

Eileen Reilly was a consummate professional and a pioneer in environmental archaeology. She single-handedly created a new field in Ireland in the study of beetles and was instrumental in the establishment of the Experimental Archaeology Centre at UCD, where she was an adjunct research fellow. In contributing to position papers, guidelines and standards, her contribution to the wider discipline cannot be overstated; Eileen served as vice-Chair, then acting-Chair of IAI, was one of the driving forces behind the IPEAN, and a member of Unite; her commitment to her profession and its standards was unwavering. Archaeology was her calling and her passion.

Eileen's love of archaeology began early, a gift from her late mother, Jo, and was nurtured at home and at school as she grew up in Donaghmede. On leaving school, Eileen studied Archaeology and Geography at UCD, graduating in 1992 with honours. She completed her masters at Sheffield University, where she specialized in the study of beetles.

Returning to Ireland, Eileen worked on numerous excavations and while employed on the Lisheen Mines Project, she completed a diploma in EIA and established her first laboratory in Killester. Throughout her distinguished career, she was involved with major multi-disciplinary projects with all of the key commercial, academic and state bodies.

In 2008, she was awarded her PhD from Trinity, for her research on woodland history and how natural and human-driven change through time affected insect biodiversity. In 2011, she secured funding to assess and catalogue the environmental remains from the iconic Viking site of Fishamble Street. This amazing archive of environmental material, which will be available for study by future generations of scientists, influenced the more recent focus of Eileen's research, and in 2013, she secured prestigious Government of Ireland funding to pursue her post-doctoral research at UCD, examining living conditions in Ireland and Europe.

At the time of her passing, she had a significant and growing international reputation, and was sought out by colleagues across Europe and, indeed, the world for her experience, expertise and insight into her specialist area.

Eileen's book, the culmination of her life's work, 'Living conditions in early medieval Europe: a case study from Viking Age Fishamble Street, Dublin' will be published shortly, along with other papers from her research, cementing her legacy as one of the truly great scholars of paleoecology and environmental archaeology and foremost scientific minds of our time.

As colleagues, we are bereft at the untimely loss, of not only a colleague with a resolute, determined, focus and commitment to our shared profession, but also of an amazing, supportive, kind and loving friend, always there with an encouraging word and balanced, articulate and well thought out advice.

Eileen is survived by her husband, Rónán, their daughter, Áine, her father, Willy, sister Abina, brothers Bill and Joe, their families and a wide circle of friends. To them, we extend our heartfelt condolences.

LORNA O'DONNELL
RÓNÁN SWAN

Material culture and identity in the southern hinterland of Hiberno-Scandinavian Dublin

GILL BOAZMAN

The material culture of the half-barony of Rathdown, immediately south of Dublin, is characterized by one of the highest densities of early medieval ecclesiastical sites in mainland Ireland (fig. 1.1), a cluster of mortared stone churches and a group of twelfth-century crosses.[1] It also possesses two exceptional elements: first, an assemblage of grave-slabs with unique incised motifs and, second, excavated evidence of rural Scandinavian settlement.[2] Extensive documentary records indicate a considerable amount of pre-Anglo-Norman ecclesiastical landholding in the area.[3] This contribution will consider the interplay of these elements in the formation of a complex multicultural identity in eleventh- and twelfth-century Rathdown.

THE EARLY HISTORY OF CUALU

Kings and overlords

The half-barony of Rathdown and part of the barony of Uppercross which form the study area for this paper include both south Co. Dublin and north Co. Wicklow. It approximates to the ancient kingdom of Cualu in the seventh century,[4] from Tallaght and Clondalkin in the west, to Delgany in the

1 The average density of the nine study areas of the 'Making Christian Landscapes' project was approximately one ecclesiastical site in 10 to 20 km^2. Rathdown had a density of one ecclesiastical site in 4 km^2 (Tomás Ó Carragáin and John Sheehan (eds), 'Making Christian landscapes: settlement, society and regionality in early medieval Ireland' (Unpublished report for the Heritage Council, 2010), p. 242; Gill Boazman, 'Theme and variations: Christianity and regional landscapes in early medieval Ireland' (PhD, UCC, 2014), p. 574; Tomás Ó Carragáin, *Churches in early medieval Ireland: architecture, ritual and memory* (New Haven and London, 2010), p. 238; Rhoda Cronin, 'Late high crosses in Munster' in John Sheehan and Michael Monk (eds), *Early medieval Munster: archaeology, history and society* (Cork, 1998), pp 138–9. 2 Patrick Healy, *Pre-Norman grave-slabs and cross-inscribed stones in the Dublin area* (Dublin, 2009); John Ó Néill, 'Excavations of pre-Norman structures on the site of an enclosed early Christian cemetery at Cherrywood, Co. Dublin' in Seán Duffy (ed.), *Medieval Dublin VII* (Dublin, 2006), pp 66–88. 3 Jocelyn Otway-Ruthven, 'The medieval church lands of County Dublin' in J.A. Watt, J.B. Morrall and F.X. Martin (eds), *Medieval studies presented to Aubrey Gwynn SJ* (Dublin, 1961), pp 54–73; Paul MacCotter, 'The church lands of the diocese of Dublin: reconstruction and history' in Seán Duffy (ed.), *Medieval Dublin XIII* (Dublin, 2013), pp 81–107. 4 The annals, as late as 1144 (AFM), refer to the area as Cualu and so I have used that contemporary title. 'Rathdown'

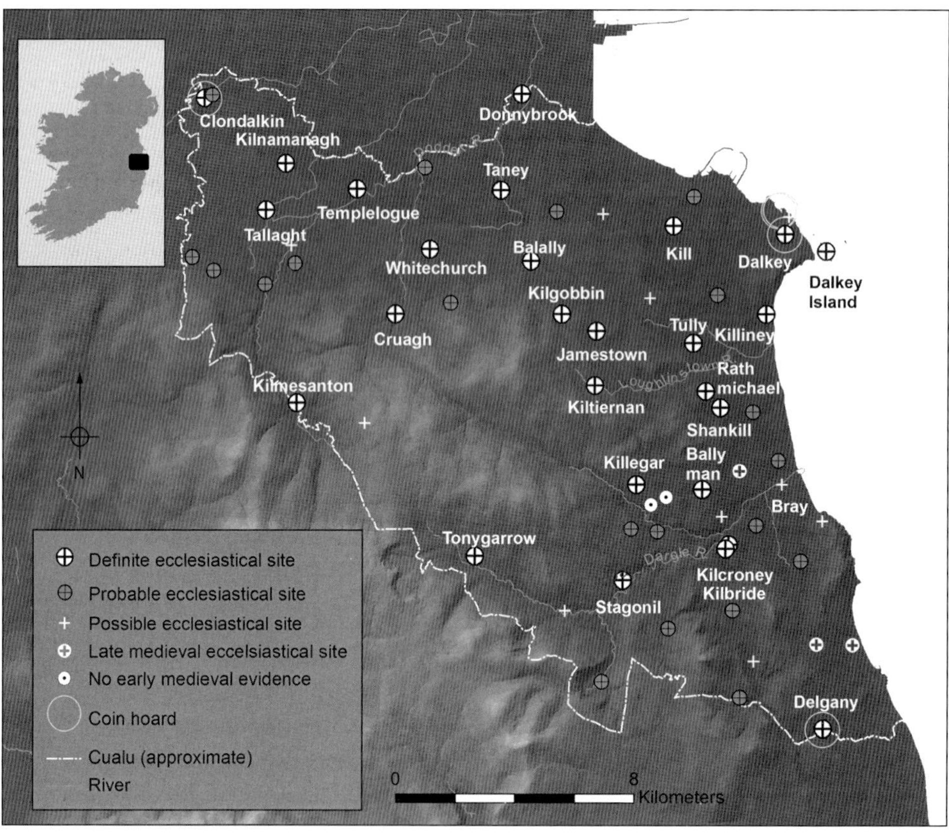

1.1 Ecclesiastical sites in Cualu, categorized by strength of evidence for early medieval foundation; also indicating coin hoards at these sites (map: G. Boazman)

southeast. As I have already published a paper on the social organization of Cualu in the pre-Viking period, a brief summary of the early period will suffice here.[5] This will stress regional characteristics that are germane to mostly later events which form the matter of the present paper.

Cualu was initially part of the kingdom of the Dál Messin Corb, whose influence in the fifth century may have extended to the Boyne in the north, to Kildare in the southwest and as far as Uisnech in Mide.[6] This area was

appears to be a post-Anglo-Norman designation (Liam Price, 'Ráth Oinn', *Eigse*, 7:3 (1955), 182–90, at 188–9). 5 Gill Boazman, 'Hallowed by saints, coveted by kings: Christianization and land tenure in Rathdown, *c*.400–900' in Tomás Ó Carragáin and Sam Turner (eds), *Making Christian landscapes in Atlantic Europe: conversion and consolidation in the early Middle Ages* (Cork, 2016), pp 22–53. 6 Henry Morris, 'Ancient Cualu, where was it?', *JRSAI*, 7 (1936), 280–3; Edward Gwynn, *The Metrical Dindseanchas*, 4 vols (Dublin, 1905; second reprint 1991), iii, p. 105; Pádraig Ó Riain, *Corpus genealogiarum sanctorum Hiberniae*

curtailed by the advance of the Uí Néill into Mide in the late fifth and sixth centuries and the rise of the Uí Dúnlainge to the west in the eighth century. Cualu was a fertile area as indicated by excavation evidence of arable cultivation over millennia. This is also emphasized by documentary references to the 'beer of Cualu (*coirm Chualann*)'.[7] A further asset of Cualu was its maritime access evidenced by finds of fifth- to seventh-century Mediterranean pottery, Frankish glassware and probably French-sourced E ware from Dalkey Island.[8] These contacts with post-Roman Europe facilitated the import of Christianity to Cualu, evinced in documented early missions from France, but also in ecclesiastical sites associated with saints from the western areas of Britain. The success of conversion is indicated by a number of sites with Dál Messin Corb founders.[9]

The evident advantages of Cualu were not lost on neighbouring kin-groups and by the seventh century the Uí Máil, who provided some overkings of Leinster up to 715 (AU), took over the governance and assets of Cualu only to be dislodged by Uí Dúnchada branch of the Uí Dúnlainge.[10] The three major branches of the Uí Dúnlainge controlled an area to the west of Cualu, roughly from Naas to Mullaghmast.[11] The Uí Dúnchada ruled the eastern part of Cualu through their underlords the Uí Briúin Chualann.[12]

Land tenure

Documentary evidence of the early Anglo-Norman period indicates a large amount of land in Cualu in ecclesiastical hands, either of the archbishop of Dublin or of reformed orders.[13] It was common for donations to these later foundations to be of land associated with pre-Anglo-Norman ecclesiastical sites.[14] At least part of this land was almost certainly granted to the ecclesiastical sites at their foundation, mostly in the late fifth to seventh centuries, but a charter of the early thirteenth century suggests that this land may have carried impost, meaning dues to the donor. This charter confirms the lands of Holy Trinity donated by local magnates before the coming of the Anglo-Normans.[15] The overlords and donors of the lands of Tully in Cualu were members of an Hiberno-Scandinavian family, the Meic Turcaill, which would suggest they had the ecclesiastical land in their gift. It seems likely that the original benefactors of these ecclesiastical sites, the Dál Messin Corb and the Uí Máil, perceived these lands as providing not only supernatural

(Dublin, 1985), p. 30; Ailbhe MacShamhráin, *Church and polity in pre-Norman Ireland: the case of Glendalough* (Maynooth, 1996), p. 186. 7 Boazman, 'Hallowed by saints', pp 26, 35. 8 Ibid., pp 26–7. 9 Ibid., pp 27–8. 10 Ibid., pp 39–43. 11 Paul MacCotter, *Medieval Ireland: territorial, political and economic divisions* (Dublin, 2008), pp 163, 176–9. 12 Boazman, 'Hallowed by saints', pp 42–3. 13 Otway-Ruthven, 'Medieval church lands'; MacCotter, 'The church lands of the diocese of Dublin'. 14 Marie Therese Flanagan, *The transformation of the Irish church in the twelfth century* (Woodbridge, 2010), p. 132. 15 *Reg. Alen*, p. 28.

dividends but also as returning capital in kind to the donor and adding value to land improved by innovatory farming methods.[16] In an insecure political situation, donating land to the church had the advantage of hopefully putting it beyond the reach of rivals.[17]

A phrase in the commentary to *Félire Óengusso* underlines the entailment of ecclesiastical foundations in Cualu.[18] The bishops of Tully are depicted travelling to Brigit of Kildare and receiving hospitality. This is almost certainly parabolic for negotiation of terms with a new landlord, in this case the Uí Dúnchada. The extension of hospitality indicates the largesse of overlordship and subsequently Tully was associated with Brigit and thus Uí Dúnchada of Kildare.

As indicated above, the lands associated with Tully were granted to Holy Trinity. There is no date for the foundation of Tully although the *Félire* commentary seems to refer to already existing bishops, which could suggest that Tully was of local importance before the visit to Kildare. With regard to the social structure of the ecclesiastical estate there were finds of bone trial-pieces with Christian connotations from the excavated ringfort at Glebe just 500m southwest of the ecclesiastical site. The townland of Glebe is demonstrated on the terrier of the Down Survey to be still part of the ecclesiastical land of Tully in the seventeenth century and the three dates from the ringfort lie in a tight cluster around AD 650–870.[19] One trial-piece has the word 'Deo' inscribed, and the other a possible Chi-Rho and *trompe l'œil* cross and a fantastic avian quadruped. These examples, of both Latin literacy and artistic accomplishment,[20] would suggest that this was the dwelling place of ecclesiastical tenants. There is now a considerable amount of evidence for ringforts on ecclesiastical land which challenges the normative perception of ringforts as solely secular and settlement forms.[21]

16 Boazman, 'Hallowed by saints', pp 37–8; Charles Doherty, 'Some examples of hagiography as a source for Irish economic history', *Peritia*, 1 (1982), 300–28, at 311–12 for various entailments imposed on ecclesiastical land. 17 Boazman, 'Hallowed by saints', p. 52. 18 Whitley Stokes, *Félire Óengusso* (London, 1905), p. 65; Pádraig Ó Riain, *Feastdays of the saints, a history of Irish martyrologies*, vol. 85, Société des Bollandistes (2006), p. 189, suggests that most of the commentary is late twelfth century but that the piece pertaining to Tully is earlier, perhaps late eleventh century. 19 Matthew Seaver, 'Interchange: excavations in an early medieval landscape at Glebe and Laughanstown, Co. Dublin' in Christiaan Corlett and Michael Potterton (eds), *Settlement in early medieval Ireland in the light of recent archaeological excavations* (Dublin, 2011), pp 261–88, at pp 267–8. 20 See discussion in Boazman, 'Theme', pp 599–600 as to whether these were the work of students or more accomplished practitioners. 21 Tomás Ó Carragáin, 'A landscape converted: archaeology and early church organization on Iveragh and Dingle, Ireland' in Martin Carver (ed.), *The cross goes North: processes of conversion in northern Europe, AD 300–1300* (Woodbridge, 2003), pp 127–52, at p. 140; Gill Boazman, 'Theme', pp 697–700; Tomás Ó Carragáin, 'Archaeology of ecclesiastical estates in early medieval Ireland: a case study of the kingdom of Fir Maige', *Peritia*, 24–5 (2013–14), 266–302; Gill Boazman, 'Inchydoney in the early medieval period', *Clonakilty Historical and Archaeological Journal*, 1 (2015), 129–48,

To sum up the early period: the fertile area of Cualu with the advantages of a position on the eastern seaboard of Ireland was characterized by a high density of ecclesiastical sites, many from the conversion period. A succession of overlords endowed these with entailed small land-parcels granted partially for material gain and partially to keep control of a contested territory. By the end of the eighth century the Uí Dúnchada branch of the Uí Dúnlainge had established overlordship in Cualu and provided the economic foundation for a prestigious spiritual powerhouse at Tallaght.[22]

THE COMING OF THE SCANDINAVIANS

Initial contacts

Although accounts of Viking relationships with Ireland usually commence with raiding, particularly of ecclesiastical sites in the early ninth century, this would not be relevant to the kingdom of Cualu. In this area south of Dublin, despite the density of ecclesiastical sites, there is only one documentary record of a Viking attack on an ecclesiastical site, Clondalkin in 833 (AU).[23] The background to this anomaly must be sought in the relationship of the earliest Viking settlements to their immediate environs, the rapid and early development of permanent settlement on the Liffey and in the idiosyncratic ecclesiastical land tenure patterns of Rathdown, described above.

From the Viking point of view raiding doubled as economic exploration. Profit was obviously one motive and the taking of slaves and hostages fulfilled this aim. However short the stay though, provisions would be required for the onwards journey, and possibly refits for ships. Gathering a viable amount of slaves and non-perishable provisions would have taken time, as would the collection of materials and perhaps the coercing of local craftsmen to assist with boat repairs. The landscape position of ecclesiastical sites was often about

at 136–7; Gill Boazman, 'The fruitful marriage: a consideration of the nature of ecclesiastical landholding in two study areas of early medieval Ireland' in James Lyttelton and Matthew Stout (eds), *Church and settlement in Ireland* (Dublin, 2018), pp 31–59. **22** John T. Gilbert (ed. and trans.), '*Gineleach Ua Dúnchada* from LL245 in TCD h.2.18' in idem, *History of the city of Dublin*, 3 vols (Dublin, 1854), pp 403–8, at pp 405–6. **23** Colmán Etchingham, *Viking raids on Irish church settlements in the ninth century* (Maynooth, 1996), pp 60–70. Perhaps the attack on Clondalkin was tactical, to establish a fortified site to defend the hinterland of Dublin. It is possible that the anomalous 'stepped barrow' and enclosure at Ballymount Great was 'Amlaíb's fort' mentioned in the annal. The burial of a horse's head could indicate a Scandinavian ritual practice (Geraldine Stout, 'The archaeology of Ballymount Great, Co. Dublin' in Conleth Manning (ed.), *Dublin and beyond the Pale: studies in honour of Patrick Healy* (Dublin, 1998), pp 145–54, at p. 145; Maeve Sikora, 'Diversity in Viking Age horse burial: a comparative study of Norway, Iceland, Scotland and Ireland', *Journal of Irish Archaeology*, 12 and 13 (2003–4), 87–97), although the second reference is concerned with horses as human grave goods but stresses the symbolic importance of horses to the Scandinavians. Certainly the horse head deposit is unusual.

communication, with sea access or on navigable rivers. As rivers formed many early-medieval territorial borders, a position on them would lead to communication with two or more polities.[24] These natural economic networks established initially in the interests of conversion were similarly advantageous to Viking exploration of Ireland's assets.[25] Taking into consideration Viking settlement in Scotland, the Western Isles and England, it is likely that the acquiring of land was a further major motive.[26]

Although the earliest annalistic record of permanent overwintering settlement on the Liffey is 841 (AU), excavations over the course of the last twenty years have indicated earlier evidence of Viking long-term activity in the Dublin area. Burials of three young men with both weapons and trading artefacts at South Great George's Street fall within a very close range of 670–880 (95% probability) and a fourth, 786–995 (95% probability). Oxygen isotope analysis showed two of them to be from close to the Atlantic, Ireland or Scotland and the other two showed values that suggested an upbringing in Scandinavia.[27] They lie around 250m northeast of the excavated site of the cemetery at Golden Lane close to the later church of St Michael le Pole. At Golden Lane, at pre-Viking levels, east-to-west-orientated, unfurnished burials were found and there were four burials with Viking artefacts, one of which had a date pre-832.[28] This almost certainly indicates Viking settlement, even if temporary, adjacent to the assets of an ecclesiastical site and close to the original course of the Poddle River and its natural pool Duiblinn before the annalistic record of the *longphort* ('ship-enclosure').

Longphuirt *and ecclesiastical settlements*

Evidence of this utilization of the existing assets of the ecclesiastical network can be seen at other proposed early Viking settlements. The *longphort* at Annagassan, Co. Louth, was recorded in 841 (AU) and is situated adjacent to the ecclesiastical site of Linn Duachaill. Similarly, Athlunkard on the Shannon estuary was close to Kilquane. A further example is the recently excavated site of Woodstown, which provided extensive evidence of the processing technologies of a bullion economy and lies just 500m from the ecclesiastical

24 Padraig Ó Riain, 'Boundary association in early Irish society', *Studia Celtica*, 7 (1972), 12–29, at 18, 26. 25 Colmán Etchingham, 'Vikings at Annagassan: the evidence of the annals and the wider context' in Howard B. Clarke and Ruth Johnson (eds), *The Vikings in Ireland and beyond, before and after the battle of Clontarf* (Dublin, 2015), pp 117–28, at pp 125, 127. 26 Christopher Morris, 'Raiders, traders and settlers: the early Viking Age in Scotland' in Howard B. Clarke, Máire Ní Mhaonaigh and Raghnall Ó Floinn (eds), *Ireland and Scandinavia in the early Viking Age* (Dublin, 1998), pp 73–103, at pp 84–7; Dawn M. Hadley, *The Vikings in England: settlement, society and culture* (Manchester, 2006), pp 84–9. 27 Linzi Simpson, 'Viking warrior burials in Dublin: is this the *longphort*?' in Seán Duffy (ed.), *Medieval Dublin VI* (2005), pp 11–62, at pp 37–53. 28 Edmund O'Donovan, 'The Irish, the Vikings and the English: new archaeological evidence from excavations at Golden Lane, Dublin' in Seán Duffy (ed.), *Medieval Dublin VIII* (2008), pp 39–108, at pp 52–3.

site of Killoteran, which possessed a horizontal mill. Dunrally, a raised mound on the Slaney, lies across the river from Cluain dá an Dobair (Cloney).[29]

So how does this association of early Viking settlement and ecclesiastical foundations pertain to Rathdown? John Bradley provided the seminal work on the hinterlands of the port-towns. His premise was that the excavations of Hiberno-Scandinavian Dublin indicated not a way station but a permanent dense settlement. This restriction of settlement to the port-towns differed from the more dispersed rural evidence of similar Scandinavian settlement in Scotland and the east of England. The corollary was that 'a town cannot exist without its hinterland'.[30] This concept of a density of population in a confined area requiring provisions from surrounding territories was a novel one in early ninth-century Ireland where settlement was dispersed and self-sufficient. Probably goods were taken by coercion initially but exploration of the hinterland for this purpose, like the original raids, must have been partly an information-gathering exercise. The information that came back must have been that, as described above, the southern hinterland of the Dublin settlement was an insecure political entity much of whose fertile land was in ecclesiastical hands. A reference from the monastery of Tallaght probably refers to this early period; the ecclesiastics complain that they are forced to break their fast and eat meat because the *geintes* (the 'heathens') took their corn.[31]

The efforts of the Irish kings in the ninth century permanently restricted Viking settlement to the towns. For example the 867 attack on 'Amlaib's fort' at Clondalkin by the Loígis and the Uí Bairrche (AU) represented, just twenty-seven years after the annalistic record of the *longphort*, a curtailment of even a localized fortified hinterland around Dublin.[32] So, instead of being sole controllers of the hinterland, the rulers of Dublin became part of the intricate weave of tribute and land tenure that comprised Cualu, joining the extant hierarchy of Uí Dúnchada and their underkings, Uí Briúin Chualann, and the remnants of the Uí Máil. However, there may have been a difference that eased their entry to land tenure. The mutual tribute scheme of early medieval Irish 'clientship' was based in the gifting of things and in-kind payment. The Scandinavians introduced the representational economy of payment in silver and this may have provided a rival incentive for negotiation. A very high percentage of coin hoards, and of ingot-hoards with some coin occurs at

29 Etchingham, 'Annagassan', p. 117; Eamonn P. Kelly and Edmund O'Donovan, 'A Viking *longphort* near Athlunkard, Co. Clare', *Archaeology Ireland*, 12:4 (1998), 13–16; Ian Russell and Maurice J. Hurley (eds), *Woodstown, a Viking-Age settlement in Co. Waterford* (Dublin, 2014); Eamonn P. Kelly and John Maas, 'Vikings on the Barrow: Dunrally, a possible Viking *longphort* in Co Laois', *Archaeology Ireland*, 9:3 (1995), 30–2. **30** John Bradley, 'The interpretation of Scandinavian settlement in Ireland' in idem (ed.), *Settlement and society in medieval Ireland: studies presented to F.X. Martin OSA* (Kilkenny, 1988), 49–78, at pp 50–1. **31** Edward J. Gwynn and Walter J. Purton (ed. and trans.), 'The monastery of Tallaght', *PRIA*, 29 (1911–12), 115–79, at 146. **32** See n. 23 above.

ecclesiastical sites and they are considered economic, as opposed to the social connotations of armrings which are associated with high-status secular sites.[33] It is probably no coincidence that the five hoards in the area of Cualu are coin hoards and associated with ecclesiastical foundations (fig. 1.1).[34]

Early Scandinavian rural settlement at Cherrywood

Possible evidence for this early period of negotiations for provisioning may lie in the excavation at Cherrywood. Cherrywood lies adjacent to the southeast of the townland of Laughanstown, which contains the church of Tully, and must have formed the demesne lands of the ecclesiastical estate.[35] The townland of Cherrywood is in the parish of Killiney on the Down Survey parish map but is cut off from the remainder of the parish by the Loughlinstown River and so lies in a liminal position.[36] The first phase of the site was an enclosed cemetery art-historically dated by a sixth- to seventh-century belt buckle. Subsequent to this the excavator notes a stratigraphical break before the next layers of evidence which appeared to be domestic structures.[37]

The earliest of these, Structure 4, was dated by a pig humerus to AD 680–890. This was a sunken area 2.75m long and, at its widest point, 1.9m wide, surrounded by a U-shaped setting of post- and stake-holes, four of which are substantial. This U-shaped setting is 4.3m long and 3.5m wide. This seems small for a house but if the area enclosed was the extent of the dwelling, it would be possible. The three 'small sunken structures' excavated by Simpson in the lower levels of Temple Bar West measured on average 2.25m by 3m, but are rectilinear.[38] These were dated to the late eighth to late ninth century, which is an overall later date range than Cherrywood Structure 4. However, the radiocarbon dates for three of the young men buried at South Great George's Street, described above, have exactly the same date range as Structure 4 at Cherrywood, 680–890. The possibility exists that Structure 4 at Cherrywood was a temporary shelter for initial negotiators from the Viking settlement around the Poddle, mentioned above, while they were assessing production from the ecclesiastical estate of Tully.

More permanent settlement, probably denoting higher-status inhabitants of the Cherrywood site with a more developed system of economic exchange with the ecclesiastical estate, is suggested by Structure 1. Structure 1 is large, 100 square metres, and has slightly bowed sides. Its date is uncertain but it is stratigraphically previous to Structures 2 and 3, whose dating and significance

33 John Sheehan, 'Social and economic integration in Viking-Age Ireland: the evidence of the hoards' in John Hines, Alan Lane and Michael Redknapp (eds), *Land, sea and home: proceedings of a conference on Viking period settlement at Cardiff, July 2001* (Leeds, 2004), pp 177–88, at pp 184–5. 34 Boazman, 'Theme', pp 518, 526–7. 35 Boazman, 'Hallowed by saints', fig. 2.3. 36 Boazman, 'Hallowed by saints', n. 70. 37 Ó Néill, 'Cherrywood', p. 70. 38 Simpson, '*Longphort*?', pp 27–9.

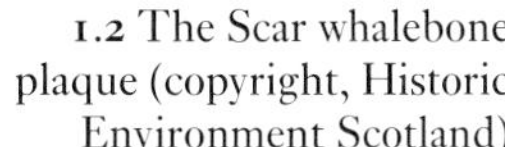

1.2 The Scar whalebone plaque (copyright, Historic Environment Scotland)

will be discussed below. The size and bowed sides of Structure 1 are reminiscent of Viking longhouses in Scandinavia. This northern European dwelling morphology was not imported into the dense urban setting of Dublin where probably available space limited house-size. There are only four possible examples in Ireland, including Structure 1 at Cherrywood.[39]

Further evidence for ninth- or tenth-century settlement at the Cherrywood site comes from another find in a refuse pit of part of a whalebone plaque, in the shape of a horse's head. Sixty of these plaques have been found in high-status Scandinavian women's burials. The majority have been found in Norway, but several in the Outer Hebrides and Orkneys and a fragment of one in Dublin.[40] A fine example comes from a boat burial at Scar on Sanday, Orkney (fig. 1.2). Whalebone plaques have been found in association with linen smoothers but do not show signs of wear which suggests they may have

39 See Rebecca Boyd, 'Where are the longhouses? Reviewing Ireland's Viking Age buildings' in Clarke and Johnson (eds), *Vikings in Ireland*, pp 325–43, particularly pp 337, 343–4, for examples and a clear and succinct discussion of how Irish Viking-Age settlement, both urban and rural, was distinct from the longhouse tradition of northern Europe. 40 Olwyn Owen and Magnar Dalland, *Scar: a Viking boat burial on Sanday, Orkney* (East

been signifiers of female primacy within the household, although in this case the plaque remnant was not found in a grave deposit. They are dated art-historically from the late eighth to the second half of the ninth century. A find of a whalebone plaque at Ribe, Denmark, was associated with a deposit dated to AD 750.[41] The excavators date the Scar boat burial to 875–950.[42] Thus it seems that at Scar the plaque may have been an heirloom.

A silver ingot was found just 200m to the east of Cherrywood. Ingots occur mainly in hoards of the mid-ninth to mid-tenth century.[43] Although it cannot be said for certain that the ingot, Structure 1 and the whalebone plaque are contemporary, an argument can be made for this. Structure 1 could be associated with permanent Scandinavian settlement at Cherrywood in the second half of the ninth century with the house morphology and the whalebone plaque privileging homeland culture. This emphasis on roots would seem to be appropriate to primary settler mind-set where the familiar traditions are a protection against the fear and insecurity of the new. Also the size of Structure 1 and the possession of the probable heirloom whalebone plaque would suggest this was the dwelling of a high-status family, while the ingot indicates the ongoing and successful economic engagement with the ecclesiastical site which was the *raison d'être* for the settlement.

BECOMING HIBERNO-SCANDINAVIAN

Terminology of hybridization

It is also possible that the Structure 1 house could have been reused in the return of the Scandinavian elite to Dublin in 917 and perhaps it was during this period that the whalebone plaque remnant was discarded. This was a time when the Scandinavians became fully embedded in their chosen Irish environment and therefore it may have seemed appropriate for some individuals to discard emblems of previous identity. Thus the meaning of the whalebone plaque shifting from totem to broken could have indicated a change in the perception of what constituted one's homeland.

Bradley's original use of the terminology of acculturation is: 'the material culture is neither purely Scandinavian nor purely Irish, but is rather a common culture which one may term Hiberno-Scandinavian'.[44] A critique suggests the current usage of the term 'Hiberno-Scandinavian' in rural contexts deviates from Bradley's concept of a common culture in that 'it refers to a distinct cultural group separate and identifiably distinct from the Irish population'.[45]

Linton, 1999), p. 83; Raghnall Ó Floinn, 'The archaeology of the early Viking age in Ireland' in Clarke et al. (eds), *Ireland and Scandinavia*, pp 131–65, at p. 142. **41** Owen and Dallard, *Scar*, p. 83. **42** Ibid., p. 165. **43** John Sheehan, 'The *longphort* in Viking-Age Ireland', *Acta Archaeologia*, 79 (2008), 282–95, at 290. **44** Bradley, 'Scandinavian settlement', pp 60–1. **45** Michael Gibbons and Myles Gibbons, 'A critique of the evidence

The process of acculturation is not a smooth transition from different to hybrid to homogenous and indeed incomers will retain facets of difference while at the same time conforming to the host culture. Bradley's conclusion that the hinterland of Dublin in the eleventh and twelfth centuries 'was different from the rest of Ireland' acknowledges this.[46] It seems self-evident that the hybridization of incomer cultures with an indigenous culture, particularly if restricted to and thus concentrated in specific areas, will result in a distinctive identity. As Bradley remarks, 'the existence of a common material culture should not be equated with a uniform one'.[47] In this paper I propose that Bradley's term 'Hiberno-Scandinavian' is appropriate to the area of Cualu with its 'settlement mosaic'[48] of cultures and I trace the manner in which this identity was promoted in the eleventh and twelfth centuries through the medium of the material culture of Christianity. This utilization of the ontology of the indigenous population to form an idiosyncratic identity demonstrates the complexity of the interplay of cultures in this period. The next sections discuss some of the contributing factors to the earlier formation of a Hiberno-Scandinavian identity in the port-town of Dublin and its southern hinterland.

Processes of acculturation

Political and genetic In the second half of the ninth century the Scandinavian elite of Dublin became an integral part of the labyrinthine power struggle between the southern Uí Néill (Clann Cholmáin), the kings of North Brega and the Northern Uí Néill. After initial, mainly unsuccessful, attempts of Irish kings to rebuff the return of the Scandinavian elite, this political integration continued after 917. During the period from the 940s to his death in 956 (AFM) Congalach of North Brega utilized both the manpower and resources of Dublin in the manner of the Uí Briain and Uí Chennselaig kings of one hundred years later, to extend his forays as far as Connacht and the Shannon.[49] During this period Amlaíb Cuarán's authority in Dublin was weakened by his focus on the kingdom of York, but his loss of the York kingship in 950, combined with the demise of Congalach, instigated a two-decade period in which Amlaíb was a credible candidate for high-kingship in Ireland. This was underlined by tactical marriage-alliances with Dúnlaith, sister of Domnall ua Néill, in 954 and that of his daughter Ragnailt around 970 to Domnall, king of North Brega.[50] The attacks by the Northern Uí Néill in

recently presented for the existence of Viking maritime havens and associated settlement', *Journal of the Kerry Archaeological and Historical Society*, 8 (2008), 28–73, at 29. **46** Bradley, 'Scandinavian settlement', p. 61. **47** Ibid. **48** Ibid. **49** See Emer Purcell and John Sheehan, 'Viking Dublin: enmities, alliances and the cold gleam of silver' in Dawn M. Hadley and Letty ven Harkel (eds), *Everyday life in Viking towns: social approaches to towns in England and Ireland,* c.*800–1100* (Oxford, 2013), pp 35–60 for a detailed account of Scandinavian and Irish alliances in the east of Ireland during the ninth and tenth centuries. **50** Margaret Dobbs (ed. and trans.), 'The Ban-senchas', *Revue Celtique*, 47 (1930), 314,

968 (AFM) on the ecclesiastical sites of Louth, Dromiskin and Monasterboice, which apparently hosted Scandinavian populations and military units, indicated the time-honoured Scandinavian tactic of using the 'facilities' of ecclesiastical sites as logistical support for an expansionist policy from Dublin.[51] This period from 918 to 980 was one of growth in the economic importance of the port-town of Dublin, reflected in both increased house numbers and artefacts indicating wide-ranging trade contacts through the Irish Sea region and Europe.[52]

The military input of the elite of Dublin into Irish political power-play in the late ninth and tenth centuries, whether as subordinates or leaders, would have necessitated communication and cooperation at many levels, not least that of language in discussion of tactics and the giving of orders. This would have included their lower-status foot soldiers. As the Dublin area supported an Irish population before the establishment of the *longphort*, it seems likely that at least some of that population were incorporated into the Dublin armies. Similarly, the recorded intermarriage of elite Scandinavians must have been mirrored at all levels of the society. Thus, on both public and personal levels the two cultures were feeding into one another.

Conversion to Christianity The victory over Amlaíb at Tara, by Máel Sechnaill of Clann Cholmáin, and the latter's subsequent imposition of control over the resources of Dublin, ended any Scandinavian designs on the high-kingship. However, the death of Amlaíb 'in penitence' on Iona indicated cognitive adjustments to the Scandinavian worldview, outside the common ground shared with the Irish of political alliance and military forays, to which both cultures were well-accustomed. Amlaíb's obit, combined with records of his baptism in 943 and of his predecessor Sitriuc's acceptance of Christianity in 926,[53] suggest a 'top–down' conversion of the Scandinavians in the tenth century and indeed these displays of royal adherence to Christianity must have been influential. However, these recorded events were only a small part of the long infiltration period in which all levels of the incomer group were exposed to an Irish political system to which Christianity was integral and also to a mnenomic landscape of small churches, particularly in Cualu.[54]

337–8; 48 (1931), 188, 227. **51** Purcell and Sheehan, 'Viking Dublin', pp 52–3. **52** Linzi Simpson, 'Forty years a-digging: a preliminary synthesis of archaeological investigations in medieval Dublin' in Seán Duffy (ed.), *Medieval Dublin I* (Dublin, 2000), pp 11–68, at pp 29–34; Patrick J. Wallace, 'The economy and commerce of Viking Age Dublin' in Klaus Düwel, Herbert Jankhun, H. Siems and D. Timpe (eds), *Untersuchungen zu handel und verkehr der vor- und frühgeshichtlichenzeit zeit in Mittel- und Nordeuropa iv: der handel der Karolinger- und Wikingzeit* (Gottingen, 1987), pp 200–45, at pp 215–20. **53** G.P. Cubbin, *Manuscript D* in David Dumville and Simon Keyes (gen. eds), *The Anglo-Saxon Chronicle, a collaborative edition*, 11 vols (Cambridge, 1996), vol. 6, pp 44, 41. **54** Bradley ('Scandinavian settlement', p. 59) hints that some of these sites may have been founded by the Scandinavians and Stout tentatively follows him with caveats (Matthew Stout, 'The

This landscape may even have had a familiar element. The manifestations of pre-Christian religion in Scandinavia were diverse with a gradual move from outside natural shrines to rituals taking place in wooden cult-houses from the fifth century.[55] The cult-houses, although not Christian, were in use in Scandinavia between AD 500 and 1000, and so the concept of indoor ritual in small wooden sacred buildings, such as the churches of Ireland, would not have been alien to the Scandinavian incomers. Although there was not a relationship between Scandinavian cult-houses and burial this may explain high-status early Viking burials close to ecclesiastical sites such as Kilmainham, Finglas and the predecessor to St Michael le Pole.[56] This desire to belong and possess the new land by incorporation in its perceived sacred places is also indicated by Viking burials in or near secular Irish burial monuments such as Donnybrook and College Green.[57]

Hadley, speaking of the tenth century in England, remarks that missionary conversion and subsequent pastoral care of the Scandinavians in England must have been hampered by the destruction of the ecclesiastical organization of northern and eastern England.[58] There is no evidence that the ecclesiastical network of Ireland was disrupted or destroyed by the events of the early Viking period. Examples could be drawn from any annalistically recorded major ecclesiastical site but both Clondalkin and Tallaght, in the south Dublin area, maintained a succession of bishops and abbots through the ninth and tenth centuries.[59] Also the density of ecclesiastical sites in England is considerably lower than in Ireland,[60] and so destruction of one site probably would have

distribution of early medieval ecclesiastical sites in Ireland' in Patrick J. Duffy and William Nolan (eds), *At the anvil: essays in honour of William J. Smyth* (Dublin, 2012), pp 53–80, at p. 74). However, both documentary and excavation evidence indicate that the vast majority of these ecclesiastical sites were founded in the pre-Viking period between the fifth and seventh century (Boazman, 'Hallowed', table 2.2, pp 30–3). **55** Anders Andrén, 'Behind *Heathendom*: archaeological studies of Old Norse religion', *Scottish Archaeological Journal*, 27:2 (2005), 105–38, at 130–1. **56** Elizabeth O'Brien, 'The location and context of Viking burials at Kilmainham and Islandbridge, Dublin' in Clarke et al. (eds), *Ireland and Scandinavia*, pp 203–22; Maeve Sikora, 'The Finglas burial: archaeology and ethnicity in Viking-Age Dublin' in John Sheehan and Donnchadh Ó Corráin, *The Viking Age: Ireland and the West* (Cork, 2014), pp 402–17; see n. 28 above. **57** Elizabeth O'Brien, 'A reassessment of the "great sepulchral mound" containing a Viking burial at Donnybrook, Dublin', *Medieval Archaeology*, 36 (1992), 170–3; Stephen Harrison, 'College Green – a neglected "Viking" cemetery at Dublin' in Andras Mortensen (ed.), *Viking and Norse in the North Atlantic* (Tórshavn, 2005), pp 229–39. **58** Dawn M. Hadley, '"Hamlet and the princes of Denmark": lordship in the Danelaw, *c*.860–954' in Julian Richards and Dawn M. Hadley (eds), *Cultures in contact: Scandinavian settlement in England in the ninth and tenth centuries* (Turnhout, 2000), pp 107–32, at p. 116. **59** For a further detailed example, see Ailbhe MacShamhráin, 'Prosopographia Glindelachensis: the monastic church of Glendalough and its community, sixth to thirteenth centuries', *JRSAI*, 119 (1989), 79–97. **60** Sam Turner, *Making a Christian landscape* (Exeter, 2006), pp 90–1, at p. 110; Gill Boazman, 'Cork and Cornwall, settlement patterns and social organization during the establishment of Christianity, AD 450–800', *Journal of Irish Archaeology*, 17 (2008), 113–36, affected ecclesiastical provision over a very wide geographical area. Although the extent of pastoral provision in Ireland for those outside ecclesiastical land is disputed,[61] in Cualu, as already indicated, a very high proportion of land was in ecclesiastical hands.[62] Missionary endeavour would have been superfluous in the face of such lavish ecclesiastical provision. The point to be drawn is that, due to the pervasive nature of the Irish church in both landscape and politics, the Scandinavians, whether making an alliance on an elite level or gathering supplies from an ecclesiastical estate on a commoner level, were informally acculturated to Christianity,[63] through the ninth and tenth centuries, by immersion in a society which conflated the entities of secular and ecclesiastical. The corollary of this is that searching for more concrete evidence of conversion of the Scandinavians of Ireland in this period may be in vain.

Eleventh-century material evidence of the practice of Christianity in Dublin Any ambivalence about the outward manifestation of Scandinavian conversion is dispelled by the material culture of Dublin in the eleventh and twelfth centuries. From the foundation of Christ Church by Sitriuc Sikenbeard in *c.*1030, up to 1170, the number of new churches within the walls of the town of Dublin multiplied to nine and these were encircled by a further eleven extramural churches and foundations of reformed orders.[64] From the meagre evidence that remains of these early churches it would seem they were innovative in design, Christ Church having aisles and St Michael le Pole an engaged round tower.[65] This would contrast with the more conservative Irish mortared stone churches of the eleventh-century period, which mostly followed the traditional small area, unicameral design of their wooden predecessors. However, a major church building, such as Christ Church, with multiple satellites in an enclosed space, also indicates assimilation of the essential design of Irish ecclesiastical sites, recalling Rome, the centre of Christianity.

It seems that following the major defeats of Tara and Clontarf the focus of the Scandinavian elite shifted from increasing territorial and political control

table 7, p. 136. **61** Richard Sharpe, 'Churches and communities in early medieval Ireland: towards a pastoral model' in John Blair and Richard Sharpe (eds), *Pastoral care before the parish* (Leicester, 1992), pp 81–109, at p. 109; Colmán Etchingham, *Church organization in Ireland, AD 650–1000* (Maynooth, 1999), p. 289. **62** MacCotter, 'Church lands'. **63** Recent research emphasizes the transformative process in Scandinavian conversion across northern Europe, rather than coercion or 'conversion moments' of kings resulting in more sudden ontological shifts, although the two are not mutually exclusive (Ildar Garipzanov, 'Introduction: networks of conversion, cultural osmosis and identities in the Viking Age' in idem (ed.), *Conversion and identity in the Viking Age* (Turnhout, 2014), pp 1–20, at pp 5–6). **64** Howard B. Clarke, *Irish historic towns atlas, No. 11, Dublin, Part 1 to 1610* (Dublin, 2002), p. 5, fig. 4. **65** Aubrey Gwynn, 'Some unpublished texts from the Black Book of Christchurch, Dublin', *AH*, 16 (1946), 281–337, at 309; Margaret Gowen, 'Excavations at the site of the church and tower of St Michael le Pole, Dublin' in Seán

of Ireland to a more limited goal: the development of Dublin as a perceived power centre with the accoutrements of a European city.[66] This was both based in and funded by the trading economy of Dublin, extending through the Irish Sea region and further and indeed looking east rather than west. These multiple church foundations may have indicated a certain amount of competitive emulation among the merchant elite of Dublin but it is significant that the Scandinavians chose to demonstrate the status of Dublin by constructing Christian monuments. This indicates that, by the eleventh century, they perceived Christianity as enhancing a valued aspect of their identity – political status. This perception would have been strengthened not only through observation of the essential contribution of ecclesiastical power to the Irish political structure but may have also been influenced by events in the homelands. The first securely dated stone church was patronized in Roskilde by the sister of Cnut *c.*1027,[67] reinforcing the message that the future of elite status lay in the patronage of Christian monuments. The poem in the Book of Leinster placing Dublin among the seven wonders of Ireland indicated that the image projected by this landmark ecclesiastical architecture was effective marketing in the Irish political sphere.[68]

To understand in what manner this very public structuring of a Christian identity in Hiberno-Scandinavian Dublin was manifest in the hinterland of Cualu it is necessary to return first to the general political structure of the area in the eleventh and twelfth centuries and then to the documentary and material evidence of its landholders before exploring ecclesiastical patronage in the context of these.

THE POLITICS OF THE SOUTHERN HINTERLAND FROM LATE TENTH TO TWELFTH CENTURY

Shifting balance of power in the Irish context

In an earlier section the Uí Dúnchada were shown to be in an apparently strong position at the beginning of the Viking Age. They continued their hold over Kildare throughout the ninth and tenth centuries providing abbots and sometimes king-abbots of that foundation.[69] Succession to the kingship of

Duffy (ed.), *Medieval Dublin II* (Dublin, 2001), pp 31–52. **66** The choice of their first bishop, Dúnán, who came bearing relics from Cologne, would support this (Raghnall Ó Floinn, 'The foundation relics of Christ Church cathedral and the origins of the diocese of Dublin' in Seán Duffy (ed.), *Medieval Dublin VII* (2005), pp 89–102; Ó Riain-Raedel in this volume, below). **67** Anne-Sofie Gräslund, 'The material culture of Christianization' in Stefan Brink and Neil Price (eds), *The Viking world* (Oxford, 2008), pp 639–45, at p. 642. **68** Howard B. Clarke, 'Conversion, church and cathedral: the diocese of Dublin to 1152' in James Kelly and Dáire Keogh (eds), *History of the Catholic diocese of Dublin*, pp 19–50, at p. 50. **69** Colmán Etchingham, 'Kildare before the Normans: "An episcopal and conventual see"', *Journal of the County Kildare Archaeological Society*, 19 (2000–1), 7–26, at

Leinster was shared between the three lines of Uí Dúnlainge – Uí Dúnchada, Uí Fáeláin and Uí Muiredaig – roughly equally through the ninth and tenth centuries but the end of the tenth century saw the Uí Dúnchada's hold on the strands of power in Laigin terminated by the ignominious capture by Sitriuc of two successive Uí Dúnchada kings, Domnall Cláen and his son Donnchad in 977 (AFM) and 999 (AU). Donnchad was deposed and replaced by Máel Mórda of the Uí Fáeláin who was allied with Sitriuc.[70] After this the Uí Dúnchada are not mentioned in the annals for forty-four years and the record of abbots at Kildare terminates.[71]

The physical adjacency, resulting in economic and genetic ties between the Uí Dúnlainge group and the Scandinavians, brought them together against the new and threatening alliance of the Clann Cholmáin and Brian Bórama in the last years of the millennium.[72] This is borne out in a reference of 995 (AFM) in which an Uí Dúnchada dynast is slain by the Uí Fáeláin, not in their own territories, but in Dublin.[73] The Uí Fáeláin and Uí Muiredaig are mentioned in the annals as fighting with the Scandinavians against Brian and Máel Sechnaill at Clontarf,[74] but not the Uí Dúnchada, showing the latter's reduced status. In the period after Clontarf the Uí Dúnlainge kingship of the Laigin was dominated by the Uí Muiredaig branch, supported by their connection with Glendalough, until 1042.[75]

The significance of the long-term control of Dublin with the multiple possibilities of its contacts in the Irish Sea zone combined with its materialization of Christianity was recognized by the Uí Chennselaig king, Diarmait mac Máel na mBó. He ended the Uí Dúnlainge dominance of the kingship of Leinster in the early 1040s, taking the throne of Dublin in 1052 (AU) and shortly after placing his son in this key position.[76] He was followed in this tactic by dominant Irish kings for the next hundred years. His obits portray him as having a wide suzerainty even extending to the kingship of Wales. Although this last may be obituary hyperbole, he pursued a policy of support by Dublin for Welsh and Anglo-Saxon magnates, such as Cynan ab Iago, king of Gwynned, who fled to Dublin in the late 1030s when unsuccessful in a dynastic challenge, and the sons of King Harold Godwinson, in their opposition to the Norman Conquest.[77] The form of this support was refuge and provision of mercenary ships.

10, 12–13. **70** Máel Mórda was the brother of Gormlaith, married to Amlaíb Cuarán; Sitriuc was the son of this union and so was Máel Mórda's nephew (Seán Duffy, *Brian Boru and the battle of Clontarf* (Dublin, 2013), p. 101). **71** Etchingham, 'Kildare', 13. **72** Glenn Máma 999 (AU); 1000 (AU). **73** See above alliance of Sitriuc and Uí Fáeláin against the Uí Dúnchada. **74** Uí Fáeláin in AU, AI, AFM, CS; Uí Muiredaig AFM, CS. **75** MacShamhráin, *Glendalough*, pp 90–5. **76** Donncha Ó Corráin, *Ireland before the Vikings* (Dublin, 1972), pp 133–4; Seán Duffy, 'Irishmen and Islesmen in the kingdoms of Dublin and Man, 1052 to 1171', *Ériu*, 43 (1992), 93–133, at 99–100. **77** Seán Duffy, 'Ostmen, Irish and Welsh in the eleventh century', *Peritia* (1995), 378–96, at 387.

An addition to lordship in Cualu: the Meic Turcaill

Returning to the microcosm of the ecclesiastical estate of Tully, adjacent to Cherrywood, it was noted above that this land was donated to Holy Trinity by Scandinavian magnates, the Meic Turcaill.[78] The origins of this Scandinavian kin-group are little understood but there are references in the Anglo-Saxon Chronicle to a Thurkil who was involved in invasions of eastern England in the early eleventh century including that of Cnut.[79] His military assistance was rewarded when he received from Cnut the jarldom of East Anglia.[80] Although relationships with Cnut were not always amicable, one entry describes Thurkil being present with Cnut, bishops and priests, at the consecration of a church at Ashingdon (Essex) in 1020.[81] Thurkil left for Denmark in 1023 but there are two mentions of later members of the family in Wales in 1039 and fighting the French at York in 1068.[82]

The next mention of a probable branch of the family is in 1093 (AI) when Turcaill, son of Eóla, is slain in the company of Rhys ap Tewdwr, fighting the Normans in south Wales. This alliance had its roots in Diarmait mac Mael na mBó's support for Cynan ab Iago who, during his exile in Dublin, married the daughter of Amlaíb, Ragnild. This latter Amlaíb (d. 1034) was the son of Sitriuc Silkenbeard, founder of Christ Church cathedral. Cynan's son, Gruffudd, returned in an attempt to reclaim the kingship of Gwynedd in 1075 after having attended the 'court of king Murcath', almost certainly Muirchertach Ua Briain.[83] He made a further attempt on the throne in 1081, where he won the battle of Mynydd Carn supported by a fleet from Waterford and Rhys ap Tewdwr. The latter was briefly expelled from his kingship and fled to Ireland where he hired a fleet and gave 'an immense sum of money to the mariners Scots and Gwyddelians'.[84] It seems likely that the Turcaill slain with Rhys in 1093 was benefitting from his family's traditional source of income, mercenary activity, but operating from Ireland.

Twelfth-century references indicate the family's gradual transition from military operators to administrators to kings of Dublin. In 1124 (AU) the obit occurs of Torfind, 'chief *óicthigen*[85] of the foreigners of Ireland' and in 1133 (ALC) and 1138 (AFM) members of the family are to be found in combat against alliances involving the Airgialla king Donnchad Ua Cerbaill. In 1146

78 See n. 15 above. 79 Katherine O'Brien O'Keefe, *Manuscript C*, in David Dumville and Simon Keyes (gen. eds), *The Anglo-Saxon Chronicle, a collaborative edition*, 11 vols (Cambridge, 2001), vol. 5, at pp 93, 98. 80 Ibid., p. 103. 81 Ibid., p. 104. The church was close to the site of the battle in 1016 at which Cnut and Thurkil prevailed over the Saxons in 1016. 82 Ibid., pp 104, 107 and Cubbin, *Manuscript D*, p. 84. 83 Thomas Jones (ed. and trans.), *Brut y Tywysogion or The Chronicle of the princes. Peniarth MS 20 version* (Cardiff, 1952), p. 16; Duffy, 'Ostmen, Irish and Welsh', 394. After the death of Diarmait mac Máel na mBó, his erstwhile protégé, the Dál Cais king, Tairdelbach ua Briain, put his son Muirchertach on the throne of Dublin in 1075 (Duffy, 'Irishmen and Islesmen', 99–100). 84 Jones, *Brut*, p. 17, n. 155; p. 18. 85 eDIL s.v. *ócthigern*: young lord perhaps with associated sense of warrior: eDIL s.v. *óc*.

(AFM) the *mormaer* of Dublin, Ragnall mac Turcaill, was slain in a battle with the old enemies, Clann Cholmáin, and two years later the family tightened their grip on governance of the port-town by assassinating a rival king of Dublin from the Isles.[86] After the initial attack of the Anglo-Normans on Dublin, Ascaill mac Turcaill, king of Dublin, having been banished, led an unsuccessful reprisal in 1171 (AU).

LAND TENURE IN CUALU IN THE ELEVENTH TO TWELFTH CENTURY (fig. 1.3)

Meic Turcaill: documentary and material evidence

There is evidence that the Meic Turcaill supported their rise in status by investing their income from mercenary activity in land and its economic benefits. The ecclesiastical estate of Tully, already mentioned, has three pieces of land associated with the Meic Turcaill: *Ballymochaine* (Ballyogan/part of Jamestown), *Balyeucharan* (Leopardstown), and *Achtillagh nun escoib Culagh*, the demesne lands of Tully in the modern townland of Laughanstown.[87] Although it cannot be categorically proven that the pre-Holy Trinity ecclesiastical estate of Tully comprised the areas approximating to the modern townlands of Leopardstown and Baliogan to the northwest, it seems likely. It is also likely that the townland of Brenanstown, containing the denomination 'Dromin' which is recorded as Holy Trinity land in 1179, was a further part of the estate.[88] The name Brenanstown, with its Welsh reference (*Baile na nBretnach*), indicates that, perhaps in 1093 or earlier, Welsh allies of the Meic Turcaill may have settled as tenants on the ecclesiastical land.[89]

Although the townland of Killiney, containing the church, is in the hands of Holy Trinity, the remainder of the parish of Killiney, including the townland of Cherrywood, is documented through the later medieval period as secular land, 'Balygodman', belonging to the Godman family, later on the Down Survey, 'Goodman'. It is likely that this innocuous surname was assumed by a Scandinavian family, probably a branch of the Meic Turcaill, as it adjoins their ecclesiastical estate of Tully.[90]

Archbishop Alen identified 'Theachnabretnach' with Kilgobbin in his notes to the confirmation of possessions by Pope Alexander III to Archbishop

86 *Mormaer*: steward. Charles Doherty, 'The Vikings in Ireland: a review' in Clarke et al. (eds), *Ireland and Scandinavia*, pp 288–336, at p. 320; Duffy, 'Irishmen and Islesmen', 121–3. 87 *Reg. Alen*, p. 28; see Boazman, 'Theme', pp 480–92 for a detailed analysis of the ecclesiastical estate of Tully. 88 *Reg. Alen*, p. 3; *CCD*, p. 345, no. 1662. 89 Brennanstown occurs in the 1326 account roll of Holy Trinity as 'Balybrenan' with Peter Howel as tenant. Howel derives from the Welsh name Hywel (James Mills (ed.), *Account roll of the priory of Holy Trinity, 1337–1346*, reprinted with an intro. by James Lydon and Alan J. Fletcher (Dublin, 1995), p. 195). 90 Mills, *Account roll*, pp 7, 13, 69; Kenneth Nicholls, 'Anglo-French Ireland and after', *Peritia*, 1 (1982), 370–403, at 383, n. 3.

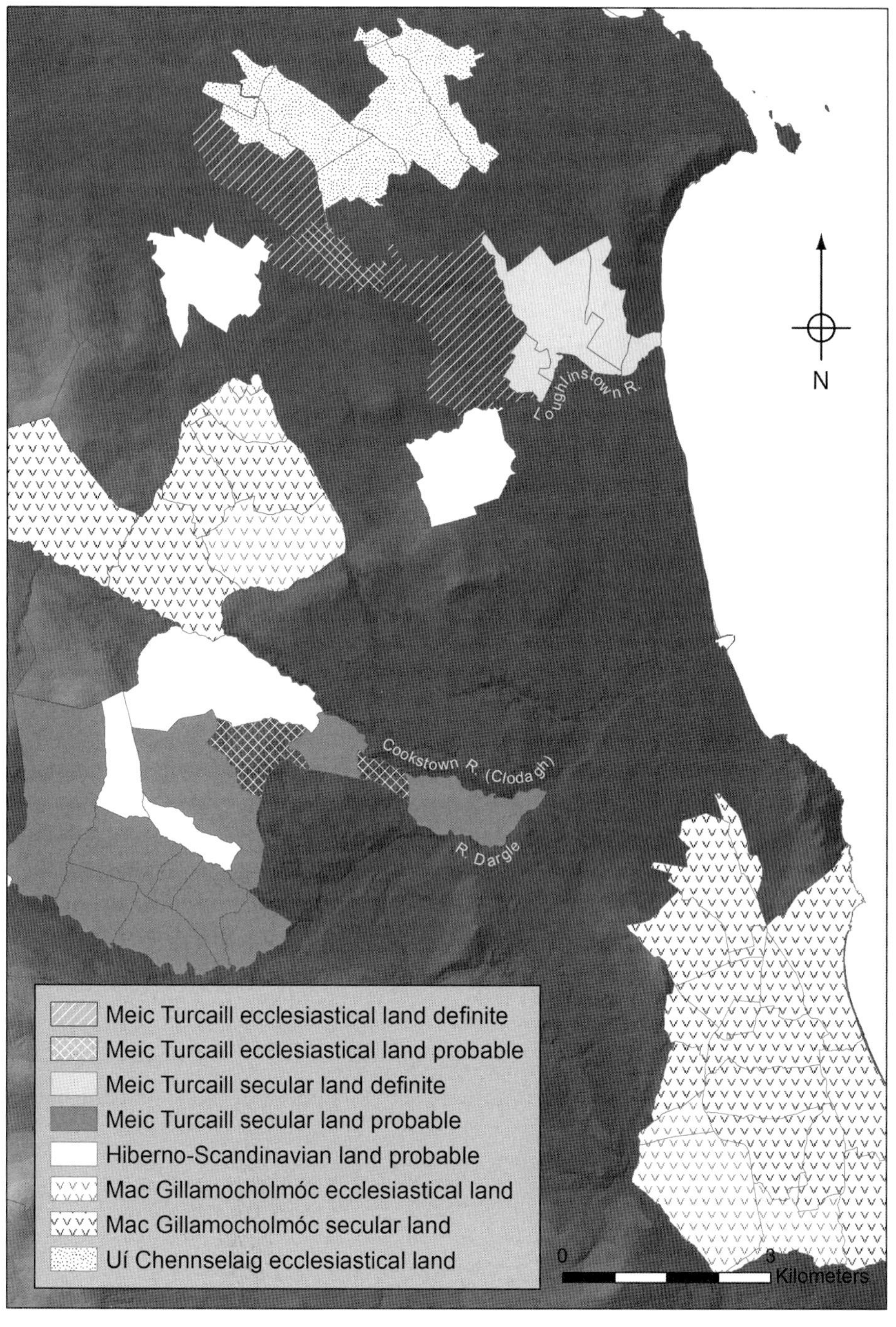

1.3 Documented landowners in Cualu in the eleventh century (map: G. Boazman)

Laurence O'Toole in 1179 and in this document it is a possession of the archbishop rather than Holy Trinity.[91] The forced donation to Holy Trinity of 'the gift of the Ostmans for their forfeit, Teachnabretnach' in the 1202 document was perceived by Nicholls as meaning that Teachnabretnach was not to be identified with Kilgobbin, because 'Kilgobbin was not a possession of Holy Trinity'.[92] However, a further confirmation document of uncertain date but around the late 1170s, places 'Terbretan' in the possessions of the canons.[93] Nicholls is correct in his assertion that Kilgobbin was a possession of the archbishop subsequent to the 1179 document, as it appears as such in the 1280 list of rural deaneries.[94] However, it may be that in the inevitable confusion of land forfeit in the initial post-Invasion period it was briefly taken by Holy Trinity in the land grab from the 'Ostmen'. The fact that it adjoined the Tully ecclesiastical estate, under Hiberno-Scandinavian lordship, would support this as well as the fact that it was held in the early thirteenth century by the Ostman family called Harold.[95] An attraction of Kilgobbin may be indicated by the evidence of cupellation of silver produced by analysis of residues on ceramic saucer crucibles at the site. Some are dated to the pre-Viking period contexts but the latest context is dated by ash charcoal to cal AD 1015–1158 2 sigma.[96]

A Hiberno-Scandinavian association is supported by the dates and morphology of the later structures at Cherrywood. Type 1 houses of Dublin with their post-and-wattle construction and three-aisled design are considered to be a compromise between Irish and Scandinavian buildings, 'worked out in a rectangular form'.[97] Both Structures 2 and 3 are similar in size to Type 1 houses in Dublin, which average 40.7 sq m.[98] Structure 2 is closer morphologically to the Type 1 houses, having a three-aisle layout and apparently rounded corners but evidence of the two sets of roof-supporting post-holes is not as clear. Boyd suggests that the substantial post-hole of the entrance may have played a part in roof support and also that the cobbled doorway and surface recall contemporary urban pathways.[99] Structure 3 is transversally divided and both have a single end-wall entrance. The variation in morphology should not surprise as there were houses excavated in Dublin that could not be classified in the typology,[100] and rural houses may have had different priorities and functions from urban.

Structures 2 and 3 are stratigraphically later in the sequence of structural evidence at the site than Structures 1 and 4.[101] Structure 2 partially overlies

91 *Reg. Alen*, p. 3. **92** Ibid., p. 28; Kenneth Nicholls, 'The land of the Leinstermen', *Peritia*, 3 (1984), 547. **93** *Reg. Alen*, p. 7. **94** John T. Gilbert (ed.), *Crede Mihi, the most ancient register book of the bishops of Dublin before the Reformation* (Dublin, 1897), p. 136. **95** James Mills, 'The Norman settlement in Leinster – the cantreds near Dublin', *JRSAI*, 24 (1894), 161–75, at 166. **96** Theresa Bolger, 'Excavations at Kilgobbin church, Co. Dublin', *Journal of Irish Archaeology*, 27 (2008), 85–113, at 94, 99. **97** Patrick F. Wallace, *The Viking-Age buildings of Dublin*, 2 vols (Dublin, 1992), for a description of the house typology and the Type 1 houses; Boyd, 'Longhouses', p. 335. **98** Boyd, 'Longhouses', p. 329. **99** Ibid., pp 337–8. **100** Ibid., p. 332. **101** Ó Néill, 'Cherrywood', pp 75, 79, 82.

Structure 1 and a post-hole from Structure 3 cuts into the backfill of a corn-drying kiln. This corn-drying kiln is dated by deposits of oats in the backfill of a post-hole of Structure 4 (dated by animal bone to the late eighth to ninth century: see above). The date of the oats is 1020–1190.[102] So, Structure 3 is later than the kiln. Structure 2 is dated by animal bone from material overlying the cobbling of the doorway which is dated to 1020–1230.[103] It is unfortunate that there are only these two dates and they are not primary structural dates. Also the dating analysis in the one article on the excavation (there is no final report) is confusing: 'Structure 2, dating to before 1020–1230; and Structure 3, both appearing to post-date the kiln and, as such, dating to after 1020–1190'.[104] However, it is very possible that primary dates from the two structures would have overlapped with the two date-ranges, and not necessarily have preceded or succeeded the whole range as suggested by the above analysis. The similarity between the two ranges would certainly suggest activity at the site in the first quarter of the twelfth century. This would coincide with mention of the Meic Turcaill in the annals: the fleet that supported Rhys ap Tewdwr in the 1093 battle and the 1124 obit of Torfinn Mac Turcaill. It is possible that the overlordship of Tully ecclesiastical estate, already associated with Scandinavian habitation (Structure 1), was a purchase with the wages of war and that Structures 2 and 3 are those of stewards of the Meic Turcaill.[105]

A further reference to Meic Turcaill landholding is in North Wicklow, where Walter de Riddlesford was granted five knights' fees lying in 'Brien and the land of the sons of Torquil' and if this amount of land was not in that area then what was missing was to be taken on one side or other of the 'Water of Brien'.[106] 'Brien' refers to the territory of the Uí Briúin Chualann, who, it was suggested above, were underlords of the Uí Dúnchada. Their territory would have extended from Tully to Delgany in the tenth century but by the eleventh was circumscribed by pressure of other interests in the area, probably to the area around Bray. The 'water of Brien' refers to the river system of the Dargle whose tributaries drain the Glencullen and Glencree valleys. As the area north of the Glencullen River is associated with other owners in documentary evidence,[107] the land of the sons of Torquil probably refers to the triangle of land formed between the Glencullen/Cookstown River and the Glencree River. This interpretation is supported by the townland Curtlestown (*Baile mhac Turcaill*) at the mouth of the Glencree valley and evidence for

102 Ibid., p. 72. **103** Ibid., p. 78. **104** Ibid., p. 83. **105** Fiona Edmonds, 'The Furness peninsula and the Irish Sea region: cultural interaction from the seventh century to the twelfth' in Clare Downham (ed.), *Jocelin of Furness: essays from the 2011 conference* (Donington, 2013), pp 17–44, at pp 26–7 on the purchase of land and generally on the complexities of land tenure in a multicultural region; the Meic Turcaill magnates were resident in Dublin (*Reg. Alen*, p. 80). **106** Eric St John Brooks, 'The de Riddlesfords', *JRSAI*, 82:2 (1951), 115–38, at 118, 119; Liam Price, 'The grant to Walter de Riddelsford of Brien and the land of the sons of Turchil', *JRSAI*, 84 (1954), 72–9, at 72. **107** *CStM*, i,

Scandinavian ownership of the townland of Ballybrew.[108] Recent research indicates that the use of oak in Dublin was restricted to shipbuilding and manufacture of artefacts rather than housing.[109] This suggests elite control over the commodity and there is documentary evidence for Anglo-Norman royal control over the forest of Glencree, for the purposes of oak timber and underwood harvest as well as hunting.[110] These Meic Turcaill landholdings in Wicklow almost certainly indicate profitable pre-Anglo-Norman domination over the supply of ship's timbers, an essential commodity in eleventh- and twelfth-century Dublin.

There is only minimal documentary evidence for a Hiberno-Scandinavian presence at Rathmichael which became part of the archbishop of Dublin's estates in 1179 but its material evidence, discussed below, would suggest patronage.[111]

Further landowners in Cualu in the eleventh and twelfth centuries

The Uí Dúnchada remained a major landowner in Cualu. Having lost control of their major asset, Kildare, as mentioned above, they seem to have moved east to the lands associated with their underlords, the Uí Briúin Chualann. They also assumed a new sobriquet: Mac Gilla Mo Cholmóc which first appears in the annals in 1044 (AFM) and they are referred to as such into the Anglo-Norman period.[112] By the end of the eleventh century they appear to possess Kiltiernan with its hinterland in the foothills of the mountains, and from Kilruddery south to Delgany (fig. 1.3). This is indicated by post-Anglo-Norman references to donations of land to St Mary's at Kiltiernan and the confirmation of Strongbow to Abbot Thomas of Glendalough, which describes the area from Killegar to Delgany as 'in terra de Macgillamochalmoc'.[113] The rise of the Uí Chennselaig in the mid-eleventh century was a further cause of the restriction of Mac Gilla Mo Cholmóc landholding. Diarmait mac Máel na

pp 35, 36, 86. **108** Price, 'Brien and the land of the sons of Turchil', 73–4; *CStM*, i, pp 38, 97, 389. **109** Eileen Reilly, Susan Lyons, Ellen O'Carroll, Lorna O'Donnell, Ingleise Stuijts and Adrienne Corless, 'Building the towns: the interrelationship between woodland history and urban life in Viking Age Ireland' in Ben Jervis, Lee G. Broderick and Idoia Grau Sologestoa (eds), *Objects, environment and everyday life in medieval Europe* (Turnhout, 2016), pp 66–91, at p. 84. **110** Aidan O'Sullivan, 'Woodmanship and the supply of underwood and timber to Anglo-Norman Dublin' in Manning (ed.), *Dublin and beyond the Pale*, pp 59–69, at pp 67–8. **111** Colmán Etchingham, 'Evidence of Scandinavian settlement in Wicklow' in Kenneth Hannigan and William Nolan (eds), *Wicklow: history and society* (Dublin, 1994), pp 113–38, at p. 130; *Reg. Alen*, p. 3. **112** This is the first mention of the kin-group since the end of the tenth century. It is surmise but maybe the choice of saint was to put a good face on their loss of Brigidine protection by invoking Colum Cille, favoured by the Scandinavians, Gruffud being fostered at Swords (Padraig Ó Riain, *A dictionary of Irish saints* (Dublin, 2011) p. 183, for saints' names deriving from Colum Cille). **113** See n. 106; Gilbert (ed.), *Crede Mihi*, p. 49. The area from Killegar to Bray is of uncertain ownership in the eleventh to mid-twelfth century and so is not affiliated on the map (fig. 1.3). It is possible that part may have been linked with the Hiberno-Scandinavian

mBó's nephew Donnchad, son of Domnall Remar (d. 1089), donated the ecclesiastical lands of Kill o' the Grange (Clonskeen) to Holy Trinity indicating that this land was in Uí Chennselaig hands by the end of the eleventh century.[114]

It seems then that the area of Cualu was possessed of a very mixed structure of lordship in the eleventh and twelfth centuries. Although it may appear that for a large part of the period the Uí Chennselaig were overlords, with an intermission of Ua Briain control from around 1072 to 1114, documentary evidence indicates that there was considerable pressure from landowners of Dublin on those in the underlord and tenant positions in the hinterland. The plea of Muirchertach Mac Gilla Mo Cholmóc on behalf of his subjects (presumably the Uí Briúin Chualann) to Diarmait Mac Murchada, although referring to the twelfth century, suggests that they suffered imposition of dues from both Dublin and the Uí Chennselaig.[115] This would support the proposition made above that the small ecclesiastical estates of Cualu were not free of impost but would also suggest that previous overlords of the area remained *in situ* but slipped down the ladder of hierarchy. This constructed a multi-cultural society of tenants spread through nominally Irish and Hiberno-Scandinavian estates.[116]

POLITICS AND ECCLESIASTICAL PATRONAGE IN CUALU

The mortared stone churches

Cualu possesses the remains of seven pre-Romanesque mortared stone churches. Although a stone church is first noted in the annals *c.*789 (AU) at Armagh, there are few other mentions in the ninth century, the next being Clonmacnoise (*daimliac*) in 909 (CS). Mention is limited to sites of regional importance up to the mid-eleventh century but at that point the word *daimliac* replaces *dairtech* (wooden church), with *tempul* also being used. Churches in stone 'became the commonest type of new church at relatively important centres by the late eleventh century'.[117] None of the mortared churches in Rathdown receive annalistic mention and the occurrence of seven in such a restricted area which is of minor ecclesiastical, and even secular, importance is notable.

holdings at Glencree. **114** *Reg. Alen*, p. 28. **115** Gilbert, 'Gineleach ua Dúnchada', p. 407. **116** Bradley, 'Scandinavian settlement', p. 61; Etchingham, 'Wicklow', p. 130. **117** Conleth Manning, 'References to church buildings in the annals' in Alfred P. Smyth (ed.), *Seanchas: studies in early and medieval Irish archaeology, history and literature in honour of F.J. Byrne* (Dublin, 2000), pp 37–52, at pp 42–5, 51; for a discussion of the chronological cut-off point between these early churches and Romanesque examples, probably sometime in the second quarter of the twelfth century, although there were overlaps, see Tomás Ó Carragáin, 'Habitual masonry styles and the local organization of church-building in early medieval Ireland', *PRIA*, 105C, 3 (2005), 99–140, at 137.

1.4a (*left*) Remains of mortared stone church at Kill o' the Grange, showing roughly coursed masonry, antae and a flat-lintelled doorway (photo: G. Boazman)

1.4b (*top right*) Remains of mortared stone church at Killegar, showing roughly coursed masonry (photo: G. Boazman)

1.4c (*bottom right*) The eastern window of the original church above the later chancel arch at Tully (photo: G. Boazman)

These churches, as a group through Ireland, share certain characteristics. They are mostly unicameral, diminutive in size, with steeply pitched roofs and sometimes antae projecting from the side walls. They possess western flat-lintelled doorways and their windows are small and narrow often with an arch formed of one piece of stone. Although some groups of these churches in the remainder of Ireland show habitual masonry styles, probably of two to three generations of masons, those of Cualu demonstrate eclectic features.[118] However, they share a style of rough coursing of slightly rounded medium-sized boulders. The churches with some evidence of belonging to this pre-Romanesque group are Dalkey Island, Kill o' the Grange, Rathmichael, Kiltiernan, Killegar, Killiney, Kilcroney and Tully.[119] Dalkey Island, Kill o' the Grange (fig. 1.4a), Kiltiernan, Killiney and Kilcroney show extant evidence of

118 Ibid., 126–9, 138, 129. 119 Palmerstown is excluded, because, although pre-Romanesque, it was probably initially founded in the early twelfth century and the others are constructed on pre-Viking sites (Ó Carragáin, *Churches*, p. 240).

a flat-lintelled doorway in the western gable. At Killegar the early church became the chancel of the later medieval church and there are no entry features in the remaining north and south walls of the early structure (fig. 1.4b). At Tully, part of the remaining features of the early church is the north and south walls, although minimal and re-constructed. It could be assumed that at Tully and Killegar the entrance was from the west. The remains of a window, above the later chancel at Tully, bears witness to the eastern gable of earlier church (fig. 1.4c).

Dalkey Island and Kill o' the Grange have antae which is, perhaps, the reasoning behind one commentator placing them in the tenth century, earlier than the remainder of the group.[120] This dating seems unlikely for several reasons. As indicated above, mortared stone churches were only occurring at major sites such as Clonmacnoise in the tenth century; neither Dalkey Island nor Kill o' the Grange would fall into the category 'major'. Although antae are considered early in the corpus, they cannot be relied on as evidence of early construction,[121] several Romanesque churches have antae, for example Kilmalkedar, Co. Kerry. Also it appears that the depth of antae reduces over time, the earliest being between 0.74m and 0.50m. Dalkey Island and Kill are at the shallow end of the table, 0.34m and 0.25m.[122] In a historical context, placing two of the churches in the tenth century would indicate they were constructed prior to the founding of Christ Church and also that Kill, documented as being patronized by the Uí Chennselaig, would have been built at least a half century before the dominance of that group over Dublin and parts of its hinterland.

It seems more probable that this group of churches was constructed within a relatively short time-period and that the variety of their style reflects the diversity of patrons and masons that would have pertained in the hinterland of the port-town. It was remarked above that the churches of Dublin were innovative and therefore it is noteworthy that the churches of the hinterland were relatively conservative, sharing the characteristics of mortared stone churches in the other regions of Ireland. The explanation may lie in their construction at pre-existing ecclesiastical sites. Five of the eight have 'kil' toponyms which would suggest pre-Viking foundation, and five are associated with early saints, two from the Dál Messin Corb period. Rathmichael has both the trace of an inner enclosure and a bullaun stone, both pre-Viking features. It may be a re-dedication as Michael was a saint favoured by the Scandinavians, and its situation on a hill would echo other more famous

120 Christiaan Corlett, 'Tully church, Laughanstown, Co. Dublin' in Christiaan Corlett and Michael Potterton (eds), *The church in early medieval Ireland in the light of recent archaeological excavations* (Dublin, 2014), pp 93–108, at p. 107. **121** Ó Carragáin, 'Masonry styles', p. 139. **122** Ó Carragáin, *Churches*, p. 115.

foundations with the same dedication.[123] Rathmichael is the most innovative of the sites, possessing the stump of a round tower, very close to the southwest corner of the church, recalling the engaged round tower at St Michael le Pole in Dublin. As suggested above, episcopal presence at Tully could indicate pre-eighth century importance. It seems then that the majority of the mortared stone churches were constructed on pre-Viking ecclesiastical sites contrasting with the churches of the port-town, which were, in many cases, on virgin ground.

It may have been their construction on pre-Viking sites that contributed to the conservative architecture of the churches. In a sense all those who controlled the land of these churches, whose donations to reformed orders are described above, were incomers to Cualu: Hiberno-Scandinavian, Uí Dúnchada and Uí Chennselaig. In early medieval Ireland even powerful incomers needed to legitimize their position in new territory by capturing the past and making it their own. How better to do this than by building new prestigious structures in stone that in general aspect recalled the earlier wooden churches whose roots were in the conversion period?[124] However, the density of these churches in a relatively unimportant area and their proposed timeframe requires further consideration. This must be sought in the specific nature of the projected Christian identity of the port-town.

Reform of the church and Dublin

The extension of the political horizons of Irish kings into the Irish Sea region, beginning with Diarmait mac Máel na mBó and continued by Muirchertach Ua Briain, instigated and encouraged by the international trade of Dublin, was paralleled by an exposure to changes in the structure of ecclesiastical organization occurring in Europe.

The first bishop of Dublin came from the background of Cologne and Muirchertach Ua Briain's apprenticeship as king of Dublin was passed in company with the Dublin bishop, Gilla Pátraic, who was consecrated in Canterbury. At this point in time the European reformers' concerns were not with the minutiae of the territorial extents of parishes but with the standardization of liturgy and the organizational hierarchy of the church. Having just fought a battle with York to assert the primacy of Canterbury, Lanfranc (archbishop of the latter) wished to establish the beginnings of a similar structure in Ireland where Dublin would become a second metropolitan with York under Canterbury's primacy. Further down the hierarchy reformers wanted to establish that bishops were appointed by two

123 Etchingham, 'Wicklow', p. 122; for example, Mont St Michel and Skellig Michael. There was an established local devotion to St Michael in Máel Ruain's eighth-century *céli Dé* foundation at Tallaght. 124 Shane Lordan, 'An Irish apostle: articulating and actualizing apostolicity in the early Irish church' (PhD, UCC, 2013), p. 45, on the legitimizing nature of origins in medieval ecclesiastical thought.

other bishops thus giving them canonical status and protecting them from secular interests.[125] Also the gift of liturgical trappings from Canterbury to Donngus, the subsequent bishop to Gilla Pátraic, indicated a reform concern with the practice of liturgy in what Lanfranc was promoting as the cathedral church of Ireland, Christ Church.[126]

The organization of the Irish church outside Dublin had a very different structure to that envisaged by the reformers. Although Irish bishoprics were territorial they were 'not characterized by long term stability but tended to fluctuate, in which respect they may have reflected the secular political scene'.[127] Similarly the abbacies of foundations with evidence of episcopal authority were staffed by the secular powerbase of the area, for example the Uí Dúnchada at Kildare, as mentioned above, or, on a more restricted level, the Uí Rónáin (Uí Bairrche) at Clondalkin.[128] It was becoming a tenet of European reform that episcopal sees should be placed in major towns,[129] which designation, in late eleventh-century Ireland, probably only described Dublin, despite attempts over the last thirty years to designate major early ecclesiastical sites as 'monastic towns'.[130] Certainly this was the image Dublin was projecting, as described above.

Around 1096, and for the remainder of his period of influence, Muirchertach Ua Briain rejected Canterbury's apparent scheme of hegemony over the ecclesiastical structure of both islands. This was almost certainly to do with Muirchertach's growing control of the Irish Sea region and also his support of the Welsh against England's new Norman kings.[131] In his self-perception as overking of a now-extensive territory, English interference at its economic heart would have been both inappropriate and destabilizing. He developed an alternative plan, which became obvious in his courting of Armagh and promotion of Cashel as a Munster metropolitan.[132] He turned his attention also to embellishment of Glendalough, its wall and gatehouse a conscious replica of Dublin whose stone walls date to *c.*1100.[133] Indeed he was

125 Martin Holland, 'Dublin and the reform of the Irish church in the eleventh and twelfth centuries', *Peritia*, 14 (2000), 111–60, at 122, nn 45, 46. **126** Ibid., 120. **127** Etchingham, *Church organization*, p. 194. **128** Charles Doherty, 'Cluain Dolcáin, a brief note' in Smyth (ed.), *Seanchas*, pp 182–8, at pp 184–7. Doherty's suggestion of parochial formation in 1076 may be premature, see Boazman, 'Theme', pp 469–70; Ó Carragáin, *Churches*, p. 241. **129** Holland, 'Reform of the Irish church', 116–17. **130** For the original pro-monastic town model, see Charles Doherty, 'The monastic town in early medieval Ireland' in Howard B. Clarke and Anngret Simms (eds), *The comparative history of urban origins in non-Roman Europe* (Oxford, 1985), British Archaeological Reports 255, pp 45–75. For an opposing view, see Colmán Etchingham, 'The organization and function of an early Irish church settlement: what was Glendalough?' in Charles Doherty, Linda Moran and Mary Kelly (eds), *Glendalough: city of God* (Dublin, 2011), pp 22–53. **131** Duffy, 'Irishmen and Islesmen', 108–10; Holland, 'Reform of the Irish church', 128–9. **132** The second had the added value of dislodging the Eóganacht Chaisil, long-term enemies of Dál Cais, from their traditional caput. **133** Tomás Ó Carragáin, 'Rebuilding the "city of angels": Muirchertach Ua Briain and Glendalough' in Sheehan and Ó Corráin (eds), *Viking Age*, pp 258–70, at pp 264–6.

probably the first proponent of the 'monastic town' model. His rationale for this became abundantly clear at the synod of Ráith Bressail in 1111 when the ecclesiastical power of Dublin was side-lined by its inclusion in a large diocese, headed by Glendalough.[134]

Mortared stone churches and the ecclesiastical reforms of Muirchertach Ua Briain

The whole group of mortared stone churches of Rathdown almost certainly lie within the context of this relationship of power politics and ecclesiastical reform in the late eleventh- and early twelfth-century period. Their patrons, a mixture of indigenous and incomer, were all domiciled in Dublin,[135] and these churches were ecclesiastical foundations whose land formed part of their country estates. As indicated above, the building of multiple churches in Dublin constructed in the psyche of the inhabitants the social identity of a city. The mortared stone churches of Rathdown mirrored and reinforced this perception in the hinterland. It is most likely that they were constructed during the late eleventh and first three decades of the twelfth century, perhaps at first in concurrence with Muirchertach's early embrace of Dublin ascendancy and some maybe in defiance after the rejection of the port-town at Ráith Bressail. Although it has been suggested that the construction of the churches was part of the establishment of a parish network,[136] this seems a premature and over-specific explanation of their initiation, as the synod of Ráith Bressail in 1111, and indeed the synod of Kells in 1152, concerned themselves with the establishment of the macrostructure of church organization, primarily the delineation of dioceses.

High crosses

Ecclesiastical patronage in the hinterland by the elite of Dublin is further illustrated in two (possibly three) high crosses, situated at Kilgobbin and Tully. These are attributed to the group of Irish high crosses dated roughly to the first half of the twelfth century which would accord with the construction of the mortared stone churches.[137] These twelfth-century crosses give prominence

134 John McErlean, 'Synod of Ráith Breasil. Boundaries of the dioceses of Ireland', *Archivium Hibernicum*, 3 (1914), 1–33, at 16. 135 John T. Gilbert, *History of the city of Dublin*, 3 vols (Dublin, 1854), i, p. 230; Duffy, 'Irishmen and Islesmen', 104; *Reg. Alen*, p. 80. 136 Hinted at by Clarke, 'The diocese of Dublin', p. 49 and stated more forcefully in Corlett, 'Tully church', p. 108. Corlett's placing of two of the mortared stone church group in the tenth century (see above) would be very early to warrant an explanation of parish foundation as a reason for their construction. 137 Peter Harbison, *The high crosses of Ireland: an iconographical and photographic survey*, 3 vols (Bonn, 1992), iii, p. 384 dates Kilgobbin to the twelfth century; Elizabeth O'Brien, 'Churches of south-east County Dublin, seventh to twelfth century' in Gearóid Mac Niocaill and Patrick Wallace (eds), *Keimela: studies in medieval archaeology and history in memory of Tom Delaney* (Dublin, 1988), pp 504–24, at pp 512–13 dates both the field cross at Tully and Kilgobbin to the twelfth century.

1.5a *(above left)* Kilgobbin high cross, showing east side with west inset (photo: by kind permission of Peter Harbison) **1.5b** *(above right)* Kilfenora West Cross (photo: G. Boazman)

to the Christ figure both in high-relief and size relative to the whole cross-head.[138] At Kilgobbin (fig. 1.5a) the crucifixion figure on the east side is in relatively high relief, feet extending below the ring with a slightly exaggerated length of thin arms. The figure has a loin cloth. On the western side is Christ triumphant with a long robe. The eastern side of Kilgobbin has a long moulding extending the length of the shaft, from the feet of Christ, similar to the West Cross at Kilfenora, Co. Clare, also dated to the twelfth century (fig. 1.5b).[139] Kilgobbin has a protuberance on top of the vertical cross arm which could have supported the stone replica of a house-shaped shrine. This particular motif may have carried over from the crosses of the ninth and tenth century, such as Monasterboice, which differed stylistically from the twelfth-century examples, being characterized by low-relief carving and scriptural representations in panels on the shaft. Kilgobbin, probably originally founded by the Uí Máil,[140] was later associated with Hiberno-Scandinavian landowners as described above.

138 Tadhg O'Keeffe, *Romanesque Ireland: architecture and ideology in the twelfth century* (Dublin, 2004), p. 37. **139** Harbison, *High crosses*, p. 384. **140** Boazman, 'Hallowed', p. 42.

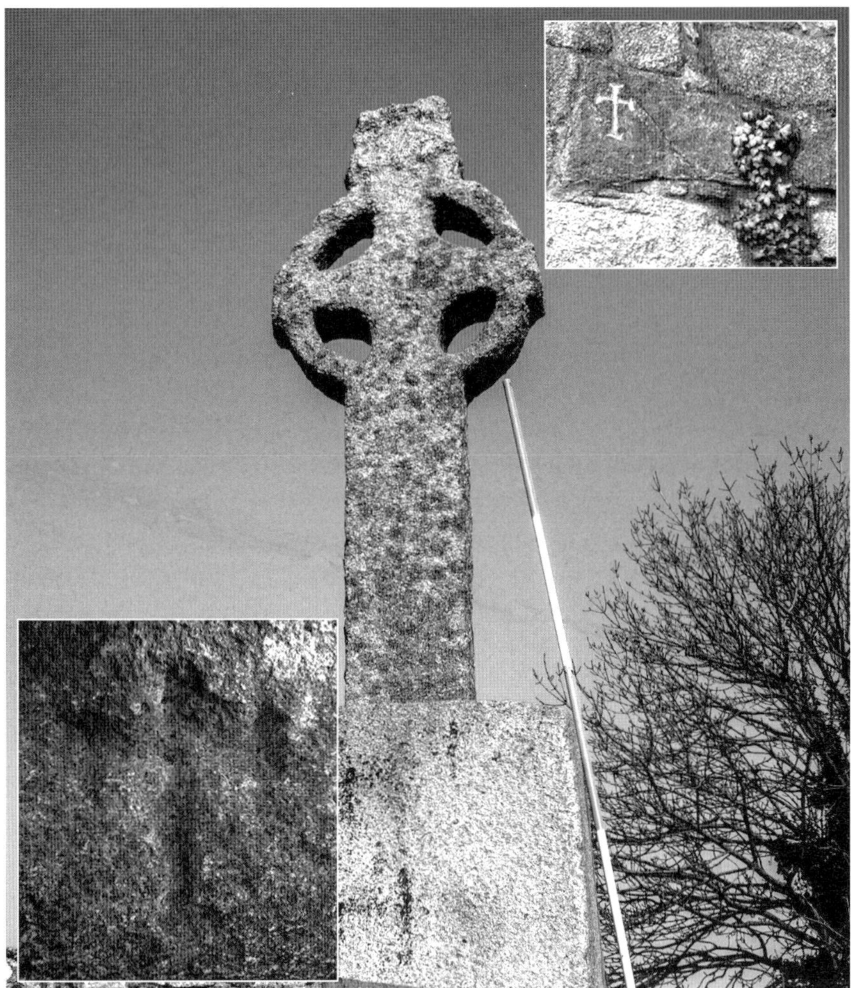

1.6 Tully Lane cross, showing incised cross with barred terminals on base (inset lower left) and similar cross on north wall of later medieval Dalkey church (inset upper right) (photos: G. Boazman)

A house-shaped shrine features on the very plain ringed cross at Tully Lane. O'Brien dates this cross to the tenth to eleventh century, based assumedly on the house-shaped shrine.[141] O'Brien also notes an incised cross with barred terminals on the Tully base, similar to an example carved on a stone built into the south wall of Dalkey church (fig. 1.6), probably from a preceding mortared stone church.[142] As discussed above, if the stone at Dalkey came from a

141 O'Brien 'Churches', pp 508, 512. If it is early it would be more likely to be ninth to tenth century as the second half of the tenth century and the eleventh represent a gap in the production of cross sculpture. **142** Ibid.

1.7a (*left*) Tully field cross: west face (photo: G. Boazman) 1.7b (*right*) Tully field cross: east face with ecclesiastic. The cross is very weathered and the inset shows Du Noyer's drawing. However, the crossover of the chasuble bottom can just be made out in the photograph as an 'X' shape which differs from the drawing (photo: G. Boazman. Drawing: George Du Noyer, by permission Royal Irish Academy)

previous mortared stone church, such a church was likely to have been built in the 1050–1130 period and so the incised cross on the Tully base could be contemporary. Although because of the lack of features on the cross it is hard to be definitive, the context, in the environs of a mortared stone church on an ecclesiastical estate controlled by the Meic Turcaill, whose floruit was late eleventh to twelfth century, would support a corresponding date.[143]

The field cross at Tully falls more clearly into twelfth-century parameters. It is not ringed and its ratio of shaft to head gives it a feeling of flow and elegance, enhanced on the west face by the roll mouldings which slightly diverge from the cross-head to the base. It has a single oval raised shape at the

143 Corlett ('Tully church', p. 106) suggests a tenth-century date for the cross because of the longhouse evidence of Structure 1 at Cherrywood. This association seems unlikely for, as discussed above, the monumentalization of Hiberno-Scandinavian conversion begins with the founding of Christ Church *c*.1030. The cross seems more likely to coincide with the two very close eleventh- to twelfth-century date-ranges of Cherrywood Structures 2 and 3.

1.8a (*right*) High ranking ecclesiastic on Dysert O'Dea high cross (photo: G. Boazman)

1.8b (*below*) High ranking ecclesiastic on Tuam high cross (photo: by kind permission of Peter Harbison)

1.8c (*above left*) High ranking ecclesiastic on Glendalough 'Market Cross' (photo: G. Boazman)

centre of the west head (fig. 1.7a). On the east face it has a high-relief figure of an ecclesiastic (fig. 1.7b), one of the defining features of twelfth-century crosses, which it shares with Tuam, Dysert O'Dea and the Market Cross at Glendalough (figs 1.8a–c). The presence of a mitre and side-facing crozier on the figure of Dysert O'Dea suggests episcopal status. Neither Tuam nor Tully have mitres, and unfortunately the Glendalough Market Cross is damaged so that the head-gear is indistinct. The croziers of these three face forward. The Dysert O'Dea figure appears to have a plain garment whereas the Tuam and Market Cross figures have a distinct chasuble with a V-neck draping over the arms, worn over a surplice. The cross at Tully differs in that the ecclesiastic is holding the crozier in both hands and the garment has a curious crossover at the bottom.[144] However, the most outstanding feature of the Tully figure is that he appears to have a beard, all the other bishops being clean-shaven.[145]

Ó Floinn places Tuam and the Market Cross at Glendalough in the same timeframe, the second quarter of the twelfth century, suggesting that they coincide with Tairdelbach Ua Conchobair's period of influence when he, like his predecessor kings, Diarmait mac Máel na mBó and Ua Briain, took over the control of Dublin in 1118.[146] This period was a tumultuous one in Dublin's ecclesiastical affairs. After Muirchertach Ua Briain's promotion of Glendalough to diocesan status, Dublin's long-serving bishop Samuel continued as incumbent until his death in 1121, after which a standoff occurred between Cellach of Armagh and the choice of some of the people of Dublin, Gréne. This concerned the status of Dublin as subservient to Armagh or as a metropolitan in its own right. Almost certainly Tairdelbach Ua Conchobar was also unhappy with the arrangements of Ráith Bressail which denied Tuam metropolitan status and as he was in control of Dublin at the time he may have supported Gréne. The name Gréne suggests Norse extraction and his obit in 1162 (AFM) indicates that he spoke several languages. It seems likely, given the context of the cross, that Gréne was supported by the Meic Turcaill and that they commissioned the cross at Tully in pursuit of metropolitan status for Dublin. An interpretation of other twelfth-century crosses such as Kilfenora and Tuam is that they were erected to raise the profile of ecclesiastical foundations which were passed over at Ráith Bressail.[147] Perhaps the beard and the unusual vestment shape indicated the multiple outside influences flowing into Dublin.

144 There is an outstanding photograph of the east face of the cross in Corlett, 'Tully church', p. 103, fig. 5.18. **145** Although the Christ figure on the Tuam cross has a beard and probably the Christ figure on the Glendalough Market Cross. **146** Ragnall Ó Floinn, 'The market cross at Glendalough' in Doherty et al. (eds), *Glendalough*, pp 80–110, at pp 101–2. **147** Cronin, 'Late high crosses in Munster', p. 145.

Sculpture and the cross

There are five examples of smaller granite crosses in the Rathdown area, three of which are disc-headed, the latter at present situated at Fassaroe, St Ann's Roman Catholic church, Shankill and Rathmichael Lane. The Fassaroe example is the only one that has survived close to full size and measures 1.40m from the base of the shaft to the top of the cross-head. In comparison, the two crosses at Tully and that of Kilgobbin measure 2m, 2.20m and 2.45m respectively. Two of the disc-headed crosses, at St Ann's and Rathmichael, have vestigial arms. All five have a crucifixion figure on one side and Rathmichael has a crucifixion on both sides. On the Fassaroe and St Ann's crosses the head falls to the figure's right, recalling the Market Cross at Glendalough and the cross at Tuam (figs 1.9a–c). The Fassaroe cross has a rounded moulding around the outer circumference and the Christ figure is in false relief on a recessed background, with four moulded quadrants in the right angles of the cross, whose curved edge forms an inner circumference moulding broken by the arms and the feet of the figure. The very thin elongated arms with large hands are reminiscent of Kilgobbin and the Market Cross. On the Rathmichael cross the head is upright, but on one side the figure is in false relief on a narrow recessed background and on the other in relief. The false relief figure appears to be wearing a loincloth and the relief figure a robe, recalling Christ crucified and Christ triumphant on the Kilgobbin cross.

The crosses at Fassaroe and St Ann's feature disembodied heads. A further cross at Blackrock, of which only the head and the top of the shaft survives, has no disc, but has a worn crucifixion in relief on a recessed background on one side similar to the disc-headed examples and an oval head in the centre on the other. There is some evidence of moulding around the edges and champfering of the shaft. Both Fassaroe and St Ann's show some champfering of the shaft.

The cross at Jamestown is eccentric to the grouping just described. It seems to have had a disc head and has an upper arm which appears to be off-centre. It has a broad shaft, tapering towards the end. On one side is a figure in high relief (fig. 1.10) with an oval head similar to the disembodied heads on the crosses described above. The figure is naked except for a loin cloth and has the hands clasped at the umbilicus. The legs are widely spaced at the hips but come together at the feet and the shoulders are hunched so that the neck is not visible. On the other side there is a circle at the meeting of the cross arms and, from this, three mouldings in high-relief descend towards the base.

As noted above, Ó Floinn dates the Market Cross at Glendalough and that at Tuam to the second quarter of the twelfth century. As these share the motif of the right-inclined head of Jesus with St Ann's and Fassaroe, it would not be too much of an assumption to place them in the same timeframe. The Rathmichael cross with an upright head may be slightly earlier. The disembodied heads on Blackrock, Fassaroe and St Ann's would also fit with the

1.9a (*top left*) Disc-headed cross now situated at St Ann's RC church, Shankill (photo: G. Boazman)

1.9b (*top right*) Market Cross at Glendalough, showing Christ's head towards right shoulder (photo: G. Boazman)

1.9c (*left*) Disc-headed cross now situated at Fassaroe, with disembodied head on rim (photo: G. Boazman)

second quarter of the twelfth century, as oval heads are a feature of the Romanesque period occurring, for example, on the outer order of the chancel arch at Cormac's chapel (1127–34) and also as a single head at Temple Cronan, Co. Clare. However, the heads in Rathdown are unlike the examples from the remainder of Ireland in that they occur on crosses rather than in the fabric of churches.

1.10 Cross at Jamestown: top left present position, right full-length sculpture, bottom left cross at Keel Chiggyrt, Maughold, Isle of Man. The Manx cross has hunched shoulders and widely placed legs (*top left photo*: G. Boazman; *right photo* by kind permission of Elizabeth O'Brien; *lower left* drawing: Kermode, *Manx crosses*)

Unfortunately, the original sites of the three disc-headed crosses are unknown. Those at Rathmichael Lane and St Ann's were found at Kiltuck, probably part of the collection of a nineteenth-century antiquarian. As Rathmichael, going by the evidence of the round tower, was a more major site than Kiltuck in the early twelfth century, it may have been the original site of at least one of these two crosses. Fassaroe is not mentioned as a church site in documentary records and a literary reference suggests that the cross may have come from Ballyman, a site connected with the Dál Messin Corb saint Sillán.[148] The cross at Blackrock may have marked the boundary of an ecclesiastical estate at Monkstown, subsequently in the hands of St Mary's.[149]

The cross at Jamestown seems to be in its original situation. Its odd figure could perhaps be referenced in a representation on a cross at Maughold on the Isle of Man, which shares the same hunched shoulders, widely spaced legs and slightly exaggerated ears (fig. 1.10).[150] However, the three mouldings descending from a circle on the other face are paralleled at a much closer location. A cross-slab built into the roof of the triforium of St Patrick's cathedral in Dublin has a motif with a cross shaft, flanked by two mouldings on each side, very similar to Jamestown but with an encircled cross at the head. There are seven of these granite slabs in Dublin, characterized by encircled Greek crosses, in relief or false relief.[151] In five of these the cross arms break the inner circle similar to the cross at Fassaroe. One of the St Patrick's slabs features, in the quadrants of the cross arms, a small triangular sinking similar to two crosses inscribed on natural rock just northeast of the mortared stone church at Dalkey Island.

The disc-headed crosses are unique in the corpus of Irish crosses, their closest parallels in shape being in Cornwall and the Isle of Man, but Manx crosses, in the vast majority, do not feature crucifixion figures.[152] Roughly a third of the Cornish crosses have a crucifixion figure but these are in relief with a single flat moulding surrounding the cross edge, unlike the false relief of the St Ann's and Fassaroe figures and the rounded moulding of Fassaroe.[153]

148 Boazman, 'Theme', p. 569 for a discussion of these nineteenth-century references. 149 Seán Ó Conbhuí, 'The lands and granges of St Mary's abbey in south County Dublin', *PRIA*, 62 (1962), 21–86, at 56–8. 150 Philip Moore Callow Kermode, *Manx crosses* (London, 1907), pl. XVIII, facing p. 128. Kermode identifies the figure with Christ but it bears a certain resemblance in bodily shape to the 'Thor' figure on the cross at Bride (ibid., facing p. 180), probably a case of syncretic fluidity in artistic representation. 151 Heather King, 'The pre-1700 memorials in St Patrick's cathedral' in Manning (ed.), *Dublin and beyond the Pale*, pp 75–83, 77–8; there are two others, at St Audoen's and in the National Museum, the second found in a culvert in Mount Street. One of the St Patrick's examples could be described as Latin but the top and side arms are within the moulded circle (ibid., fig. 4). 152 David Wilson, 'The conversion of the Viking settlers in the Isle of Man' in Garipzanov (ed.), *Conversion and identity*, p. 125. Also, in the majority, the Manx crosses are partially in relief, partially incised on slabs, the disc heads are not three dimensional. 153 Arthur G. Langdon, *Old Cornish crosses* (Truro, 1896).

The disembodied head feature, as indicated above, does not occur on crosses in the remainder of Ireland.[154] It could reference bishops and be concerned with the diocesan rivalry between Dublin and Glendalough. The cross-slabs in Dublin also form a characteristic group dissimilar to cross-slabs at even relatively close ecclesiastical sites such as Glendalough. However, they share stylistic motifs with the five hinterland crosses and the inscribed crosses on Dalkey Island. The hinterland crosses embody eclectic influences, from inside and outside Ireland, but reproduce them in a distinctive style. They are also relatively unsophisticated, compared to the Tully or Kilgobbin crosses, which could indicate non-elite production. Ó Floinn sees the famous relic of the Speaking Crucifix in Christ Church as engendering a 'cult of the Cross' in the hinterland evidenced by both groups of crosses, large and small, which is quite possible.[155] However, to broaden the implications of this observation it could be said that the crosses, similar to the churches, represent at all levels in the society of the hinterland, an investment in the construction of a distinct identity, compounded of elements of traditional and innovatory Christianity, both reflecting and nourishing the reform image of the port-town from the late eleventh century into the first three decades of the twelfth.

Rathdown slabs

Further material evidence of the interaction between tradition and innovation that formed the particular identity of the hinterland are the series of inscribed slabs, whose description, 'Rathdown slabs', indicates their provenance. They occur only in the area east of the parish of Tallaght, north to Taney and south to Killegar and Kilbride in north Co. Wicklow. There are twenty-eight extant, possibly eight built into the fabric of later medieval churches and seven non-extant but recorded.[156] All the slabs were situated in the context of the early ecclesiastical sites discussed in this article and sixteen of the extant slabs are in the graveyards of the mortared stone churches (fig. 1.11). It is likely, therefore, that they are commemorative grave-slabs and, as they are decorated on one side only, that they were recumbent.

154 There are heads on the Cross of the Scriptures, Clonmacnoise, Muiredach's Cross, Monasterboice and the cross at Durrow. However, these are small and inconspicuous, in low relief, under the cross arm in the first two cases and on the south side of the third. They are entwined in serpents and are part of the overall iconographic design. 155 Ó Floinn, 'Market cross', p. 102. Ó Floinn considers the Speaking Crucifix to be included in the relics first brought to Christ Church from Cologne by Donngus in the second quarter of the eleventh century. However, it should be noted that Marie Therese Flanagan proposes the Speaking Crucifix to be a later acquisition as it is not mentioned among the relics re-enshrined by Gréne, perhaps in 1152, but is mentioned in the later Book of Obits (*Transformation*, p. 233). Perhaps as the relationship of worshippers with the crucifix entailed its total visibility, it may not have been enshrined but remained separate from the smaller relics. 156 I am indebted to Patrick Healy's comprehensive research on the Rathdown slabs summarized in idem, *Pre-Norman grave-slabs*.

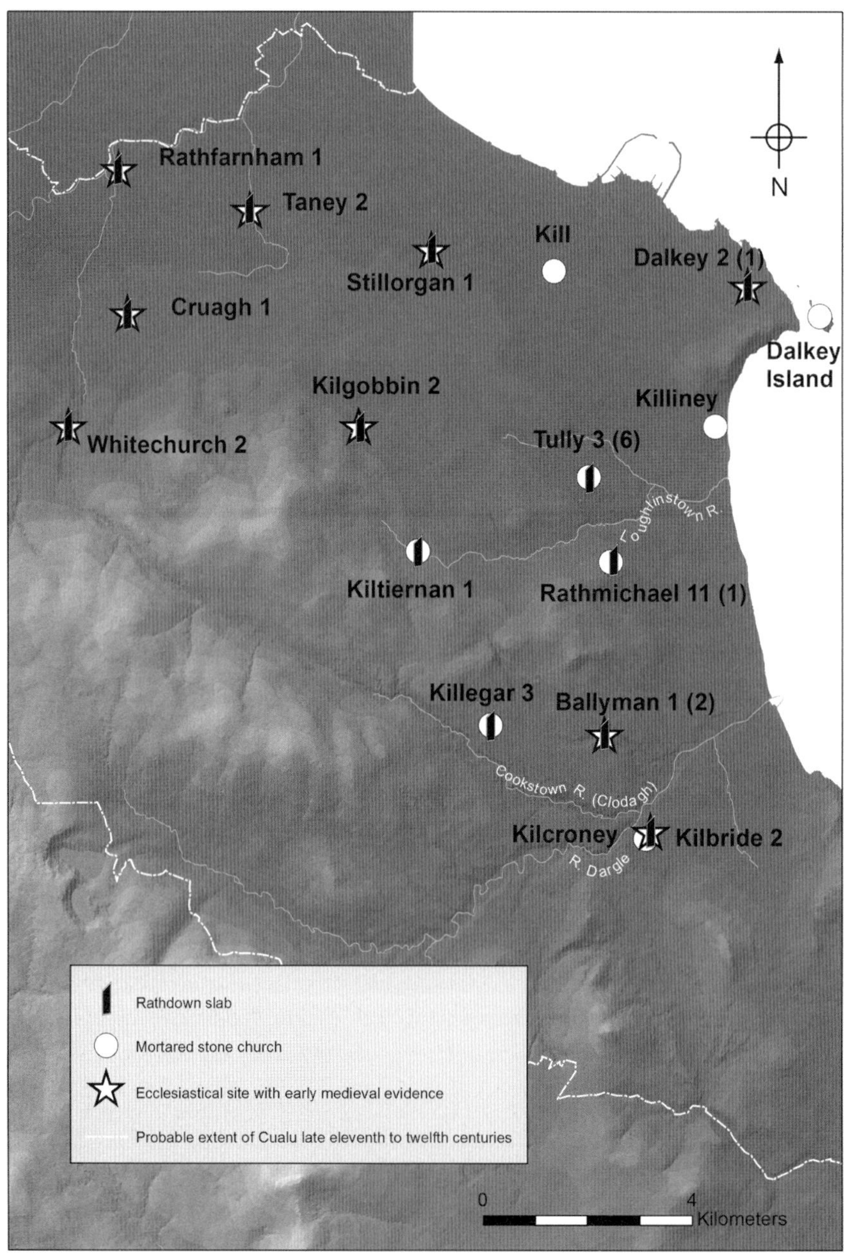

1.11 Distribution of Rathdown slabs. The figures in brackets are those slabs identified by Healy as being built into the fabric of later medieval churches (Healy, *Pre-Norman grave-slabs*, 68–9) or recorded but now non-extant (map: G. Boazman)

The decoration of twenty-five of the slabs is cryptic, being formed of incised symbols that occur throughout the corpus but are never combined in the same manner, each slab being unique in pattern. These motifs are a cup-mark surrounded by two to four equally-distanced concentric circles (fig. 1.12a), diagonal herring-bone emanating from a central rib (fig. 1.12b), 'C' shapes (fig. 1.12c), in two of three cases only on the edge of the slab, as well as various rectilinear shapes. Four of the slabs have been described as bearing 'saltire' crosses, although the 'X' shape is bisected in three cases by a longitudinal line and in the fourth the 'X' is formed into a triangle by the addition of a horizontal line. These four crosses also carry different examples of the motifs of the rest of the group, one 'C' shapes, one herring bone and two central cup-marks.

It was initially suggested that some of the slabs, particularly those with Christian symbolism, were pre-Viking. This referred to slabs at Whitechurch, Tully and Kilbride, where two small bosses below the cross arms were interpreted as sun and moon symbols.[157] The cross at Tully, however, has herring-bone patterning on the lower section, using the cross shaft as central rib (fig. 1.12a) and the double cross at Kilbride has two deep cup-marks at the cross centre.[158] This use of motifs common to the corpus of the slabs would suggest that all the monuments, with or without crosses, lie within the same chronological framework. The remainder of the slabs, despite the lack of Christian iconography, have their context in the sanctified ground of ecclesiastical sites founded in the sixth to seventh centuries which often contain a later mortared stone church. This would suggest their connection with the monumentalization of Hiberno-Scandinavian Christian belief beginning with the foundation of Christ Church, discussed above. The choice of individuals in Rathdown to commemorate their relations, in this manner, in these places would have further substantiated the changing social identity of the inhabitants of Dublin and its hinterland, both in their own eyes and in the perception of others.

As the slabs occur in the graveyards of the churches of the small ecclesiastical estates in the gift of local magnates, it seems likely that they commemorate those tenants who worked land on the estates. From a very early period the tenants of ecclesiastical estates in Ireland could be secular families who retained a certain autonomy in the management of their land.[159] It cannot be assumed then that the slabs commemorated only ecclesiastics. Also, although precise dating of grave-slabs is almost impossible, the use of rectilinear recumbent monuments for commemoration of secular individuals at Glendalough seems to be a feature of the eleventh and twelfth centuries.[160]

157 Healy, *Pre-Norman grave-slabs*, 43, 47. **158** The cross at Whitechurch echoes two of the cross slabs (Healy, *Pre-Norman grave-slabs*, nos 3, 13) at St Patrick's which, it was suggested above, share stylistic attributes with the disc-headed crosses of Rathdown. **159** See n. 21 above; Etchingham, *Church organization*, p. 438. **160** Lorcan Harney, 'Glendalough, the evidence of the crosses and cross-slabs' in Doherty et al. (eds), *Glendalough*, pp 112–36, at pp 123–8.

1.12a (*top left*) The Tully slab featuring a Latin cross, herringbone and bosses (photo: G. Boazman)

1.12b (*top right*) Herring bone at Rathmichael (photo: G. Boazman)

1.12c (*bottom left*) Latin cross and 'C' shapes at Killegar (photo: G. Boazman)

Ó Floinn notes annalistic records of the death and probable burial of eminent secular individuals at Glendalough in this period.[161] As one of these was the mother of Muirchertach Ua Briain,[162] and acknowledging the input of Muirchertach into Glendalough, it would not be surprising to find a similar perhaps competitive trend in the hinterland of Glendalough's rival, complementing the new mortared stone churches and the crosses. One stone fragment links the slabs with the smaller crosses.[163] At Killegar there was found what appears to be the remains of a cross. It has part of a crucifixion figure on one side, in relief on a recessed background, which has an upright head, and an umbilicus, similar to the figure on the cross at Rathmichael. It is smaller, being 0.33m in diameter whereas Rathmichael is 0.65m in diameter. The cross at Killegar also has vestigial arms similar to St Ann's and Fassaroe. On its other side it has, incised, two concentric circles around a cup-mark similar to the slabs.

However, the technical execution of the Rathdown slabs, despite its boldness and vigour, lacks the uniformity and subtlety of the elite slabs at Glendalough. This would lend support to both these and the small crosses being produced locally to commemorate individuals in the mid-range of early medieval society, probably well-to-do tenants of ecclesiastical land as suggested above.

This does not elucidate the derivation and meaning of the symbols on the Rathdown slabs. Firstly, there is no precedent for the Rathdown symbols, or indeed the manner of their execution, in Scandinavia. The production of rune-stones increased hugely in Scandinavia, particularly eastern Sweden, in the eleventh century, seemingly in tandem with Scandinavian conversion.[164] These are characterized by rune inscriptions in narrow bands often close to the outside edges of the stones and later with zoomorphic detail within the bands. Crosses are more prevalent in the initial period of conversion.[165] The Gotland picture-stones, whose production period runs from the fifth/sixth to the eleventh centuries, include earlier complex figural scenes whereas the later picture-stones which feature Christian crosses are more abstract.[166] In both cases the incision is lighter and more accomplished than the Rathdown examples. However, the use of stone to materialize and give permanence to a readjustment of identity is similar, although in Cualu this took place in an ethnically diverse context where Christianity had been extant for six centuries.

There are parallels for the Rathdown symbols in eleventh- and twelfth-century craftwork on other materials. Healy pointed out the dot and circle (or

161 Ó Floinn, 'Market cross', p. 110 and n. 10 to same page. **162** 1098 (ATig, AFM). **163** Boazman, 'Theme', pp 625–6; Christiaan Corlett, 'The Rathdown slabs revisited' in Clarke and Johnson (eds), *Vikings in Ireland*, pp 438–50, at pp 445–6. **164** Anne-Sofie Gräslund and Linn Lager, 'Runestones and the Christian missions' in Stefan Brink and Neil Price (eds), *The Viking world* (London, 2008), pp 629–38, at pp 634–6. **165** Ibid., p. 634. **166** Laila Kitzler Ahfeldt, Magnus Kallstrom and Per Widerstrom, 'Introduction' in Maria Herlin Karnell (ed.), *Gotland's picture stones: an enigmatic legacy* (Gottland, 2012), circles) motif on combs from the Dublin excavations and there is a further example of two concentric circles around a circle on a metal object from Inishbofin, Co. Westmeath.[167] Hatching or herring-bone is well-evidenced on metalwork such as the Cross of Cong and on woodwork from Dublin.[168] However, it is important to keep in mind Laing's conclusions on the Dublin woodwork: 'In the broadest terms all the decorated wood from Dublin is "Insular" for its eclecticism shows it emerging from contacts with parts of England at particular times, always preserving its native sources by revivalism or tradition'.[169] This stresses two related points germane to this discussion. First, the use of what appear to be Irish ('native') motifs does not mean a pre-Viking date and, second, these motifs are neither Irish nor Scandinavian in derivation but emanate from the creative integration of diverse Insular sources.

Recently Corlett made the ingenious suggestion that the concentric circles represented round Viking shields and that the combination of symbols was heraldic, indicating affiliation to different Scandinavian families in the vicinity.[170] Although there is no archaeological proof of the round shield, found in very early Viking warrior-graves in Dublin, continuing in use into the twelfth century, Corlett uses Cambrensis' description of the Dublin and Irish Sea area attack on Dublin as a documentary reference to the use of round shields.[171] Although this is possible, for example it is suggested above that elite Dublin families of the eleventh and twelfth centuries based their income on mercenary activities, the reference to heraldic symbols is misleading as it suggests a tighter organization of representation than is demonstrated by the Rathdown slabs. A reference to a specific group would seem to suggest some recognizable patterning, at least, on several slabs in the same graveyard. Also, although there is some indication of early heraldic symbols in the Bayeux tapestry, it is thought that heraldry proper only commenced at an elite level in the thirteenth century.[172] It is possible that the symbols, similar to the rune-stones, indicate generational ties amongst the families in the area,[173] but the shield reference isolates Scandinavian ethnicity in what was, by the late eleventh century, a multi-cultural area.

Going back to ancient divisions, the examples of Rathdown slabs west of Two Rock Mountain would fall in Uí Chellaig Chualann and the remainder in

pp 6–9, at p. 7. **167** Pádraig Ó hÉailidhe, 'Early Christian grave-slabs in the Dublin region', *JRSAI*, 103 (1973), 51–64, at 58–9; Liam de Paor, 'Antiquities of the Viking period from Inishbofin, Co. Westmeath', *JRSAI*, 92 (1962), 187–91, pl. XV facing p. 187. **168** Griffin Murray, *The Cross of Cong: a masterpiece of medieval Irish art* (Dublin, 2014); James Lang, *Viking Age decorated wood: a study of its ornament and style*, Medieval Dublin Excavations, 1962–81, ser. B, vol. 1 (Dublin, 1988), pp 21, 30. **169** Ibid., p. 48. **170** Corlett, 'Rathdown slabs', pp 447–8. **171** Ibid.; A.B Scott and F.X. Martin (ed. and trans.), *Expugnatio Hibernica: the conquest of Ireland by Giraldus Cambrensis* (Dublin, 1978), p. 77. **172** Charles Stothard, 'Some observations on the Bayeux Tapestry' in Richard Gameson (ed.), *The study of the Bayeux Tapestry* (Woodbridge, 1997), pp 1–6, at pp 3–4. **173** Birgit Sawyer, *The Viking Age runestones, custom and commemoration in early medieval Sweden*

Uí Briúin Chualann, minus the extent of that territory south to Delgany. In the late eleventh and first part of the twelfth century, as described above, the land of the area was controlled by a complex hierarchy of sometimes Uí Chennselaig overkings, a constant Uí Dúnchada presence in the shape of the Mac Gilla Mo Cholmóc kings, remnants of the Uí Briúin Chualann and Hiberno-Scandinavian and Welsh magnates. Corlett suggests the slabs represent a privileging of Scandinavian roots by the 'Norse' of Rathdown in an 'identity crisis' caused by an influx of Welsh settlers in the 'early to mid-twelfth century'.[174]

Links between Leinster and Wales had existed from the conversion period: Mo Gorróc of Delgany and Mo Chonnóc (Kilmacanoge) were reputedly sons of a Welsh king,[175] and as detailed above both Diarmait mac Máel na mBó and Muirchertach Ua Briain supported exiled Welsh royalty from north and south Wales. More specific to Rathdown the alliance of the Meic Turcaill and Rhys ap Tewdwr is annalistically recorded. It would seem that it would not be a cultural shock to the Hiberno-Scandinavians who controlled land in Rathdown that Welsh allies settled among them. In fact, it is likely that they rented the land to them.[176] As Corlett points out himself, the Archbold family retained the use of Holy Trinity land at Laughanstown and, as indicated above, the Goodmans retained ownership of most of Killiney. These were both Hiberno-Scandinavian families who continued to live cheek by jowl with the Hiberno-Welsh Howels and Walshes into the later medieval period.

One question is why the Rathdown slabs or a similar example of material culture are not found in the Hiberno-Scandinavian hinterland north of Dublin. It could be said that the same mixture of cultures pertained in the northern hinterland, after all it was there that Cynan ab Iago and his son Gruffudd were almost certainly domiciled and members of the Meic Turcaill family are documented as owning land.[177] However, there is an essential difference in political history between the two areas. This is that Cualu was, from antiquity to the twelfth century, associated with the Leinster kingship,[178] while the hinterland north of Dublin, although possibly once part of Leinster,

(Oxford, 2000), p. 146. **174** Corlett, 'Rathdown slabs', p. 449, although he also refers, in the next sentence, rather confusingly, to an intensification of this phenomenon after the coming of Cambro-Normans in 1169. Although it may be a relevant comment for the post-1169 period, it does not help with the contextualizing of the Rathdown slabs, which he has variously dated to 'late eleventh to mid-twelfth century' (ibid., p. 444) and 'early twelfth to mid-twelfth century' (ibid., p. 448). **175** MacShamhráin, *Glendalough*, p. 124. **176** See n. 89 above. **177** Duffy, 'Ostmen, Irish and Welsh', 394; *CStM*, i, p. 83. **178** Edel Bhreathnach, 'Kings, the kingship of Leinster and the regnal poems of *laidsenchas Laigen*: a reflection of dynastic politics in Leinster, 650–1160' in Alfred P. Smyth, (ed.), *Seanchas: studies in early and medieval Irish archaeology, history and literature in honour of Francis J. Byrne* (Dublin, 2000), pp 299–312, at pp 309–12, for a discussion of the contribution of past tradition contained in symbol, place and origin legend to the legitimization of the Leinster kingship, even in the case of a 'politically astute and hardened' king such as Diarmait Mac

was for most of the early medieval period a tributary kingdom of the Southern Uí Néill. Cualu was the residence of the Uí Máil kings of Leinster, and then came under Uí Dúnlainge rule from the eighth century, becoming the relict kingdom of the Uí Dúnchada in the line of the Mac Gilla Mo Cholmóg kings in the eleventh century. It seems that probably because of an alliance of Leinster's age-old enemies, the Clann Cholmáin, with the Dál Cais, Leinster's interests came to coincide with Dublin's which led them to be main allies of Dublin at Clontarf. This coincidence of interest from the beginning of the eleventh century, which was epitomized by the two Uí Chennselaig kings, Diarmait mac Máel na mBó and in the twelfth century Diarmait Mac Murchada, gave the southern hinterland a security and confidence that the northern hinterland lacked. This consciousness of a relationship, both with the past ancient kingdom of Cualu and the present powerful kingdom of Dublin, combined with incomer settlement, almost certainly promoted the idiosyncratic material culture of the area.

CONCLUSION

The Rathdown slabs may indeed be an expression of identity but perhaps not with the specific ethnic connotations that have been assigned to them. There is a tendency, springing from John Bradley's characterization of the hinterland of Dublin, to see the Rathdown slabs as mapping out an area of Scandinavian settlement, although Bradley is careful to designate the term 'Hiberno-Scandinavian' to them.[179] In the above interpretation, Corlett uses the terms 'Hiberno-Norse' and 'Norse' interchangeably, and so the connotations of the 'Hiberno-' part of the label become meaningless.[180] Ethnic identity is not essentialist, it shifts imperceptibly over time,[181] and if it is accepted that the slabs are a feature of the late eleventh to early twelfth century it seems more appropriate to view them in the context of the process of social reorientation that was taking place in north Leinster described above. In this approach the slabs become an element, along with the mortared stone churches and crosses, in the gradual construction of a distinct regional identity from a multiplicity of discourses.

In the three hundred years of Scandinavian contact with the area of Cualu considered in this contribution, there is a myriad of evidence for the manner in

Murchada (ibid., 311). **179** Bradley, 'Scandinavian settlement', p. 60. **180** Corlett, 'Rathdown slabs', pp 446, 450 for a categoric association of the slabs with purely Norse identity. The shield argument shifts between characterization of the shields as 'early Viking' used by the 'Norse' on p. 447 to round shields used by the 'Hiberno-Norse' on the following page. **181** Philip von Rummel, 'The fading power of images: Romans, barbarians and the uses of a dichotomy in early medieval archaeology' in Walter Pohl and Gerda Heydemann (eds), *Post-Roman transitions: Christian and barbarian identities in the*

which this identity was reproduced. Initially there does seem to be a privilege of roots in the Scandinavian home countries, given the example of the whalebone plaque and the possible longhouse (Structure 1) at Cherrywood and, similarly, the warrior burials in the port settlement, albeit adjacent to traditional Irish burial places. Up to the battle of Clontarf, at which Dublin and Leinster were allied, the occupants of Dublin and its hinterland,[182] had a more fluid identity, joining the Irish in a series of military and marriage alliances but with a focus often deflected towards the east – Cumbria, Chester and York. The relationship of the Scandinavian-derived population of Dublin with one of the defining strands of Irish identity, Christianity, was ambivalent and invisible in material culture. However, the process of alliance, whether political or personal, must have engendered a conversion by osmosis at all levels of Scandinavian-derived society. Similarly, from the very establishment of the *longphort*, economic relations with the hinterland to support the settlement brought the negotiators into close contact with a social organization to which Christianity was integral. This was particularly well-represented in the area of Cualu, where a plethora of small productive ecclesiastical estates must have contributed considerably to the provisioning of Dublin. Although initially probably coercive, the entailed nature of these estates could have resolved itself into a more formal but symbiotic arrangement, from which new overlords and the ecclesiastical tenants of the estates both profited.

Identity is reflexive, composed of the interplay of our self-perception and the perception of us in the eyes of others. After Clontarf, beginning in the second quarter of the eleventh century the Scandinavians began to monumentalize a Christian identity in the port-town. This materialization of that which had previously been low-key and invisible changed both their self-perception and the perception of them by others. As well as its economic assets, well-known to Irish kings such as the Clann Cholmáin and the Dál Cais for two centuries, Dublin came to represent a new and desirable form of the traditional Irish ecclesiastical centre, a *civitas* for this world and the next. This manifestation of Christianity conveyed the security of familiarity for Irish observers. However, another attractive facet of the port-town for ambitious Irish kings of the eleventh and twelfth centuries – connections and

early medieval West (Turnhout, 2013), pp 365–406, at p. 365. **182** It could be said that these were a mixed population ethnically from the initial arrival of the Scandinavians. The area would have been characterized by dispersed Irish settlement, possibly partly on the ecclesiastical estates of Kilmainham and somewhere in the area between St Michael le Pole and St Peter's. See Barra Ó Donnabháin and Benedikt Hallgrimsson, 'The biological identity of the Hiberno-Norse town' in Seán Duffy (ed.), *Medieval Dublin II* (2001), pp 65–86, at p. 76 for the 'significant contribution' of the pre-contact population to the gene pool. Also the Scandinavians, arriving through the ninth century and after, were themselves ethnically diverse, with possible Danish and Norwegian backgrounds but with more recent personal histories of domicile throughout the Irish Sea region and further.

opportunities across the Irish Sea – introduced a note foreign to Irish ecclesiastical organization, that of European church reform.

It is in the context of this self-confident Hiberno-Scandinavian Christian identity in the port-town that the mortared stone churches, crosses and commemorative slabs of Cualu should be viewed. This southern hinterland of Dublin was a multi-cultural community and it was in the interests of all to reflect back the prestige of Dublin with a distinct material culture. This assertion of an identity interwoven of traditional and innovatory strands became particularly pressing after the promotion of Glendalough at Ráith Bressail. It could be said, that rather than one element causing an ethnic identity crisis, the whole material culture of Cualu both constructed and maintained an idiosyncratic and inclusive identity, Bradley's 'common culture', the significance of which was acknowledged by the promotion of Dublin to metropolitan status in 1152.

ACKNOWLEDGMENTS

I would like to thank Dr Tomás Ó Carragáin (UCC) for supervising the thesis on which the article is based and John Sheehan (UCC) who gave invaluable help and advice on the Viking Age; Dr Paul MacCotter, Kenneth Nicholls and the late Professor Donnchadh Ó Corráin who discussed territorial boundaries and interpretation of documents with me. I am most grateful to Dr Elizabeth O'Brien, Margaret Gowen and Dr Mark Clinton who allowed me to examine unpublished work, Tommy Halton and Brian Murray of the OPW who were so helpful in facilitating my access to the Tully Rathdown slabs, Nick Hogan (UCC) for unfailingly patient technological support and members of Rathmichael Historical Society for information and discussion on sites. Finally, thanks to the Irish Research Council and the Heritage Council who funded the research for my thesis.

New light on the beginnings of Christ Church cathedral, Dublin

DAGMAR Ó RIAIN-RAEDEL

Despite the many alterations made to its fabric since its foundation, and particularly the 'restoration' undertaken by George Edmund Street in 1871, Christ Church cathedral is the only extant building that references back to Hiberno-Norse Dublin. Now, however, thanks to studies by Howard Clarke, Roger Stalley, Tadhg O'Keeffe, Rachel Moss, Michael O'Neill and Stuart Kinsella, as well as excavations undertaken by Helen Kehoe and Linzi Simpson, parts of the medieval plan of the building can be re-envisaged.[1] The sparse documentary sources, and in particular the late fourteenth-century *Liber Niger* or Black Book of Christ Church, can now be augmented by architectural consideration, and an outline reconstruction of the footprint of the crypt, church, chapels and precinct of the conventual buildings of the original Benedictine chapter has become possible.[2]

It is generally agreed that the earliest building activity followed on from the pilgrimage to Rome in 1028 of the Hiberno-Norse king Sitriuc 'Silkenbeard', which is recorded in the Irish annals.[3] The *Liber Niger* names Sitriuc as the *fundator* who provided the site and money for the cathedral's construction, and who set the scene for the appointment of Dúnán (Donatus) to the role of its first bishop. We do not know where, or by whom, Donatus was consecrated but, following an incumbency lasting some forty years until his death in 1074, his successor, Gilla Pátraic (Patricius) – who was accidentally drowned a mere ten years later – became the first bishop of Dublin to be consecrated by an archbishop of Canterbury, a custom that was to be followed by three more

1 For these, see the essays in Kenneth Milne (ed.), *Christ Church cathedral, Dublin: a history* (Dublin, 2000); James Kelly and Dáire Keogh (eds), *History of the Catholic diocese of Dublin* (Dublin, 2000); also, Tadhg O'Keeffe, *Romanesque Ireland: architecture and ideology in the twelfth century* (Dublin, 2003); Rachel Moss, 'Tales from the crypt: the medieval stonework in Christ Church cathedral' in Seán Duffy (ed.), *Medieval Dublin III* (Dublin, 2002), pp 95–114; Michael O'Neill, 'Christ Church cathedral and its environs: medieval and beyond' in Seán Duffy (ed.), *Medieval Dublin XI* (Dublin, 2011), pp 298–319; For an overview, see Linzi Simpson, 'Fifty years a-digging' in Seán Duffy (ed.), *Medieval Dublin XI* (Dublin, 2011), pp 9–112. 2 On the *Liber Niger*, see H.J. Lawlor, 'A calendar of the *Liber Niger* and *Liber Albus* of Christ Church Dublin', *PRIA*, 27C (1908), 1–93, and Colmán Ó Clabaigh, 'The *Liber Niger* of Christ Church cathedral, Dublin' in Raymond Gillespie and Raymond Refaussé (eds), *The medieval manuscripts of Christ Church cathedral, Dublin* (Dublin, 2006), pp 60–80. 3 'Sitriuc grandson of Amlaíb, king of the foreigners, and Flannacán Ua Cellaig, king of Brega, went to Rome': AU s.a. 1028.

bishops, until Dublin was eventually incorporated into an Irish diocesan structure.[4] Primarily on the basis of papers published by the Jesuit scholar Aubrey Gwynn, with reference to the evidence of Canterbury documents, it has become generally accepted that the creation of the new diocese of Dublin formed part of a plan by England's chief church to exert primacy over the Irish church.[5]

While there is no uncertainty about Canterbury interest in Dublin from the late eleventh century onwards, particularly during the tenures of archbishops Lanfranc (d. 1089) and Anselm (d. 1109), the publication of two papers in *Medieval Dublin* (2005, 2006) has led to changes in our understanding of the origins of Christ Church. Pádraig Ó Riain demonstrated that the church's martyrology, still extant in a thirteenth-century copy (MS TCD 576, fos. 75–132), had come to Dublin from Metz via one of the two Benedictine monasteries at Cologne – Gross St Martin and St Pantaleon – which in the early eleventh century were home to Irish monks.[6] While the extant manuscript now contains the Rule of St Augustine, adopted by Archbishop Lorcán Ua Tuathail on his accession in 1162, when he introduced Arrouasian canons regulars to the cathedral, its martyrology reflects the Benedictine observance of the Cologne monasteries, as must have been the case since its foundation.[7]

Around the same time, Raghnall Ó Floinn made a study of the list of relics entered into the martyrology at 31 July and showed that a substantial part of what appear to have been the foundation relics of Christ Church had been procured in Cologne. According to Ó Floinn, the staff of St Peter and the chains that had bound him – relics originally acquired by Archbishop Brun, brother of Emperor Otto II and *archidux* of Lotharingia – 'bore powerful witness to the apostolic succession of the archbishops of Cologne' and, together with a number of episcopal relics, would have been most appropriate to underline Dublin's claim to be the first territorial cathedral in Ireland.[8] In a subsequent publication, Ó Floinn drew attention to a second list of relics contained in the Book of Obits, apparently dating to a later phase and

4 The names of the two bishops will be given in Latin, in the form in which they appear in most records. 5 For a reconsideration of Dublin-Canterbury connections, see Martin Brett, 'Canterbury's perspective on church reform in Ireland, 1070–1115' in Damian Bracken and Dagmar Ó Riain-Raedel (eds), *Ireland and Europe in the twelfth century: reform and renewal* (Dublin, 2006), pp 13–35. 6 Pádraig Ó Riain, 'Dublin's oldest book? A list of saints "made in Germany"' in Seán Duffy (ed.), *Medieval Dublin V* (Dublin, 2004), pp 52–72; idem, 'The calendar and martyrology of Christ Church cathedral, Dublin' in Gillespie and Refaussé (eds), *Medieval manuscripts of Christ Church*, pp 33–59; idem, *A martyrology of four cities: Metz, Cologne, Dublin, Lund* (London, 2008); J.C. Crosthwaite (ed.) and J.H. Todd (intr.), *The book of obits and martyrology of the cathedral Church of the Holy Trinity, commonly called Christ Church, Dublin* (Dublin, 1844). 7 Ó Riain also showed that additions made to the martyrology in Cologne bear witness to the interest in their native saints maintained by the Irish Benedictines there. 8 Raghnall Ó Floinn, 'The foundation relics of Christ Church cathedral and the origins of the diocese of Dublin' in Seán Duffy

displaying the wide-reaching connections of Dublin's cathedral. Although now no longer verifiable, as all relics perished in the aftermath of the Reformation, the majority of the second list's items could likewise have been procured in Cologne. In addition, the cathedral's miraculous Speaking Crucifix, mentioned in the second list and attested from the twelfth century onwards and now also lost, might, as Ó Floinn argued, have been sourced at Cologne, and later used as a model by the stone masons who fashioned the 'Market Cross' at Glendalough which shows stylistic similarities with Rhenish metal work of the eleventh century.[9] Both lists begin with Christ-connected relics, the Speaking Crucifix in the second list and a piece of the True Cross in the first, a direct allusion to the cathedral's role as a *basilica sancti Salvatoris* (later translated into Christ Church), to which the dedication to the Holy Trinity was added when Archbishop Lorcán Ua Tuathail introduced Augustinian canons after his accession.

The two aforementioned publications thus established independently that at least some of the liturgical requirements for the Dublin cathedral were acquired in the course of Sitriuc's Roman pilgrimage. He evidently stopped over at Cologne and was received there by Helias (d. 1042), who then held the abbacy of both Benedictine communities in the city, Gross St Martin and St Pantaleon. Donatus, alias Dúnán, who was subsequently to be the first bishop of Dublin, may have been a monk at one of these monasteries and have returned with the king to Dublin with a view to cooperating with him in the establishment of Ireland's first territorial diocese.

Continental connections of this kind had already been noticed by Tadhg O'Keeffe in 2003 when he proposed that the nearest parallels to the Christ Church crypt were to be found in Lotharingia and the Rhineland.[10] Crucially, as O'Keeffe argued, this influence had come to Dublin both early and directly, bypassing England where comparable examples did not begin to appear until the latter part of the eleventh century. As the crypt's architectural features belonged in the foundation phase of the cathedral, the Continental influences on them thus pointed to the same timeframe as that proposed by Ó Riain and Ó Floinn.

The Cologne connection has featured in a number of other important studies, notably those of Marie Therese Flanagan on the transformation of the Irish church in the twelfth century, and Stuart Kinsella's reconstruction of the medieval cloister at Christ Church.[11] Kinsella reconstructed the layout of the

(ed.), *Medieval Dublin VII* (2006), pp 89–102, at p. 98. 9 Raghnall Ó Floinn, 'The late-medieval relics of Holy Trinity church, Dublin' in John Bradley, Alan J. Fletcher and Anngret Simms (eds), *Dublin in the medieval world: studies in honour of Howard B. Clarke* (Dublin, 2009), pp 369–89; idem, 'The "Market Cross" at Glendalough' in Charles Doherty, Linda Doran and Mary Kelly (eds), *Glendalough: city of God* (Dublin, 2011), pp 80–111. 10 O'Keeffe, *Romanesque Ireland*, pp 97–102. 11 Marie Therese Flanagan, *The transformation of the Irish church in the twelfth century* (Woodbridge, 2010); Tadhg O'Keeffe, cloister and conventual buildings located to the south of Christ Church and, crucially, showed these to be coeval with the first cathedral.[12] While no major excavations have been conducted in recent years within or without the cathedral, a number of exploratory digs found traces of previous structures beneath the present crypt floor but their evidence needs to be examined in more detail.[13] For much of the archaeology we have instead to depend on the somewhat unreliable nineteenth-century comments of Edmund Street and the cathedral architect Thomas Drew.[14]

The evidence of the late fourteenth-century *Liber Niger* of Christ Church shows that Sitriuc's church was wholly innovative in an Irish context.[15] Following on a fictitious foundation-story involving St Patrick, who was said to have celebrated mass in the arches and vaults (*fornices sive volto*) previously erected by the Danes, it relates how 'Sitriuc, king of Dublin, son of *Ableb* [Amlaíb], earl of Dublin' gave to the 'Holy Trinity and to Donatus, the first bishop of Dublin, a site on which to build a church and he also gave gold and silver sufficient to build a church with all its court (*curia*)'. It then goes on to state that Donatus built the nave with two aisles (*cum duobus collateralibus structuris*) and the base for the image of a crucifix (*solium ymaginis crucifixi*), together with the chapel of St Nicholas in the northern part with other buildings, in addition to a chapel of St Michael 'in his palace' (*in palacio suo*), the income of the latter being later used to provide for the table of the canons. When a new route-way was introduced west of the cathedral in 1234, the chapel (later St Michael's parish church) within the *placea palatii* was separated from the western range, which functioned as an episcopal palace and later as the prior's chambers. Kitchen and refectory were situated in the

Medieval Irish buildings, 1100–1600 (Dublin, 2015); Stuart Kinsella, 'Mapping Christ Church cathedral, Dublin, *c*.1028–1608' in John Bradley et al. (eds), *Dublin in the medieval world*, pp 143–67. 12 Some of the conventual buildings were redesigned with the advent of the Augustinian canons; by the early-modern period they were being utilized as the Four Courts and, after the relocation of these to the Gandon-designed new building across the Liffey in the late eighteenth century, they were used for commercial buildings and eventually fell into disrepair. 13 For the archaeological reports, see Helen Kehoe, 'Archaeological monitoring at Christ Church cathedral Dublin 8' (Unpublished report, licence no. 99E0539, 29 July 2000; http://www.excavations.ie/report/1999/Dublin/0004072); Linzi Simpson and Helen Kehoe, 'Excavation in the crypts of Christ Church cathedral, Dublin'; 'Archaeological assessment in the crypts of Christchurch cathedral, Dublin' (Licence Reference 99 E 0091/ Planning Reference 1886/98), 2 April 1999. I would like to thank Linzi Simpson for providing me with the reports. 14 Thomas Drew, 'On evidences of the plan of the cloister garth and monastic buildings of the priory of the Holy Trinity, now known as Christ Church cathedral, Dublin', *PRIA*, 16 (1879–86), 214–18; idem, 'The ancient chapter-house of the priory of the Holy Trinity, Dublin', *JRSAI*, 20 (1890–91), 36–43; for Street, see Roger Stalley (ed.), *George Edmund Street and the restoration of Christ Church cathedral, Dublin* (Dublin, 2000). 15 For a discussion of the two versions contained in the *Liber Niger*, which are here taken together, see Stuart Kinsella, 'From Hiberno-Norse to Anglo-Norman, *c*.1030–1300' in Milne (ed.), *Christ Church*

southern range with, in the customary manner, chapter-house and dormitory above it in the eastern range.

This plan of the basilica with its tripartite eastern end, mirroring that of the crypt, is further supported by an entry in the annals of St Mary's, which records the death of Bishop Donatus in 1074 and his subsequent burial at the 'right side of the high altar (*iuxta magnum altare ad dexteram ipsius est sepultus*)'.[16] Equally innovative was Donatus' choice of St Nicholas as patron for one of his chapels at a time when the saint's cult had not yet spread widely in the West, but was already present at Cologne, as was the dedication to St Michael. While the location of the cathedral complex in relation to Sitriuc's stronghold and the rest of the Hiberno-Norse town remains poorly understood, the archaeological evidence confirms the position of the earliest level of both the cloister complex and the cathedral.

Moreover, since the *Liber Niger* makes no reference to Donatus having built both a crypt and church above it, it may well be that the church was positioned on the ground-level and later used as a crypt; in other words, the plan of the present crypt may reflect that of the original church rather than that of a crypt. Late twelfth- and early thirteenth-century building activity would then have involved the partial or complete demolition of the original church building and the construction of the piers needed to hold the weight of the substantial Romanesque structure to be built over it. Further tests of extant crypt walls will no doubt determine the accuracy of this suggestion but, in its support, the sloping side of the present structure shows that most of the crypt was and is above ground, and particularly so on the northern side, where the upper church later had to be reached by a stairway. On the southern side, only a few steps lead from the crypt (i.e., the earlier church) up to the cloister and its surrounding ranges. Intriguingly, Archbishop John Cumin (1180–1212) appears to have been willing to adopt the confined eastern apsidal arrangement of the crypt as part of his cathedral at a time when such arrangements would long have been outdated and replaced by spacious eastern choirs and chancels. Arguably, he was aware that what he copied was the plan of the church rather than the *crypt* and decided to honour the achievements of Dublin's first bishop.

cathedral, pp 25–52, at pp 30–1. **16** Aubrey Gwynn, 'Some unpublished texts from the Black Book of Christ Church, Dublin', *AH*, 16 (1946), 281–337, at 333: *Dunanus episcopus Dublinie civitatis in Christo quievit, et in ecclesia sancte Trinitatis iuxta magnum altare ad dexteram ipsius est sepultus*; O'Keeffe, *Romanesque Ireland*, p. 102; in his obituary, the 'Christ Church annals', as recorded in the 'First Register of Christ Church', mention that Donatus was 'buried in the Choir, at the right hand side of the altar, where his body has been found some years since' and record for the year 1545 that a stone coffin was discovered containing the body of a bishop in episcopal dress, 'said to be that of Donat': Colm Lennon and Raymond Refaussé (eds), *The registers of Christ Church cathedral* (Dublin, 1998), pp 123, 125; Gilbert recorded that 'on repairing the choir some years since, his [Donatus'] body was found there with his mitre, which was an exquisite work of art': J.T. Gilbert, *A history of the*

The multi-disciplinary research to date, as outlined above, has yet to be brought together in the wider context of the background influences at work on Dublin's first two bishops, Donatus and Patricius.[17] However, research to date has gone some way towards supporting the view already expressed by Aubrey Gwynn in 1940, namely that the main purpose of his essay on the Irish monks and Cluniac reform

> has been to discuss the possibility of other influences outside Canterbury as causes of the Irish reforming movement which took shape in the last quarter of the eleventh century. What has been said should be sufficient to prove that Ireland was much more in contact with continental reformers than seems to have been understood by most of our recent historians.[18]

The complexity of this issue has since been stressed by Marie Therese Flanagan, who commented that:

> assessing the relative influence of Cologne and Canterbury on the foundation of the cathedral church of Dublin, and more generally of Continental and Irish influence on the wider Irish church, remains frustratingly difficult owing to the fragmentary nature of the evidence, but there is little doubt that sources generated by, or preserved at, Canterbury may have distorted perceptions about its impact on the Irish church.[19]

In the remainder of this essay I propose to bring to bear some hitherto neglected eighteenth- and nineteenth-century Continental evidence that throws new light on Dublin–Cologne associations in the early eleventh century.

THE NECROLOGY OF GROSS ST MARTIN: THE LOST 'PFARRBUCH NR. 12'

When Peter Opladen finished his history of the Benedictine monastery of Gross St Martin in 1944 (subsequently published in 1954), three *Memorienbücher* – manuscripts that contained the names of the monastery's community and its benefactors – were still available to him. Two of these, one from the year 1323,

city of Dublin, 3 vols (Dublin, 1854–9; reprinted 1973), i, p. 101. 17 For an earlier summary of the evidence, see Dagmar Ó Riain-Raedel, 'Irish Benedictine monasteries on the Continent' in Martin Browne and Colmán Ó Clabaigh (eds), *The Irish Benedictines: a history* (Dublin, 2005), pp 25–63, at pp 28–35. For subsequent research, see Pádraig Ó Riain, *Feastdays of the saints: a history of Irish martyrologies*, Société des Bollandistes, Subsidia Hagiographica, 86 (Brussels, 2006), and idem, *A martyrology of four cities*. 18 Aubrey Gwynn, 'Irish monks and the Cluniac reform', *Studies*, 29 (1940), 409–30, reprinted in idem, *The Irish church in the 11th and 12th centuries*, ed. Gerard O'Brien (Dublin, 1992), p. 15. 19 Flanagan, *Transformation of the Irish church*, 9.

and another from 1789, are still extant and, though since published, contain little of interest for the Irish phase of the monastery. The third and most important manuscript, Pfarrbibliothek St Martin Nr. 12, which contained a necrology, a *Martyrologium Romanum* (possibly similar to the Christ Church martyrology) and the Rule of St Benedict, transcribed by 'frater Henricus Zonsbeck' in 1474 under the abbacy of Adam Meyer, has since been lost.[20] Although the library of Gross St Martin was transferred to the Cologne Diocesan Library (Erzbischöfliche Diözesan- und Dombibliothek Köln) in 1908, the manuscript appears not to have been part of the move and may subsequently have been lost during the difficult war years. The necrology in Zonsbeck's *Memorienbuch* was based on an older necrology, possibly reaching back to its foundation. Fortunately, an alphabetical list of the entries in Zonsbeck's autograph, the *Necrologium Martinense*, was compiled by the Benedictine historian Oliver Legipont (d. 1758), while librarian at Gross St Martin.

In 1731, Legipont had composed a *Chronicon Abbatiae S. Martini Maj. Coloniae vulgo in insula Scotorum ordinis S. Benedicti Congregationis Bursfeldensis* (now Landes- and Universitätsbibliothek Darmstadt MS 2701), which attributed an Irish beginning for the monastery that reached back to the seventh-century reign of Pippin, king of the Franks from 751 and father of Charlemagne. Elements of this fictitious foundation-history, which established links between the Irish at Cologne and alleged missions led by their countrymen in Lotharingia, had already been the subject of comments by Cologne historians of the sixteenth and seventeenth centuries.[21] However, Legipont's account, which he expanded on in a number of subsequent versions, was presented in much greater detail, so much so that the text was accepted for publication by the renowned Bruno Krusch in the *Monumenta Germaniae Historica* series, only to have a stinging rebuke published in 1900 by Otto Oppermann, who uncovered Legipont's fraudulent approach.[22] While the foundation-story indeed appears to be wholly spurious, Legipont's use of the two now-lost necrologies is, of course, to be welcomed. Oppermann also

20 For these, see Peter Opladen, *Groß St. Martin. Geschichte einer stadtkölnischen Abtei* (Düsseldorf, 1954), pp 9–10, 179–80. Heinrich von Zonsbeck is known to have written other manuscripts, among these a Missale Benedictinum, an Antiphonarium Benedictinum-Coloniense, and an illuminated Officium-Antiphonary: Opladen, *Groß St. Martin*. According to Oppermann, Legipont was still in a position to consult the older necrology and added from there names into Zonsbeck's *Memorienbuch*: Otto Oppermann, 'Kritische Studien zur älteren Kölner Geschichte I' in *Westdeutsche Zeitschrift für Geschichte und Kunst* XIX (1900), 271–344, at 320–1. **21** Kaspar Bruschius, *Monasteriorum Germaniae praecipuorum ac maxime illustrium Centuria prima* (Ingolstadt, 1551); Aegidius Gelenius (ed.), *De admiranda Sacra et civili magnitudine Coloniae Claudiae ...: libri IV* (Cologne, 1645); the relevant excerpts from these are discussed by Oppermann, 'Kritische Studien zur älteren Kölner Geschichte I'. **22** MGH SS 2, pp 214–15; Oppermann, 'Kritische Studien zur älteren Kölner Geschichte I', 271–344.

provided a number of readings of Zonsbeck's manuscript, which he was then obviously still able to consult. Although all the names were taken out of their intended liturgical context, we can be grateful to both for having salvaged at least part of the legacy of what appears to have been a considerable Irish community in Cologne.

Unfortunately for historians, when abroad Irish monks routinely Latinized their names or adopted those of biblical figures, so that most cannot now be recognized. As the names of the abbots of Gross St Martin alone prove, only a minority can be identified as Irish at first glance, namely, Mimborinus, Kylianus, Helias, Maiolus, Foelanus. However, Legipont and Oppermann listed names which suggest an Irish provenance, namely, Amchinakus sacerdos (22 February) and Anamchadus (26 May) (neither of them identical with the *inclusus* of Fulda whose obit is given by Marianus as 30 January), Brendanus, Flanghus, Sumcadus, Ketlachus, Krukanus, Maelbridus (22 February; apparently not identical with Marianus sacerdos (Marianus Scotus the chronicler) who is commemorated as such on his usual day of 22 December), Mailmichel, Mirabrinus, Columbanus, Furseus, Kellachius, Muridachus, Aidanus, Kieranus and Kynaidus. Some of these names occur more than once, as, for example, Aidanus four times, Columbanus twice, Kellachius twice, Kylianus abbas twice, Kieranus four times, Muridachus twice (once on 21 April, close to the day of Muiredach mac Robartaig of Regensburg (23 April)), and Patricius three times, one of them Patricius abbas.[23]

Some entries in Legipont's *Chronicon* (MS 2701), allegedly taken from a *vetus obitualis liber*, perhaps Zonsbeck's source, were singled out by Legipont as they referred to monks of Gross St Martin who were also described as bishops. While he identified two of these (17 August: *Witakerus episcopus noster conversus*; 3 October: *Dñus Heynianus episcopus ecclesiae Coloniensis et monachus nostre congregationis*) as archbishops of Cologne – an opinion hotly repudiated by Oppermann – he did not attempt an identification of the other three. These are listed on 9 November (*Magnoaldus et Johannes episcopi et monachi* (MS 2701, fo. 221)), an entry to which Legipont added that Magnoaldus may have arrived as a pilgrim (to Cologne) together with Marianus Scotus in 1056. Machantinus/Magnoaldus and Johannes are indeed named as companions of Marianus Scotus, though not of the chronicler, as Legipont assumed, but of his contemporary, the *other* Marianus Scotus, alias Muiredach mac Robartaig, and while these may well have stayed over at Cologne in 1067 x 1070 on their way to their eventual final destination of Regensburg, they are not described as bishops in any of the Schottenklöster texts.[24] The name of another of the

23 These names are taken from Legipont's alphabetical *Necrologium* and from Oppermann, who was still able to consult Zonsbeck's autograph. 24 Pádraig Breatnach, *Die Regensburger Schottenlegende-Libellus de fundacione ecclesiae consecrati Petri. Untersuchung und Textausgabe* (Munich, 1977), pp 49–50.

episcopi et monachi mentioned by Legipont (XVIII kal. Januarii [15 December] *Kynaidus episcopus et monachus noster conversus* (MS 2701, fo. 16v)), is entered for the same date in the necrology of St Maximin in Trier, indicating that he was a monk in both of these Benedictine monasteries. The first abbot of St Pantaleon, Christianus (d. 1001), had also previously been a monk there and his name appears in the necrologies of both houses. Whether Kynaidus (presumably Cináed) was already a bishop before he came to the Continent, as was probably the case with the grammarian *Israel episcopus Scotigena*, who had been a monk at St Maximin in the tenth century, is not known.[25]

Fortunately, for two out of Legipont's three next entries we have corroborative evidence from Irish sources, sufficiently strong to identify them as the two first bishops of Dublin:

> *Nonus maii* [6 May]: *obiit Donatus episcopus noster conversus, de quo habemus annuatim dimidiam amam vini.*[26] (MS 2701, fo. 16)
>
> *VI id. Octobr.* [10 October]: *Patricius et Christianus episcopi et monachi nostri conversi* (MS 2701, fo. 16)

Donatus' death is vouchsafed by a number of notices. The annals recorded his death for the year 1074, calling him '*epscop Atha Cliath*' (CS), '*ardescop Gall*' (AU) and '*airdescop Atha Cliath*' (ATig, AFM), the honorific titles being bestowed at a time when there were no archbishops in Ireland. As Martin Holland has pointed out, the seventeenth-century translation of the Annals of Clonmacnoise called him 'archbushop of Dubline both of the Irish and of Danes', a description which will find its confirmation in the discussion below.[27] In the Book of Obits of Christ Church he is remembered on 6 May as '*Donatus primus episcopus Dublin, et fundator ecclesie nostre*', for whom nine lessons were to be read on his anniversary. The dates are further confirmed for the year

25 Rainer Reiche, *Ein rheinisches Schulbuch aus dem 11. Jahrhundert. Studien zur Sammelhandschrift Bonn UB. S 218 mit Edition von bisher unveröffentlichen Texten* (Munich, 1976), pp 20, 269. For a recent discussion of Israel, variously described as Irish or British, see Seppo Heikkinen, 'Poet, scholar, trickster: Israel the Grammarian and his "Versus de arte metrica"', *Journal of Medieval Latin*, 25 (2015), 81–110. **26** This entry may be connected with the bequest of vineyards at the Moselle by Archbishop Heribert, issued before his death in 1021 and confirmed in 1022: Leonhard Ennen and Gottfried Eckertz, *Quellen zur Geschichte der Stadt Köln*, 6 vols (Cologne, 1860–79), i, Nr. 17–20, pp 435–75; Opladen, *Groß St. Martin*, p. 165. Such bequests became more prevalent from the twelfth century onwards and were more often recorded in *Libri anniversarii*, where the memory of the deceased donor was celebrated on the day of his death. The exact meaning of 'conversus' is not clear here. The term is often used for lay brothers but, as Kracht has shown for St Pantaleon, equally so for professed monks: Hans-Joachim Kracht, *Geschichte der Benediktinerabtei St. Pantaleon zu Köln 965–1250* (Siegburg, 1975), pp 166–9. Legipont (MS 2701 fo. 17) explains: *Episcopus et monachus noster converses: id est professus.* **27** Martin Holland, 'The synod of Dublin in 1080' in Seán Duffy (ed.), *Medieval Dublin III* (Dublin,

1074 in the chronicle of Marianus Scotus, as '*Dunatus episcopus Dulini* [sic] *obiit Idus Mai*'.[28] In a list of early bishops of Dublin, copied on fo. 78 of the fourteenth-century *Liber Niger* or Black Book of Christ Church, Donatus' name also takes pride of place.[29] We can be certain, therefore, that the obit provided by Legipont from the necrology on 6 May refers to the death in 1074 of Donatus, alias Dúnán, first bishop of Dublin and previously a monk of Gross St Martin in Cologne.

While the Annals of Ulster and the Annals of the Four Masters merely report for 1084 that 'Gillaphadraig, Bishop of Ath-cliath, was drowned' (AU *Gilla Pátraic espoc Atha Cliath do bathadh*), a fuller entry is provided by the 'Annals of St Mary's Abbey', which were based on Christ Church material. Here we read:

> *Patricius, Dublin[ensis] episcopus, cum sociis in Britannie oceano, VI Id. Octobris fuit submersus* (Patrick, bishop of Dublin, was drowned with his companions in the ocean of Britain on the sixth day before the Ides of October) [10 October].[30]

The *oceanus britanniae* in general denotes the sea around Britain, but, like the *mare Britannicum*, it was more often used for the English Channel. Were the reference to the Irish Sea, *mare Hybernicum* would have been expected.

The entry in Legipont's excerpts from the Cologne necrology for 10 October applies, therefore, to Patricius, second bishop of Dublin, who, to merit the commemoration, must also have been a monk of Gross St Martin. *Christianus episcopus*, who is mentioned in the same entry and evidently had the matching Cologne connection, is not known from other sources but may have been one of the companions who, according to the Irish annals, drowned with Patricius in the 'British Sea' on 10 October 1084. Judging by the October date, both bishops and their companions may have been on their return journey from a Continental visit. At this point, in view of the new evidence, it may be opportune to re-examine some aspects of the careers of Dublin's first two bishops.

2002), pp 81–94, at p. 81. **28** MGH SS V, 561. The obit of 'Donatus episcopus primus Dublin.' entered on 9 Kal. Dec. in the Christ Church calendar is a mistake for the third bishop, Donatus or Domgall Ua hAingli, who died in 1095: Crosthwaite and Todd, *Book of obits*, pp xxxii, 23, 51. **29** Gwynn, 'The first bishops of Dublin', *Reportorium Novum*, 1 (1955–6), 1–26; repr. in Howard Clarke (ed.), *Medieval Dublin: the living city* (Dublin, 1990), pp 37–61, at p. 39; idem, 'Some unpublished texts from the Black Book of Christ Church'. **30** *CStM*, ii, p. 250, s.a. 1084; see also, Elizabeth Boyle, 'On the wonders of Ireland: translation and adaptation' in Elizabeth Boyle and Deborah Hayden (eds), *Authorities and adaptations: the reworking and transmission of textual sources in medieval Ireland* (Dublin, 2014), pp 233–61, at p. 238.

A BREGA LINK?

As Ó Riain has suggested on the basis of his name, Donatus, alias Dúnán, may have been a member of the Uí Dúnáin of Tuilén (Dulane), near Kells, one of the learned families of Brega, an area then encompassing most of the present-day county of Meath and parts of Louth and Dublin. This may explain why Cairnech, patron saint of Dulane, was added to the list of saints in the martyrology during its sojourn at Cologne.[31] Sitriuc's companion on his pilgrimage to Rome, Flannacán Ua Cellaig, king of Southern Brega, might well have been involved in the choice of a candidate from one of the families in his kingdom with long-standing ecclesiastical credentials. This would explain why a man as young as Donatus, who, after all, enjoyed a more than forty-year-long incumbency, should have been selected for what was going to be an ambitious undertaking, the creation of a new diocese and the building of a new cathedral.

It may also mean that the 1028 visit to Cologne and the subsequent setting up of a Dublin diocese was a combined venture, between Brega and Hiberno-Norse Dublin, that had been planned well in advance. According to the annals, just a year before Ua Cellaig's visit, the abbot of Dunshaughlin, Donnchad son of Gilla Mo Chonna, king of Southern Brega, and 'the most learned of the Irish' had died in Cologne (AU 1027: *Donnchad m. Gilla Mo Conna, comarba Sechnaill, sapientisimus Scotorum*). In the same year, Ruaidrí son of Fócartach, king of Southern Brega, a probable brother and successor of Gilla Mo Chonna, died 'on his pilgrimage' (AU 1027), possibly also on the way to Cologne, and Sitriuc's companion, Flannacán Ua Ceallaig, may well have been his successor as king.[32] The association between Dublin and Brega may have arisen from the king of Dublin's authority over some of Brega's Columban churches, a connection that went back to his father Amlaíb.[33] Regardless of this, however, there was clearly an already existing royal Brega connection with the Irish monasteries in Cologne and Donatus may have been prepared for his future role by Donnchad mac Gilla Mo Chonna, *sapientisimus Scotorum*, in Cologne.

31 The name is omitted in the Christ Church martyrology but appears in its sister copy of the cathedral of Lund: Ó Riain, *Feastdays*, pp 140, n. 100, 138, Donnchadh Ó Corráin, 'Mael Muire Ua Dúnáin (1040–1117), reformer' in Pádraig de Brún, Seán Ó Coileáin and Pádraig Ó Riain (eds), *Folia Gadelica: essays presented by former students to R.A. Breatnach, MA, MRIA* (Cork, 1983), pp 47–53, at p. 51. Máel Tuile mac Dúnáin, who died in 943, held the abbacy of Dulane together with that of Clones. This may be significant as the latter's patron, Tigernach, appears in the martyrology on the same day as Cairnech (16 May). To this can be added St Ultán of Ardbraccan in Meath (4 September: Ultanus abbas) in the Memorienbuch of 1323: Köln Stadtarchiv A 179, fo. 51; Ó Riain, *A martyrology of four cities*, 150. 32 Sitriuc may have continued an alliance with Brega, based on their mutual hostility to Clann Cholmáin and the Uí Néill, already fostered by his father Amlaíb Cuarán. 33 Alex Woolf, 'Amlaíb Cuarán and the Gael, 941–81' in Seán Duffy (ed.), *Medieval Dublin*

Given the obvious companionship of the kings of Brega and Hiberno-Norse Dublin on the 1028 pilgrimage that led to the founding of Christ Church, there must have been close cooperation between the two in the choice of the community's personnel. Furthermore, given these circumstances, at least some of the Irish monks in Gross St Martin and St Pantaleon very probably originated in the area covered by the modern counties Meath, Louth and Monaghan, where Muckno, the church from which Helias, abbot of the two Cologne abbeys, had come. Arguably, therefore, Dúnán may indeed have belonged to the same Brega family as Máel Muire Ua Dúnáin (d. 1117), who is named in a charter written into the Book of Kells between 1087 and 1094 as *ind epscop Oa Dunan .i. senior Leithe Cuind* ('the bishop Ua Dúnáin, i.e. the elder of the Northern Half [of Ireland]'). Máel Muire's role in the reform movement, including his involvement in the establishment of Waterford as Ireland's second earliest territorial diocese, rendered him, in the words of Donnchadh Ó Corráin, 'court bishop, counsellor and grand old man of the new order' in the service of Muirchertach Ua Briain.[34]

In light of this evidence, it is tempting to visualize the meeting that took place in Cologne in 1028 as a gathering of like-minded people that included abbot Helias, King Sitriuc, Flannacán Ua Cellaig and Dúnán, two Benedictines and two kings, all united in the common goal of setting up a cathedral in Dublin complete with a Benedictine chapter. Clearly, this portrayal of a well-planned cooperative effort, rather than a spontaneous decision made by Sitriuc on his return from pilgrimage, depends for its main support on evidence originating in Cologne. Adding further support to it, however, is the hitherto unrecognized evidence to show that Donatus' successor, Gilla Pátraic, alias Patricius, appears also to have served as a Benedictine monk at Cologne.

BISHOP GILLA PÁTRAIC, ALIAS PATRICIUS

Unlike Dublin's first bishop, Patricius has been the subject of much previous discussion; yet, notwithstanding the Patrician allegiance implied by his name, clues as to his background still have to be found. Aubrey Gwynn was foremost in drawing particular attention to the second bishop of Dublin, which culminated in an edition of a corpus of writing attributed to a *sanctus Patricius episcopus* in mainly English twelfth-century manuscripts.[35] Dublin's second bishop is known to have sworn an oath of obedience to Lanfranc of Canterbury

III (2002), pp 34–43; Gwendolyn Sheldon, 'The conversion of the Vikings of Dublin' in Seán Duffy (ed.), *Medieval Dublin XIV* (2015), pp 51–97, at pp 86–8. 34 Ó Corráin, 'Mael Muire Ua Dúnáin', p. 47. 35 Aubrey Gwynn (ed.), *The writings of bishop Patrick, 1074–1084*, Scriptores Latini Hiberniae 1 (Dublin, 1955).

and was professed at St Paul's in London, allegedly on the basis of a letter sent by 'Godericus [Gofraid], king of Dublin, together with the people and the clerics of the city', petitioning the archbishop of Canterbury for a new bishop to replace the one recently deceased and recommending Patricius as the preferred candidate. A copy of the letter is preserved in the Canterbury archive, as is the new bishop's vow of obedience at his subsequent consecration at St Paul's in London.[36] The letter reads, in Gwynn's translation:

> We therefore have chosen the priest named Patrick, who is sufficiently well known to us as one who is of noble birth, and character, formed by apostolic and ecclesiastical discipline, Catholic in his faith, skilled in the meaning of the Scriptures, well versed in the Church's doctrines; and we beg that he may be ordained as bishop as soon as possible, so that with God's blessing he may rule over us and help us according to law, and we may be able to fight unto Salvation under his rule.[37]

As Philpott and Brett have pointed out, the wording follows closely that of other Canterbury professions, with the bulk of the phrasing taken from the *decretum* of the Romano-German Pontifical.[38] Philpott therefore proposed that the letter, rather than having been sent from Dublin, was drawn up in Canterbury on the basis of names supplied by Patricius, in what Martin Brett called a 'piece of contemporary Canterbury drafting on the basis of Irish information'.[39] Crucially, there are some omissions from the usual text of the *decretum* but these in themselves may furnish vital information. Thus, there is no use of the customary formula expressing the consecrator's awareness of the vacancy, which would have been expected if Canterbury had been involved in the diocese of Dublin and the position previously held by Donatus. Nor is there the usual stipulation that the 'elect is a priest of this province'. Thus, Lanfranc's words make it obvious that at the time of his consecration Patricius was not a priest 'of this province', that is, of Canterbury (although the

36 Gwynn, 'Some unpublished texts from the Black Book of Christ Church', 333–4; see Mark Philpott, 'Some interactions between the English and Irish churches' in Christopher Harper-Bill (ed.), *Anglo-Norman Studies XX: Proceedings of the Battle Conference in Dublin 1997* (Woodbridge, 1998), pp 187–204, at p. 193; Brett, 'Canterbury's perspective on church reform in Ireland', p. 21. 37 Gwynn, *Writings of Bishop Patrick*, p. 2; for a recent discussion, see Mary Kelly, 'Twelfth-century ways of learning from Worcester or Cologne to Glendalough', *JRSAI*, 141 (2011), 47–65, at 53–4. 38 The Romano-German Pontifical had only recently been introduced into England, most probably from Cologne where Archbishop Ealdred of York (d. 1069) had spent a year in 1054/55: Michael Lapidge, 'Ealdred of York and MS. Cotton Vitellius E.XII', *Yorkshire Archaeological Journal*, 55 (1983), 11–25; repr. in idem, *Anglo-Latin literature 900–1066* (London, 1993), pp 453–67. As it happens, depending on the age of Patricius at his consecration, he could well have been at Cologne at the same time as Ealdred. 39 Philpott, 'Some interactions', p. 197; Brett, 'Canterbury's perspective on church reform and Ireland', p. 21, n. 16.

Benedictine monastery at Worcester, in which – according to Gwynn, on the basis of glosses contained in some of the manuscripts – Patricius had been a monk, lay within it).

Patricius' authorship of the bulk of the writings attributed to him has recently been challenged by Elizabeth Boyle, who, on the basis of discrepancies in style and subject matter within the texts, argues against a single authorship and instead proposes at least one 'Pseudo-Patricius', if not more.[40] Furthermore, as regards Patricius' Worcester connections, Martin Brett judged Gwynn's arguments to be 'extremely precarious' and based on premises 'which are in their nature very fragile'. He went on to conclude that Patricius 'was a monk, a man of sufficient learning to impress Lanfranc', and that he 'may well have had friendly contacts with Worcester, but there is no evidence that he had been a monk there'. Brett suggested that he had arrived in Canterbury directly from Dublin, but, in view of the new evidence, he may well have arrived from Cologne instead.[41]

Gwynn had assumed that Donatus had started the trend of consecration by the archbishop of Canterbury, 'for this would explain why the people of Dublin turned to Canterbury for a replacement', but King Gofraid of Dublin may instead have turned to the very place from which the previous bishop had come.[42] It is not known where Donatus was consecrated but even if Gwynn were right, consecration by Lanfranc did not automatically mean that Dublin was then, or had ever been, under the control of Canterbury. As has become clear through publications by Flanagan, Philpott and Brett, Lanfranc had ambitious plans, but these were primarily focused on the archbishopric of York, with the see of Dublin being used as a mere pawn in his strategy.[43]

Legipont's excerpts provide a fleeting glimpse of the community of Irish monks in Cologne. Through his writings a respectable number of their names has been preserved and, although some thirty or so are immediately

40 On the writings associated with 'Ps.-Patrick', see Donnchadh Ó Corráin, *Clavis Litterarum Hibernensium: medieval Irish books and texts (*c.*400–*c.*1600)*, Corpus Christianorum Claves, 3 vols (Turnhout, 2017), ii, 851–3; Elizabeth Boyle, 'The authorship and transmission of De tribus habitaculis animae', *Journal of Medieval Latin*, 22 (2012), 49–65; eadem, 'On the wonders of Ireland', pp 233–61, at p. 255; eadem, 'The twelfth-century English transmission of a poem on the threefold division of the mind, attributed to Patrick of Dublin (d. 1084)' in Wolfram R. Keller and Dagmar Schlüter (eds), '*A fantastic and abstruse Latinity?' Hiberno-Continental cultural and literary interactions in the Middle Ages*, Studien und Texte zur Keltologie 12 (Münster, 2017), pp 102–16, at pp 105, 107, 113–16. **41** Brett, 'Canterbury's perspective on church reform and Ireland', p. 35. **42** For the following, see Sheldon, 'Conversion of the Vikings of Dublin', pp 74–5, 79. **43** For a recent appraisal which however stresses a Canterbury link, see Elizabeth Boyle and Liam Breatnach, '*Senchas Gall Átha Cliath*: aspects of the cult of St Patrick in the twelfth century' in John Carey, Kevin Murray and Caitríona Ó Dochartaigh (eds), *Sacred histories: a festschrift for Máire Herbert* (Dublin, 2015), pp 22–55, at pp 24–8. For comparable aspects of the cult in twelfth-century Germany, see Dagmar Ó Riain-Raedel, 'Patrician documents in medieval Germany', *Zeitschrift für Celtische Philologie*, 49–50 (1997/8), 712–24 and

identifiable as Irish, many more may lurk in his list under Latinized names. Most importantly, perhaps, through Legipont's quotations from the now lost necrology, we now know that Dublin's first two bishops, Donatus, alias Dúnán, and Patricius, alias Gilla Pátraic, had been members of the Benedictine monastery of Gross St Martin.

ABBOT HELIAS OF GROSS ST MARTIN AND ST PANTALEON

Much of the evidence for the Irish at Cologne is provided by the chronicler Marianus Scotus (Máel Brigte), who was professed at Gross St Martin on *5 Feria Kal Augusti* (28 July) 1056, perhaps not by chance the feast-day of St Pantaleon.[44] He was keenly interested in Abbot Helias of Gross St Martin and St Pantaleon, whose reputation at Cologne was clearly still very much alive when he arrived more than a decade after the abbot's death. Helias had held the abbacy of Gross St Martin from 1005 and that of St Pantaleon from 1019/1021 until his death in 1042, and he is one of the very few Irish *peregrini* of this period to receive a mention in the native annals. The Annals of Ulster record his death for the year 1042, noting that 'Ailill of Mucnám, head of the Irish monks in Cologne, rested'.[45] Apart from his connection with the church of Muckno, Co. Monaghan, nothing else is known of his early life but, presumably, he had been a Benedictine monk at Cologne for some time prior to his consecration as abbot. While there, he kept the memory of his native locality alive, as it was most probably through him that St Medoldus of Muckno (13 May) and St Tigernach of the nearby Clones (4 April) were included in the community's martyrology.[46]

At Gross St Martin, Helias' term as abbot followed on those of Mimborinus (975–88) and Kilianus (988–1005) and he was succeeded by Maiolus (1042–62) and Felanus (1062–8). The abbots that then followed bore the German names of Wolfhard, Hezelin and Isaac. At St Pantaleon, Helias had succeeded Christian (964–1001), Reinbert (1001–15), Kilian (1015–19) and Folbert (1019–21) and he was followed by Aaron (1042–52); of these only Kilian and Aaron may have been Irish.

Our main sources of information on Helias' term of office in Cologne are the account of Helias given by Marianus Scotus the chronicler (who spent two years following his profession in 1056 at Gross St Martin under the abbot Maiolus) and the 'Life and Miracles of St Heribert', archbishop of the city and

eadem, 'The other paradise: perceptions of Ireland in the Middle Ages' in Rudolf Simek and Asya Ivanova (eds), *Between the Islands and the Continent. Papers on Hiberno-Scandinavian-Continental contacts in the early Middle Ages* (Vienna, 2013), pp 167–92. 44 Ó Riain, *A martyrology of four cities*, p. 129. 45 AU, s.a. 1042. 46 Ó Riain, *A martyrology of four cities*, p. 8. The feast-days now only survive in the sister manuscript, the Martyrology of Lund.

diocese from 999 to 1021, with whom Helias appears to have enjoyed a very close relationship.[47] Charters granted to the monastery by Heribert speak of the valuable contribution made by the Irish monks, the *pauperes*, who spent their lives serving the Lord, and, in order to alleviate their poverty, Heribert is said to have confirmed his predecessor's donations to the community and added to them his own. Moreover, as an outward sign of his support he is described as placing his staff on the altar of St Martin.[48]

The archbishop's close relations with Helias became especially apparent during the prelate's last days when, conscious of his approaching death, Heribert made one last journey through his diocese but fell ill while at Neuss, north of Cologne. Messengers were immediately sent to summon Helias (*domnus abbas Helyas*) and, after some conversation on religious subjects, the abbot proceeded to dispense the last unction, after which the archbishop was brought to Cologne by boat. Here, he was brought to his cathedral where he prostrated himself before the holy crucifix – presumably the famous Gero-Kreuz – and prayed for the intercession of St Peter. Subsequently brought to his residence, Helias and others gathered around the dying archbishop in learned and religious conversations, in the course of which Helias is said to have experienced two visions that saw the archbishop being received into the heavenly Jerusalem.[49] Heribert died on 16 March 1021 and was buried in his newly built monastery at Deutz, facing his cathedral across the Rhine. Although sanctification of the archbishop did not begin officially until the 1040s, it is no surprise that a piece of Heribert's vestments should have entered the relic-list of Christ Church, Dublin.

Respect for Helias continued at Deutz, if the interest in the abbot's name taken by Heribert's biographer, Lantbert, is any guide. Following 4 Reg. 2, 11, he explained the name as meaning the sun: *Helyas qui nomine solis interpretatur*, an interpretation no doubt given to him by Helias himself. The erudite conversations Helias conducted with the archbishop during the latter's last hours are indications of their shared attitudes to learning and religion. And having been educated at the famous reform centre of Gorze, Heribert had probably become acquainted with Irish monastic life long before he was called to the see of Cologne.

Abbot Helias' scholarly interests are attested by a number of references. In a contemporary catalogue of the Dombibliothek in Cologne, now preserved at Erfurt, Helias is noted as having borrowed a treatise of Augustine on John, 'completely newly and well written'.[50] A book-related anecdote, this time

47 Bernhard Vogel, *Lantbert von Deutz. Vita Heriberti. Miracula Heriberti. Gedichte. Liturgische Texte*, MGH Script. rer. Germ., 73 (2001), pp 193–200, 203–5. 48 For the following, see Opladen, *Groß St. Martin*, pp 19–21. 49 Bernhard Vogel, *Lantbert von Deutz. Vita Heriberti. Miracula Heriberti. Gedichte. Liturgische Texte*, MGH Script. rer. Germ., 73 (2001), pp 193–200, 203–5. 50 On the *Hi sunt libri praestiti de armario sancti Petri*, a list of manuscripts on loan from the Dombibliothek entered on fo. 117v in Cod.CA 2° 64,

supplied by Marianus Scotus, shines further light on Helias' personality. According to Marianus, Helias threw into the fire, in the presence of the whole community, a beautiful missal written by a monk of St Pantaleon (*monachus Francus*) because it had been written without his permission. This can be taken to reflect the abbot's stern demand of absolute obedience at a time when local monks may have outnumbered the Irish in the community, and this would have probably given rise to tensions between Irish and German ('Frankish') monks, a situation later reflected in Archbishop Pilgrim's attempt to expel both Helias and the Irish monks from St Pantaleon, on the pretext that Helias' rule was too strict.[51] Helias is said to have prophesized that the archbishop, who was away on imperial business, would die before returning to his city, which turned out to be the case.[52] On his own death, Helias was buried in the chapel of St Benedict at Gross St Martin, where the inscription on his tomb paid due homage to his fame, proclaiming that miracles had proved his sanctity: *Haec tumuli fossa conduntur praesulis ossa / Heliae miri mirificique viri* ('Under this stone are the remains of Abbot Helias, miracles have shown that he was a holy man').[53]

It was during Helias' long abbacy that the future diocese of Dublin was planned. In 1028, the date of the Irish royal visit to Cologne, the abbot was at the height of his career, ruling over the two Benedictine episcopal *Eigenklöster*. Through his connections he was enabled to secure for Dublin's cathedral and chapter a collection of magnificent foundation relics, including a part of the Holy Cross, together with parts of the highly valued staff and chain of St Peter, as well as a piece of garment worn by the soon to be sanctified Heribert. In addition, Helias arranged for the provision of such liturgical requisites as the

Wissenschaftliche Allgemeinbibliothek, Bibliotheca Amploniana, in Erfurt, and first published by Ernst Dümmler, 'Cölner Bücherkatalog', *Zeitschrift für deutsches Altertum und deutsche Literatur* 19 (N.F. 7) (1876), 466–7 and on the library generally, Joachim M. Plotzek, 'Zur Geschichte der Kölner Dombibliothek' in idem (ed.), *Glaube und Wissen im Mittelalter. Katalogbuch zur Ausstellung* (Munich, 1998), pp 15–64, at p. 30. The list begins with: *abbas Elias habet Augustinum super Iohannem novum ex toto bene scriptum.* **51** *Mariani Scoti Chronicon* (MGH SS V, 557): *Helias Scottus abbas obit 3. Idus Aprilis, vir prudens et religiosus, et ideo monasterium sancti Pantaleonis cum suo id est sancti Martini, sibi datum est. Ipse optimum missalem librum monachi etiam Franci, sine licentia conscriptum, in commune monachorum in monasterio sancti Pantaleonis igne consumpsit, ne alius sine licentia conscriberet aut tale aliquid fecisset;* the few Irish names listed in the St Pantaleon necrology (Totenbuch) and in Kracht's catalogue of known personnel, are 'Kilianus sac.' (2 April) and Kilradus sac. (6 March). There is no certainty whether those using biblical or non-Germanic names (Johannes, Peligrinus, Paulus, Petrus, Salemon, Mauritius, Nicolaus, etc.) were Irish: Kracht, *Geschichte der Benediktinerabtei St. Pantaleon zu Köln*, pp 211–38. **52** MGH SS V, pp 556–7; Kessel, *Antiquitates*, XII. This course of events provided Marianus Scotus with the opportunity for his well-known pun: *Si Deus in nobis est peregrinis, vivus Coloniam non veniat Piligrinus* ('If God is with us pilgrims, Pilgrim will not return alive to Cologne'). It also shows that, as was to be the case in the Schottenklöster literature, the card of the *peregrini* was regularly played. **53** Opladen, *Groß St. Martin*, p. 21.

martyrology needed for daily reading in the monastery at prime. To procure all this, preparations must have been ongoing for quite some time and Donatus, alias Dúnán, may well have been specifically sent to Cologne to receive the necessary instruction. If he was a member of the Uí Dúnáin ecclesiastical family of Dulane (Tuilén), near Kells, this would sit well with the obvious connection of Sitriuc's family's with the king of Southern Brega, which presupposes the possible existence of a hitherto unnoticed alliance between the native king and the Hiberno-Norse king of Dublin. As Tadhg O'Keeffe has shown for the architecture of Dublin's cathedral, all these procurements in Cologne bypassed England, and one day it may be possible to identify more possible sources in the Rhineland. All this should be sufficient to prove, as Aubrey Gwynn remarked in 1940, 'that Ireland was much more in contact with continental reformers than seems to have been understood by most of our recent historians'.[54]

54 Gwynn, 'Irish monks and the Cluniac reform', 15.

Wood Quay and later waterfront revetments in Anglo-Norman Dublin: a reappraisal of their carpentry

MÁIRE GEANEY

INTRODUCTION

It is now over thirty years since the excavations carried out at Wood Quay were first published (Wallace 1982, 263–98). Yet, despite the wealth of comparative evidence recovered in more recent times, especially on the London waterfront, no attempt has been made to reassess the evidence, and the carpentry of Revetment 1 is still described as conservative (O'Sullivan 2000, 87; Wallace 2016, 154) and reflective of improvisation (Wallace 2016, 154). Moreover, the general belief (largely unspoken) that the Anglo-Normans introduced fully-framed structures into Ireland (O'Sullivan 2000, 87–8; Brigham 1992, 105) needs to be challenged.

Using Wallace's seminal paper on Wood Quay, this study will attempt to identify significant differences between the carpentry techniques used on Wood Quay and those exhibited on contemporary revetments on the London and Bristol waterfronts (Milne 1992; Ponsford 1985; Good 1990; Fulford et al. 1992). It will be shown that, compared with contemporary riverfront structures in England, the carpentry of the late twelfth-century Wood Quay revetments was not only technically more accomplished than their English counterpart, but that the carpenters responsible for their construction had a remarkable knowledge of structural mechanics. The carpentry of the later revetments on Winetavern Street (Halpin 2000) and Usher's Quay (Swan 2000, 126–58), as well as Strand Street Great (Walsh 2005, 160–87) and Arran Quay (Hayden 2004, 149–242) on the northern shoreline, is equally informative and suggests that the further out from Wood Quay, both in time and space, the greater the decline in carpentry skills.

The late twelfth-century Wood Quay revetments (Wallace 1982; 2016) were mainly front-braced, a method of bracing probably introduced into Ireland by the Anglo-Normans but which the carpenters on Wood Quay brought to a very high technical level – a level, it is suggested, not yet achieved by contemporary carpenters in Britain. Indeed, this paper goes further and suggests that, with a number of notable exceptions, the carpentry techniques used on Revetment 1 on Wood Quay were carried out, not by Anglo-Norman carpenters, but by Gaelic Irish or, more likely, Hiberno-Norse carpenters. In fact, apart from Section B on Wood Quay (Wallace 1982, 275–7, 283–5; and 2016, 159), it is not until Strand Street Great on the northern shoreline (Walsh 2005, 160–87) that waterfront revetments incorporating construction techniques similar to those recorded on the London waterfront (Milne 1992, 40, 59, 63) are recovered on the Dublin riverfront sites. That is not to say, however, that Anglo-Norman carpenters were not employed on the construction of the Dublin revetments, merely that, initially at any rate, their role appears to have been a secondary one. At the turn of the century, however, and the construction of the revetments on Winetavern Street (Halpin 2000), it is clear that the demarcation lines between the Hiberno-Norse tradition of carpentry and that of the Anglo-Normans are already blurring as carpenters from both sides of the 'cultural divide' continue to work side by side.

According to Yeomans (1999, xix), understanding the construction process depends in part upon the jointing methods used. To this end, the main focus of this paper is Wood Quay – the range of carpentry techniques employed and the joints used in the construction of the waterfront revetments following the Anglo-Norman conquest. Accordingly, the construction details of each revetment will be briefly described and commented on. Comparisons will then be made between this evidence and the evidence for carpentry techniques on contemporary revetments on the London waterfront and the two isolated examples of waterfront revetments recorded on the Bristol waterfront. Other evidence, such as the carpentry of the Hemington Bridges (Ripper and Cooper 2009), will also be discussed. First, however, a brief summary is required of the evidence for the development of carpentry in Ireland and Britain up to the late twelfth–early thirteenth century.

PRE-ANGLO-NORMAN WOODWORKING TECHNIQUES IN IRELAND

It is not generally appreciated that the coming of Christianity to Ireland in the fifth century brought with it not only literacy and learning but also new technologies, including new timber-framing techniques incorporating advanced Roman carpentry joints: a technology that is best represented in Ireland in the carpentry of the early medieval watermills, over 153 of which have been recorded in Ireland and dated by dendrochronology, radiocarbon dating or associated finds from AD 612 to AD 1124 (Rynne 2015, 70). Although a small number of these early mills were of earthfast-post construction, the majority were founded on squared baseplates with rectangular mortises supporting the tenoned uprights of the mill, a post-Roman tradition of carpentry that also included the tusk tenon, the lap-dovetail joint and the chase mortise-and-tenon joint (fig. 3.1, A–C) – carpentry joints that we now know continued in use in Ireland alongside the indigenous method of post-and-wattle construction. At Deer Park Farms, for example, the doorframe of an eighth-century round post-and-wattle structure was framed using a tusk tenon joint (Lynn and McDowell 2011, 421). Earlier in AD 630, the tusk tenon was

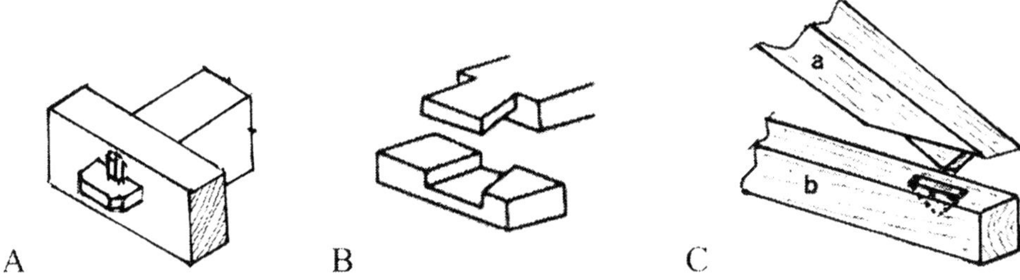

3.1 Joint types: (A) tusk tenon; (B) dovetail; (C) chase mortise-and-tenon.

used to frame the horizontal and vertical tidal mills at Little Island, Co. Cork (Geaney 2014, 125–8, 149–51). The tusk tenon joint was also used to secure the piles pinning the baseplates of the Cashen Bridge to the bed of the river. It is noteworthy, however, that while square mortises were used to secure the tusk tenons of the piles, long rectangular mortises were used to support the principal uprights of the bridge (O'Kelly 1961, 135–51; Geaney 2016, 89–104). Long rectangular mortises are much more efficient than square mortises, in that, in a strong flow of water or in a high wind, a rectangular tenon in a rectangular mortise is better able to resist torsion and wind pressure whereas a square tenon in a square mortise has a tendency to twist and destabilize the structure. The Cashen Bridge was never dated, however, but from the jointing techniques used and the similarities between the carpentry of the bridge and that of the early mills, a date between the late ninth and early eleventh centuries is likely, that is to say, well before the Anglo-Norman conquest (Geaney 2016, 89–104). And interestingly, a wooden bridge recently recovered from the River Dargle in Bray returned two dendro dates ranging from AD 972 to AD 1084 and AD 933 to AD 1068. The bridge was founded on squared baseplates with rectangular mortise-and-tenoned uprights (O'Sullivan and Downey 2015, 37–40). Also in the tenth century, a pegged, edge-halved scarf joint with vertical butts (fig. 3.2A) was used to repair the doorframes of two Hiberno-Norse post-and-wattle houses on adjacent plots on Fishamble Street, Dublin (Wallace 1992, 42). The most important evidence for continuity, however, comes from a late eleventh-century Hiberno-Norse site on South Main Street, Cork, where a reused baseplate, F146, T62, dated to AD 1057, was recovered. The baseplate had a rectangular mortise at either end with a smaller sub-rectangular mortise in the middle into which a centre post supported by diagonal bracing was tenoned (Geaney 2014a, 538, fig. A1.4.3). At some point, however, the diagonal braces, which were lap-jointed and pegged to the front face of the baseplate, were replaced by two reused timbers with evidence for lap-dovetail joints. On the same site, evidence for a quay structure, dendro-dated to AD 1166, was also recovered (fig. 3.2). The quay, which was built using

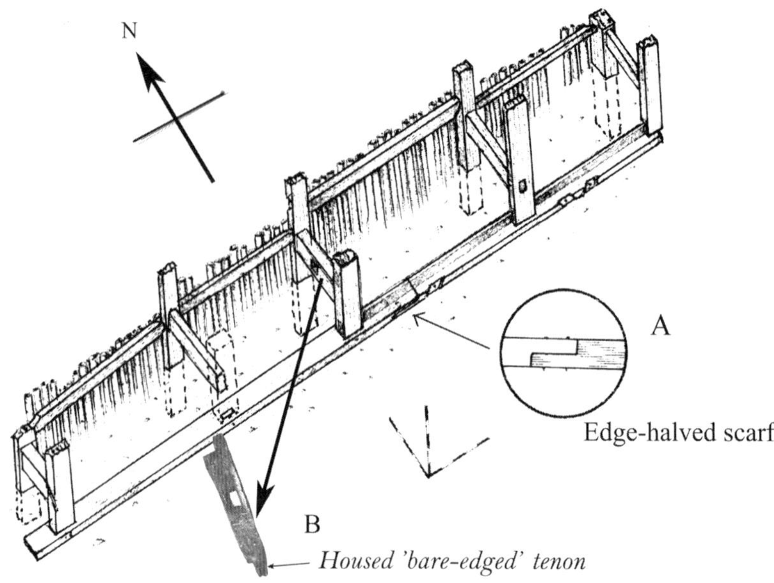

3.2 Hiberno-Norse quay structure, AD 1166, South Main Street, Cork (after Sutton 2014).

two very different methods of construction, was braced to the rear by a solid sheet-wall of piles supporting five earthfast posts. To the front of the structure, that is, on the riverward side, five opposing uprights were mortise-and-tenoned into two baseplates jointed together using a pegged edge-halved scarf joint (fig. 3.2A). Horizontal east–west cross-beams jointed into the side face of each upright were used to brace the uprights to the rear and also those on the riverward side. Additional crossbeams aligned north–south were then tenoned into mortises in the front face of the earthfast-posts to the rear and into mortises in the upright posts jointed into the baseplates to the front. These latter crossbeams were set on edge to reduce deflection. In other words, and despite the use of earthfast-posts to the rear, this quay structure was fully framed three years before the Anglo-Norman conquest (Geaney 2014a, 539–42).

WOODWORKING TECHNIQUES IN BRITAIN UP TO THE THIRTEENTH CENTURY

In England, the transition from earthfast-post construction to fully framed structures with baseplates, squared timbers and long rectangular mortises did not take place until the late twelfth/early thirteenth century (Milne 1992, 82). This, despite the evidence for full framing in Roman Britain and a range of

Roman carpentry joints at Cannon Street, London in the late first century AD (Goodburn 1992) and at Courage's Brewery in Southwark in the late second century (Brigham et al. 1995). With the withdrawal of the Roman army, however, and a decline in the money economy, the building tradition of the Romans gradually disappeared, to be replaced by that of the Anglo-Saxons. The building tradition of these Germanic peoples was one of earthfast-post construction, a method of construction that was very different to the full framing techniques introduced into Britain by the Romans and which were commonplace in Claudio-Neronian Colchester and Verulamium (Perring 2002, 87). That earthfast-post construction persisted in England into the late twelfth century and beyond is attested by the evidence for earthfast arcade-posts at Fyfield Hall and in the rebuilding of the hall in a similar archaic style *c.*AD 1400 (Walker 1999, 112–42). The sequence of riverfront structures from the tenth to the fifteenth centuries on the London waterfront also demonstrate the continued use of earthfast-post construction (Milne 1992, 80). In broad terms, however, the transition from earthfast-construction to structures with mortised baseplates is now generally assigned to the late twelfth century with full framing techniques introduced in the early thirteenth century (ibid., 82). In Bristol, because of the extreme range of the tides, from the mid-twelfth century, waterfront structures were built mainly in stone and, apart from two massive timbers at Dundas Wharf with mortises to take upright posts (a possible loading platform), there is little evidence for timber structures (Good 1990, 29–36). Nevertheless, a thirteenth-century back-braced post-and-plank revetment, broadly similar to several recorded on Trig Lane, was recovered at Penner Wharf close to Bristol Bridge (Ponsford 1985, fig. 5). At Woolaston Grange on the Pill, due to the narrowness and steepness of the channel, similarly, a very different structural approach to that used on the Dublin and London waterfronts had to be taken and two quay structures, the Upper and Lower Quays, were built. Constructed in the mid-twelfth and early thirteenth century respectively, both quays appear to be founded on stone-filled compartments, with the Upper Quay built on massive timber baseplates and the Lower Quay retained by posts and planks (Fulford et al. 1992, 101–27). Indeed, contrary to O'Sullivan's assertion that Bristol strongly influenced the construction of the Dublin revetments (O'Sullivan 2000, 88), apart from the mortised baseplates, the methods of construction used on the Severn estuary generally are very different from those of Dublin and, in fact, the London evidence is eminently more comparable.

The Hemington Bridges, discovered in 1993 during quarry works near Castle Donnington in Leicestershire (Ripper and Cooper 2009), provide invaluable information on the introduction and development of framing techniques in Britain. Between *c.*AD 1100, when Bridge I at Hemington was built, and *c.*AD 1200, when Bridge III was built, there is clear evidence for a

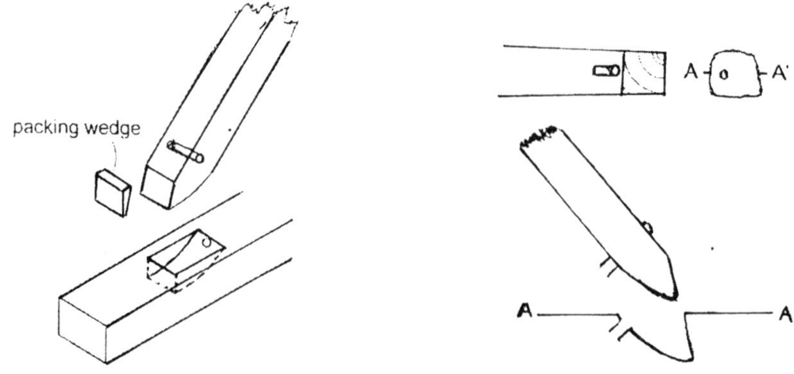

3.3 Saxo-Norman chase mortise-and-tenon joint (after Darrah 2009).

change in the carpentry of these bridges (Darrah 2009, 111). For example, on the trestle-and-caisson structures of Bridge 1, the mortise-and-tenon joints are square, poorly cut and loose-fitting with the carpenters relying on a combination of massive joints, earthfastness and bracing to support the load (ibid. 112). Darrah refers to these joints as Saxo-Norman mortise-and-tenon joints to distinguish them from later medieval joints of the same name, which by Bridge III, are now rectangular in shape, the tenons having proper shoulders that evenly distribute the load across the entire bearing surface of the joint (ibid.). The so-called Saxo-Norman chase mortise-and-tenon joint is also very different from that of the later medieval period. While in the latter, the joint is a rectangular slot with at least one angled end to take the tenon of a diagonal brace (fig. 3.1C), in the former the chase mortise is just a notch housing the entire section of the brace. That is to say, there is no tenon and the end of the brace is pegged into a mortise that is curved rather than flat bottomed (fig. 3.3).

THE WOOD QUAY EVIDENCE

The three oak revetments, Revetments 1, 2 and 3 on Wood Quay (Wallace 1982, 275–89; 2016, 157–68), are part of a general trend of revetted waterfronts in northwest Europe from the late eleventh century, in which dumped infill to the rear of the revetment was used to advance the foreshore further out into the riverbed (Hobley 1981, 1–9). Revetment 1, which Wallace originally dated to *c.*AD 1210, but which Halpin suggested is earlier and dated to AD 1195–1201 (Halpin 2000, 37; Wallace 2016, 165), can be traced for 60m in an east–west line along the southern foreshore of the River Liffey (fig. 3.4). Revetment 1 also had what Wallace termed a 'buffer' or 'floating' outer revetment (see fig. 3.6).

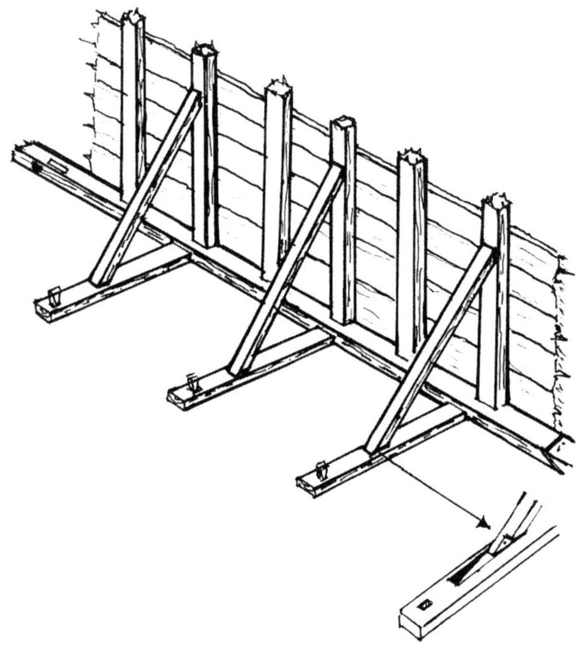

3.4 Reconstruction of Revetment 1 on Wood Quay, Dublin (redrawn, after Wallace 1982).

Freestanding and without horizontal planking or front-braces, Wallace saw these 'buffers' as shock absorbers that rose and fell with the tide and prevented ships from damaging the revetments as they docked alongside (Wallace 2016, 160). Revetments 2 and 3 on Wood Quay are later and back-braced rather than front-braced with the back-bracing of Revetment 3 technically superior to that of 2. According to Wallace, reused timbers on Revetment 2 had evidence for more advanced jointing techniques, but without detailed drawings specifically identifying these joints, it is not possible to comment further.

Revetment 1

Five sections (A, B, C, D and E) of Revetment 1 were excavated as well as an extension to Section C roughly 20m further out into the riverbed. Founded on squared oak baseplates (*c*.4.82m L x 0.25m W x 0.20m Th.), each section was *c*.12–15m in length and scarf-jointed together using a simple pegged, through-splayed scarf joint (fig. 3.5). A through-splayed scarf joint is not very efficient, however, in that it has to rely entirely on the pegging to resist sliding and rotation. And while Wallace concluded that this joint may have been a local development (Wallace, 1982, 279; Wallace 2016, 174), it is now known that, by the mid- to late twelfth century, a rough unpegged through-splayed scarf joint

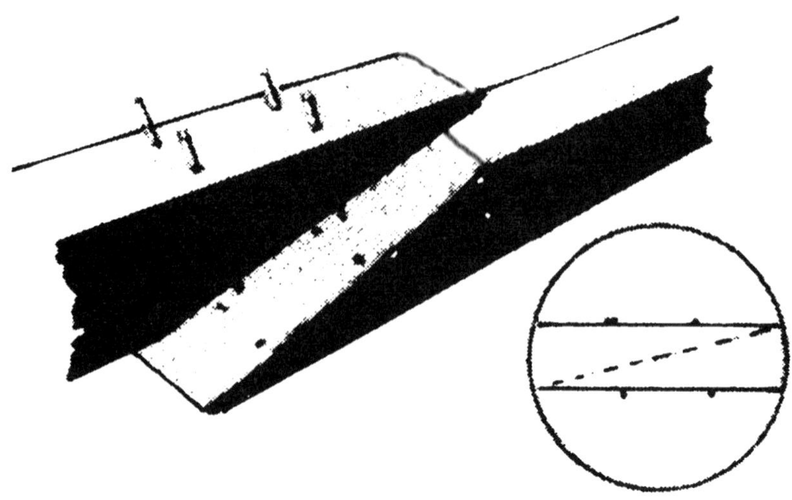

3.5 Through-splayed scarf joint.

was already in use on BG12 at Billingsgate on the London waterfront, at which time it was probably also introduced into Ireland by the Anglo-Normans. A through-splayed scarf joint was also used on SH3 on the Seal House site in AD 1202/3 and, as late as AD 1250, a pegged example of a through-splayed scarf joint was used on BG16 at Billingsgate. Indeed, the through-splayed scarf joint is not replaced on the London waterfront until *c.*AD 1239 when the more efficient pegged stop-splayed scarf joint was used on the Thames Exchange site TX9 (Milne 1992, 30–63).

In contrast, the pegged edge-halved scarf joint with vertical butts seems to have been preferred in Ireland from at least the tenth century when it was used to repair the doorjambs of two adjacent houses on Fishamble Street (Wallace 1992, 42). More importantly, a pegged, edge-halved scarf joint (fig. 3.2A) was used in AD 1166 (i.e., three years before the Anglo-Norman invasion) to joint together the two baseplates of the Hiberno-Norse quay structure on South Main Street, Cork (Geaney 2014a, 539–42). The edge-halved scarf joint appears not to have been used on Wood Quay, however, even though it would have been much more efficient than the through-splayed scarf joint. Indeed, apart from a possible edge-halved scarf joint recorded on F166 on Winetavern Street (O'Sullivan 2000, 86, ill. 21), there is no evidence for this joint anywhere on the Dublin waterfront. This negative evidence could suggest that the scarfing of the Wood Quay baseplates may have been the responsibility of Anglo-Norman carpenters, a conclusion that is supported by the continued use of the through-splayed scarf joint on the London waterfront into the mid-thirteenth century. Indeed, the edge-halved scarf joint with vertical butts does not appear to have been used on the London waterfront until the late thirteenth century when it was used on revetment TL3 at Trig Lane (Milne 1992, 68).

In Revetment 1 on Wood Quay, rectangular through-mortises cut at *c.*1.0m intervals into the principal baseplates supported the principal uprights, as well as the posts at mid-span in Section D. The mortises were pre-drilled with an auger, a technique also used on a reused baseplate (F146.T62) on South Main Street, Cork and which has been dendro-dated to the mid-eleventh century (Geaney 2014a, 347). Although the upright posts in all sections of Wood Quay were generally mortised, tenoned (using bare-faced tenons) and pegged into the baseplate, in Section D (where the best evidence survived), at least half of the joints were wedged rather than pegged. According to Wallace, the carpentry of Section D was of such a high standard that pegging was probably seen as unnecessary (Wallace 1982, 280). Traditionally however, mortise-and-tenon joints in the carpentry of the early medieval mills in Ireland were not pegged. Indeed, apart from the eighth-century vertical mill at Morett, Co. Laois – the carpentry of which was exceptional in any case and included the dovetail joint and the chase mortise-and-tenon joint (Lucas 1953; Geaney 2014, 151–4) – and the pegged end-posts of the Cashen Bridge (O'Kelly 1961; Geaney 2016, 89–104), the earliest evidence to date for the pegging of mortise-and-tenon joints in Ireland was recorded on the mid- to late twelfth-century quay structure on South Main Street, Cork (Geaney 2014a, 539–42).

The standard of workmanship evidenced on Section D was higher than that of other sections on Wood Quay, especially Section B. For example, while the principal posts in Sections D and B were generally squared with an axe, in Section B a number of lightly trimmed half-round logs were also used. Moreover, while in Section D the principal posts and posts at mid-span were similar in size and well fitted, in Section B the principal posts were not only lighter than those in D, but the posts at mid-span were also very poorly fitted. In fact, in Section B the mid-span posts were without tenons and simply set into shallow hollows in the baseplate. Posts without tenons were used on the London Billingsgate site in the eleventh century where they were used in association with square mortises (Milne 1992, 15). And in a discussion on the carpentry of Bridge 1 at Hemington, posts without tenons that are set into mortises are described as Saxo-Norman tenons (Cooper and Ripper 2009, 102). In other words, the use of mid-span posts without tenons in Section B appears to be part of a Saxo-Norman tradition of carpentry.

In all Sections of Revetment 1 on Wood Quay, the head of a diagonal front-brace was tenoned into a mortise at the top of each principal post, while the foot of the brace (with the exception of Section B) was mortise-and-tenoned into a subsidiary baseplate set at right angles to the principal baseplate (fig. 3.6). A second mortise in the subsidiary was used to stake the baseplate to

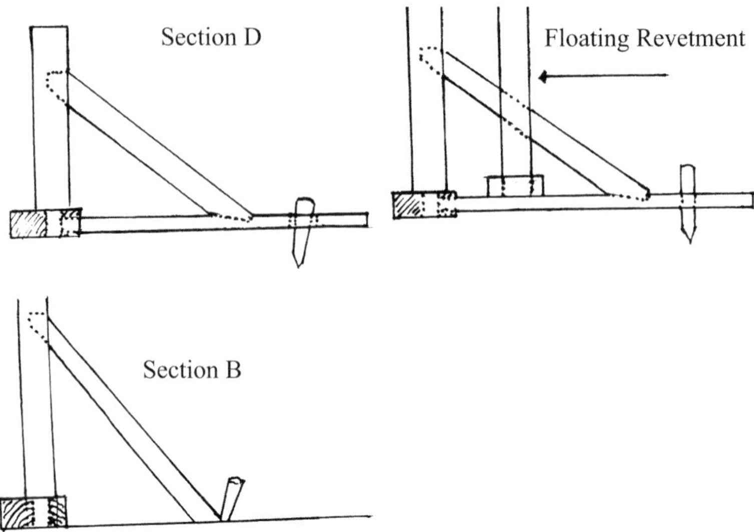

3.6 Sections D and B of Revetment 1 and outer floating revetment (redrawn, after Wallace 1982).

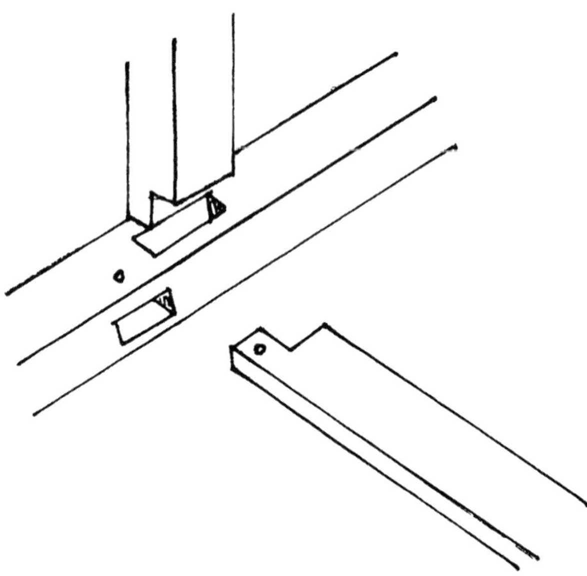

3.7 Subsidiary baseplate tenoned into mortise on front face of principal baseplate (redrawn, after Wallace 1982, fig. 15.4).

the foreshore. In Sections B and D, the tenon at the top of the brace was cut at right angles to the upright post which, in D, Wallace describes as frustum-shaped with a level upper face tightly fitted into the mortise (Wallace 1982, 285), a description that strongly suggests that these tenons were in effect chased, a suggestion supported by Wallace's drawings (Wallace 1982, figs 15.3, 15.6; redrawn in fig. 3.6 in this volume). On the other hand, the chase tenons at the foot of the front-braces in Section D were triangular in shape and well formed, with a vertical front face fitting neatly into chase mortises cut into the subsidiary baseplates.

A significant characteristic of the Wood Quay revetments, especially in Section D, is that the subsidiary baseplate was jointed into the principal baseplate using a pegged mortise-and-tenon joint, a method of front-bracing not recorded on the London waterfront (fig. 3.7). Wallace was incorrect, however, when he referred to the tenon on the end of the subsidiary as haunched (Wallace 1982, 280, 286, fig. 15.4). From his drawing, it is clear that the tenon in question was formed from the full thickness of the subsidiary and then housed into a mortise cut into the front face of the principal baseplate, a technique that would rule out haunching. The main function of haunching is to give greater strength to a joint by helping to prevent the tenon from twisting within the mortise (Bates 1997, 56; Hewett 1980, fig. 303). However, a tenon very similar to that used on Wood Quay (but used on edge rather than on the flat) was recorded on the north–south crossbeams of the Hiberno-Norse quay on South Main Street, Cork (see fig. 3.2B). Because the tenon does not belong to any known set of mortise-and-tenon joints, in that it was simply cut from the end of the crossbeam, the term 'housed bare-edged tenon' was used to describe the joint (Geaney 2014a, 540).

In Section B, instead of using a subsidiary baseplate, the foot of the front-brace was earthfast and retained by a pile driven into the foreshore, a method of front-bracing also used on stave revetment TL1 at Trig Lane on the London waterfront (fig. 3.8) in the early thirteenth century (Milne 1992, 66). In one instance on Section B, however, the foot of the front-brace was wedged into a mortise cut into a short log or base-pad (Wallace 1982, 285). While no further details are given, this latter method appears to be very similar to that used on a near contemporary London revetment TX4 (AD 1198–1224) on the Thames Exchange site, where the subsidiary baseplate is perpendicular to the principal baseplate but not jointed to it. Instead, the subsidiary is staked to the riverbed up to 1m further out on the foreshore (fig. 3.9). Moreover, on TX4, while the foot of the front-brace was cut to a chase tenon and wedged into a mortise in the subsidiary baseplate, the head of the brace was simply tapered and set into a splayed recess cut into the front face of the upright post; such a shoring technique is technically rudimentary, especially when compared with the frustum-shaped chase mortise-and-tenon joints used on the head of the

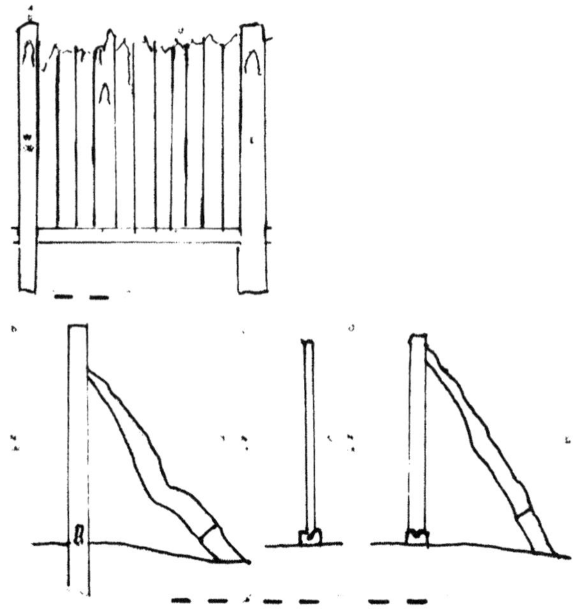

3.8 Revetment TL1 at Trig Lane on the London waterfront (after Milne 1992).

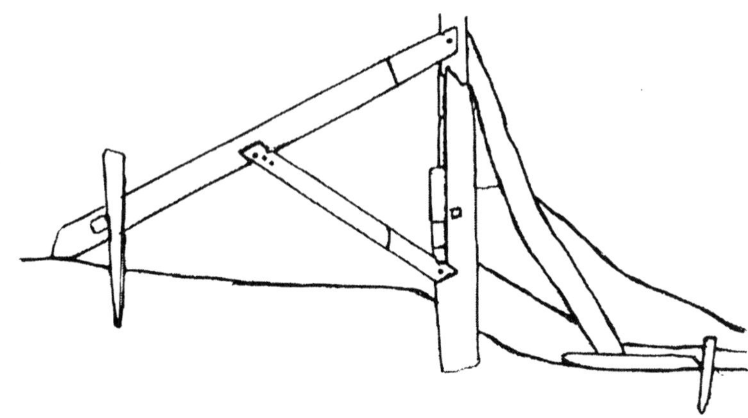

3.9 TX4 on the Thames Exchange site, London (after Milne 1992).

front-braces in all sections of Wood Quay, including Section B. Indeed, the splayed recess continued in use on BG14 (*c.*AD 1220) at Billingsgate (fig. 3.10), and it is not until the mid- to late thirteenth century on TX6 on the Thames Exchange site that the splayed recess was finally replaced by the more efficient chase mortise-and-tenon joint (Milne 1992, 59). It is also worth noting that in

3.10 BG14, Billingsgate, London: front elevation showing splayed recesses (after Milne 1992).

the early thirteenth century, TL1 and TX4 (*c.*1200) were still reliant on earthfast-post construction, in addition to which, the front-braces of BG14 on Billingsgate, at least twenty years after Wood Quay, were barely modified branches, often curved and still in the round (Milne 1992, 32). In Section B on Wood Quay, on the other hand, the angle of the front-brace was described as very steep (Wallace 1982, 283), which could explain why auxiliary posts were needed to reinforce this section of the revetment. This also suggests that the carpenters involved in the front-bracing of Section B were not as competent as those responsible for the front-bracing of Sections A, C, D and E, but especially Section D.

But it is the jointing of the subsidiary baseplate into the principal baseplate that emphatically distinguishes the carpentry of Revetment 1 on Wood Quay from that of London and Bristol. For example, on the London waterfront, subsidiary baseplates supporting the front-braces of early to mid-thirteenth-century revetments, such as TX4, TX7, TX8, TL2, TL3 and BG14, were staked to the foreshore at least 1m out from the principal baseplate and not jointed to it (Milne 1992). In contrast, on Sections A, C, D and E on Wood Quay (but not on Section B), the subsidiary baseplates were jointed into the front face of the principal baseplate which in turn was jointed to the upright posts, which, together with the subsidiary baseplate, supported the front-braces. In other words, these timbers are triangulated and it is this triangulation, this jointing together of these timbers – that is, the upright posts, the front-braces, the subsidiary baseplates and principal baseplate – that creates a truss and stiffens the revetment. And even in today's world, the applications of trussing are extensive and extend to shipbuilding, bridge-building and even aircraft. In effect, the engineering of Sections A, C, D and E of the Wood Quay revetments is significantly more advanced than that of their English counterpart. The carpenters appear to have a good grasp of tension and compressive forces and used this knowledge to stiffen and improve the docking facilities at Wood Quay in a manner that is very different to that used on contemporary and later revetments on the London waterfront.

Revetments 2 and 3

Built further out into the riverbed, Revetment 2 was built sometime in the early thirteenth century (Wallace 2016, 163). According to Wallace, this revetment was back-braced. Apart from the baseplates and a 2m-high A-frame that may have been connected to another revetment, no further evidence was recovered (ibid., 163–6). The use of a pegged lap-joint at the top of the A-frame as well as the pegging of the legs into notches in the principal baseplate suggests, however, that this feature was probably part of a later repair. Revetment 3 was also back-braced using a pegged horizontal tie-back fitted with short cross-pieces (Wallace 1982, 275). Although back-bracing was used by Dublin carpenters in the tenth, eleventh and twelfth centuries (Wallace 2016, 166), the technique used on revetment 3 seems to be closer in character to that used from the early to late twelfth century on the London waterfront, e.g., BG10, SH1, TX3 and TX4 (Milne 1992). The use of the through-splayed scarf joint also continued into Revetment 3, where, in one instance at least, an upright post was tenoned into a mortise cutting right through a scarf-joint in the baseplate. Although it is generally thought that this technique weakened the scarf-joint, if the tenon in question continued right through the mortise and into the foreshore, the post would then be earthfast and capable of strengthening the joint.

WINETAVERN STREET

To the west of Wood Quay, and clearly a continuation westwards of the reclamation process, F166 (AD 1190–1208), an east–west revetment on Winetavern Street, was also excavated (Halpin 2000). Front-braced and similar in construction to Revetment 1 on Wood Quay, Revetment F166 had a substantial baseplate set into a pre-dug slot on the foreshore. The baseplate incorporated three oak timbers jointed together using through-splayed scarf joints but with a possible edged-half scarf joint between F166.54 and F166.55 (O'Sullivan 2000, 86). Using a variety of pegged tenons ranging from the housed bare-edged tenons recorded on Wood Quay, to two-shouldered tenons or, in some instances, timbers with simple tapered ends, the subsidiary baseplates were jointed and pegged into the front face of the principal baseplate, in a manner similar to that recorded on Wood Quay (fig. 3.11). Also

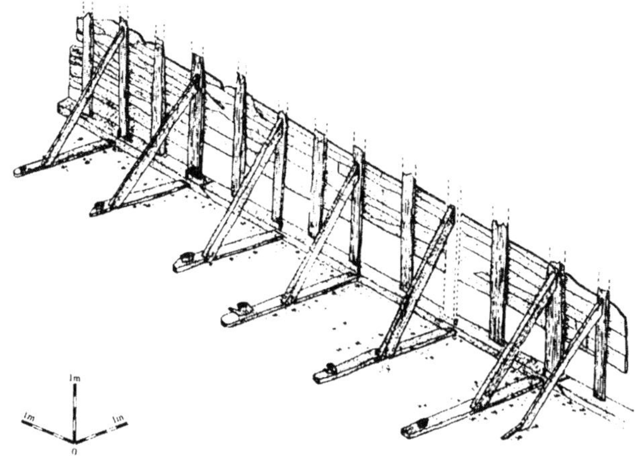

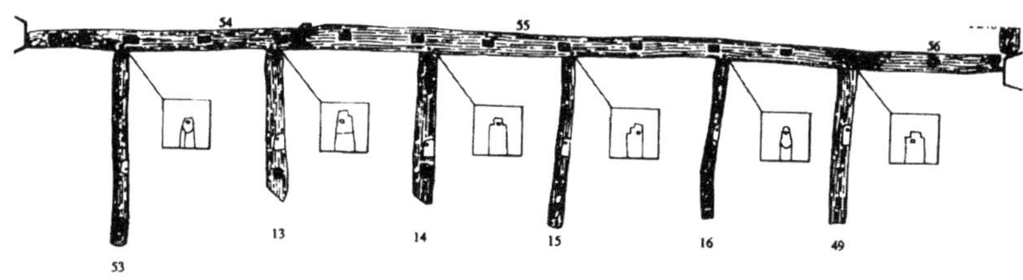

3.11 Reconstruction and plan of Revetment F166, Winetavern Street, Dublin (after Halpin 2000).

as on Wood Quay, a number of the housed bare-edged tenons at the end of the subsidiary baseplates were cut through by the mortises supporting the upright posts (Halpin 2000, ill. 2). The use of three different types of tenon, however, especially the use of tapered ends to joint the subsidiaries to the principal baseplate, strongly suggests that carpenters from different carpentry traditions are now working side by side preparing the subsidiary baseplates. For example, the so-called tapered end on two of the subsidiaries is not too dissimilar to the Saxo-Norman tenon used on Bridge 1 at Hemington, in which the full cross-section of the timber is housed into a mortise (Ripper and Cooper, 2009, 102) – evidence that could suggest that Anglo-Norman carpenters are now more involved than previously in the construction of the Dublin revetments and are working alongside Hiberno-Norse carpenters on the same section of the revetment, a phenomenon also recorded on the ninth/tenth-century site at Billingsgate in London (Horsman et al. 1988, 71), where baseplates and earthfast-posts, two very different construction methods, were employed in the same structure.

3.12 Foot of front brace of Revetment F166 (after O'Sullivan 2000).

From the only surviving front-brace still *in situ* (Halpin 2000, ill. 13, 53; O'Sullivan 2000, 67), it would appear that the front-braces (like Wood Quay) were chase mortise-and-tenoned into the top of every alternative vertical post. Most unlike Wood Quay, however, the foot of the front-brace was simply tapered and pegged into a notch in the subsidiary baseplate (fig. 3.12) – a very inferior joint, especially when compared with the chase mortise-and-tenon joint used at Wood Quay, a joint, moreover, that would have seriously compromised the trussing action of the front-bracing. The suggestion by O'Sullivan, however, that the tapered foot of the front braces was pegged into a notched-lap joint is most unlikely (O'Sullivan 2000, 67). A notched-lap joint, as the name implies, usually has a distinctive V-shaped notch to prevent the withdrawal of one timber from another, in this instance, to prevent the front-brace withdrawing from the subsidiary baseplate. However, a photograph of the front-brace 'foot' (O'Sullivan 2000, ill. 20) would seem to indicate that the tapered end of the brace was simply inserted and pegged into a crudely cut 'notch' in the subsidiary baseplate – a type of joint more reminiscent of the Saxo-Norman chase mortise-and-tenon joint (see fig. 3.3 above) used on Bridge 1 at Hemington in the eleventh century (Ripper and Cooper 2009, 103). If this conclusion is correct (and this is where detailed drawings are essential), the use of this joint, together with the use of tapered ends on two of the subsidiary baseplates, further supports the argument that Anglo-Norman carpenters are now playing a greater role in the construction of the Liffey waterfront revetments.

On the western side of Winetavern Street and contemporary with F166, two parallel post-and-plank revetments, F246 and F1055, marked the boundary of the reclamation site. Running north–south and founded on baseplates *c.*0.80m apart, the revetments were unbraced with evidence for two traditions of jointing. Baseplate F246, for example, had stopped mortises, 0.60m apart, while F1055 had through-mortises at 0.40m intervals, mortise types that were part of the repertoire of carpentry joints used in the early medieval watermills in Ireland (Geaney 2014, 125–37).

USHER'S QUAY

On Usher's Quay, evidence for two timber revetments, *c.*AD 1217–19, was interpreted as the remains of an enclosed stone and timber dock, *c.*18m x 20m, built to the south of an existing riverfront wall. Subsequently, a third revetment was built on the northern side over the remains of the riverfront wall (Swan 2000, 126–58).

Revetment 1 was essentially a front-braced revetment founded on baseplates (fig. 3.13). As on Wood Quay, the baseplates were jointed together using a through-splayed scarf joint, with rectangular through-mortises supporting four upright posts. Only two of the upright posts (U2 and U3) were front-braced, however. Two subsidiary baseplates, jointed into the front face of the principal baseplate, supported the diagonal braces of both these uprights. A substantial earthfast-post (UA), *c.*0.10m sq., also supported a series of overlapping planks immediately inside the riverfront wall.

Revetment 2 continued the line of revetments southward. Built at a higher level, Revement 2 was unbraced with carpentry techniques that are very different to those of Revetment 1 and also those of Wood Quay. The baseplate was massive and, like Wood Quay, the upper face was grooved to take the lower planks. Unlike Wood Quay, however, only one of the six uprights (U5) was mortised-and-tenoned into the baseplate. Two other uprights, U7 and U9, were, to quote, 'shaped like an inverted "L"... set with their longer edges protruding across the line of the groove, somewhat in the manner of barefaced tenons' (though unfortunately there are no accompanying drawings with these details) (Swan 2000, 150). This is a technique that sounds very similar to that used on the mid-ninth-century Saxon mill at Tamworth in Staffordshire, in which two of the earthfast-posts supporting the mill-house were notched over the main foundation timbers (Rahtz and Meeson 1992, 128). The other three uprights (U6, U8 and U10) on Usher's Quay were earthfast and set firmly into the mud to the rear of the baseplate, carpentry techniques that are archaic and regressive by contemporary standards, including the standard of carpentry on the London waterfront where, in the early thirteenth century, carpenters were finally adopting framing techniques (Milne 1992, 83). Indeed, the carpentry of Revetment 2 on Usher's Quay could suggest that a considerable number of Anglo-Norman carpenters now based in Dublin were out of touch with developments in London and medieval Britain generally.

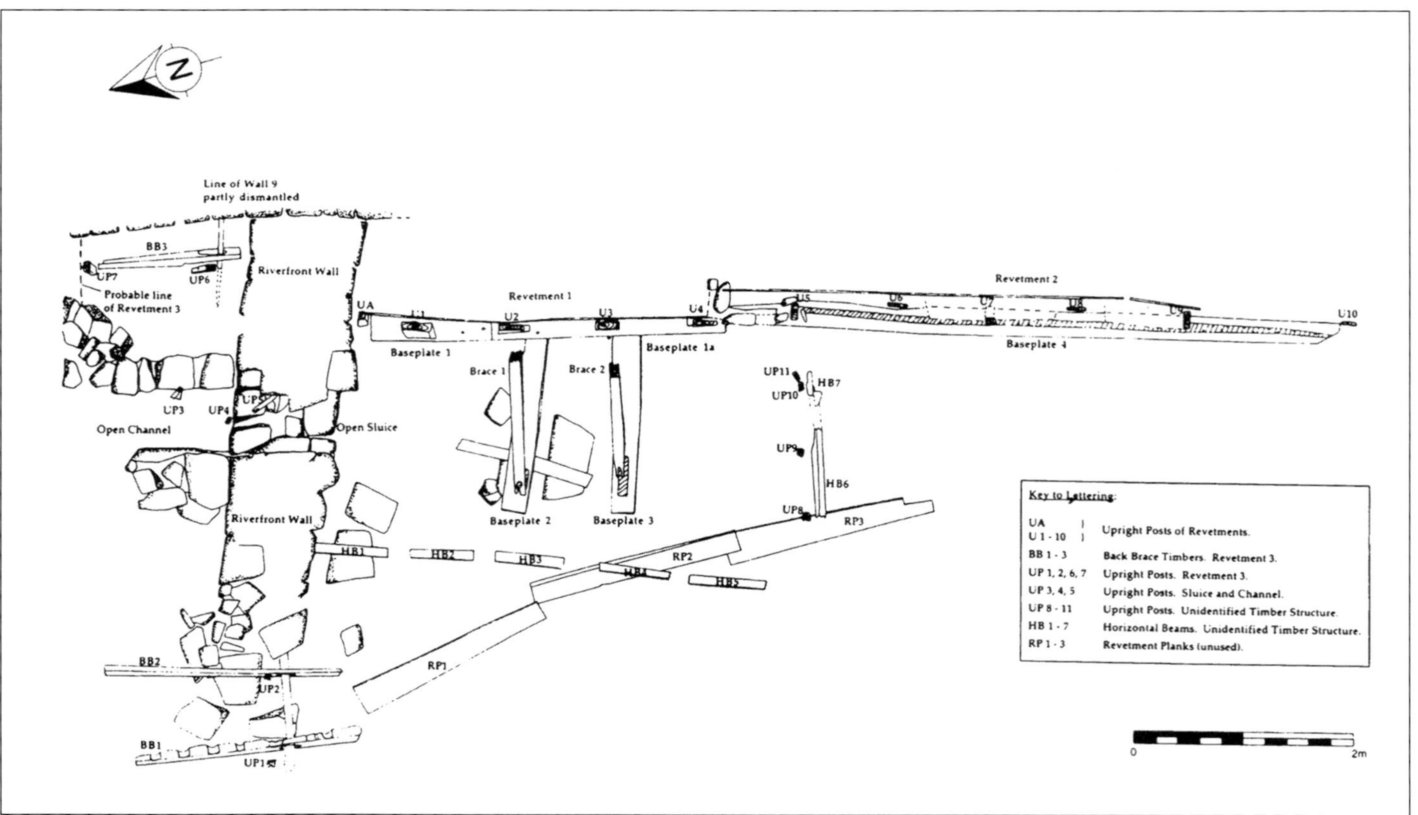

3.13 Revetments 1, 2, 3 on Usher's Quay, Dublin (after Swan 2000).

Revetment 3 on Usher's Quay was back-braced and built out into the Liffey, to the north of an earlier riverfront wall. Only the back-bracing timbers of the revetment survived. These had been wedged into the riverfront wall, which had been partially demolished to accommodate them. The back-braces consisted of two large timbers, each perforated at one end to receive a single curved timber to tie back the braces and lock them into the collapsed wall. A third pair of back-braces with a similar tie-back arrangement, but slightly forward of the riverfront wall, were also recorded. Although Revetment 3 has not been dated, nevertheless it is possible that this revetment is roughly contemporary with Revetment 3 on Wood Quay, with both reflecting a new strategy of using back-bracing only on the Liffey waterfront.

After the mid- to late twelfth century, revetments that were back-braced only seem to have been abandoned on the London waterfront, at which time revetments that were front-braced only or, more generally, revetments that were both front- and back-braced, were introduced, with the latter continuing to be built into the late thirteenth century, after which, in the early fourteenth century, we again see a return to back-bracing only on Trig Lane. Two tiers of horizontal back-bracing, tied back by pile-retained crosspieces, were used on TL7 on Trig Lane. In the top tier, where the horizontal braces passed through the front face of the revetment, the protruding end of the brace was pierced to take a long horizontal bar and pull back the revetment in a manner similar to that used in the mid-twelfth century on BG10 (Milne 1992, 28–70). And, in the eleventh century, a somewhat similar technique was used on pathway fences along Fishamble Street, where a crook at the end of the back-brace clasped a wailing beam and pulled back the vertical staves (Wallace 1982, 275; Wallace 1992, fig. 189). By the mid-fourteenth century, further developments in back-bracing technology can be identified on the London waterfront and, on the stave revetment TL10 on Trig Lane, two timbers inclined towards each other are jointed into a rear subsidiary baseplate using pegged chase mortise-and-tenon joints (Milne 1992, 72).

THE LIFFEY'S NORTHERN BANK: STRAND STREET GREAT

On the northern bank of the Liffey, evidence for land-reclamation and waterfront revetments has been recorded on Strand Street Great (Walsh 2005, 160–87) and Arran Quay (Hayden 2004, 149–242). Classified as a front-braced revetment, Strand Street Great incorporated a very different structural technique to that used on Wood Quay and on the Liffey waterfront generally. Whereas on Wood Quay the subsidiary baseplates were jointed into the front face of the principal baseplate, on Strand Street Great the subsidiaries were set beneath the principal baseplate with the soffit of the latter seated into the upper face of the former (fig. 3.14). In simple terms, the subsidiary baseplates,

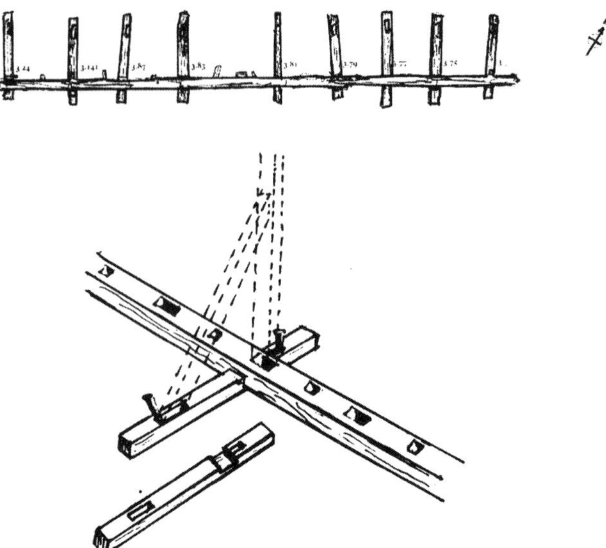

3.14 Plan and reconstruction of revetment on Strand Street Great, Dublin (redrawn, from Walsh 2005).

which were aligned north–south and regularly spaced, had a rebate cut into their upper face at the south end, into which the principal baseplate was then trenched and tightly fitted – a technique broadly similar to that recorded on one of the baseplates on SH3 at Seal House on the London waterfront in the early to mid-thirteenth century (Milne 1992).

On Strand Street Great, the principal baseplate, which extended east–west, comprised seven oak timbers jointed together using pegged through-splayed scarf joints. Rectangular mortises, cut into the upper face of the principal baseplate at regular intervals, supported the upright posts of the revetment, with smaller square mortises in between probably supporting lighter studs at mid-span. The principal posts of the revetment were front-braced, with the foot of the front-brace simply wedged and pegged into a mortise at the northern end of the subsidiary baseplate. How the braces articulated with the top of the principal posts is not known. The foot of the front-brace, however, is described as tenoned but not well-fitted and generally unshouldered (Walsh 2005, 174). What Walsh seems to be describing here is a raking strut that is either fully housed into the mortise or, alternatively, a raking strut with a tapered end, a technique that appears to be very similar to the Saxo-Norman tenons used on Bridge 1 at Hemington (Ripper and Cooper 2009, 102). Either way, the technique is crude and archaic, especially when compared with the chase mortise-and-tenon joint used on the foot of the front-brace on Wood

Quay and also, in fact, with the chase mortise-and-tenon joint used on the foot of the front-brace of SH3 at Seal House on the London waterfront (Milne 1992, 40). In common with other thirteenth-century revetments on the London waterfront, however, the head of the front-brace on SH3 was simply set into a splayed recess.

The use of square mortises on Strand Street Great in the early thirteenth century is surprising. Another archaic feature, this joint was also recorded on baseplate 203.1 on Site D, a contemporary revetment on the River Poddle (Walsh 1997, 47). Although square mortises were used in early medieval Ireland, they were generally used in secondary positions only. On the horizontal mill at Little Island (*c.*AD 630), for example, while the rectangular mortise was used to take the tusk tenons of the principal posts, the square mortise was used to joint the baseplates to the support beam of the flume (Geaney 2014, 125–9). Square mortises were also used on Cashen Bridge to take the tusk tenons of the bridge piles (Geaney 2016, 96), after which there appears to be no further evidence for square mortises and certainly not in an area where structural strength was important. On the other hand, on the eleventh-century bridge at Hemington, the square mortise was used to support the uprights of the timber caissons (Ripper and Cooper 2009, 19), an area where river flow would have put considerable stress on the structure and where the rectangular mortise-and-tenon joint would have been much more efficient. Instead, to stabilize the bridge caissons, the Hemington carpenters relied on the sheer weight of the timbers, the use of pegs and, to a certain degree, the fact that the corner posts of the caissons were also earthfast (ibid., 28, 20). Indeed, the square mortise continued in use in England into the mid-twelfth century when it was used on the moat bridge at West Derby (Rigold 1972, 89, fig. 23) and it is not until the thirteenth century that tight-fitting joints and the efficiency of the rectangular mortise-and-tenon joint was fully appreciated (Ripper and Cooper 2009, 28).

THE LIFFEY'S NORTHERN BANK: ARRAN QUAY

The two timber revetments recorded on Arran Quay (Hayden 2004, 149–242) belong to the same category of front-braced, vertical revetments recorded on Section B of Wood Quay. The Arran Quay revetments are much later, however, with Revetment 1 dated to *c.*AD 1305 and Revetment 2, which was built at right angles to Revetment 1, constructed only slightly later (Hayden, 2004, 160–74).

Revetment 1

Front-braced, Revetment 1 comprised three oak baseplates, 52, 53, 54, jointed together, using pegged through-splayed scarf joints (fig. 3.15). Only baseplate 53 (4.02m L x 0.26m W x 0.11m Th.) survived to its full extent, however. Nine

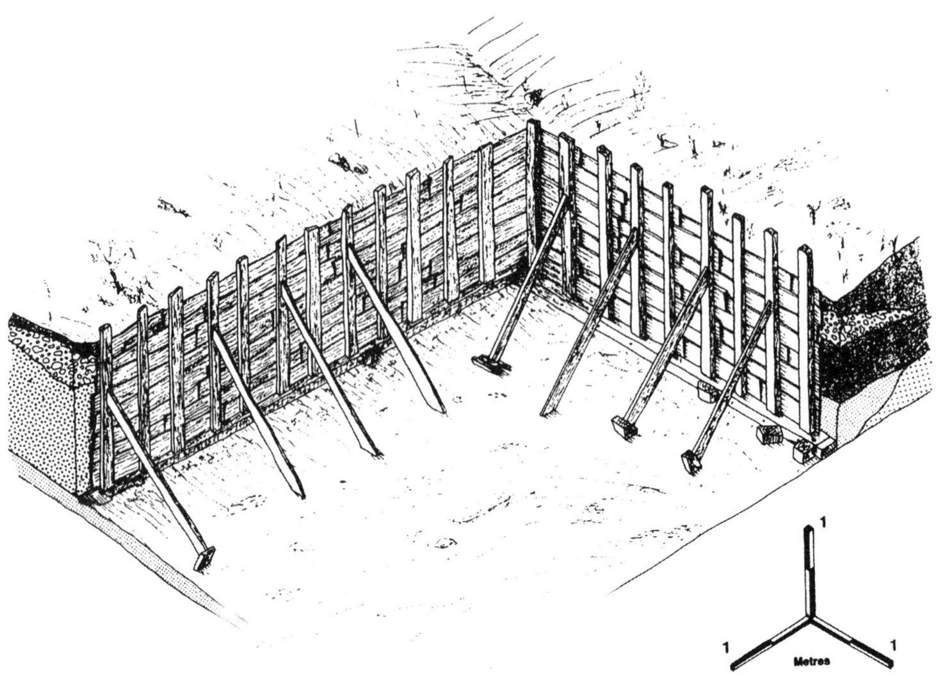

3.15 Revetment 1 (*right*), Revetment 2 (*left*), Arran Quay, Dublin (after Hayden 2004).

3.16 Composite base-pad on Revetment 1, Arran Quay, Dublin (after Hayden 2004).

mortises supported the upright posts of the revetment, only five of which survived *in situ* – one of ash, the remainder of oak. Three of the posts were squared timbers, the remaining two were split half-round logs. Although none of these posts had tenons, nevertheless, except for the ash post, all were tightly fitted and pegged. A row of posts, *c.*0.80m out from the baseplates and opposite every second upright, were interpreted as anchors for diagonal front-braces, none of which survived. That is to say, the front-braces were earthfast and retained by a pile in a manner very similar to that used in the late twelfth century on Section B on Wood Quay (see fig. 3.6). At the south end of the revetment, a single squared oak timber *c.*1.07m in length, 0.95m wide and 0.70m thick, was interpreted as a composite base at the foot of a diagonal front-brace (fig. 3.16). The base had a long central cavity with an ash plant lapped and pegged across one end. The base was set at right angles to the revetment but not jointed to it, a feature that appears to be reminiscent of the single base-pad recovered on Section B on Wood Quay over a century earlier. While Wallace in his later work describes this composite base as unique to Dublin (Wallace 2016, 171), in truth, the base was probably a reused timber in which an ash plant was used to reduce the length of the cavity in order to secure the foot of the front-brace in a manner similar to that used on subsidiary baseplates such as TX3 on the London waterfront in the late twelfth century (Milne 1992, 50–51). And generally speaking, on the London waterfront, an over-long mortise in a subsidiary baseplate was often just packed with wedges once the final adjustments to the posts had been made (ibid., 17).

Revetment 2

Apart from the two baseplates 54 and 55, little survived of Revetment 2. A redundant scarf joint at one end suggested that baseplate 54 had been lifted from Revetment 1 and reused in Revetment 2 with five of its original six mortises supporting the upright posts (fig. 3.15). Baseplate 55 was also a reused timber, but of ash. Crudely finished, the baseplate varied from rectangular at one end to a half round log at the other end. Both baseplates were jointed together by a poorly made scarf joint, with a mortise cutting through the joint supporting a pegged upright post. The pegging of the post is interesting, however, in that a single peg was driven at an angle of 45° through the baseplate, down into the post and out into the silts below – a technique that would have been very difficult to execute, especially *in situ*, but one which would have produced a very strong joint. In other words, despite the general lack of good carpentry joints in both revetments, overall the carpenters seem to have appreciated the importance of tight fitting, pegged joints, and at least one carpenter had a sound knowledge of structural strength and how to achieve it.

SUMMARY AND CONCLUSIONS

Using the revised date of AD 1195–1201 (Halpin 2000, 37; Wallace 2016, 165) for the construction of Revetment 1 on Wood Quay, it is clear that the carpentry of these front-braced revetments is not only very different from contemporary revetments on the London waterfront but it is also considerably more advanced. Indeed, while the concept of front-bracing was probably introduced into Ireland by the Anglo-Normans, the technology used to construct and brace the Wood Quay revetments was not. The Wood Quay revetments were founded on squared baseplates with rectangular through-mortises supporting the tenons of the principal posts – framing techniques that are not used on the London waterfront until the early thirteenth century (Milne 1992, 83). And in Section D on Wood Quay, where the best evidence survives, the joints were accurately cut and tight-fitting, characteristics that are the hallmark of good carpentry. On all sections of the Wood Quay revetment, a chase mortise-and-tenon joint was used on both the head and (except on Section B) on the foot of the diagonally set front-braces. On the London waterfront on the other hand, while a chase tenon was used on the foot of the front-brace in the early thirteenth century, the head of the brace was simply set into a splayed recess, a feature more usually associated with temporary shoring. And it is not until the late thirteenth century that the chase tenon was used on the head of the front-brace, almost a century after it was first used on Wood Quay.

But it is the development of the trussed timber revetment with its ability to sustain greater loads that best represents the technical achievements of the Wood Quay carpenters – evidence that emphatically refutes the claim that the carpentry of these revetments was conservative (Wallace 2016, 154; O'Sullivan 2000, 87) and reflective of improvisation (Wallace 2016, 154). In fact, the use of the front-braces to triangulate the other three components of the revetment is a very advanced framing technique, one, moreover, that is not recorded at any stage on the London revetments and certainly not in the late twelfth century. Instead, following the introduction of front-bracing on the London revetments in the mid- to late twelfth century, front-braces were either earthfast or, by the early thirteenth century, set into a subsidiary baseplate that was simply pegged to the foreshore c.1m out from the principal baseplate. In other words, the front-brace of these revetments would have been vulnerable to damage caused by scouring due to tidal action or by debris brought down by periodic floods. Furthermore, the timbers of these front-braces were often barely modified branches.

The trussing of the Wood Quay revetments, together with the use of a floating revetment as a buffer protecting the main revetment, was, in the late twelfth century, an exceptional piece of engineering that may have allowed ships to dock against a front-braced revetment. This was an engineering solution that required not only a high standard of carpentry (indications for which were already evident in Cork in the mid- to late twelfth century) but one that required great experience in dealing with water-related problems – problems such as might have occurred during the construction of the tidal mills in the early medieval period, or the building of the early ninth-century pile bridge across the Shannon at Clonmacnois and the later Cashen Bridge (Geaney 2016, 89–104), or in the design and construction of the Viking boats in Dublin (McGrail 1993).

While this paper has argued that Revetment 1 on Wood Quay was mainly the work of Hiberno-Norse carpenters, the use of the through-splayed scarf joint together with the evidence for earthfast front-braces and a front-brace jointed into a base-pad in Section B, as well as the lack of tenons on the mid-span posts, are all indicative of a different carpentry tradition. It is a tradition that is also attested on the London waterfront and which supports the view that these elements were probably the work of Anglo-Norman carpenters – evidence which in turn suggests that both Anglo-Norman and Hiberno-Norse carpenters were involved in the construction of the Wood Quay revetments, but with the Hiberno-Norse, initially at least, the main contractors. And although it is now known that, in the medieval period, carpenters from different backgrounds frequently worked alongside each other on the same site (Horsman et al. 1988, 71), in late twelfth century Dublin, relations between the Anglo-Normans and the Hiberno-Norse are far from clear. For example, according to the traditional view, the Hiberno-Norse were driven out of Dublin following the Anglo-Norman invasion and forced to settle north of the Liffey in an area known as Oxmantown (Simpson 2011, 49). It is now known, however, that Oxmantown was already well-established prior to the invasion (ibid., 54) and, in fact, following the conquest the Hiberno-Norse sought fraternization, recognition and privileges from the new order. However, a massive influx of English immigrants ultimately undermined the position and security of Dublin Hiberno-Norse who, by 1300, had lost their identity as Northmen (Ryan 1990, 126).

The reclamation process that began on Wood Quay continued westwards into Winetavern Street with the construction of revetment F166 in AD 1190–1208. Although the construction techniques used on Wood Quay are generally replicated on Winetavern Street, closer inspection reveals a number of significant differences in the jointing methods used – evidence that not only suggests that carpenters from different traditions were involved here, but also demonstrates the great disparity in the level of skill between these carpenters. But it is the replacement of the 'true' chase mortise-and-tenon joint at the foot of the front-brace by the technically inferior Saxo-Norman joint of the same name (which seriously undermines the triangulation and trussing action of the revetment timbers) that strongly suggests that the Hiberno-Norse carpenter was no longer the lynch-pin in the construction of the Dublin revetments. Even more significantly, the use of the Saxo-Norman joint also suggests that

Anglo-Norman carpenters in Dublin are not keeping pace with developments in London where, from the early thirteenth century, the 'true' chase mortise-and-tenon joint was used on the foot of the front-brace (Milne 1992, 85).

Like Wood Quay, Revetment 1 on Usher's Quay was front-braced and founded on squared baseplates with rectangular mortise-and-tenon joints. In contrast, Revetment 2 was unbraced, with five of the six upright posts of earthfast-post construction – a radical shift away from the complex jointing techniques used on Revetment 1 and a lowering of carpentry standards – evidence that could suggest that carpenters with a background in Saxo-Norman carpentry techniques are steadily replacing Hiberno-Norse carpenters on the Dublin waterfront. And although little survived of Revetment 3, the evidence for back-bracing on both Usher's Quay and Wood Quay and possibly also on Winetavern Street (Halpin 2000, 48) would seem to support the suggestion that a second generation of Hiberno-Norse carpenters have either succumbed to Saxo-Norman construction techniques or are no longer employed on the Dublin revetments.

Wallace's dismissal of Claire Walsh's report on Strand Street Great on the grounds that it has no unique traits (Wallace 2016, 172) is to misunderstand the evidence presented. While on Wood Quay the carpenter relied on good jointing and triangular trusses to improve the stiffness and strength of the revetments, on Strand Street Great the carpenters relied on the weight of the principal baseplate, trenched into and bearing down on the subsidiary baseplate, to create a rigid and stable support for the revetments – a technique also used on SH3, a contemporary revetment recorded at Seal House on the London waterfront (Milne 1992, 40). Seal House, however, does not explain the use of square mortises and the lack of tenons on the front-braces of Strand Street Great, especially as Saxo-Norman techniques such as these had, by the early thirteenth century, been largely abandoned on the London waterfront. But perhaps the greatest dilemma posed by the Strand Street Great revetments is this: why, in an area traditionally thought to be Hiberno-Norse, were they using what appear to be Anglo-Norman carpenters to build the revetments? And although there is good evidence to show that both Gaelic Irish and Hiberno-Norse frequently adopted English names and English ways to protect their position in society (O'Byrne 2003, 20–35), the way in which a carpenter is trained during his apprenticeship has a lasting influence on his work. That is to say, if Hiberno-Norse carpenters were involved in the construction of Strand Street Great, there should be some supporting evidence.

The carpentry of the two revetments on Arran Quay is poor, not only in comparison to the carpentry of Wood Quay in the late twelfth century, but also in comparison to contemporary carpentry on the London waterfront. London carpenters, having adopted full-framing techniques in the early thirteenth century, had by the early fourteenth century advanced their craft significantly (Bond 1998, 16–21). On Arran Quay, the opposite appears to be the case and the innovative skills of the Wood Quay carpenters appear to be irrevocably lost. Indeed, the use of earthfast front-braces similar to Section B on Wood Quay in the late twelfth century, as well as the lack of tenons on the ends of the upright posts, all suggest that carpentry in Dublin is now the preserve of the Anglo-Norman carpenter, but one who is now out of touch with developments in England and possibly also in Gaelic Ireland.

BIBLIOGRAPHY

Bates, D.R. 1997 *Carpentry and joinery: book 1*. Longman, London.

Bond, R. 1998 'Timber-framed building in the London region'. In D.F. Stenning and D.D. Andrews (eds), *Regional variations in timber-framed building in England and Wales down to 1550*, 16–21. Essex.

Brigham, T. 1992 'Re-used house timbers from the Billingsgate site, 1982–3'. In G. Milne (ed.), *Timber building techniques in London* c.*900–1400*, 86–105, London and Middlesex Archaeological Society.

Brigham,T., Goodburn, D., Tyers, I. and Dillon, J. 1995 'A Roman timber building on the Southwark Waterfront, London'. *Archaeological Journal* 152, 1–72.

Darrah, R. 2009 'The tools and joint types in the construction of the Hemington Bridges'. In S. Ripper and L. Cooper (eds), *Hemington Bridges*. Leicester Monograph Series no. 16, 96–113.

Fulford, M.G., Rippon, S., Allan J.R.L. and Hillam, J. 1992 'The medieval quay at Woolaston Grange, Gloucestershire'. *Trans. Bristol & Gloucestershire Arch. Soc.* 110, 101–27.

Geaney, M. 2014 'Structural carpentry in medieval Ireland: continuity and change'. PhD, UCC.

Geaney, M. 2014a 'A review of the evidence for waterfront developments at 40–48 South Main Street, Cork'. In M. Hurley and C. Brett (eds), *Archaeological excavations at South Main Street, 2003–2005*, 534–43. Cork.

Geaney, M. 2016 'Timber bridges in medieval Ireland'. *Journal of Irish Archaeology* 25, 89–104.

Good, G.L. 1990 'Some aspects of the development of the Redcliffe waterfront in the light of excavations at Dundas wharf'. *Bristol and Avon Archaeology* 9, 29–42.

Goodburn, D. 1992 'A Roman timber framed building tradition'. *Archaeological Journal* 148, 182–204.

Halpin, A. 2000 *The port of medieval Dublin*. Dublin. Four Courts Press.

Hayden, A. 2004 'Excavation of the medieval river frontage at Arran Quay, Dublin'. In S. Duffy (ed.), *Medieval Dublin V*, 149–242. Dublin. Four Courts Press.

Hobley, B. 1981 'The London waterfront; the exception or the rule?' In G. Milne and B. Hobley (eds), *Waterfront archaeology in Britain and northern Europe*, CBA Report no. 41, 1–9.

Horseman, V., Milne, C. and Milne, G. 1988 *Aspects of Saxo-Norman London 1: building and street development near Billingsgate and Cheapside, London*. London and Middlesex Arch. Society. Monograph no. 11.

Lynn, C. and McDowell, J.A. 2011 *Deer Park Farms: the excavation of a raised rath in the Glenarm Valley, Co. Antrim*. Belfast. Northern Ireland Environmental Agency.

Lucas, A.T. 1953 'The horizontal mill in Ireland'. *JRSAI* 83, 1–36.

Lydon, J. 2003 'The defence of Dublin in the Middle Ages'. In S. Duffy (ed.), *Medieval Dublin IV*, 63–78. Dublin. Four Courts Press.

Milne, G. and Milne, C. 1982 *Medieval waterfront development at Trig Lane, London*. London. London and Middlesex Archaeological Society.

Milne, G. 1992 *Timber building techniques in London* c.*900–1400*. London.

O'Byrne, E. 2003 *War, politics and the Irish of Leinster, 1156–1606*. Dublin. Four Courts Press.

O'Kelly, M.J. 1961 'A wooden bridge on the River Cashen, Co. Kerry'. *JRSAI*, 91, 135–51.

O'Sullivan, A. 2000 'The wooden waterfronts: a study of the construction, carpentry and use of trees and woodlands'. In A. Halpin (ed.), *The port of medieval Dublin*, 62–92. Dublin. Four Court Press.

O'Sullivan, M. and Downey, L. 2015 'Historical bridges'. *Archaeology Ireland*, Winter, 37–40.

Ponsford, M.W. 1985 'Bristol's medieval waterfront: the Redcliffe project'. In A. Herteig and E. Asbjørn (eds), *Conference on waterfront archaeology in north European towns no. 2. Bergen 1983*, 112–17

Perring, D. 2002 *The Roman house in Britain*. Oxford. Routledge.

Rahtz, P. and Meeson, R. 1992 *An Anglo-Saxon watermill at Tamworth*. CBA Report 83. Oxford.

Rigold, S.E. 1975 'Structural aspects of medieval bridges'. *Medieval Archaeology* 19, 48–91.

Ripper, S. and Cooper, R. 2009 *Hemington Bridges: the excavation of three medieval bridges at Hemington quarry near Donnington, Leicestershire*. University of Leicester Archaeological Services, Monograph no. 16. Leicester.

Ryan, J. 1990 'Pre-Norman Dublin'. In H. Clarke (ed.), *Medieval Dublin: the making of a metropolis*, 110–27. Dublin. Irish Academic Press.

Rynne, C. 2013 'Mills and milling in early medieval Ireland'. In N. Jackman, C. Moore and C. Rynne (eds), *The mill at Kilbegly*, 115–48. Dublin. National Roads Authority.

Rynne, C. 2015 'The technical development of the horizontal waterwheel in the first millennium AD: some recent archaeological insights from Ireland'. *International Journal for the History of Engineering and Technology* 85, 70–93.

Simpson, L. 2011 'Fifty years a-digging: a synthesis of medieval archaeological investigations in Dublin City and suburbs'. In S. Duffy (ed.), *Medieval Dublin XI*, 9–112. Dublin. Four Courts Press.

Swan, D.L. 2000 'Archaeological excavations at Usher's Quay'. In S. Duffy (ed.), *Medieval Dublin I*, 126–58. Dublin. Four Courts Press.

Wallace, P.F. 1981 'Dublin's waterfront at Wood Quay: 900–1317'. In G. Milne and B. Hobley (eds), *Waterfront archaeology in Britain and northern Europe*, CBA Report 41, 109–18. Oxford.

Wallace, P.F. 1982 'Carpentry in Ireland, AD 900–1300: the Wood Quay evidence'. In S. McGrail (ed.), *Woodworking techniques before AD 1500*. BAR International Series 129, 263–97. Oxford.

Wallace, P.F. 1992 *The Viking Age buildings of Dublin*. Dublin. Royal Irish Academy.

Wallace, P.F. 2016 *Viking Dublin: the Wood Quay excavations*, 154–91. Dublin. Irish Academic Press.

Walker, J. 1999 'Fyfield Hall: a late twelfth century aisled hall rebuilt *c.*1400 in the archaic style'. *Archaeological Journal* 156, 112–42.

Walsh, C. 1997 *Archaeological excavations at Patrick, Nicholas and Winetavern Streets*. Dublin. Dublin Corporation.

Walsh, C. 2005 'Archaeological excavation of the Anglo-Norman waterfront at Strand Street Great, Dublin'. In S. Duffy (ed.), *Medieval Dublin VI*, 160–87. Dublin. Four Courts Press.

Yeomans, D. 1999 *The development of timber as a structural material*. London. Ashgate.

Archaeological excavation of the medieval church of St John of Bothe Street, Fishamble Street, Dublin 8

LINZI SIMPSON

INTRODUCTION

This paper describes the results of an archaeological monitoring programme at Dublin Civic Offices, carried out on behalf of Dublin City Council, which included an area of excavation in and around the Fishamble Street main entrance, Licence ref. 08E42 (fig. 4.1). A total of five projects were carried out on the grounds of the Dublin Civic Offices, which are located in the centre of the medieval city (figs 4.2–6; pls 4.1-6):

> *Works 1*: The replacement of the plantar box and retaining wall along Fishamble Street in preparation for the construction of a gate.
>
> *Works 2*: The reduction in levels of introduced soil around the basement fire-exit, at the Fishamble Street entrance.
>
> *Works 3*: The replacement of some of the slabs in the Amphitheatre, in the central area of the complex, and some of the lighting along the northern side.
>
> *Works 4*: Ground preparation for the erection of a fence (east–west) in the western sector of the complex.
>
> *Works 5*: Excavation of masonry remains at the top (southern end) of Fishamble Street.

Works 1–4 found no archaeological remains of significance, which was nonetheless useful as an indicator of where archaeological deposits do not survive in the complex (fig. 4.2); however, Works 5 did produce significant findings (fig. 4.5). This area was archaeologically excavated after a modern low retaining wall running along the western side of Fishamble Street, at the southern end, collapsed over a weekend. The water-main had burst and, as part of the repair works, an emergency excavation was carried out, which revealed masonry at the junction of Fishamble Street and John's Lane East (figs 4.6–8). However, it was immediately apparent that two major interventions had occurred previously. The first was that the structure had been exposed, probably as part of the Wood Quay excavations in the 1980s, and the second

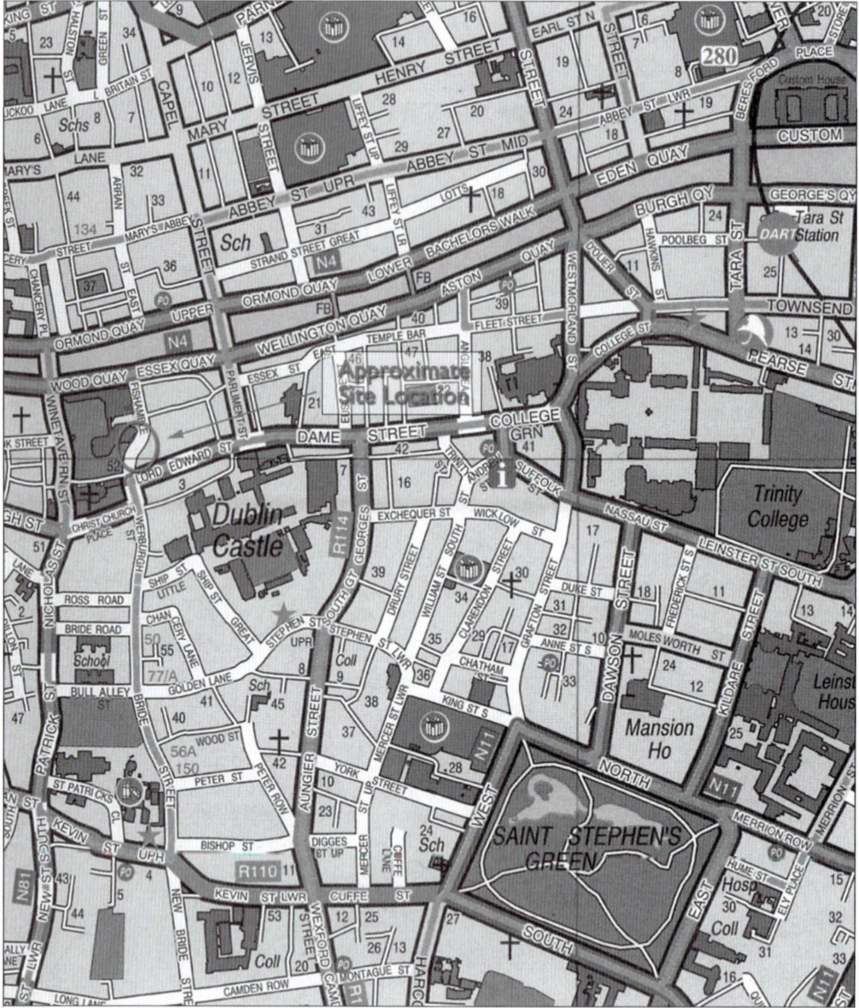

4.1 Site location.

was that a large service trench had been cut through the medieval foundations, running parallel to Fishamble Street, and causing considerable damage (pl. 4.5).

The Dublin Civic Office complex is centrally positioned within the Viking town of Dublin and was the location of the major Wood Quay excavations, carried out in the 1970s and 1980s. These excavations confirmed that Fishamble Street was an early street, dating from at least the early tenth century, the archaeological levels made up of house plots, with post-and-wattle houses, fronting onto the street (fig. 4.3). This settlement was subsequently enclosed by a stone wall *c.*1100, the northern section of which was found

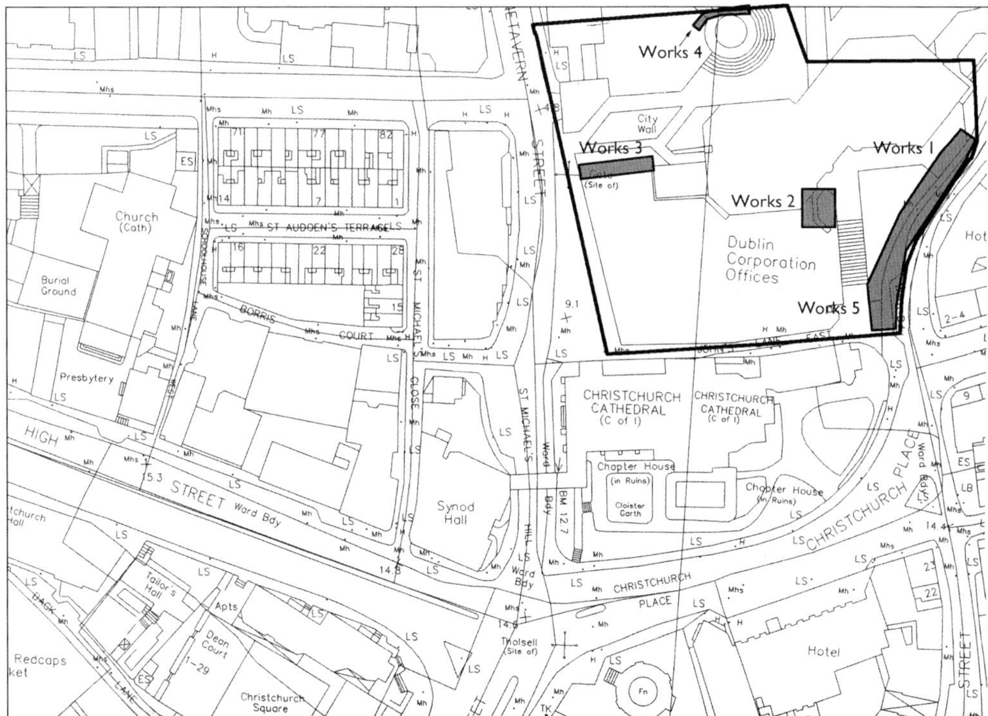

4.2 Works detail.

during the Wood Quay excavations. A significant stretch was subsequently preserved *in situ* within the basement of the offices, now forming the backdrop of an exhibition and conference centre called the Wood Quay Venue. The medieval church of St John the Evangelist was located at the top of Fishamble Street, on the western side of the street, at the junction with John's Lane East, which runs along the southern side of Christ Church cathedral. This church is first mentioned in the twelfth century and served as an important parish church with a large parish. It underwent significant rebuilding programmes throughout the medieval and post-medieval period culminating in a new build in the eighteenth century with a fine Palladian façade fronting onto Fishamble Street. The church was only demolished in 1877 and was replaced by a Mission Hall, which was subsequently demolished in the early 1960s.

The excavation for the water-pipe repair was in and around the known site of the church and, after the removal of slabs and soils in this area, the foundations of what appeared to be a medieval stone structure were found and immediately interpreted as forming part of this church. The extant remains consisted of a small, almost square, structure measuring externally 6.14m north–south by 5m wide, with evidence of a rebuild in some locations

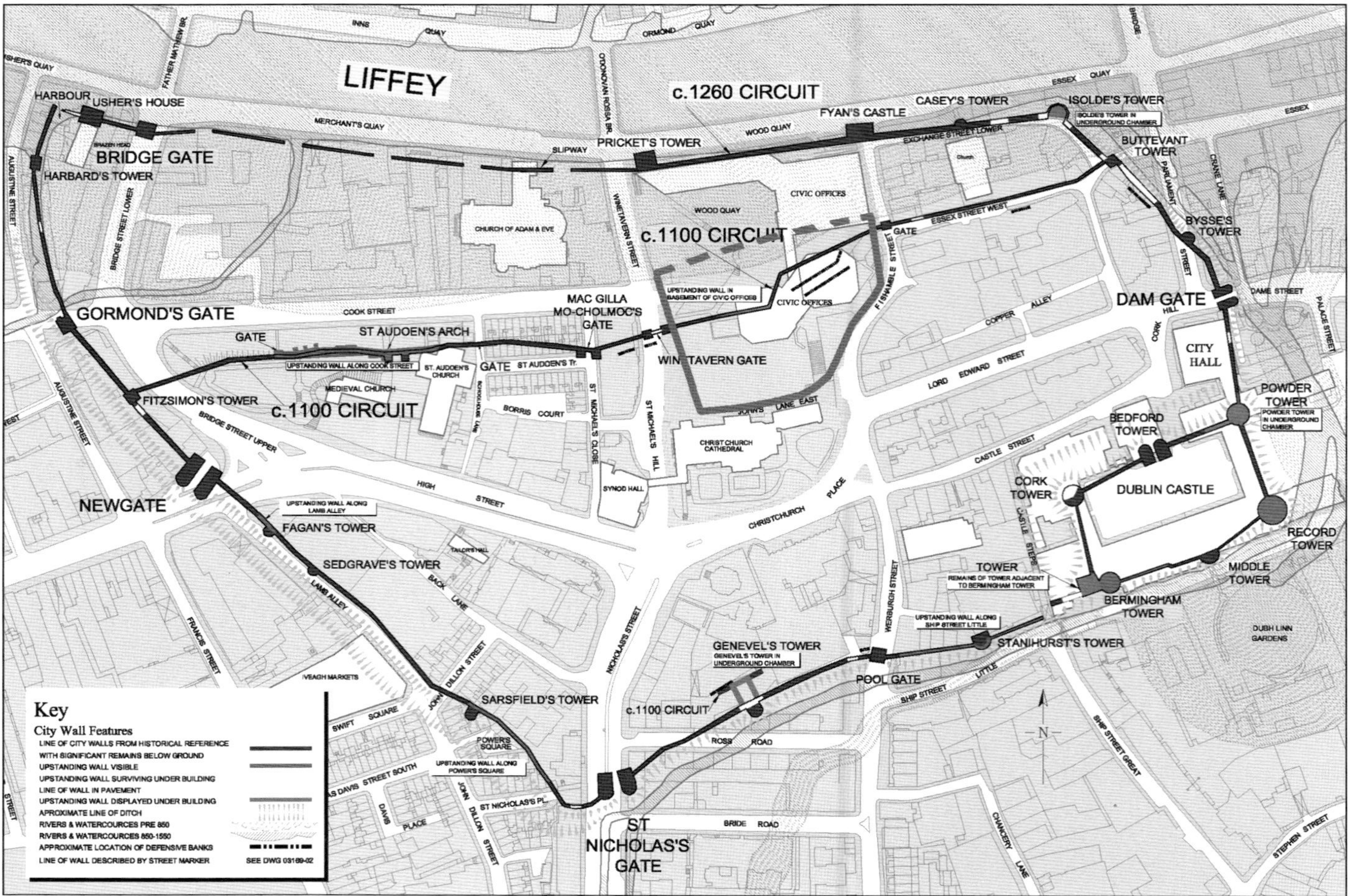

4.3 Medieval Dublin, 1170–1540 (after Clarke).

(figs 4.8–11; pls 4.2–4). The small size immediately suggested that this may have represented the chancel of the stone church, likely to have been built in the twelfth century, as suggested in the documentary sources. This type has been classified as a double-cell church, comprising a nave and a separate chancel, the latter housing the altar, which separated the liturgical ceremonies from the congregation, sitting in the nave. The chancel had been demolished to a single level, probably in the eighteenth century, but the foundations were substantial and at least two additional medieval walls were also identified, which can probably be related to a rebuild in either the fourteenth or fifteenth century, both of which are documented in the surviving sources. The footprint of the nave was not investigated and it is not known whether any remains are present beneath the modern ground surface. However, there was evidence of an additional brick wall along what would have been the western chancel wall and of other fragments of walls related to the rebuilding works of the eighteenth century. At least one later wall was identified which contained a fine cut sandstone, evidently harvested from the church, part of which was evidently demolished by this time.

The recording of the archaeological remains involved limited hand excavation of the infill clays to further expose and define the walls but, as stated previously, much of the investigation was restricted by Health and Safety restrictions. During the course of this excavation, substantial amounts of redeposited human bone, probably from the adjacent graveyard attached to St John's, were noted but not disturbed. The redeposition of this disarticulated bone probably occurred in the rebuilding programme in the eighteenth century, as it also contained fragments of clay-pipe stems and brick. The excavation also found that the foundations of the church had previously been exposed during the Wood Quay excavation campaign in the 1970s and 80s but was sealed by plastic and left *in situ*. This was exposed during the excavation under discussion.

Following discussion with Dr Ruth Johnston, Dublin City Archaeologist, a method statement for preservation *in situ* was agreed as the area formed one of the main entrances into the Civic Offices and scope for additional investigation was limited, along with the fact there were existing live services running through the middle of the site. However, the masonry remains were re-exposed in an attempt to establish the nature and extent of the surviving building in a cutting that eventually measured 12m in length north–south by between 4.50m in width at the northern end, widening to 6m in the southern. After this was completed the masonry remains were covered with a protective terrum and then sealed with 804 lime-free stone, which was then gently packed. As part of these works the church walls were surveyed on CAD, which will facilitate their re-exposure, should this be required, at a later date (fig. 4.12).[1]

1 National Grid Reference for the survey station (at the southern side of the excavated area): 315253.439m E 233982.956m N (fig. 4.12).

The monitoring programme was carried out by the writer and Kevin Weldon under licence to the National Monuments Service within the Department of Environment, Heritage and Local Government, and the National Museum of Ireland (Licence ref: 08E42). The on-site works were conducted between December 2007 and February 2008 with a team of four (Linzi Simpson, Kevin Weldon, Peter Kearns and Eric Simpson).

SITE WORKS 1–4 (figs 4.2 and 4.4)

Works 1

Works 1 involved the reduction in depth of artificial plantar boxes along the Fishamble Street frontage and this was carried out by hand and machine. The plantar boxes measured 38m north–south by 20m in width at the northern end, narrowing to 3m in width at the southern end (fig. 4.4). Each had an artificial base at the northern end. All works were monitored and the clays were found to be a modern infill deposit. The stone cladding along the eastern side of the plantar (along the Fishamble Street frontage) had to be removed suddenly and as a matter of urgency when a 12-inch water-pipe burst during the night, causing extensive flooding in the basement of the Civic Offices (pl. 4.1). The pipe was found to be set back between 0.40m and 1.50m from the street frontage, positioned within a modern clay mix containing rubble material and modern debris, which was over 1.50m in depth. A large manhole was also located, the upper levels of which were removed and rebuilt as part of this programme of works. The clay fill, evidently dumped in this area after the archaeological excavations in the 1980s, originated on the site and it contained disarticulated human remains, presumably from St John's graveyard. At the southern end of the excavation cutting, on the western side, medieval masonry was located under thin blue plastic as part of these works and an investigation was subsequently carried out. The results of this are listed below as Works 5 9; pls 4.2–3).

Works 2

Works 2 involved removing the clay and earth material on the western side of the Fishamble Street entrance, which partially extended over the basement, to facilitate rebuilding and repairs to the fire-exit. The clay infill in this location was found to contain medieval and post-medieval ceramics, as well as fragments of human bone. The latter evidently originated in the preserved graveyard of St John's and were carefully collected and reinterred within the medieval structure. No *in situ* archaeological layers were located during this phase of the works.

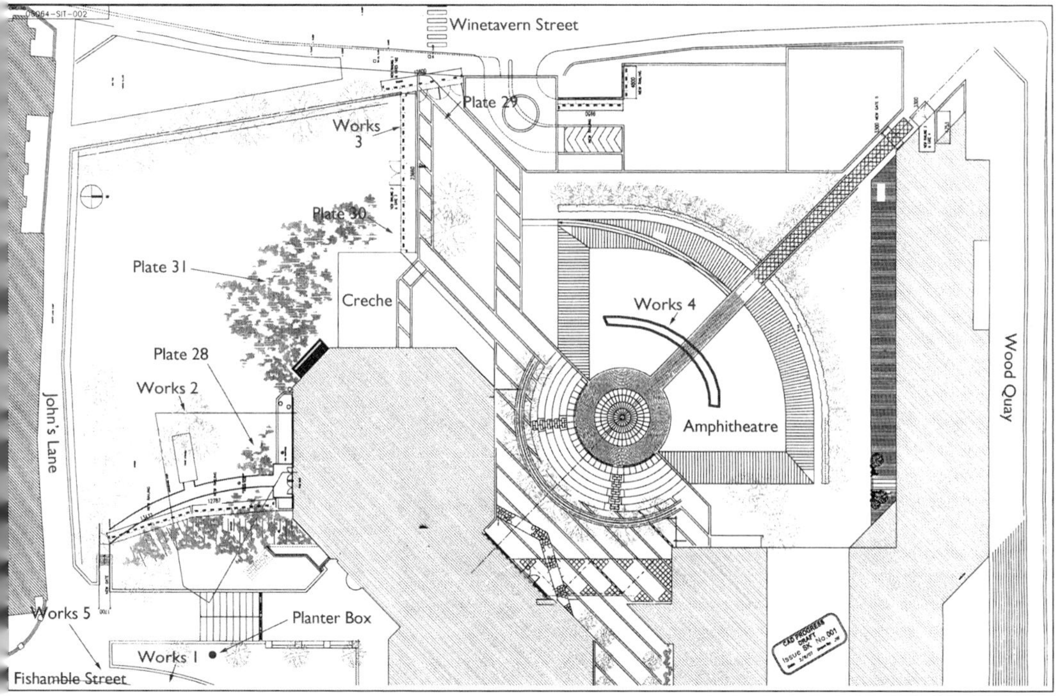

4.4 Detail of site on medieval map (after Clarke).

Plate 4.1 Site from the southeast.

Plate 4.2 (*top*) Structure F4, from the south.

Plate 4.3 (*bottom*) Structure F4, looking north.

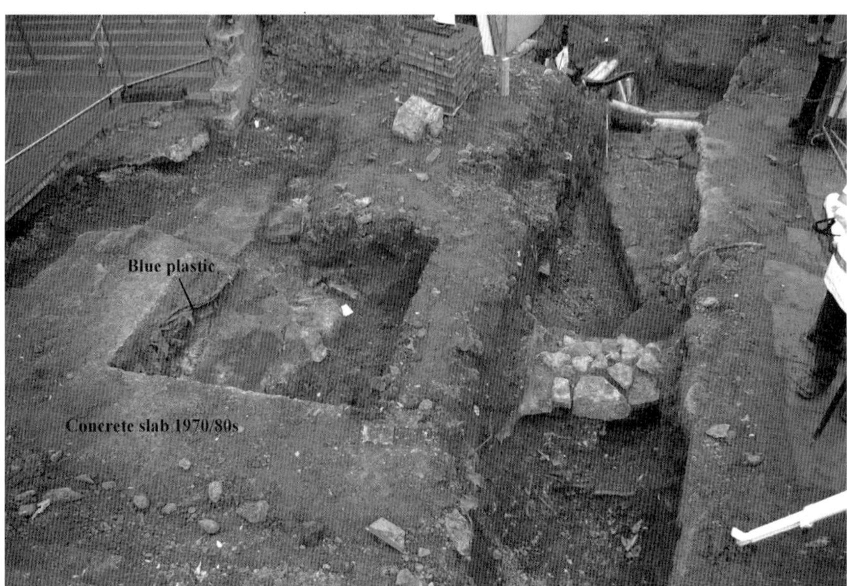

Works 3

Works 3 involved the excavation of a footing trench for a galvanized fence, orientated east–west, at the western side of the complex, extending from the Dublin City Council crèche as far west as Winetavern Street. This fence was located 1.5m north of the known line of the *c.*1100 city wall in an area that was partially resolved during the archaeological excavations between 1974 and 1976. The initial works consisted of a series of test-trenches excavated in advance by machine along the route of the railings, under archaeological supervision. After this was completed, the trench proper was excavated and this measured 0.50m in width by 0.45m in depth, deepening to 0.80m in depth at the western end, close to the entrance of the basement carpark on Winetavern Street. The ground was found to be an infill brown soil layer, introduced after the Wood Quay excavations and as part of the landscaping works. No archaeological finds or features were located during this phase of the works. It should be noted, however, that additional monitoring along the line of the city wall by the writer did locate the city wall incorporated into what appeared to be an eighteenth-century building. This indicates that a significant stretch of city wall probably does survive, incorporated within later remains, along the line of the wall (west of the Dublin City Council crèche).

Works 4

Works 4 involved the removal of the modern gravel layer in the modern Amphitheatre and the replacement of some of the existing slabs (figs 4.2 and 4.4). A series of small pits, 1m square by 0.30m in depth, was also excavated around the northern side of the Amphitheatre to facilitate the insertion of flood lights. The ground was found to be introduced soil, comprising made-up ground (excavated between 1974 and 1976) and no archaeological levels were encountered.

WORKS 5: ARCHAEOLOGICAL EXCAVATION (AT THE JUNCTION OF JOHN'S LANE EAST AND FISHAMBLE STREET) (figs 4.6–12; pls 4.1, 4.2, 4.6)

Introduction

The western side of Fishamble Street contains a large number of services and part of the programme of works was to re-expose these services – most notably a water-main – for repair, which was duly carried out (figs 4.5–6). Most of services were found to be within a large service trench, which ran up the hill, parallel to the street. Unfortunately, this trench had been excavated right through the middle of an earlier masonry build immediately identified as possibly forming part of the eastern end of the church of St John the Evangelist, known to have been located in this position (fig. 4.7). As a result,

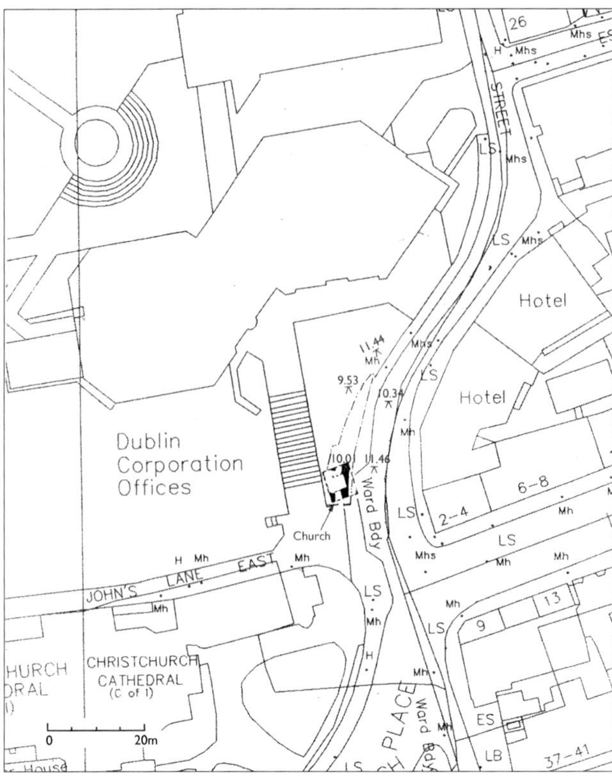

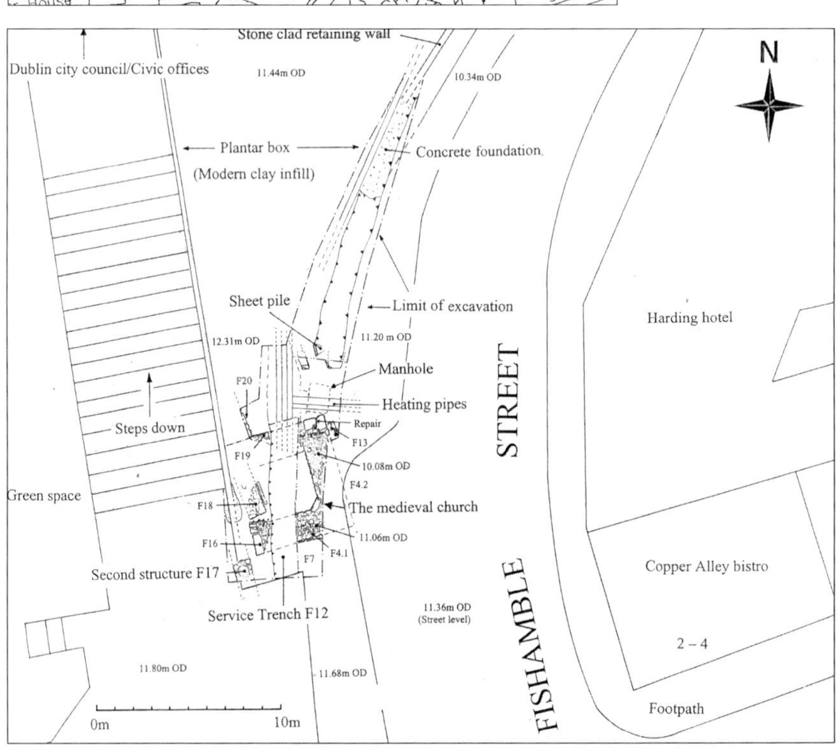

4.5 (*top*) Excavation area, site location.

4.6 (*bottom*) Excavation area, detail.

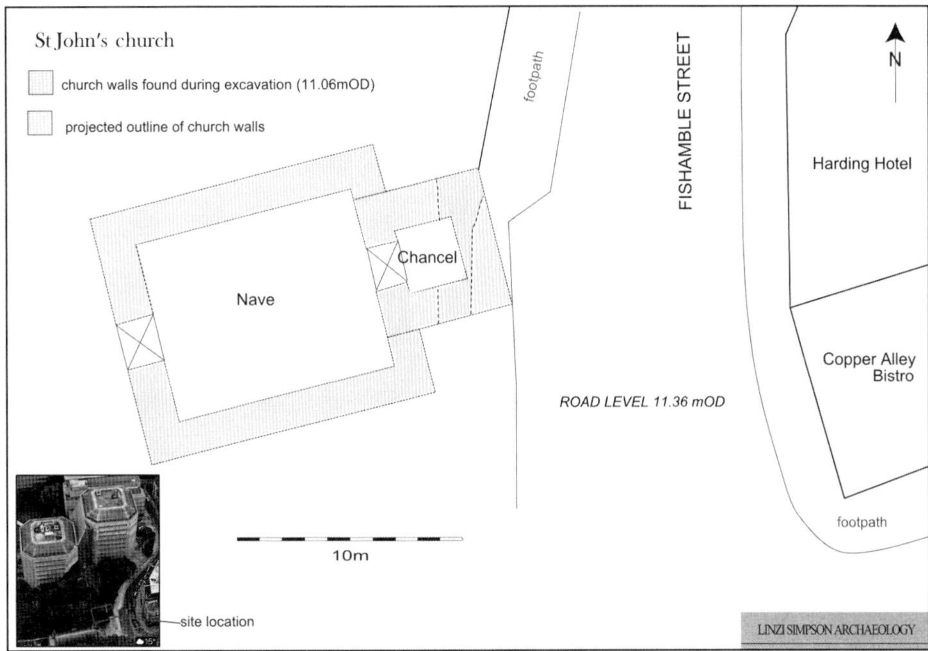

4.7 Proposed church layout.

careful management was required to re-expose these services, which was carried out as an archaeological excavation. The initial fragment that had been exposed of masonry build lay approximately 0.60m below the existing ground level at the southern end of the cutting but it was immediately apparent that the continuation northwards had been badly damaged at the northern end by the service trench, F12 (pls 4.6–7). Thus, on locating the potential medieval structure, the excavation brief was immediately expanded, not only to locate the service pipes and to facilitate the construction of a new wall and railings, but also to clarify the nature, extent and exact position of the structure, through the excavation of an expanded cutting.

These investigations located a rectangular build, the northeast corner of which lay between 9.65m O.D. and 10.08m O.D. while the southern wall was higher, positioned between 11.08m O.D. (east) and 11.10m O.D. (west), reflecting the sharp rise in the street (figs 4.8–12; pls 4.1–4, 4.7). When exposed the build was found to measure externally 6.14m north–south by 5m wide and was well built, composed of solid limestone blocks, the internal dimensions measuring almost 3m north–south by 2.8m wide. The deposits removed to define the structure were all modern and consisted of fill material containing a large amount of medieval material redeposited in the nineteenth and twentieth centuries. Thus, it was established that the medieval remains had been exposed before, probably during the Wood Quay excavations.

Plate 4.4 Northern end of the site.

Plate 4.5 The service trench F16 from the South.

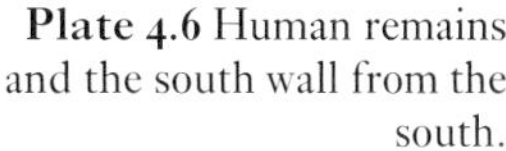

Plate 4.6 Human remains and the south wall from the south.

The service trench (pl. 4.6)

Excavation of the trench began at the northern end of Fishamble Street, almost opposite Essex Street West, and this was found to be cut through backfill material, containing concrete block, brick and plastic material, establishing a modern date for these deposits (pl. 4.1). When completed the final trench measured 16m in length, north–south, and was between 1.50m in width at the northern end, widening to 3.50m at the southern end. Works progressed carefully at the southern end, towards John's Lane East, as this was the known location of the church and graveyard, and photographs and plans of the Wood Quay excavations demonstrated that this entire corner, comprising the graveyard attached to the church, was held in position by sheet piling throughout the Wood Quay excavations and was therefore preserved *in situ*. As the trench progressed southwards, evidence of *in situ* material quickly came to light and the trench was widened.

The excavation site (figs 4.6 and 4.8; pl. 4.3)
The site was located between the path on the western side of Fishamble Street and the modern steps leading down to the Civic Offices and encompassed the western side of the path and the existing shrubbery. It was situated on ground that sloped from south to north towards the Liffey, with the street level dropping from 11.68 O.D., on the southern side of excavation area, to 9.84m O.D. on the north side, over a distance of 27m (fig. 4.12). The excavation area measured 12m in length north–south by between 4.50m in width at the northern end, widening to 6m in width at the southern end. A large manhole was also uncovered and this was found to neatly abut a solid medieval wall on the southern side. While the manhole appeared to have been carefully positioned to avoid the remains, the service trench described above was inserted through the medieval stone walls causing significant damage. At the southern end of the trench a thin layer of concrete sat directly on a protective covering of blue plastic, which covered some of the medieval walls (pl. 4.9). This was probably carried out during the Wood Quay excavations when the area was being preserved *in situ*.

Historical background
Medieval Dublin was well serviced by a large number of parish churches, a total of twenty-one, positioned both within and without the city walls (fig. 4.3). The church of St John the Evangelist occupied a prime position just north of Christ Church cathedral, at the top of the modern Fishamble Street, known originally as 'Bodestret' (Gilbert 1854–9, i, 153; Mc Neill 1950, 80; Clarke 1978; Bradley 1992, 49). The graveyard lay to the northwest of the church. A second church, St Olave's, which was also pre-Anglo-Norman in date, was located just north of St John's, opposite the junction at Essex Street West (Clarke 1950, 120). This was an important church, which became known as St Tullock's and was eventually unified with St John's in 1538 (ibid., 121). The church is not depicted on John Speed's map of Dublin published in 1610, which may suggest that it was demolished between these dates although a grant dated to 1587 records a complex there that included the rectory, the church or chapel of St Olave's, otherwise St Tullock's, with the site and churchyard and two houses. Included in this was a 'priest's chamber', a building which, unlike the church, did survive the late medieval period as it was still standing as late as 1774 (no. 40 Fishamble Street) (ibid., 122).

St John's church was granted to the priory of the Holy Trinity (at Christ Church cathedral) by 'Gillamichell, son of Gillamurri', along with a second church, St Paul's, which was located somewhere east of Dublin Castle (Mc Neill 1950, 29). The grant – which appears in a list of similar donations in rough chronological order – can probably be dated to the 1160s or 1170s, suggesting that Gillamichell was an Ostman of some means living in Dublin

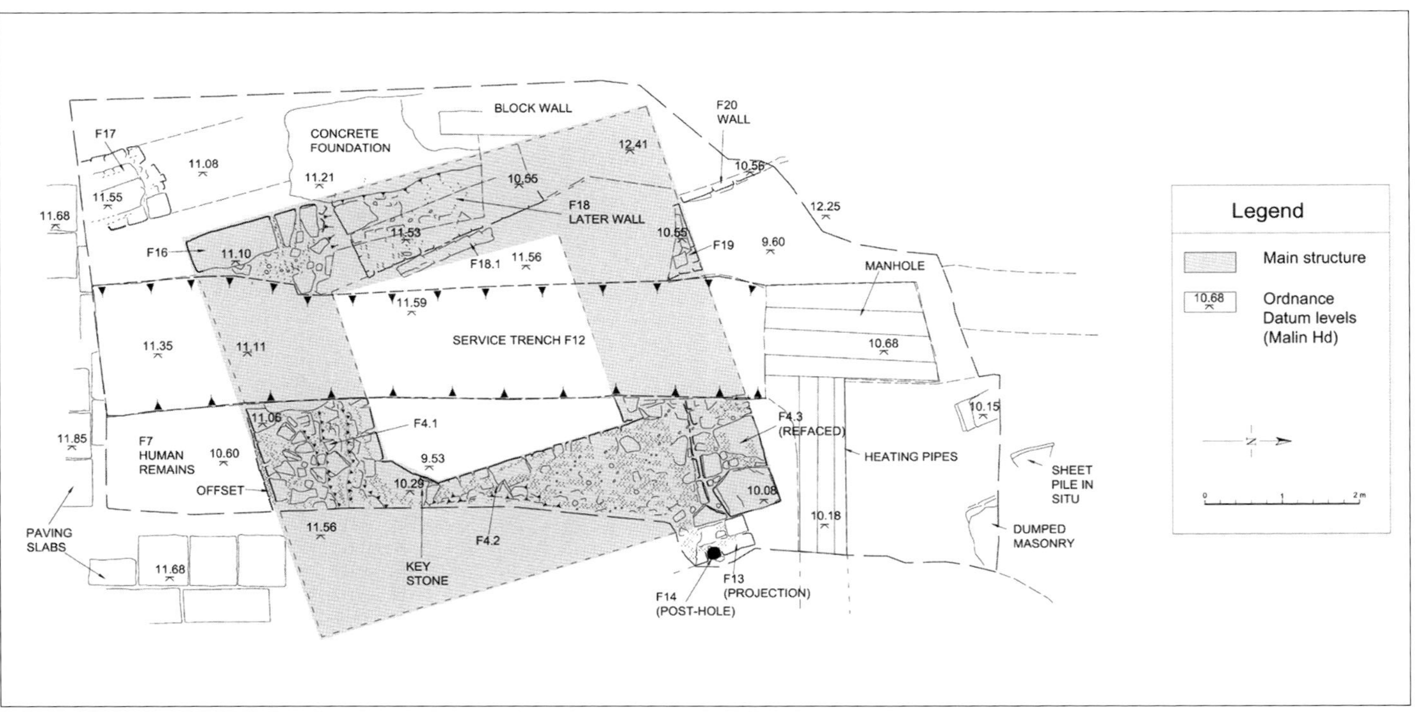

4.8 Plan of the build.

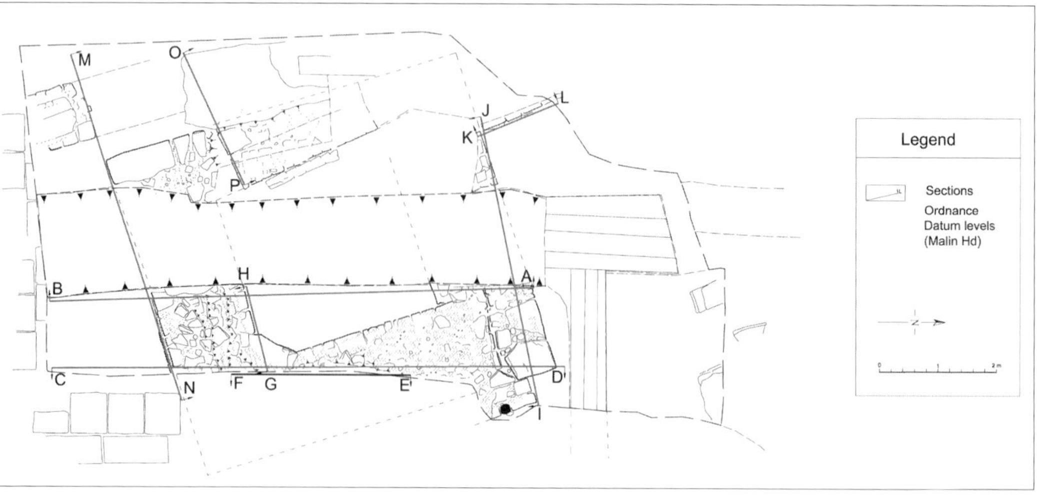

4.9 Sections lines.

during and after the English invasion (perhaps father of the Richard Gillemichel who was a relatively prominent citizen of Dublin in the early decades of the thirteenth century (see, e.g., Brooks 1936, nos. 13, 116, 157, 309)). While it is likely that Gillamichell was a benefactor who paid towards the churches, it may also be the case that one of the churches functioned initially as a private family chapel before being granted to the priory, as often happened in contemporary England. The church was originally dedicated to St John the Baptist but this was later transferred to John the Evangelist (Mc Neill 1950, 16; Gilbert 1854–9, i, 48). It appears in the confirmation grants of Pope Alexander III *c.*1179 and again in 1186 (Mc Neill 1950, 7, 15).

The parish was large, covering an area measuring just under 12 acres. It stretched from Winetavern Street in the west, to Lower Exchange Street in the east, and from Wood Quay along by the Liffey at the north to Christchurch Place in the south; and the parish expanded further when it was merged with St Olave's parish in 1538. In the modern period the parish records of 1851 reveal that it was a very congested tenemented area, containing a total of 296 dwellings, and housing a documented 3,483 inhabitants (Gilbert 1854–9, i, 48). The graveyard was large and in use throughout the medieval period into the early modern period with an estimated 12,500 people in total reputedly buried there. According to Dublin tradition, Molly Malone was baptized in St John's in 1663 and subsequently interred there on 13 June 1699 while Henry Grattan (1746–1820), of Grattan's Parliament fame, was also baptized in the church on 3 July 1746, having been born in Fishamble Street. The last documented person buried in the graveyard was Elizabeth Causland in 1859 (Bennett 1991, 192).

The church formed one of a large number of churches both within and without the walls of Dublin. St John's was listed as a possession of the priory

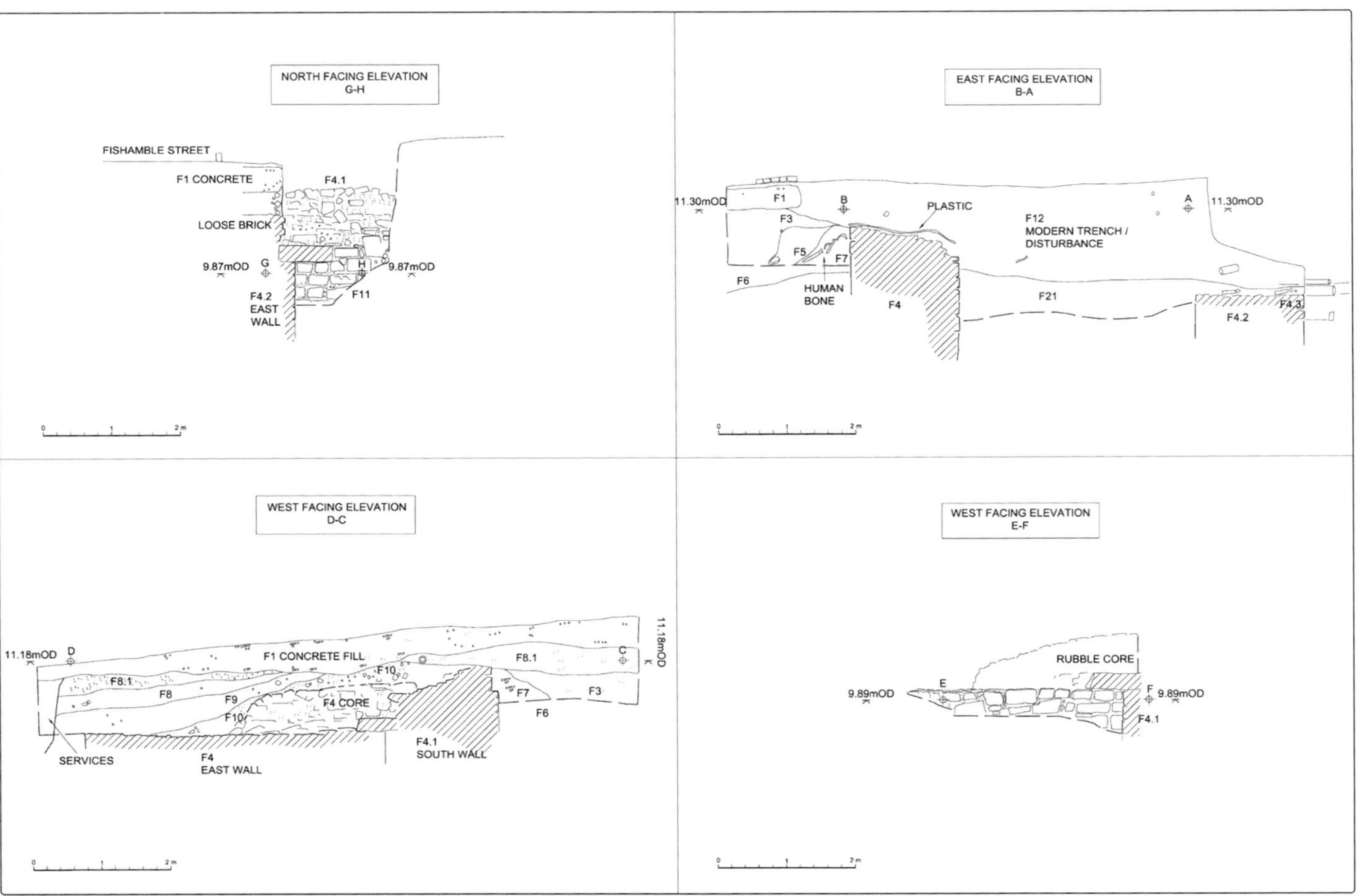

4.10 Section lines A–H.

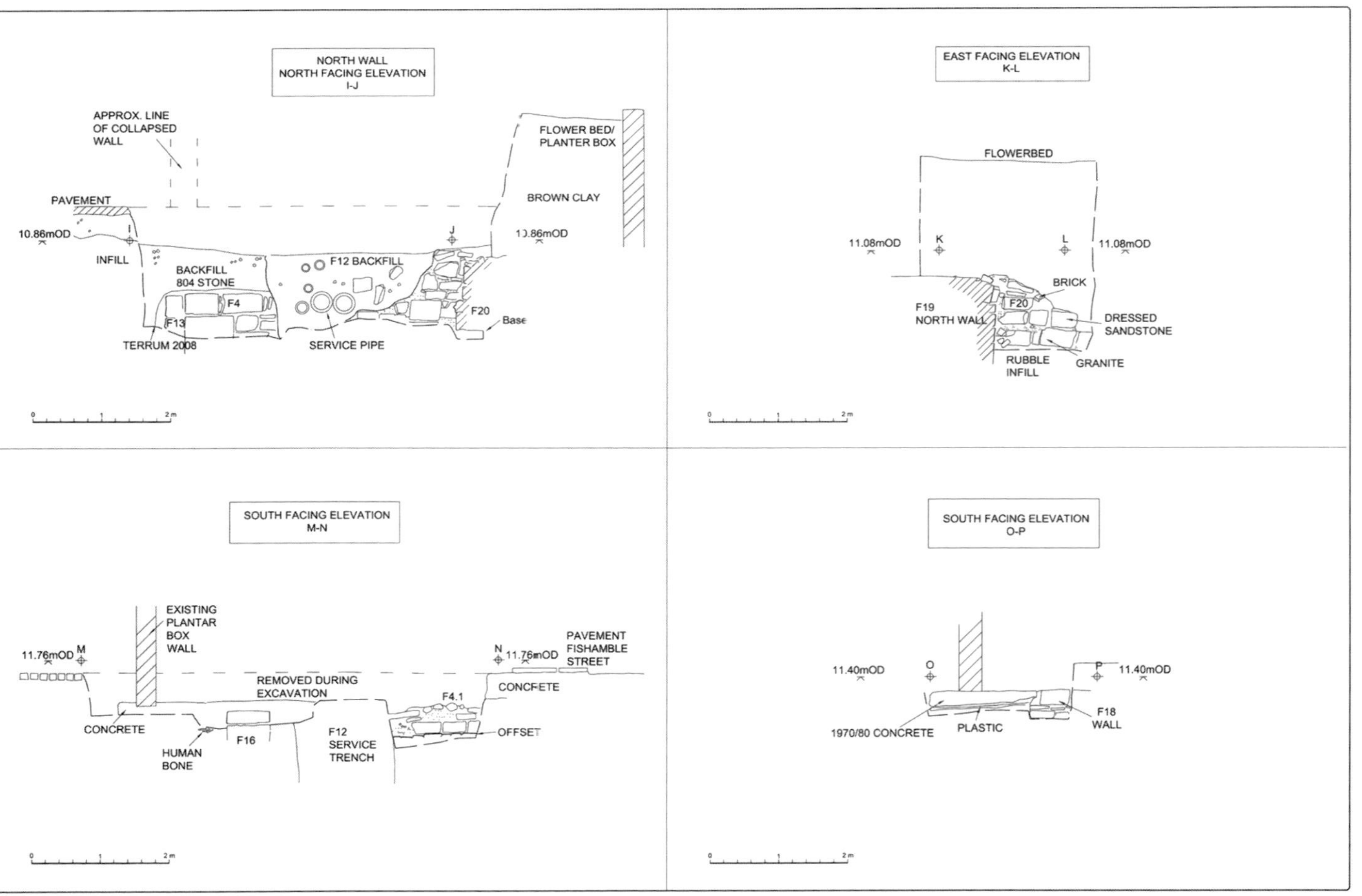

4.11 Section lines I–P.

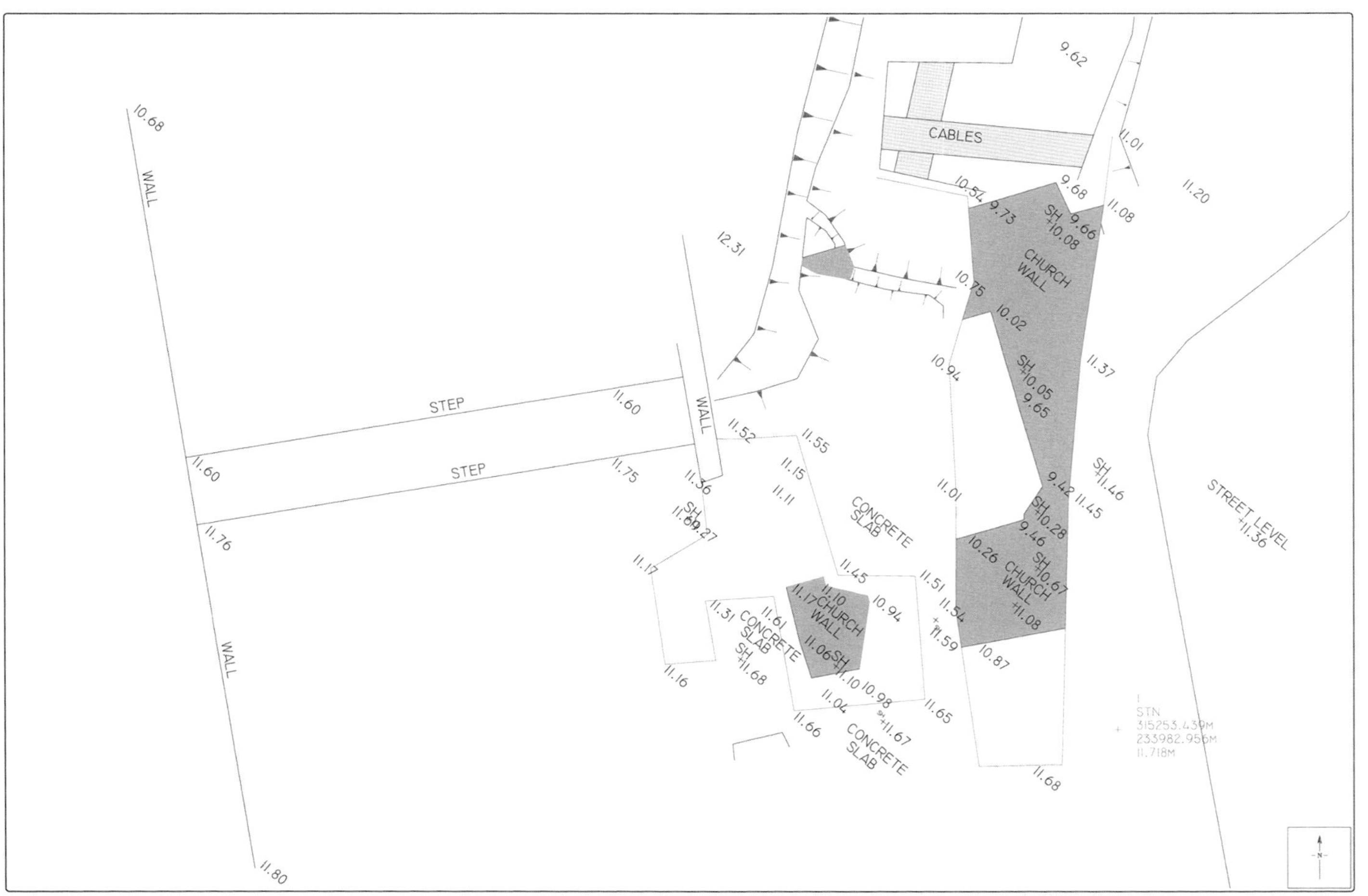

4.12 CAD survey.

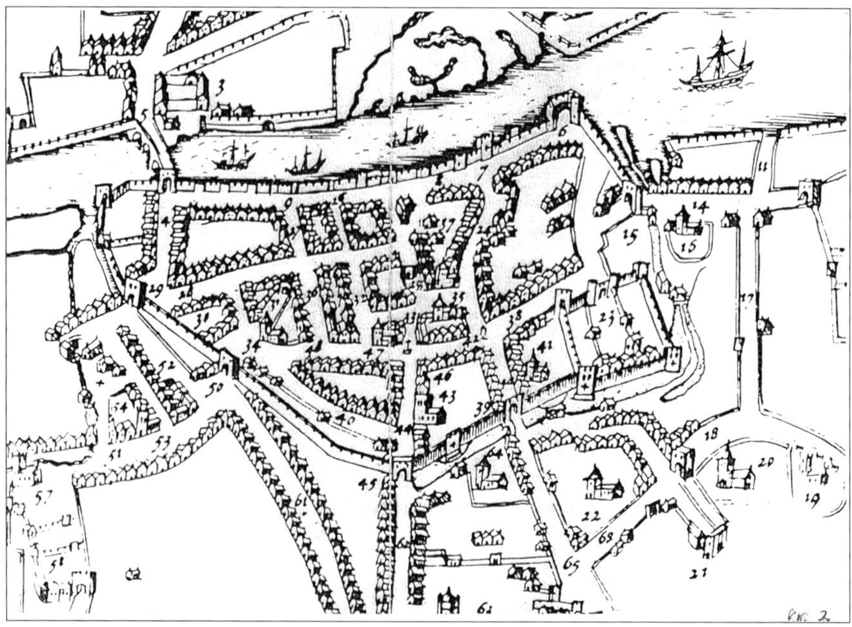

4.13 Speed's map of Dublin, dated 1610.

of the Holy Trinity in the confirmation charters throughout the late twelfth and the thirteenth century and in *c.*1230 it was recorded as being 'too poor to be taxed', although this was possibly an exaggeration in a bid to reduce the parishioners' contribution (Clarke 2002, 17). The situation had not improved by 1294 when there was a plea that the church was too 'poor to support brethren' (Gilbert 1854–9, i, 48); this latter assertion is perhaps more likely to be true as the English colony was beginning to decline somewhat by this stage. In 1306, however, the church was valued at 100 shillings a year, suggesting that it was in a good state of repair. The surviving ancient deeds of the parish of St John preserve a document dating to 1349 which records plans for the enlargement of the church and for a new chapel, dedicated to the Blessed Virgin Mary (Robinson and Armstrong 1916–17, no. 45). The following year, 1350, Edward III granted a mortmain licence to Richard Knight, chaplain, assigning him a dwelling house for the enlargement of the church and graveyard and the erection of a new chapel in honour of the Virgin Mary (ibid.). Further expansion occurred when a charter was granted in 1417 to the Corporation of Tailors to found a chantry church at St John's for which the church received an annual rent of 20 shillings (Gilbert 1854–9, i, 48).

The church was under restoration again in 1477 after damage was caused in a storm and the chapel was rebuilt and repaired in 1495 as one of the deeds refers to property granted for the 'repair of the fabric of the chapel of St

Mary's in St John's church' (Clarke 2002, 17; Robinson and Armstrong 1916–17, no. 148). The church was again under repair in 1500, by Arland Usher, at which point the church is recorded as being composed of a chancel, nave and two aisles with vaults underneath, and a belfry that contained three bells (probably at the western end) (Hughes 2009, 22). After the Dissolution of Christ Church in 1539, St John's was re-granted as a prebendal church to the cathedral by Archbishop Browne and the chancel was enlarged fifty years later, in 1589, when it was recorded that the parishioners were 'greatly increasing' (ibid.). In 1604, a charter of James I names Branabus Boulger as the first canonical prebendary of St John and in 1630 the church is recorded as being in 'a good state of decency with most of the parishioners Protestants although there was a great store of papists' (Gilbert 1854–9, i, 51).

St John's is depicted on Speed's map of Dublin, dated 1610, but fronting onto what was a large rectangular space, now the east end of John's Lane East but originally opening out onto the rear of the cathedral. The stylized depiction shows the tower at the western end, with an entrance in the south wall (fig. 4.13). There is no indication of an enclosure or graveyard but this is not surprising as graveyards are generally not depicted on this map. In 1639, a spire was added onto the northeast end of the church but this is likely to have been constructed from the roof. Bernard de Gomme's map, dated 1673, depicts the church with a tower at the western end and a cross on either end, presumably on the spire on the east and the tower on the west (fig. 4.14). However, like Speed, there is no indication of a graveyard (de Gomme too tended not to depict graveyards).

Despite de Gomme's formal depiction, the church was evidently in a poor state of repair by that period as in 1680 it was recorded as being in 'great decay' and was to be pulled down 'as far as there was absolute necessity and that it should be rebuilt with all convenient speed' (Gilbert 1854–9, i, 51). The deeds of the church record the agreement between Rice Lewis and John Lawrence, merchants, who were evidently funding the repairs, with William Middlebrook and Samuel Wiggen, joiners, which specifies that

> the chancel to be paved to the chancel rails with black stone, the ground within the rails with white French stone, and the altar steps with black stone (the stones to be polished with water, sand & oil, as the chancel of St Michael's is done); the nave & aisles to be paved with good flag-stones (all except the bottom of the pews), the gravestones being placed in convenient places, & stone steps to be built from Fishamble Street up to the level of the church. The work to be done within two months after the carpenter, joiners & slaters finish their work. The said Rice Lewis to have for his own use the old flag-stones & the old pews (Robinson and Armstrong 1916–17, no. 196).

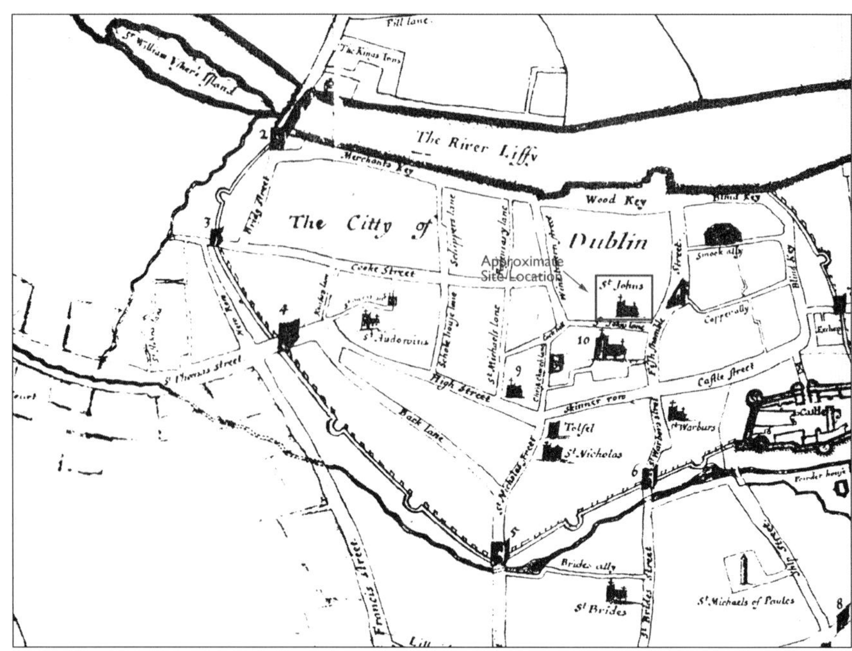

4.14 De Gomme's map of Dublin, dated 1673.

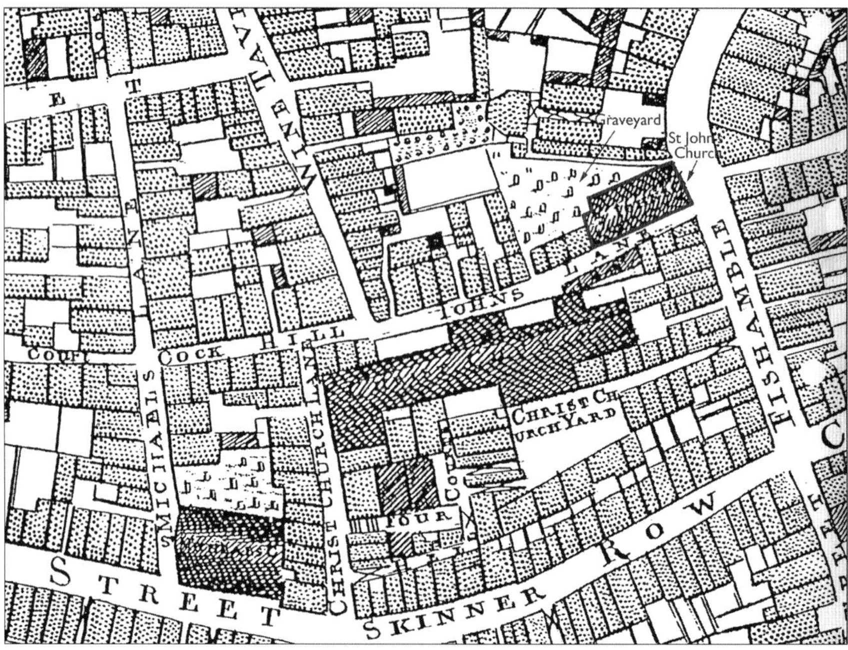

4.15 Rocque's map of Dublin, dated 1756.

4.16 Front façade of the church.

A fee of 50 pounds for the works formed part of the agreement which added that the grave stones in the church were to be lifted up, 'if any of them should be broken, to make them good' (added in another hand). All the 'old monuments' had to be removed for this rebuilding programme, which was completed in 1682 and this included other works such as gilding and painting the church: at this date the walls are recorded as being 24ft in height (7.5m) (ibid.).

The improvement works continued into the eighteenth century as, in 1704, a clockmaker Thomas Newman was paid £30 for maintaining 'one wath with two dyalls' that he had set up on a seventeenth-century tower on the east side of the church (Gilbert 1854–9, i, 52; Pearson 2002, 243). The next depiction of St John's is on Rocque's map, dated 1756, and on this source, the church is a substantial building, orientated east–west and fronting onto the Fishamble Street frontage on the east (fig. 4.15). The building plan has a return at the southwest corner, which is probably the tower, and is built directly against

4.17 Photograph of St John's church.

three terraced houses that front onto the lane, on the western side. While Rocque is unscaled, a rough estimation of the church size would suggest the nave (double-aisled) measured approximately 30m long by 15m in width with the return in the southwest corner measuring about 10m north–south by 5m in width. A large trapezoidal property to the north contains the graveyard (headstones depicted) and there is an entrance, via John's Lane East, at the western end (fig. 4.18). The graveyard was not excavated during the Wood Quay archaeological campaigns and was preserved *in situ* as a green space. This is currently marked by six grave-slabs, which are laid out on the grass (Pearson 2002, 232).

Rocque's plan captures the ground plan of the church just before the major revamp, between 1766 and 1769, to the designs of architect George Ensor (Dwyer 1981, 107) but the church was already a considerable size. The spire, which had been added in 1639, was not retained in the new plan but an impressive classical façade at the eastern end was constructed with the main entrance onto Fishamble Street via a colonnaded porch behind the altar (figs 4.15–17). The new façade consisted of four ionic columns in antis, supporting a classical temple style with the main frontage onto Fishamble Street, rather than John's Lane East. The round-headed doorway was centrally-placed, flanked by rectangular windows on either side, accessed up a flight of steps that

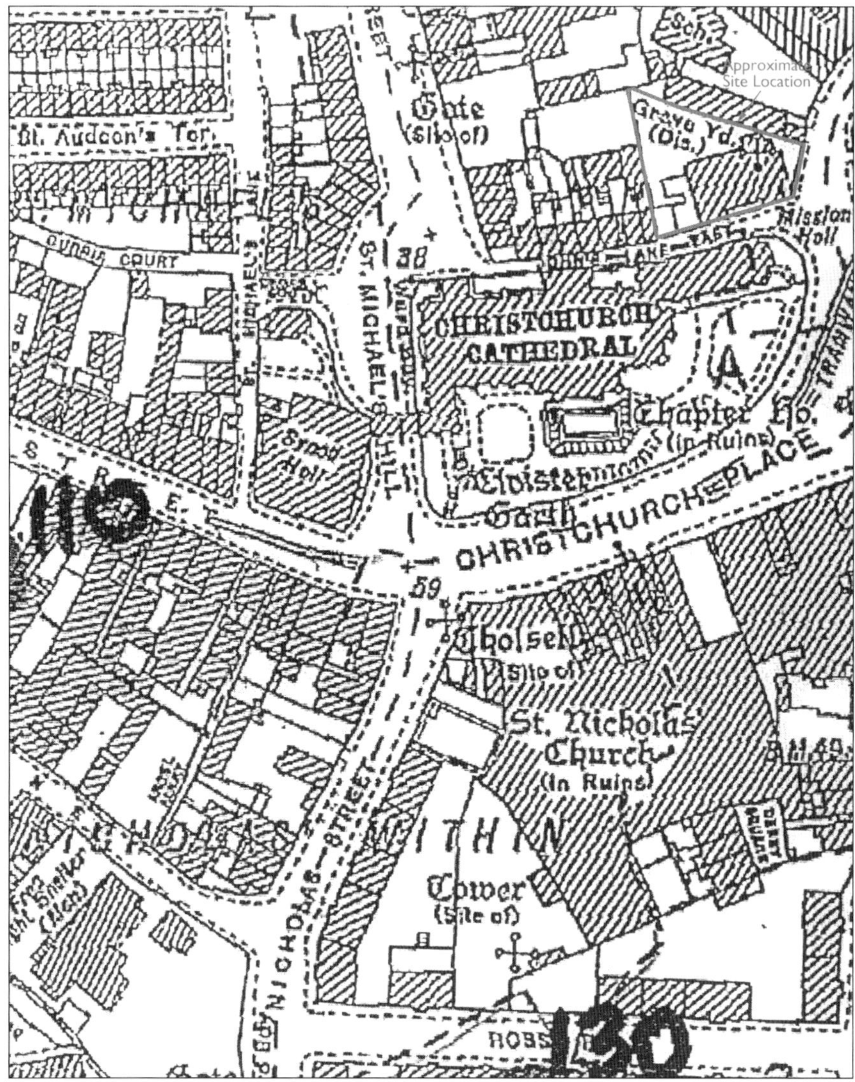

4.18 Ordnance Survey, dated 1911.

extended across the full width of the building. The upper level was lit by three round-headed windows. The Ordnance Survey 1909 depicts the floor-plan of the church in detail, including the colonnaded front façade supported by matching internal columns (fig. 4.19). The columned side aisles are also evident, probably reflecting the original layout of the expanded medieval church. Gilbert records the grant of £1000 given in 1763 for the new Ensor redesign and also recounts that it contained 'neither monuments or remains of antiquity' (Gilbert 1854–9, i, 52).

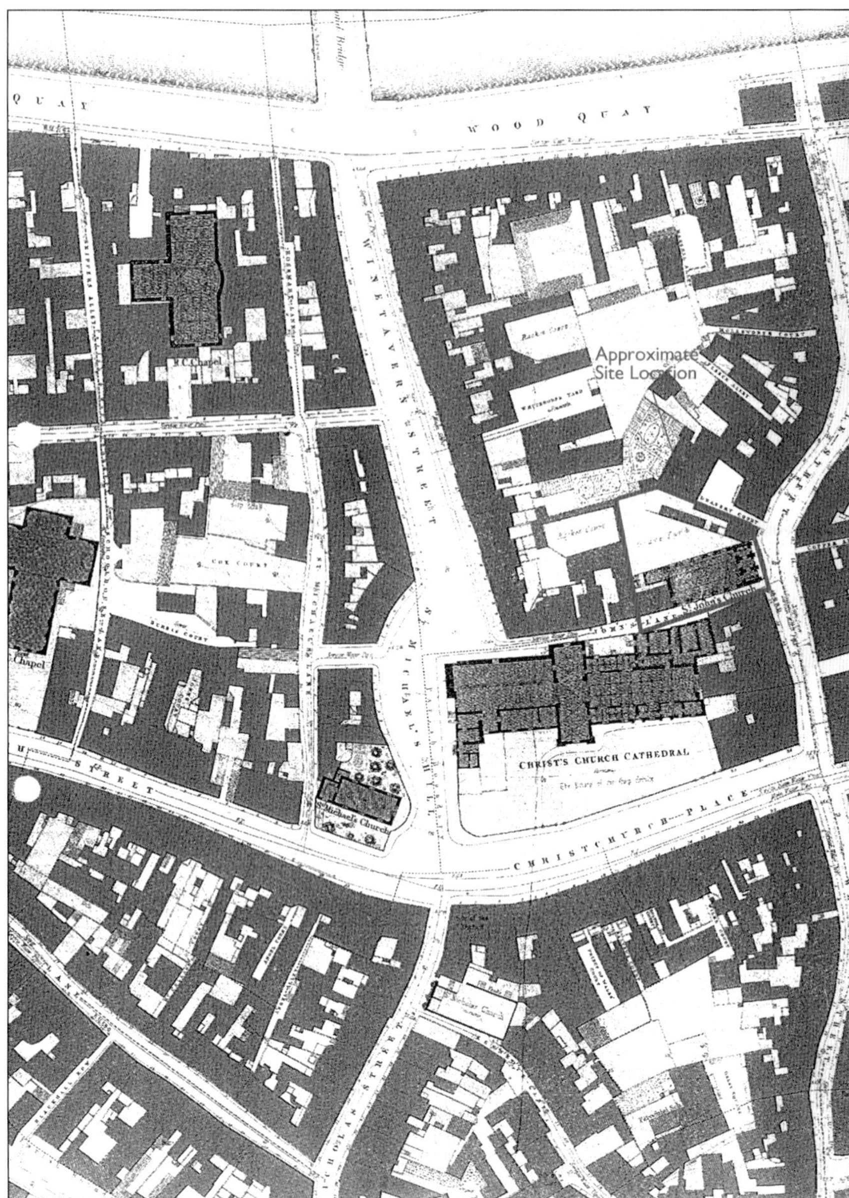

4.19 Ordnance Survey, dated 1909.

The church continued to function as the parish church throughout most of the nineteenth century, serving a congested part of the city, but gradually the area declined, with a subsequent loss in population, with many houses being demolished and converted into industrial yards and premises. The dwindling congregation eventually resulted in the church being closed in 1878 and the

4.20 The Mission Hall from the northeast (*c*.1961)

4.21 John's Lane East from the east (*c*.1961).

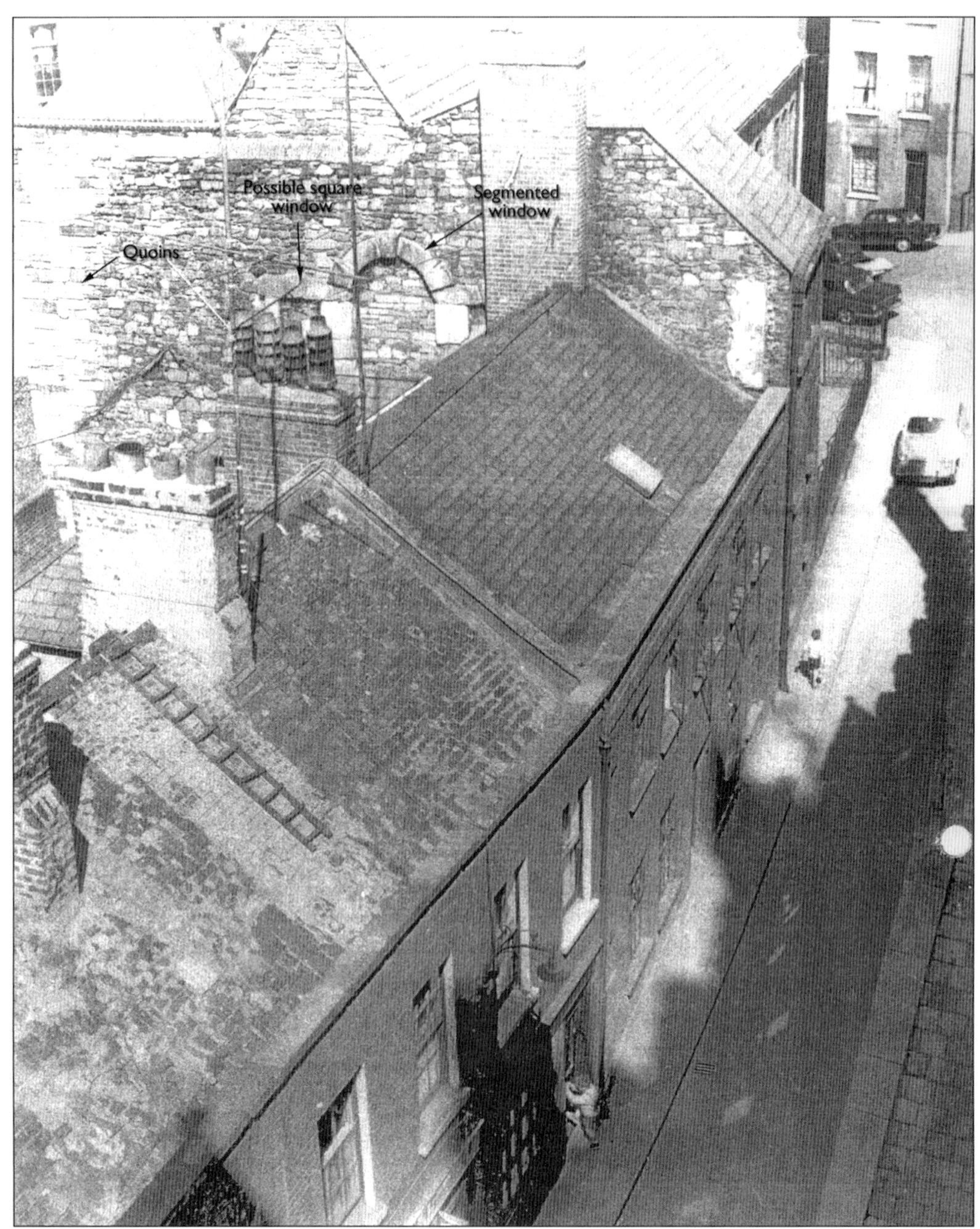

4.22 John's Lane East, from the west (*c.*1961).

4.23 The graveyard from the south east (*c.*1961).

4.24 Detail of the graveyard from the northeast (*c.*1961).

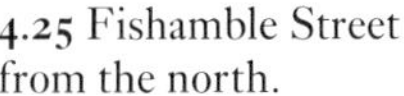
4.25 Fishamble Street from the north.

parish merged with the parish of St Werburgh. Finally, in 1884, the church was demolished and some of its monuments were moved to St Werburgh's church (Casey 2005, 345–6). The streetscape was completely altered in 1886 when Lord Edward Street was constructed, linking Dame Street directly to Skinner's Row (now Christchurch Place). A Mission Hall was constructed on the site but, despite the fact that the church is recorded as being demolished, the western wall was clearly left intact, presumably as it formed part of the party wall of the adjoining dwelling on this side. This surviving wall was then incorporated into the new Mission Hall, which appears on the 1909 Ordnance Survey and was only demolished *c.*1961 (figs 4.19–21). This building, built of limestone with long rectangular windows with brick surrounds, occupied the same plot and almost the same footprint of the church but was set back from both Fishamble Street and John's Lane East, fronting onto the latter. It had three pitched roofs with chimneys on either gable and an expanded western end. A photograph, taken from Christ Church cathedral at the western end, depicts the houses fronting onto the laneway and the rear wall (western) of the Mission Hall revealing earlier features, which suggests that it was the original west wall of the church (fig. 4.22). A segmented window, probably dating to the early to mid-eighteenth century, is clearly visible at first-floor level, in a central location which was part of some sort of square window feature. Also of note are the well-dressed quoins on the northern end of the wall (where the belfry/tower was located), usually a feature of medieval buildings, and these are not present at the southern end. On demolition of the Mission Hall in 1961, part of the west wall was again left standing as it was still abutting the dwellings on John's Lane East.

Photographs taken after the demolition of the Mission Hall *c.*1961 depict the graveyard space with a series of headstones placed upright against the main western boundary wall (fig. 4.23). The space was then used as a carpark (fig. 4.24) replacing an earlier walled area in front of the Mission Hall (fig. 4.25).

STRATIGRAPHIC REPORT FOR WORKS 5

LEVEL 1 *(Medieval Phase 1)*

The excavation of the trench along Fishamble Street exposed the remains of a solid rectangular limestone build (F4) at the southern end of the site, just north of the junction of Fishamble Street and John's Lane East (fig. 4.6). This build was orientated northeast–southwest, now set at an angle to Fishamble Street but reflective of an earlier alignment evident in the orientation of the house and plots that originally fronted onto the northern side of John's Lane East, before the eastern end of the lane was realigned in more modern times (figs 4.7–12). The build measured externally 6.14m north–south by 5m wide and was exposed to 2m in depth, a test-pit in the southeast corner suggesting that it extends for at least another 1m, giving an estimated combined depth in places of 3m. The interior measured 1.80m by 3m square. Unfortunately, the structure was very badly damaged by the large service trench, F12, containing a large number of services, as mentioned above. All the walls were keyed into each other and were clearly contemporary but with some evidence of re-facings and/or rebuildings along with a small projection at the northeast corner, extending eastwards (but not fully excavated due to the presence of live services). The structure had evidently been exposed previously, as a blue plastic sheeting was identified lying beneath a modern concrete slab, which extended over the medieval build on the western side. On the eastern side the structure was back-filled with a rubble and brick deposit, while a clay layer was found on the southern side, filled with disarticulated human remains, mostly long-bones, piled neatly against the southern wall (F7: see below).

Unfortunately, the stone remains were only exposed to retrieve the ground plan and then carefully backfilled with stone. Thus, excavation was limited in this location. However, the likelihood is that more extensive remains of the church, at foundation level, survive to the west of the site, attached to the preserved section of the graveyard. The modern steps leading down to the entrance to the Civic Offices, however, are likely to have caused some damage in the central area.

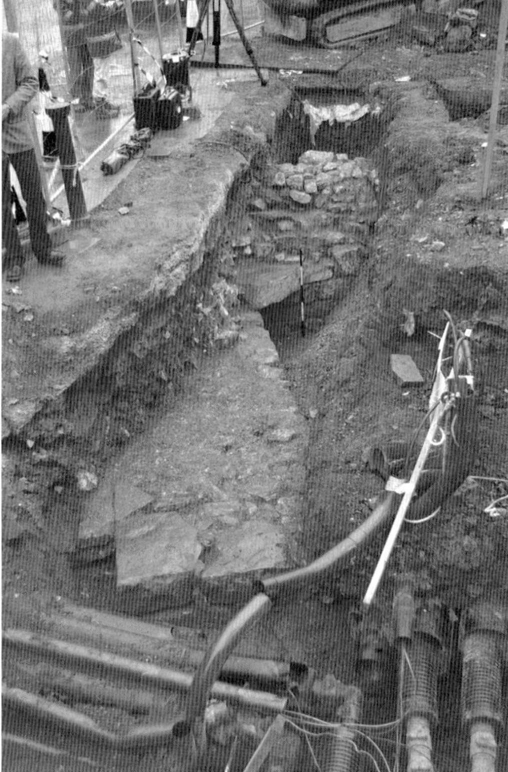

Plate 4.7 (*top*) Site with feature numbers.

Plate 4.8 (*bottom*) East wall from the north.

Plate 4.9 (*opposite, left*) South wall from the south.

Plate 4.10 (*opposite, right*) Structure 4, looking north.

The south wall F4.1 (pls 4.7–10)

The southern wall F4.1 survived to over 2m in depth on the inner (northern) side but the upper levels had no facing stones and consisted of just a robbed-out core, the top of which lay at 11.06m O.D., just 0.70m below present ground level. This core was composed of small irregular-shaped limestone blocks measuring, on average, 0.15m by 0.20m, which were strongly mortared with a distinctive crumbly grey/off-white lime mortar. The lower facings were intact, on both the north and south side, demonstrating that the wall originally measured between 1.50m and 1.60m in width in total. Only two courses were exposed on the southern side, extending to a total of 0.45m in depth and composed of large limestone facing stones, averaging 0.40m by 0.22m, which were tightly and neatly coursed. The wall had an external off-set or plinth on this side, lying 0.40m below the top of the wall, which projected out by 60mm suggesting that the wall may not have extended down much further on this side, although it continued in the northern face for at least another 1.50m, perhaps because it was straddling the steep slope from south to north. The interior of the rectangular build was at a lower level at approximately 9.90m O.D. and had been demolished to this level in a single event.

Plate 4.11 Southeast corner of Structure 4 from the north.

The upper facing, on the northern side of the wall, had also been removed to a depth of 0.60m and the core was exposed, the top surviving course on this side lying at 10.29m O.D. The northern side survived to at least five courses in depth, measuring collectively 0.75m in depth but was not fully exposed. This side was similar to the southern face and was also neatly coursed, composed of large rectangular limestone blocks, measuring, on average, 0.20m by 0.35m with smaller stones filling the interstices. The wall also contained a very substantial and unusual bridging slab of limestone in southeast corner, which spanned the corner of the southern and eastern wall and was obviously structural in nature (pls 4.8–10). This was a significant stone, measuring 0.75m north–south by 0.50 wide, by between 0.20m and 0.25m in depth, which was keyed into both walls. The upper face of the slab was very smooth and had probably been worked, although the sides were less so. The unusual feature was part of the original construction and was designed to span or bridge the gap, providing structural support to the upper level.

The central area of the southern wall was removed in part by the service trench (F12) but the western end was located, although only at the upper level. This revealed that the southwest corner was broken through at the northern end (see below, F16). The southwest corner may also have been rebuilt (F16)

Plate 4.12 Overview of east wall, from the southwest.

Plate 4.13 Southeast corner of Structure F4 looking east.

Plate 4.14 (*top*) Projection F13 looking south.

Plate 4.15 (*bottom*) Projection F13 looking southwest.

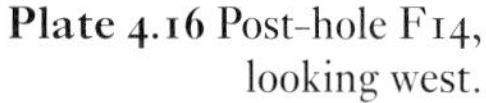

Plate 4.16 Post-hole F14, looking west.

although this is less obvious than the northeast corner, in an area measuring 1.70m north–south by 1.20m in width by at least 0.21m in depth (pl. 4.4–10). The upper face of the medieval wall was dominated by a large flagstone, set at a higher level and measuring 1m north–south by 0.60m in width by 0.21m in depth, which did not appear to be a grave-slab although there was a square recess in the northwest corner. This stone may have been a later addition, as it was bedded in a beige crumbly mix with visible mortar fleck, which differed from the main southern wall, F4.1. This wall appeared to continue south into the section comprising what might have been the nave wall to the south but this had clearly been rebuilt as the upper levels were comprised of handmade early brick (F16.1), which was badly damaged but clearly represents a rebuild in this location (see below).

The east wall F4.2

The eastern wall was evenly demolished to a lower level than the southern wall, the top lying 1.40m below present ground level, at 10.08m O.D. (pls 4.4, 4.10 and 4.13). Only the western face was visible at the upper level as the bulk of the wall lay under the footpath. The wall was exposed for 3m in length, north–south, and measured 1.50m in width by at least 0.45m in height but the full depth was not ascertained in a bid to preserve the lower deposits *in situ*. The western face consisted of between two and three courses of wall, with the bridging flag mentioned above positioned on top of the intact section. The blocks, as with the southern wall, were rectangular cut limestone, the largest of which measured 0.70m by 0.12m. The wall was bonded with a mix of mortars: a hard grey/off-white mortar with patches of a yellow/gritty mortar, and hard white mortar along the upper face. The northeast corner was dominated by a distinctive change in masonry, with two large slabs forming the corner, lying at 10.06m O.D. The corner-piece flagstone was well-cut and smoothly faced on the two presenting edges, measuring 0.70m north–south by 0.45m in width by 0.22m in depth. A second flag lay to the west and this was a similar size and depth although not fully exposed. This general area contained other large flattish slabs with open joints and was visibly different from the original wall, as it was mortared with a yellow gritty mortar as opposed to a hard grey/off-white mortar. The slabs were not unlike the bridging slab in the southeast corner although there is a possibility this area represented a repair, as the joints between the limestone core and limestone slabs appeared different. A similar repair may have been carried out in the southwest corner also (F16 see below).

The projection F13 (pls 4.14–15) The northern end of the east wall had what appeared to be an eastern projection, at least three courses deep, the base of which was contemporary with the main structure (10.08m O.D.). This measured 0.90m north–south by 0.40m in width but was set back by 0.50m from the northern face of the northern wall. While the upper two courses abutted the main eastern wall the third course was keyed directly into the main wall. The block-work was composed of hewn limestone similar to the main wall but was dominated by two large blocks, measuring, on average, 0.40m by 0.38m by 0.26m while the other courses averaged blocks measuring 0.20m by 0.20m by 0.10m. The mortar was also identical to the eastern wall. There is a possibility this projection was created by the addition of the flags at the northeast corner but not enough of the structure was exposed to clarify the exact relationship in this location.

Post-hole F14 While excavation was very limited in this area a large post-hole F14 was located, set into the F13 projection and this measured 0.15m north–south by 0.14m wide and was at least 0.40m in depth (pl. 4.16; fig. 4.8). It contained an upright stone on the southern side, which was probably used to wedge the post in place. The post-hole was filled with silty clay containing tiny flecks of crushed bone (not enough to date) and a corroded iron nail was found at the base. A deposit of dark brown friable organic deposit with charcoal and shell fleck, along with lenses of yellow mortar, F15, abutted the northern and eastern face of F13 and this had no brick, an indication it may be medieval in date. A small section was excavated (0.20m in depth) but the remainder was left *in situ*. This produced no artefacts or finds but is likely to be medieval in date.

Plate 4.17 North wall, looking west.

Plate 4.18 North and west wall, looking north.

Plate 4.19 West wall and F16.1 brick wall on top, looking south.

Plate 4.20 F16, west wall of Structure F4, looking east.

The north wall F4.3/F19 (pls 4.17 and 4.18)
The north wall F4.3 was visible in two sections, at the eastern end where it was keyed into the eastern wall F4.2, and a small section west of the service trench F12, namely F19, lying between 10.55m O.D. and 10.08m O.D. (fig. 4.8). The western end F19 stood 1.10m in height, comprising five courses of blockwork and composed of neatly-cut limestone blocks, measuring on average, 0.42m by 0.30m by 0.18m. The mortar was similar to elsewhere but also contained lenses of dark grey mortar with sandy gritty inclusions and occasional charcoal fleck. The eastern end, keyed into the east wall F4.2, was of similar build, measuring 1.55m in width, and was clearly contemporary. The remains of a medieval clay deposit F15 were also found to abut the northern face at this end and this was a brown friable organic deposit with charcoal and shell fleck, along with lenses of yellow mortar. No brick was found in this deposit suggesting that it is likely to be medieval in date.

The west wall F16 and F16.1 (pls 4.19 and 4.20; fig. 4.8)
Only a small section of the western wall face was exposed at the southwest corner of the structure, lying at 11.10m O.D. and this extended for 0.70m north–south. The wall was slightly smaller measuring 1.10m in width, with a large slab forming part of the build and this was similar to the slabs used in the northeast corner (see above). It was only exposed to 0.20m in depth and this may have been the base but had been cut through on the northern side as there was a void filled with loose fill where the rough core was exposed. Immediately north was another possible medieval wall F18, later in date, which appears to have replaced the northern wall. Interestingly, this wall was jointed at the southern end and neatly coursed, as if it abutted a similar joint in the original western wall, before it was damaged and filled with rubble. If this is the case, this suggests there was a joint at the southern end of the west wall, which is likely to represent the entrance into the chancel.

This wall is likely to have been replaced in the eighteenth century as the upper level of an early brick wall F16.1, along the same alignment, could be identified in the southern section (pl. 4.19). This was composed of early handmade orange brick, measuring 0.22m in length by 0.15m by 0.07m and mortared with grey-coloured beige mortar. It measured 55m in width and stood three courses in height (0.45m), collapsing to the east. The wall sat on a dark grey clay and mortar deposit on the western side but a small section of limestone build was located on the eastern side suggesting that it may be the rebuilding of the east wall of the nave, at foundation level. However, the wall appears to be very insubstantial and may have been an internal wall. Excavation to the south of the F16 did not reveal any more masonry but this was a very basal layer and it might have been removed.

Conclusion of LEVEL 1

The main rectangle of masonry was very substantial but, unfortunately, the removal of deposits in this area, both when it was excavated previously (probably in the 1980s) and more recently when the service trench was put through, made dating practically impossible. However, the limestone blockwork and the general substantial width of the walls, along with an absence of brick, suggests that it is likely to date to the medieval period and therefore to be associated with the medieval church of St John. The general external width of 6.14m by 5m with an internal width of 3m by 2.80m is small but the masonry suggests a robust structure and one that was clearly structurally independent. It may have been repaired at some date but had certainly been demolished by the eighteenth century, the foundations sealed by brick deposits.

Initial considerations were that this may have represented some sort of steeple or bell-tower and it should be noted there was a structure added to the northeast side of the church in the seventeenth century. However, the archaeological evidence suggests this is too late for this building, based on the build technique, intact medieval deposits and the complete absence of brick. Consideration was also given to whether this represented the basal foundations of the Ensor frontage, dated to the early eighteenth century, specifically the columns, but this was discounted for the same reason and also because the front columns were engaged and therefore part of the front wall rather than independent structures that might require pier foundations. What is more far more likely is that this formed part of the medieval church of St John, which was subsequently built over and subsumed into the later church. The small size of the interior does not preclude this possibility as the most likely layout in the twelfth century is a small two-cell structure comprising a nave leading to a smaller chancel at the eastern end. The general dimensions of the rectangle, 6.14m by 5m, on the basis of comparisons, may suggest that the nave was likely to measure approximately 12m by 8m (fig. 4.7). There was a no indication of what would have been the west wall of the nave, extending south from the chancel, but the foundation of the chancel was only two courses in depth in this location thus it may not have survived. However, there was a brick wall, F16.1, which continued southwards along what would have been the original alignment. On the opposite side, the northwest corner was damaged by the construction of a later wall, F18, built almost along the same line and, as a result, there was no evidence of the nave wall on the northern side either.

The northeast corner and southwest corners may have been repaired at some date although this is not certain and these works are likely to have been associated with the rebuilding programmes documented in the historical sources. The projection F13 at the northeast corner may be of some significance in trying to define what this structure was as a suggestion was made that it may represent some sort of anta on the eastern side of the build. Antae are features

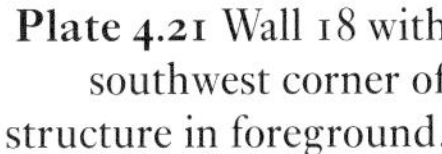
Plate 4.21 Wall 18 with southwest corner of structure in foreground.

of early pre-Romanesque churches and usually present as extensions of the northern and southern wall, which project out from the gable of the building. However, in this instance, the projection F13 was not flush with the northern line of the northern wall, as one would expect, and was set back from this line with the possible evidence of repair obscuring things in this location.

A large amount of disarticulated human remains found within the rubble deposits (F7 see below) presumably originated from within the medieval graveyard attached to the church or maybe even from the church itself, disturbed when the church at this end was substantially rebuilt in the eighteenth century. This collection was dominated by long-bones, comprising arms and legs, and are likely to represent the remains of burials interred within the church, disinterred and then reburied south of the masonry build. Other disarticulated remains had been disturbed at a later date, probably during the excavations in this area in the 1980s.

LEVEL 2 *(Medieval Phase 2)*

The main rectangle appears to have been partially demolished in Level 2, possibly in the late medieval period, as a new masonry wall F18 was

Plate 4.22 Wall F18 from the south.

Plate 4.23 Wall F17 looking south.

Plate 4.24 Wall 17, from the north.

constructed on the western side, roughly along the line of the original western wall of the rectangular build and presumably extending across what was originally the entrance into the chancel from the nave (fig. 4.8). Thus, either the chancel was demolished by this date or the ground level was raised up. The F18 wall was orientated slightly northwest–southeast following the orientation of the west wall and had evidently been found during the Wood Quay excavations, as it was sealed by modern blue plastic at the northern end. As there was to be little impact in this location, excavation was confined to establishing the footprint of the wall in this area and it was left *in situ*.

The north wall F18 (pls 4.22 and 4.23)

The F18 wall lay 0.70m below present ground level and extended for 2m in length, north–south, extending northwards into the section. Thus, the full length was not ascertained. The wall measured 0.95m in width and was thus narrower than the original west wall but was only exposed to 0.48m in depth at the southern end; here it was found to be at least two courses in depth and jointed, possibly where it originally abutted the west wall of the chancel arch. It was exposed in two sections, the eastern side exposed after the western end. The wall appeared to extend further north as it continued into the northern section. It was a well-constructed wall, dominated by a large limestone block measuring 0.50m by 0.30m but, on further excavation, was found to comprise at least two main courses, interspersed with a smaller narrower levelling course. The wall was mortared with a soft white mortar at the lower levels, which was the original mortar but the demolished upper levels were sealed with hard white cement-like mortar with brick fleck, where it had been previously exposed. A thin concrete slab was laid on the eastern side, on blue plastic sheeting, presumably during the Wood Quay excavations. The wall, by type and width, appeared to be medieval in date and may have been inserted as a blocking wall, blocking the chancel arch, at foundation level at least. It certainly followed the orientation of the original western wall and represents some sort of rebuild. A modern skim wall, F18.1, was of concrete and was built up against the eastern side of the F18 wall in modern times. This measured 0.12m in width (east–west) by 1.20m in length and was exposed to a depth of 0.30m during the backfilling process.

Second structure F17 (fig. 4.10; pls 4.23 and 24)
The remains of a second very badly truncated wall, F17, were located 0.80m west of the main square, on the southern side and this was later in date than the rectangular build. Only a short length, 1.60m north–south, survived *in situ* and, unfortunately, the wall was very badly truncated. The upper course (F17.1) lay 0.30m below existing ground level, at 11.55m O.D. but this appeared to have been built on a wider wall (F17.2), both possibly medieval in date. The upper wall measured 0.70m wide by 0.47m in height and was composed of roughly rectangular limestone blocks but including a granite stone, measuring 0.50m by 0.40m. It was bonded with a dark grey mortar, with visible inclusions of lime and grit. The lower wall was significantly wider measuring 1.10m in width by 0.52m in depth and this was composed of limestone blocks measuring, on average, 0.30m by 0.28m, but bonded with a soft yellow mortar with lenses of grey mortar throughout, rather than the dark grey of the upper portion. This build had also been previously exposed and was covered with blue plastic.

Conclusion of LEVEL 2
The two walls F18 and F17 are likely to have been medieval in date as neither wall contained any brick. Both could have been standing at the same time as the chancel. F18 appears to be a blocking wall, narrower than the chancel walls but nevertheless a substantial wall, which continued northwards, thus removing the western wall of the chancel at this end. This may suggest that this area of the church was widened. The F17 is a somewhat different wall in terms of construction and type but this too was a very solid wall, which followed the orientation of the chancel and which, if slightly further east, may have been a contender for the eastern nave wall. However, it displayed none of the well-built and neat construction found in the rectangular build and is most likely to be later in date, representing one of the rebuilding programmes

Plate 4.25 Wall F20, from the northeast.

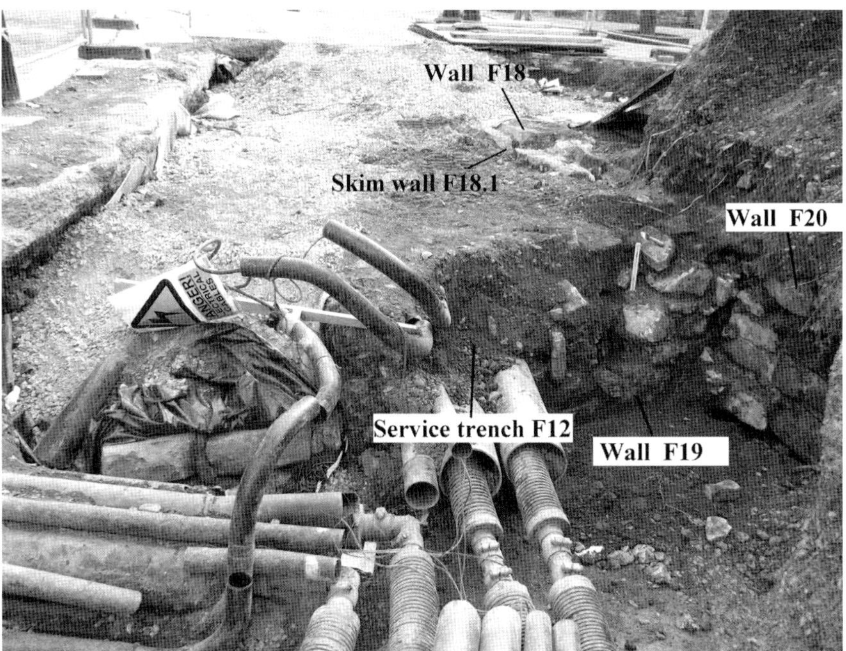

Plate 4.26 F19 and F20, looking south.

Plate 4.27 Dressed sandstone.

documented in the historical sources. Certainly, by the early sixteenth century, the church had additional aisles and underground crypts which are not likely to have been original to the building.

LEVEL 3 *(post-medieval in date)*

This phase is represented by a single wall that was exposed on the northern side of the site, almost along the line of what would have been the northern end of the west chancel wall.

Additional wall F20 (pls 4.25 and 26)

The remains of a very poorly-preserved wall, F20, were located on the northern side of the main rectangle, on the western side, but this was very badly damaged. The wall was also orientated northwest–southeast, very close to the projected orientation of the western chancel wall but positioned slightly to the east. At the southern end it did not actually abut the north wall (F4.3) of the chancel but rather stopped 80mm off it, the gap filled with loose black silty clay containing redbrick and human bone fragments. Only a small section of the eastern face was exposed, in a stretch measuring 1.30m north–south by 1m in depth at the southern end. In general, the wall was found to be composed of large limestone blocks with open joints containing hard white/grey gritty mortar. A very orange dressed sandstone oolite (possibly Dundry) was identified within the build of the wall and this was evidently one of the moulding of the original church, which was reused in the new build (pl. 4.27). The wall and stone moulding was left *in situ*. The entire wall was founded on a rubble deposit, which contained brick and mortar and can probably be related to the rebuild in the late eighteenth century.

Conclusion of Level 3

This was a badly built wall which could be dated to the post-medieval period and may have been related to the rebuild in the eighteenth century. The reuse of the dressed sandstone is interesting as it was the only dressed stone found during the excavations, which is somewhat unusual.

LEVEL 4 *(post-medieval demolition)*

The demolition deposits

The eastern section of the cutting escaped both the service trench and excavation carried out during the Wood Quay campaign. Thus, this section is of great significance as it retained the sequence of demolition rubble and debris over the church although undisturbed natural ground was not exposed. The primary deposit on the south side, F11/F21, was of crushed brick rubble, comprising small fragments, less than 0.10m in diameter, which was used to infill the rectangle (fig. 4.10, BA, GH). This was a mixed deposit that was at least 1m in depth and contained slate fragments, mortar and disarticulated human bone. Although post-medieval, this deposit also contained fragments of medieval floor-tiles, dated to the fourteenth and fifteenth centuries, suggesting that some sort of re-flooring occurred at this time at this end, perhaps related to either the restoration in 1477, or the rebuilding in 1495 and 1500 (pl. 4.26).

The equivalent deposit on the southern side of the rectangle, up against the face of the southern wall, was of almost pure crushed rubble F6, which had purple aggregate brick, pure orange brick and lumps of off-white mortar with visible mortar fleck mixed throughout (fig. 4.11, D-C). In the eastern section the exposed core of the church wall was found to be sealed directly by loose dark grey silt, F10, which contained mottled lenses of beige mortar/silt along with frequent amounts of mortar, small limestone and red brick fragments up to 0.60m in depth. It also contained some crushed fragments of human bone and occasional larger bone pieces. On the northern side this deposit was sealed by loose dark grey clay, F9, which also contained frequent amounts of mortar and pure orange redbrick fragments up to 0.60m in depth and this was clearly a demolition deposit as it also included a large amount of plaster as well as some human bone. The upper deposit F8 sealing the clay deposits F9 rubble was clearly demolition debris deposits but may have been later in date, related to the demolition in the nineteenth century, although this was difficult to establish. It represented a mix of rubble and brown clays but contained cinder fragments usually associated with 'cellar fill' or dumped domestic refuse. A layer of limestone shale, F8.1, was dumped down over the F8 deposits, which was between 0.20m and 0.40m in depth, extending on both sides of the wall, the origins of which are not clear. It may represent the remains of a stone shingle roof of some description.

The F6 deposit on the southern side of the church was sealed by mixed sticky grey/brown clay F3, which contained shell fragments and mortar fleck, as well as human bone but this was noticeably less fragmented than it was in the other deposits and most of the long-bones were almost complete. Interestingly, this mixed deposit also included fragments of medieval floor-tiles, as well as local glazed medieval pottery but, while this suggests it was inherently medieval in date, it must have been a redeposited layer as it extended over the crushed brick deposit F6. The third significant find was a collection of various human bones, F7, laid up against the base of the southern wall. This collection included adult leg bones, arm bones, vertebrae and skulls, which were laid out very neatly, parallel to the southern wall of the church. They sat within a distinctive mixed grey clay and lenses of silt and mortar fleck but which also contained small fragments of wood (possibly coffins) along with several nails. This deposit also contained one medieval ridge-tile and two fragments of medieval pottery, which could be dated to the early thirteenth century. The human remains had evidently been gathered up manually and stacked neatly against the base of the southern wall but the smaller bones were evidently not retrieved at the time. In the western section F7 was sealed by a deep deposit F5, of mixed demolition debris, 0.50m in depth, which contained mortar and human bones, similar to the F7 deposits.

Conclusion of Level 4

The documentary sources record that the church was substantially rebuilt in the eighteenth century as part of the renovations by Ensor but the chancel may have been demolished before this, to accommodate a growing church. During the eighteenth-century rebuilding the new construction disturbed existing graves, the careful collection of the bones, especially on the southern side of the church, suggestive of deliberate disinterment. The masonry from the rectangular build appears also to have been robbed out, seen especially in the southern wall where the exposed core was left *in situ*, and this may suggest that, either the build was still standing, or the demolished foundations had been re-exposed. Apart from the southern wall of the structure, the rest of it was demolished to a consistent level. The church was only demolished in 1877 and some of the rubble from this final phase of activity was dumped over the demolished foundations of the church, possibly even re-exposing the earlier rectangle. Thus, while the lower deposits were related to the Ensor rebuild, the upper levels (F8 and F8.1) may be later in date. The west wall of the church was left standing however, partially as it formed the party wall with the dwelling along John's Lane East and was therefore physically inaccessible. This is confirmed in the cartographic sources and also by photographic evidence on the western side, taken from Christ Church cathedral in the 1960s. This photograph indicates that the west wall is an old wall containing a blocked up segmented window, in addition to possibly earlier medieval features, i.e., a square window and door.

LEVEL 5 *(the modern period)*

The excavation site had been exposed previously, possibly as part of the archaeological excavations carried out in the 1970s and 1980s at Wood Quay and the medieval structure was carefully sealed with blue plastic sheeting and thin concrete slab, which was poured directly on top. The attached graveyard on the western side was also preserved *in situ* and this was very visible throughout the excavation, as the area was sheet-piled and fenced off. More recently, a series of modern services were inserted, running along the western side of Fishamble Street and cutting right through the medieval remains. All were placed within a wide service trench (F12), which measured 2m in depth by between 1.50m and 2m in width and included a large manhole constructed just north of the church, measuring 5m square.

The modern wall running along the western side of Fishamble Street was a block wall that extended as far south as the stepped entrance into the Dublin Civic Offices. The emergency works involved the removal of a stretch of this wall measuring approximately 25m north–south (including the concrete foundations). The wall averaged 1.20m in height, stepping down the slope from south to north and it was founded on a concrete foundation measuring 0.70m in width by 0.40m in depth. The top of the foundation was roughly level with the existing road level of Fishamble Street at 11.36m O.D. On removal of the wall, several plastic service pipes were revealed extending to a depth of approximately 1m and sealed by sand and hardcore. These fed into the manhole just north of the church. The removal of the wall also exposed the dumped deposits within the raised area west of Fishamble Street, within the Dublin Civic Offices grounds, and these consisted of mixed brown clays, which were up to 1.20m in depth. Additional service pipes were visible at the base of dumped deposits close to the inner face of the wall, lying approximately the same depth as the wall foundation. The clays contained frequent fragments of concrete and plastic and there was waste electrical cable visible throughout the section face. However, there were also fragments of human bones evident, suggesting that this material was probably redeposited shortly after the completion of the Civic Offices in the early 1980s as part of the new landscaping programme. As previously stated, the remains of the church were carefully covered in a protective terrum and then packed in lime-free 804 stone and gently packed (pls 4.20 and 4.27).

GENERAL CONCLUSIONS

The small emergency excavation at the top (southern end) of Fishamble Street, at the junction with John's Lane East, unexpectedly exposed what is likely to be the basal remains of the chancel of St John's church, confirming its location and type and linking it directly with the graveyard, preserved *in situ* to the northwest in the grounds of the Dublin Civic Offices. The major discovery was a solid rectangular build, dated by type to the medieval period, which had been demolished down to one level in what appeared to be a single event. Additional walls of both medieval and post-medieval date were also exposed and are representative of the long evolution of the church, from its foundation in the twelfth century right up to when it was finally demolished in 1877. The earliest masonry was quickly identified as potentially part of the foundations of the church, known to have been located on this site, and further investigation demonstrated that it had been exposed previously, most likely as part of the Wood Quay archaeological campaigns in the 1980s. Thus, many of the deposits originally associated with the foundations have been removed previously, the masonry itself carefully sealed with blue plastic. Unfortunately, despite this protection, a more modern service trench was cut through them in the relatively recent past, damaging them badly. Despite this, the footprint of the medieval rectangle could be immediately identified on the ground and, on examination, was found to be of substantial construction, externally measuring 6.14m north–south by 5m wide, with the internal chamber measuring just 3m north–south by 2.8m wide.

The original church of St John was almost certainly constructed just before the English conquest of Dublin in 1170 and is highly likely to have been of stone (Stalley 2000, 54–6). It was located within the city walls, adjacent to Christ Church cathedral, this prime location presumably a reflection of the wealth and status of its founder, an Ostman called Gillemichell, son Gillamurri. The church became a parish church and its importance is again reflected in the size of the parish, which by the sixteenth century encompassed most of the area from north of the cathedral down to the Liffey (having been recently united with St Olave's). From its twelfth-century beginning, by 1500, the church had expanded considerably and is recorded as having a nave with side aisles and a chancel at the eastern end, along with underground vaults and a belfry (Hughes 2009, 22). Speed's map, dated 1610, is the earliest plan of the church and this depicts the building as a rectangular church with a square tower/belfry at the western end (fig. 4.13). However, this is clearly a stylized version as all the other churches on the map are similarly depicted. But what is interesting is that it shows the position of the church, fronting onto what was a larger rectangular open space, set back from the cathedral.

By the time of the de Gomme map of Dublin, dated 1673, the church is shown fronting onto what is now annotated 'S John's Lane' running along the northern side of the cathedral, the church somewhat relegated to back-lane status (fig. 4.14). This second depiction also shows the tower at the western end, complete with cross, but with a second cross on the eastern end. Less detail is given on Rocque, dated 1756, but the general size can be calculated, a rough estimation suggesting the church was approximately 35m long by 15m wide at the eastern end, with a return or tower on the southwest corner (fig. 4.15). This, therefore, was the aisled church with a chancel at the eastern end, underground crypts and a tower at the western end, as described in 1500, and may be compared directly with St Audoen's church in the late thirteenth/fourteenth century when the double aisled church measured approximately 22m long by 16m wide with a tower in the southwest corner that measured approximately 4m square (McMahon 2006, 86). Rocque does not show a narrow chancel, which had probably been expanded to the full width of the church by this date. The church was extensively renovated between 1766 and 1769 by George Ensor who probably retained the actual structure adding a new façade, facing onto Fishamble Street and thus the orientation of the church was altered (Dwyer 1981, 107). The first edition Ordnance Survey map of 1847 captures the plan after Ensor, revealing a substantial church, slightly longer than that depicted on Rocque, at an estimated 42m in length, east–west (including two returns at the western end) by approximately 13m in width (fig. 4.18). While the western end may consist of add-on buildings that expanded the length of the church, the east end of the medieval rectangle found during the works under discussion corresponds exactly to the east end of the church as denoted on the first Ordnance Survey.

The rectangular masonry build is something of a mystery. It presents as a small but defined build at what must have been the altar end of the church. At first it was thought this could represent the base of a tower as there is a record of a seventeenth-century tower at the northeast end of the church, which contained a clock (with two dials) in 1704, and there is a record of the addition of a spire in 1639 (Pearson 2002, 243). However, on investigation, the walls were identified as medieval in date, sitting on medieval deposits and containing no brick, which was used copiously in Dublin from the seventeenth century onwards. The stone remains, then, may represent the chancel of the original twelfth-century stone mortared church, a significant survival if this is the case. While the chamber appears small, there are parallels: St Kieran's church in Glendalough is a double-cell church with a chancel that measured externally 4m square but with internal dimensions of just 2.80m east–west by 2.50m wide, while a similar example can be found on Friar's Island, Co. Clare, where the chancel was only 3m square (Ó Carragáin 2010, 192–3).

The Early Christian period saw the construction of mortared stone churches, single-cell structures that can be found all over the country. Early characteristics included antae, plinths, square-headed doorways, and one or two small windows (Ó Carragáin 2010, 192; Walsh 2008, 21–35; Ní Mharcaigh

1997, 249; Corlett and Potterton 2014). By the end of the eleventh century, however, the early Romanesque double-cell starts to emerge, which, by the creation of a chancel, effectively separated the altar from the congregation by placing it in another chamber. While there was open access via the chancel arch, there were still two separate cells. Some of the churches were built as double-cell originally but others were developed from existing single-cell churches by the addition of a chancel. Concentrations of the early double-cell have been identified by Ó Carragáin in the Hiberno-Norse towns and the ecclesiastical foundations at Killaloe, Co. Clare and Glendalough, Co. Wicklow (see Ó Carragáin 2010, fig. 1). He suggests that the emergence and concentration of the double-cell typology in these locations is reflective of direct contact with Canterbury, the strong ecclesiastical links perhaps providing the architectural impetus for the introduction of this new type. In Killaloe, the high-status St Flannan's church, built *c.*1100, is a double-church (and double-vaulted), confirming that the new plan was considered to be the height of sophistication, while in Glendalough the cluster of double-cell churches can be attributed to a substantial rebuilding programme between 1096 and 1111, the ecclesiastic authorities presumably commissioning the most fashionable builds of the day (Ó Carragáin 2010, 193).

The introduction of the double-cell type in Dublin must also have been influenced by the strong political and mercantile links between Dublin and the towns in England, where, by and large, the churches were double-cell in type. By the twelfth century, Dublin boasted over twenty such churches, located inside and outside the newly constructed city walls, with many more in the immediate hinterland, all clearly reflective of the large population-base in Dublin. While appearing initially to be a very large number, when examined against the English towns the numbers of churches, mostly of nave-and-chancel types, compares very favourably. Winchester had a total of 57 medieval churches, eleven of which had been founded by 1100 while York, which had such strong links with Dublin in the pre-Anglo-Norman period, had some 24 churches established by the eleventh and twelfth century (Scholfield 1995, 41; Steane 2015, 84–5). Bristol, a trading partner with Dublin before the English invasion, had in and around fifteen churches by this time while, further afield, the medieval city of London had over 100 churches, 27 of which were established by 1100. In England, many of the small churches began life as private chapels to wealthy families and these eventually became parish churches; this may have happened at St John's, as it was granted to the priory of the Holy Trinity by a private individual. However, this man also granted St Paul's to the priory, as previously stated, and may simply be a benefactor, providing funding for both churches. In any event, the evidence from England suggests the growing urban populations living in and around the towns were often serviced by a myriad of small churches.

The evidence for the churches of the Hiberno-Norse ports in Ireland, however, is very limited and is confined at the moment to Waterford and Dublin. In Waterford the foundations of the church of St Peter were found through archaeological excavation and revealed to be a double-cell church (with a later apse), which was built in the late eleventh/early twelfth century. Thus, this type of church was certainly being constructed in the Ostman port of Waterford at an early date. The evidence from St John's demonstrates that there were also double-cell churches being constructed in Dublin but, in this instance, probably at a slightly later date, in and around the mid-twelfth century. Nevertheless, the foundation remains suggest a double-cell church with a chancel measuring externally 6m by 5m attached to a nave probably approximately 9m wide by 12m in length (based on St Ciarán's church in Glendalough (see Ó Carragáin 2010, figs 194, 193).

Unfortunately, the evidence for the other churches in and around the walled city is extremely limited. The largest ecclesiastical foundation, Christ Church cathedral, can be dated to the rebuilding programme of the late twelfth century and, as a result, nothing survives of the original eleventh-century plan. St Patrick's is of a similar date. Of the parish churches, only St Audoen's is still extant but this large church is dated predominantly to the thirteenth century (although there are earlier remains: see below). Archaeology, however, has started to provide some answers, although the evidence is somewhat limited.

The church and round tower of St Michael le Pole was always considered an important church in Dublin, located outside the city walls in the southeast suburb (Simpson 2000, 17–18). This was also a pre-Anglo-Norman foundation that had been rebuilt throughout the medieval and post-medieval period, eventually being converted into a schoolhouse but managing to survive in the modern landscape up until 1975 when it was unfortunately demolished. The site was well known and in 1981 a research excavation was carried out exposing the significant remains of, not only the church and schoolhouse rebuilding, but also evidence of habitation which, at the time, were the earliest levels uncovered in Dublin (Gowen 2001, 29). Two eighteenth-century depictions of the church survive when it was in use as a schoolhouse and both these show a small rectangular stone building. There is no indication of a narrower chancel at the eastern end, which is probably more suggestive of a single-cell church than a double cell, although there may have been a chancel that extended the full width of the church. Two cuttings were opened up at either end of the known footprint but only the western end produced evidence of the medieval church, exposing the original western wall and part of the southwest corner, indicating a small church 7.50m in width. The church had an off-centre west doorway with a plinth, and was constructed of limestone block facings with a heavily mortared random rubble core (ibid., 38). Only a short stretch of the medieval southern wall was exposed, less than 3m in length, but this wall was clearly rebuilt, as part of the construction of the schoolhouse in 1706. This new wall, only 0.80m in width, was actually keyed into the southern medieval wall and also displayed a similar plinth but, more importantly, continued along the alignment of the original medieval southern wall. The cutting put across the eastern end of the church to try to find the east wall did not reveal medieval masonry but did locate the 1706 eastern wall, which, if still on the alignment of the medieval build, would suggest this represents the end of the medieval church. If this is the case, this may suggest that St Michael le Pole was a single-cell church, measuring 17.50m in length by 7.50m in width rather than a double-cell as one might expect. However, this might be connected with the fact that St Michael le Pole also produced evidence of the earliest habitation in Dublin, dating from the late seventh to the late ninth century, which possibly links this church with the monastic settlement of Dubhlinn, thought to be in the general location. This habitation was followed by a phase of burial, which was subsequently sealed by the church, suggesting that St Michael le Pole may have been very early in the sequence. This may help explain the single-cell rather than the double-cell morphology.

A second pre-Anglo-Norman church is under archaeological investigation while going to press and this is the church of St Peter's of the Hill, also in the southwest suburb of Dublin, a short distance from St Michael le Pole. Here, ongoing excavations are starting to uncover substantial medieval walls associated with a graveyard but the findings are at a very preliminary stage as the entire structure has not yet been uncovered. A brief initial summary is provided here by the director, Paul Duffy, which is subject to change:

> The masonry remains consist of two parallel walls that may represent the foundations of an eleventh or twelfth-century simple nave church (single-cell) with dimensions of *c.*16m east–west by 6m in plan. Evidence for a later (twelfth-century in date?) subdivision of the church into double-cell nave and chancel arrangement may also be emerging but the site is still [September 2018] under excavation. This structure is located at the highest surviving point of the site and is therefore consistent with contemporary descriptions of the church being located on a mount or hill. However, several stratigraphic complications challenge a simple interpretation of this structure. In particular, the walls overlie a curving ditch of probable eleventh-century date, which has long been suspected to represent an ecclesiastical enclosure surrounding the church. Extensive burials of approximate fourteenth-/fifteenth-century date occur within the footprint of the structure and, while these burials appear, on current information, to respect the walls, they illustrate that the structure was no longer a place of worship at this time. This picture is further complicated by the retrieval of numerous fragments of Gothic

> masonry from secondary contexts across the site, which are broadly contemporary with the burials. Excavation is ongoing but a working interpretation suggests that the remains represent an early stone church with a period of activity between the eleventh and thirteenth century followed by a substantial and relatively lavish rebuild somewhere in the immediate vicinity.

St Peter's church, then, may have started life as a single-cell church but was possibly converted into a double-cell by the addition of a chancel in the twelfth century, a development more in keeping with the churches of the hinterland of Dublin where some of the earlier churches were expanded into double-cells.

The third and fourth churches in Dublin for which there is archaeological evidence are both double-cell churches and are slightly later in date than St John's but probably only by a couple of decades. However, they span that critical date of 1170, the year the English conquered Dublin. St Audoen's church, mentioned previously, is located within the city walls at the western end of the city and represents the only extant medieval church in Dublin, the main build dating to the early to mid-thirteenth century (McMahon 2006, 23, 85–8). However, excavations within the body of the church exposed the foundations of an earlier church, dated to the late twelfth/early thirteenth century, incorporated within the southern end of the existing church. These masonry remains presented similarly to St John's and consisted of a narrow build at the eastern end, interpreted as a chancel, which measured approximately 4.20m square (internally). The main survival was the main east wall, measuring over 1.10m in width and faced with limestone block with a mortared rubble core, although the mortar had all but disappeared. Unlike St John's there was no foundation course or offset. McMahon concluded that this represented the 'narrower, chancel end of an aisleless church', the nave measuring an estimated 15.5m long by 8m in width (based on the existing southern wall of the church) with the smaller contemporary chancel at the eastern end. This double-cell church, then, was only slightly larger than St John's.

There is archaeological evidence of a third church outside the walls of the city in the western suburb but this is within a wholly English foundation, St Thomas's abbey, founded in 1177. The limited but detailed investigations revealed masonry remains that could be identified as the southern wall of the church, measuring a massive 2.75m in width and traced for over 22m in length, east–west, indicating that the church was at least this in length. While mostly robbed-out, the wall was found to be composed of limestone/calp rectangular block with a mortared rubble mortar core, as was typical for this period and found in the churches discussed above (Walsh 2000, 193–5). Within the church, two sections of tiled pavement and cobbling were found, suggesting that much of the interior of the church may survive beneath the existing ground, an exciting prospect. Walsh suggested the church was a double-cell plan, consisting of a nave and chancel, although dimensions could not be ascertained. This church, then, was of similar plan to both St John's and St Audoen's built soon after the English took over Dublin.

Mention should be made of a fourth pre-Anglo-Norman church, St Michael's of the Hill beside Christ Church, which is the subject of a paper by Dooley in this volume. This paper attempts to trace the layout of the church in the present nineteenth-century Synod Hall and retrieves what may be a double-cell layout of a church preserved within the modern build. Dooley suggests that the nave measured 9.83m in length by 7.35m in width, with a chancel at the eastern end measuring 4.55m giving a combined length of 15.22m. A depiction of the church on a piece of ornamental silverware in 1667 was suggestive of a rectangular build with no obvious chancel but this was after extensive rebuilding in this later period.

FINAL THOUGHTS

The limited evidence from the city of Dublin perhaps does suggest that nave-and-chancel double-cell churches were being constructed in Dublin, both before the English invasion and certainly after, which is not surprising given the European trend in favour of the double-cell church type and the well-documented ecclesiastical, trading and political links with England. Despite generations spent in Ireland, the Hiberno-Norse of Dublin managed to retain their distinct Scandinavian identity as the 'Ostmen' (the men from the east), and their churches, then, one would think, were unlikely to show significant 'native' influences in the form of the single-cell model. However, both the church of St Michael le Pole and St Peter's of the Hill may skew this picture somewhat as both these churches may have been of single-cell construction initially.

Interestingly, Dublin's hinterland also displays this dichotomy, with a concentration of stone mortared churches, as identified by Ó Carragáin, but with ample evidence of both types, the single-cell church, such as Drimnagh in southwest Dublin and Kilternan, in south Dublin, along with the double-cell type such as that at Killiney, also in south Dublin. In some cases, the single-cell expanded was into a double-cell by the addition of a chancel, such as at Tully, in south Dublin, and in Palmerston, in southwest Dublin. Others had an addition of a third cell, abutting the nave such as Killiney, south Dublin (Walsh, 2008, 28–9; Ní Mharcaigh 1997, 257). There is also evidence that single-cell churches continued to be built alongside double-cells and that once the parish church system was established in the twelfth century, many of the earlier single-cell churches were expanded in size by the addition of a chancel, in some cases followed by the addition of side aisles, common in the thirteenth century.

The different styles and types are somewhat perplexing but perhaps it all suggests something of cultural mix, from the ecclesiastical sites at Glendalough, Clonmacnois, and so on, and from Britain, with which Dublin was linked so intricately that eventual colonization was arguably inevitable. The identification of St John's as a double-cell church carries with it significant connotations, especially when one considers what a small area was investigated. It may be the case that the medieval rectangular build was something else entirely. However, the monumental nature of the walls uncovered signals that this must have been an important stone building, the foundations of which managed to survive the rigours of the Early Modern period though not without considerable damage.

The good news is that Dublin City Council has preserved the cemetery attached to the church to the west of the chancel remains, where grave-slabs are still visible, lying in the grass and commemorating this once great Dublin landmark. Thus, this area has not been damaged and should be relatively intact, containing burial soils to the rear (north) of the terraced houses that originally fronted onto John's Lane East. Recent archaeological testing by the writer did locate both burials and what is likely to be the footprint of the later church and part of the houses along the lane and, even more importantly, the remains of the tarmacadam carpark that followed the demolition of the Mission Hall in the early 1960s. Thus, the area immediately west of the chancel was clearly not excavated completely as part of the Wood Quay excavations and may still be relatively intact, although the steps down to the Civic Offices are likely to have caused damage. But, despite this, it is likely the Wood Quay archive will contain the records of this excavation carried out by the careful archaeologists who covered the masonry remains with blue plastic, alerting us in advance to the earlier remains when machinery was working in this area. Further work in this location may reveal what must have been one of the most important churches within the city walls.

ACKNOWLEDGMENTS

Thanks, as always, to Kevin Weldon, who helped direct on the site and also produced the photography and the figures, and also to Dr Ruth Johnson who assisted with the excavation along with Peter Kerins and Eric Simpson. Thanks also to Mags Gowen for her thoughts at the time of excavation and to Paul Duffy who was asked for information far too early in his excavation process.

BIBLIOGRAPHY

Bennett, D. 1991 *Encyclopaedia of Dublin*. Dublin.

Bradley, J. (ed.) 1992 'The topographical development of Scandinavian Dublin'. In F.H.A. Aalen and K. Whelan (eds), *Dublin city and county: from prehistory to present*, 43–56. Dublin.

Bradley, J., Fletcher A., and Simms, A. (eds) 2009 *Dublin in the medieval world: studies in honour of Howard B. Clarke*. Dublin.

Brady, J. and Simms, A. (eds) 2001 *Dublin through space and time (c.900–1900)*. Dublin.

Brooks, E. St J. (ed.) 1936 *Register of the hospital of S. John the Baptist without the New Gate, Dublin*, IMC, Dublin.

Casey, C. 2005 *Dublin: the buildings of Ireland*, New Haven.

Clarke, H.B. 1978 *Dublin* c.*840*–c.*1540: The medieval town in the modern city*. Dublin.

— 1997 'The topographical development of early medieval Dublin'. *JRSAI* 107, 29–51.

— 1998 '*Urbs et suburbium*: beyond the walls in medieval Dublin'. In C. Manning (ed.), *Dublin and beyond the Pale: studies in honour of Paddy Healy*, 45–58. Bray.

— 2002 *Dublin part 1, to 1610. Irish historic town atlas, no. 11*, RIA. Dublin.

Clarke, J.H. 1949–50 'The parish of St Olave's'. *DHR* 11, 116–23.

Corlett, C. and Potterton, M. 2014 *The church in Early Ireland in the light of recent excavations*. Dublin.

Craig, M. 1980 *Dublin, 1660–1860*. London.

— 2 1989 *The architecture of Ireland from the earliest times to 1880*. London.

Dwyer, F. 1981 *Lost Dublin*. Dublin.

Gilbert, J.T. 1854–9 *A history of Dublin*, 3 vols (repr. 1972). Dublin.

Gowen, M. 2001 'Excavations at the site of the church and tower of St Michael le Pole, Dublin'. In S. Duffy (ed.), *Medieval Dublin II*, 13–52. Dublin.

Haworth, R. 1988 'The site of St Olave's church'. In J. Bradley (ed.), *Settlement and society in medieval Ireland*, 177–91. Kilkenny.

Hughes, S.C. 1889 *The church of S. John the Evangelist, Dublin*. Dublin (repr. 2009).

Leask, H.G. 1955–60 *Irish churches and monastic buildings*. 3 vols, Dundalk.

McCullough, N. 2007 *Dublin: an urban history: the plan of the city*. Dublin.

McMahon, M. 1991 *Medieval church sites of north County Dublin*. Dublin.

— 2006 *St Audoen's church, Cornmarket, Dublin: archaeology and architecture*. Dublin.

O'Brien, E. 1988 'Churches of south-east County Dublin, 7th to 12th century'. In G. Mac Niocaill and P.F Wallace (eds), *Keimelia: studies in medieval archaeology and history in memory of Tom Delaney*, 504–24. Galway.

Ó Carragáin T. 2010 *Churches in early medieval Ireland*, New Haven and London.

O'Donovan, E. 2008 'The Irish, the Vikings, and the English: new archaeological evidence from excavations at Golden Lane, Dublin'. In S. Duffy (ed.), *Medieval Dublin VIII*, 36–130. Dublin.

O'Keefe, T. 1999 'Architectural tradition of the early medieval church in Munster'. In M.A. Monk and J. Sheehan (eds), *Early medieval Munster: archaeology, history and society*. Cork.

Pearson, P. 2002 *Heart of Dublin: resurgence of an historic city*. Dublin.

Robinson, J.L. and Armstrong, E.C.R. 1916–17 'On the ancient deeds of the parish of St John'. *PRIA* 33, 175–224.

Platt, C. 1981 *The parish churches of Medieval England*. London.

Schofield, J. 1994 'Saxon and medieval parish churches in the city of London: a review'. *Transactions of the London and Middlesex Archaeological Society* 45, 23–146.

Simpson, L. 2000 'Forty years a-digging: a preliminary synthesis of archaeological investigations in medieval Dublin'. In S. Duffy (ed.), *Medieval Dublin I*, 11–68. Dublin.

— 2010 *The archaeological remains of Viking and Medieval Dublin: a research framework*. Irish National Strategic Archaeological Research (INSTAR), available at www.heritagecouncil.ie.

— 2011 'Fifty years a-digging: a synthesis of medieval archaeological investigations in Dublin city suburbs'. In S. Duffy (ed.), *Medieval Dublin XI*, 9–112. Dublin.

Stalley, R. 2000a 'The construction of the medieval cathedral, *c.*1030–1250'. In K. Milne (ed.), *Christ Church cathedral, Dublin: a history*, 53–74. Dublin.

Steane, J. 2015 *The archaeology of medieval England and Wales.* London and New York.

Wallace, P.F. 1981 'Anglo-Norman Dublin, continuity and change'. In D. Ó Corráin (ed.), *Irish antiquity: essays and studies presented to Professor M.J. O'Kelly*, 247–66. Cork.

— 1988 'Archaeology and the emergence of Dublin as the principal town in Ireland'. In J. Bradley (ed.), *Settlement and society in medieval Ireland*, 123–60. Kilkenny.

— 1990 'The origins of Dublin'. In H.B. Clarke (ed.), *Medieval Dublin: the making of a metropolis*, 70–97. Dublin.

— 1992 'The archaeological identity of the Hiberno-Norse town'. *JRSAI* 122, 35–66.

Walsh, N. 2008 'Pre-Romanesque churches in Dublin and its hinterland: the Golden ratio'. In S. Duffy (ed.), *Medieval Dublin XVIII*, 21–35. Dublin.

APPENDIX I

Fishamble Street ceramic finds

SIOBHÁN SCULLY

Introduction

Five floor-tiles, one roof-tile and three sherds of pottery were recovered from the excavations at Fishamble Street (08E42). All of the material appears to be medieval in date, although one of the floor-tiles (08E42:7:2) is very fragmentary (fig. 4.26).

Floor-tiles

Five floor-tiles were recovered from the excavations at Fishamble Street (08E42) and these included three medieval line-impressed tiles, one fragment of a plain, glazed tile and a small fragment of an unglazed tile. These were all dated to the fourteenth and fifteenth century. Line-impressed tiles have their decoration applied to the surface of the tile by means of a wooden, or possibly metal, stamp, although occasionally it was done by hand. This was done while the clay was leather-hard. The tile was then glazed and fired (Eames and Fanning 1988, 32–3). Three line-impressed tiles were recovered from

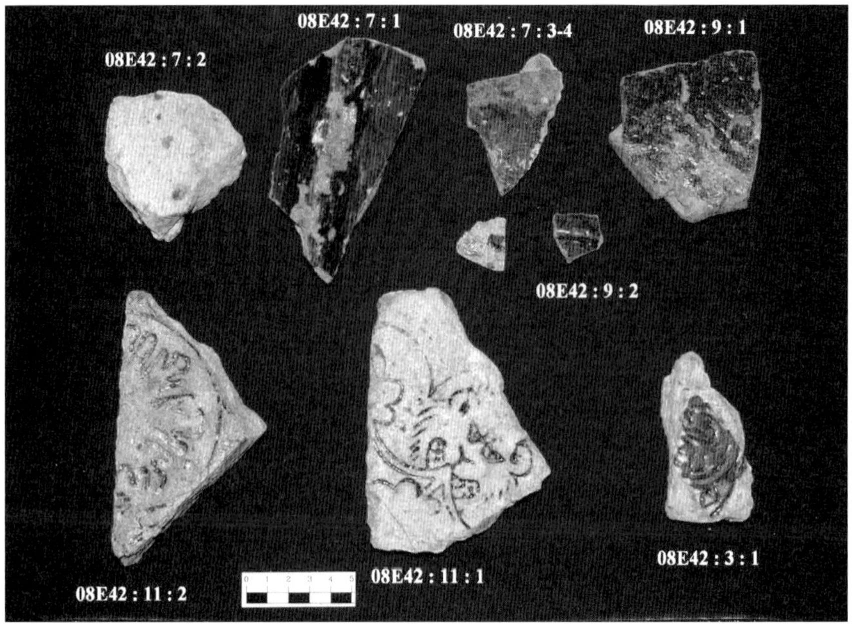

4.26 Floor tiles.

Fishamble Street, which can be related to the Eames and Fanning (1988) catalogue, which contains an index of medieval tile-designs found in Ireland. Only one of the tiles from Fishamble Street (08E42:11:1) could be identified among the designs they recorded and this tile dates to the fourteenth/fifteenth century (see below).

L6 Lion's face with leaves. A corner fragment of a tile (08E42:11:1) displays this design and is dated to the fourteenth and fifteenth century. It is from a 4-tile design and consists of a lion with foliage gripped in his teeth. Above the lion's head is a cusped band which forms a circle when all four tiles are together. However, only one of these cusps is visible in the tile from Fishamble Street as the tile is incomplete (a complete tile would have had a trefoil in the corner above the cusped band). This design has been found on tiles from a number of sites in Dublin such as Christ Church cathedral, Dublin Castle, Fishamble Street, Kilmainham, Wood Quay, St Audoen's church and St Patrick's cathedral. It has also been found on tiles outside of Dublin at Kildare cathedral, St Canice's cathedral in Kilkenny, and at the Dominican Friary, James Street, St Peter's church and Shop Street in Drogheda (Eames and Fanning 1988, 86–7). Eames & Fanning (ibid., 42) suggest, as this design has not been found on tiles in Chester, that it was a local

Plate 4.28 Medieval finds.

design and made in Ireland. In support of this, wasters (tiles that did not fire properly) of this design were found at Kilmainham and in Drogheda (ibid.).

Unidentified foliage design, triangular tile A triangular line-impressed tile (08E42:11:2) is almost complete except for damage along one of the shorter edges. Most of the upper surface of the tile is taken up with the large foliage design, which is half a leaf with serrated edges and a possible semi-circular border around this. This tile was probably part of a 2-tile design and there were traces of a yellow lead glaze remaining in the impressed lines. It dates to the fourteenth and fifteenth century.

Unidentified design, small fragment of tile A small fragment of a line-impressed tile (08E42:3:1) has an unidentified design, but probably dated to the fourteenth and fifteenth century. The design is possibly of tightly-curled foliage and it has a green/yellow lead glaze.

Undecorated tiles The collection included one fragment of a glazed undecorated floor-tile and a small fragment of an unglazed tile. The glazed tile (08E42:9:1) is thinner than the other tiles and has a red earthenware fabric with a grey core. It has a mottled green and yellow lead glaze. The unglazed tile (08E42:7:2) has a red earthenware fabric banded with yellow clay.

Roof-tile One U-shaped medieval ridge-tile fragment (08E42:7:1) was also found. It had a red earthenware fabric with inclusions of quartz and a streaky green/brown glaze on the exterior. This type of decorative roof furniture was introduced into Ireland in the early thirteenth century, possibly as part of the expansion of Anglo-Norman building at the time (Wren 2006, 180).

Pottery Two sherds of Dublin-type medieval pottery were found during excavations (08E42:7:3–4). This locally produced ware was wheel-thrown, with a less coarse fabric than the earlier Dublin-type coarseware but it still has visible inclusions of mica. The sherds have an orange/red fabric with a mottled dark green/brown external glaze. This pottery began to be produced from the mid-thirteenth century onwards (McCutcheon 2006, 61). The third pottery sherd was a small body sherd (08E42:9:2) of Ham Green pottery. This has a beige coloured fabric with a grey core and a mottled green glaze. Ham Green A wares began to be imported into Ireland in the early twelfth century, and the B wares from the late twelfth century, and continued in use until the late thirteenth century when it was replaced by Bristol Redcliffe wares (Gahan and McCutcheon 1997, 294). It was not clear whether this sherd was Ham Green A or B.

Catalogue (*dimensions in brackets are incomplete)

Find no.	Description	Dimensions	Weight
08E42:3:1	Line-impressed tile. Red earthenware fabric. Green/yellow glaze. Small fragment of tile.	(78mm) x (38mm) x 23mm	93.3g
08E42:7:2	Small fragment of tile. Undecorated. Red earthenware fabric with banded yellow clay. Sandy base.	(68mm) x (64mm) x 29mm	125.6g
08E42:9:1	Undecorated tile. Red earthenware fabric with a grey core. Sandy base. Glazed with mottled green and yellow lead glaze.	(73mm) x (68mm) x 10mm	100.2g
08E42:11:1	Line-impressed tile. Red earthenware fabric. Lion's face with leaves (L6). Green glaze remaining in impressed lines. 4-tile design. Also found in Dublin at Christ Church, Dublin Castle, Fishamble St, Kilmainham, Wood Quay, St Audoen's church, St Patrick's cathedral. Also found at Kildare cathedral, St Canice's cathedral Kilkenny, and Drogheda.	120mm x (84mm) x 23mm	279.6g
08E42:11:2	Line-impressed tile. Triangular in shape, one corner is broken off. Appears to have a large-leafed foliage design. Probably from a 2-tile design. Yellow lead glaze remaining in the impressed lines. Sandy base.	121mm x (83mm) x 25mm	206.7g

Roof-tile

Find no.	Description	Dimensions
08E42:7:1	Fragment of U-shaped ridge-tile. Red earthenware fabric with inclusions of quartz. Streaky green/brown exterior glaze	L (118mm); Wth (64mm); H (38mm)

Pottery

Find no.	Description	Date
08E42:7:3	Dublin-type ware. Bf	mid-13thC onwards
08E42:7:4	Dublin-type ware. Bf	mid-13thC onwards
08E42:9:2	Ham Green Bf	12th-13thC

BIBLIOGRAPHY

Eames, E.S. and Fanning, T. 1988 *Irish medieval tiles*. Dublin. RIA.

McCutcheon, C. 2006 *Medieval pottery from Wood Quay, Dublin*. NMI, Medieval Dublin Excavations, 1962–81, ser. B, vol. 7. Dublin RIA.

Wren, J. 2006 'Medieval and post-medieval roof tiles'. In C. McCutcheon, *Medieval pottery from Wood Quay, Dublin*, 177–95. NMI, Medieval Dublin Excavations, 1962–81, ser. B, vol. 7. Dublin. RIA.

‘The laws and usages of Dublin’: a complete translation of *Les leys et les usages de la cite de Diveline*

PHYLLIS GAFFNEY AND YOLANDE DE PONTFARCY SEXTON

INTRODUCTION

The source text and its location

Included in the so-called Chain Book of Dublin, housed in the Dublin City Archives in Pearse Street, Dublin, is a substantial text entitled *Les leys et les usages de la cite de Diveline* (‘The laws and usages of Dublin’).[1] This document in medieval French lays down a set of regulations, prescribed by custom and law, for the inhabitants of the city of Dublin. In more or less random order, it indicates norms of conduct and sanctions for a range of human activities within the franchise of the municipality. Inhabitants might learn, for example, of what bailiffs could do lawfully to a pig left wandering too long in the street, or what distance it was required to leave between one’s latrine and an adjacent dwelling. There are rules governing various forms of trade, buying and selling goods and property, laws on criminal liability, and detailed protocols on matters such as the customary privileges, liberties and status of burgesses, the election of public representatives or the recommended restrictions on donations of land to clerical orders.

Dublin’s *Laws and usages* are to be seen within the broader context of a group of legal texts prescribing similar norms and practices pertaining to scores of boroughs throughout the Anglo-Norman realm. These custumals were comprehensively analysed more than a century ago by Mary Bateson.[2] Sixty years later, Gearóid Mac Niocaill outlined the history of medieval boroughs in Ireland, and printed (in the original French) the custumals of Dublin, Waterford and Cork, together with over seventy Irish borough charters.[3] In general, custumals are to be read as guidelines, or codes of practice, for municipal clerks and bailiffs engaged in urban administration. To quote Bateson: ‘Their purpose is practical; they are destined to serve as guides to the procedure of the borough court. They form the proper introduction to

1 Chain Book, fos 6–26, or pp 64–105. Online access to the manuscript is now available at http://databases.dublincity.ie/chainwhite. 2 Mary Bateson, *Borough customs*, 2 vols, Selden Society (London, 1904–6). 3 Mac Niocaill, *Burgéisí*.

the study of the borough court-rolls, which cannot be understood without them … and they scatter their information, if in disorderly and scrappy fashion, still over a very wide field of law.'[4]

Editions

Dublin's *Laws and usages* were transcribed from the Chain Book and printed by John Thomas Gilbert in 1870.[5] The custumal for Waterford, a copy of which lies in a fourteenth-century manuscript in Corpus Christi College, Cambridge (MS 405, fos. 203–32a), is also in medieval French, and is, to all intents and purposes, a copy of the Dublin text. Both of these custumals – Dublin's and Waterford's – were published in parallel, in facing page format, by Mac Niocaill.[6] The juxtaposition reveals their substantial similarity, apart from name changes, linguistic differences – the Waterford scribe is from Picardy – and some amendments to chapter divisions and numerical values.

Dating

A single precise date for the Dublin custumal is difficult to determine. Bateson dated the text as a whole *c.*1300, but believed it to incorporate material that spans several decades of the thirteenth century. Towards the end of the text,[7] a list appears of the names of certain prominent citizens of Dublin, purchasers of the franchises of the city, who can be traced to the mid- to late 1220s. That part of the document could therefore refer to the period before the grant of the mayoralty to the city of Dublin by King Henry III in 1229.[8] However, elsewhere the evidence suggests a more appropriate dating of some seventy years later. Bateson concludes that 'there is nothing to fix dates definitely. The whole collection is disorderly, and may possibly represent a selection taken from borough records of many earlier years.'[9] She claims that the Waterford custumal was copied and adapted from the Dublin text in the early 1300s.[10] Mac Niocaill seems to concur with this dating.[11]

This translation: completing the pioneering work of Mary Bateson

As far as we are aware, no complete English translation of Dublin's *Laws and usages* has hitherto been published. On foot of a suggestion that this gap in Dublin's medieval sources ought to be filled, we agreed to embark on the task.[12] The difficulty of translating the text was soon evident to us as scholars of medieval French literature, whose normal fare is twelfth- and thirteenth-century chivalric romance. Although the syntax, by and large, is clear, the lexical challenges posed by its technical legal vocabulary are multiple. A literal

4 Bateson, *Customs*, i, pp xvi–vii. 5 Gilbert (ed.), *Hist. & mun. docs*, pp 240–69. 6 Mac Niocaill, *Buirgéisí*, i, pp 2–59. 7 See ch. 97. 8 Bateson, *Customs*, i, pp liv–lv. 9 Ibid., pp xxiv–v. 10 Ibid., p. liv. 11 Mac Niocaill, *Buirgéisí*, ii, p. 335, n. 18. 12 The suggestion originated from Eoin C. Bairéad, via Professor Rick Caldicott.

translation was relatively easy to produce, but from there to making our translation intelligible was another story. Meaning derives from context. Many individual words and phrases remained semantically opaque, despite our best efforts to penetrate them.

Help came from an unexpected source. Having borrowed Mary Bateson's two-volume study, already mentioned, in order to understand the necessary context for making sense of our document, we soon realized that her *Borough customs* contained much more than useful background. Her vast compendium gives examples of precise points of law in urban settings throughout the Anglo-Norman realm. Instead of proceeding town by town, her study treats the subject topic by topic, taking a thematic and comparative approach, and citing extracts from the custumals of some 130 boroughs in England, Wales, Scotland and Ireland. Significantly for our purpose, whenever Bateson quotes extracts in Latin or in French, she adds a plausible rendering in formal modern English. In addition, whenever she refers to examples from the Dublin custumal, Bateson cites and translates from the corresponding part of the Waterford text, because the two custumals are so very similar and (unlike Dublin's) the Waterford custumal, which she considered linguistically interesting, had not yet been published.[13]

Availing of Bateson's extensive index, we combed her volumes to note and copy all the instances when she cites and translates the Waterford text. These extracts were the key to the translation of our Dublin source text, once we had rearranged them into a sequence that corresponded to it. Thanks to Mac Niocaill's facing-page edition of the two custumals, the job of cross-checking the Dublin French, the Waterford French and Bateson's English was greatly facilitated. The somewhat cumbersome process of assembling the textual jigsaw paid a handsome dividend: we found, when it was done, that Bateson's translations from the Waterford text had in effect provided us with a readymade trustworthy English version of about four-fifths of the Dublin custumal. All that remained was to fill the gaps by translating those extracts that had been omitted by Bateson.

In bringing this translation to the light of day, therefore, we stress that our work merely rearranges and completes the translation work of a remarkable Victorian scholar. Medievalist, suffragist and fellow of Newnham College, Cambridge, Mary Bateson (1865–1906) was one of the most esteemed and dedicated medievalists of her generation. Her tragically brief career, entirely devoted to lecturing and publishing on medieval history, produced a vast output of research.[14] *Borough customs* was her last work. It is a testament to her

13 Bateson, *Customs*, i, pp liii–lv. 14 Thomas Frederick Tout, 'Bateson, Mary' in *Dictionary of national biography*, second supplement, vol. I (London, 1912), pp 110–12; Mary Dockray-Miller, 'Mary Bateson (1865–1906): scholar and suffragist' in Jane Chance (ed.), *Women medievalists and the academy* (Madison, WI, 2005), pp 67–78.

painstakingly methodical mind and complete command of her complex, multilingual and heterogeneous material. Her mentor and Cambridge colleague, the preeminent legal historian F.W. Maitland, in an appreciation following her untimely death, remarked that Bateson's 'knowledge of the history of our medieval towns was almost, if not quite, unrivalled'.[15] Of *Borough customs* he said that he could not see how it could have been done better, or who else could have done it.[16] For a person not entitled, on grounds of her sex, to be awarded the Cambridge degree for which she had taken a first class result in 1887, this was praise indeed. Needless to add, we have found her translations thoroughly reliable, and respect them for the most part. In knitting together her translated fragments of our text into a complete version in English, we pay homage to her exemplary source-based scholarship.

Interest of the Dublin custumal: linguistic and historical

The text is of interest as a minor linguistic curiosity, particularly in its lexical range. It illustrates a regional variety of late medieval French, demonstrating that the legal language of medieval Dublin can contain calques, when required, from the Irish vernacular (e.g., the term *betagh*, chapter 7), as well as rare terms specific to the Irish context (e.g., *dernehundred*, ch. 92, which Bateson glosses at length,[17] and *tounderie*, appearing in several places and also glossed by Bateson).[18] It also uses a number of archaic and legal terms that require elucidation, such as *fresche force* ('fresh force') (chs 9, 21, and passim), *miskennyng* (ch. 33), *landgable* (chs 3, 75 and passim), *fraunk amoisne / frankalmoign* (ch. 78), and so forth.

The *Laws and usages of Dublin* is conceivably more important for other spheres of enquiry. In the introduction to her study of borough customs,[19] Bateson claims that the primary historical interest of these texts, in general, has less to do with local history than with the legal history of these islands. Custom law has long been considered, together with common law and statute law, to be one of the three keystones of the English legal system. In Bateson's view, borough customs afford a glimpse into a remote past, and allow folk memory and practice to live on, because they reflect a period when unwritten archaic local customs and procedures had not yet been made uniform by central government or the rule of common law. For example, she interprets the Dublin rule 'which burned the incendiary in the fire which he had made, if he could be caught' as an expression of 'the ancient horror of arson'.[20]

The closing decades of the twelfth century and the early decades of the thirteenth coincided with the growth of borough charters, which in Ireland

15 F.W. Maitland, 'Mary Bateson', *The Athenaeum*, 1906, reprinted in H.A.L. Fisher (ed.), *The collected papers of Frederic William Maitland*, 3 vols (Cambridge, 1911), iii, pp 541–3, at p. 541. 16 Ibid., p. 542. 17 Bateson, *Customs*, i, pp 321–2. 18 Ibid., p. 322. 19 Ibid., p. ix. 20 Ibid., ii, p. xxxv; cf. ch. 61 below.

were a means of consolidating the power of the Anglo-Norman crown and baronage after the invasion. These formal legal instruments, granting rights and privileges to towns in exchange for money, helped to delineate the respective jurisdictions of crown and municipalities where local government was concerned. Some charters reflected or even derived from custumals, and thus chartered boroughs safeguarded older customs and privileges by grafting them onto the ban, the royal jurisdiction first used with the king's authority by his ministers, which was later exercised 'in the borough by mere burgesses, admitted by royal charter to stand in the place of the King's reeve'.[21]

What do these *Laws and usages* reveal about the particular case of Dublin? To what extent do they reflect pre-Conquest conditions in the city? How do they relate to the various royal charters granted to Dublin between 1171 and the grant of the mayoralty in 1229?[22] We hope that this completed English translation may prove useful in answering questions such as these, and may indeed prompt other speculations. Given the abundance of ground-breaking research produced in recent decades by historians of the medieval Irish capital, they will be in a particularly strong position to estimate the text's value as a source.

Presentation of the text

The chapter-headings are those of the Dublin custumal; square brackets indicate that the chapter-heading is absent from the Dublin version and has been supplemented by headings preserved in the Waterford text.

The chapter numbering is that of Mac Niocaill's edition in *Na buirgéisí*. The earlier edition in Gilbert's *Historic and municipal documents* did not introduce chapter-numbers but, for readers who may wish to work back from our translation to Gilbert's text, we supply references to his pages in bold within square brackets (hence **[p. 240]**, etc. below).

Since our translation of the great bulk of the chapters is, as discussed above, derived from Bateson's translation of extracts from the Waterford custumal, a note at the end of such chapters indicates the location of Bateson's translation in her *Borough customs*.

Since our field is not legal studies, for our own benefit and perhaps for that of others, we have looked for explanations of unfamiliar terms, and these too are provided in the notes as they occur.

21 Ibid., ii, p. xvi. **22** Seven royal charters pertaining to Dublin were published by Mac Niocaill, *Buirgéisí*, i, pp 75–89; cf. Howard B. Clarke, 'The 1192 charter of liberties and the beginnings of Dublin's municipal life', *DHR*, 46 (1993), 5–14; Seán Duffy, 'Town and crown: the kings of England and their city of Dublin' in Michael Prestwich, Richard Britnell, and Robin Frame (eds), *Thirteenth century England X. Proceedings of the Durham Conference 2003* (Woodbridge, 2005), pp 95–117.

[p. 240] LAWS AND USAGES OF THE CITY OF DUBLIN

THESE ARE THE LAWS AND USAGES OF THE CITY OF DUBLIN, WHICH EVERY CITIZEN IS BOUND TO KEEP WELL AND FREELY, WITHOUT INFRINGEMENT, FOR THEY WERE ESTABLISHED IN ANCIENT TIME.

1. **Of [trial by] battle:** According to the laws and customs of the city of Dublin, be it known that if a citizen wound a foreigner[23] whereby he [the foreigner] dies, and thereby cause for battle may arise, the citizen shall purge himself with forty loyal men,[24] whereby against a citizen the [appellant's] weapon[25] of every foreigner is broken, since a citizen shall never come to battle.[26]

2. **Of [compurgation[27] for] murder:** Further, even though it be a case of murder, still one ought to acquit oneself in this same manner.[28]

3. **Of landgable:**[29] Further, each burgage within the city must not exceed 64 feet, and will pay yearly landgable of 15 pence.

4. **Of assize of beer:** Further, every woman brewer[30] must pay 2 shillings per annum for the beer she sells, unless exempted by the bailiffs. Further, if she does not provide as good a beer as she should, or respect the assize like her neighbours and others, as declared throughout the city, she is fined 15 pence.

5. **Of summons:** Further, if any townsman, whoever he may be, has been summoned and fails to appear, the fine is 15 pence, unless he be exempted by the bailiffs.

6. **Of bakers:** Further, if any baker makes faulty bread, the first time he will be fined 15 pence, the second **[p. 241]** time 30 pence. The third time, he will stand on the pillory and will leave the city for a year and a day. If he wants to come back, he must leave his trade if he has no forgiveness from the mayor and the commonalty; and if he has the chance to go back to his trade, his stamp will be

23 *un foreyn*. 24 Bateson, *Customs*, i, p. 37, n. 1: 'The Waterford charter of 1205 gave compurgation by 12, that of 1232 by 24; no charter exists giving the oath by 40 [...] but in the MS from which the custumal is taken, Corpus Christi College Cambridge, MS 405 f.191, it seems to be claimed as a Waterford liberty conferred by Henry II, when he gave Waterford the liberties of Bristol. Dublin (to which Henry II did in November 1171 give the laws of Bristol) had the oath of 40 by John's charters of 1192 and 1200. The rule at Bristol is not known. Limerick had the oath of 40 by charter ... [Mac Niocaill, *Buirgéisí*, i, 238, §6]. In 1276 the king was advised to withdraw this liberty, which allowed a man to purge himself of a charge of murder by the oath of 40 men ... [Maurice Lenihan, *Limerick: its history and antiquities* (Dublin, 1866), p. 55]'. 25 Bateson, *Customs*, i, p. 37, n. 2; 'the [appellant's] weapon' is Bateson's translation of *le bastun de* (which in fact is omitted from the Waterford version). Bateson suggests: 'The reference is no doubt to the *baculus cornutus*, the combatant's weapon in trial by battle'. 26 Bateson, *Customs*, i, pp 36–7 (Waterford, ch. 1). 27 The action of clearing an individual man from a charge or accusation by the oaths of a number of others. 28 Ibid., i, p. 37 (Waterford, ch. 2). 29 A land tax akin to ground rent payable annually. 30 *chescune braceresce*, mistranscribed by Gilbert as *chescune ki aceresce*.

put on his bread. Further, even bakers who have not made faulty bread must add their stamp and names on their bread under a penalty of half a mark; and each master-baker who owns an oven must be responsible towards the mayor and the commonalty for the misdeeds and all sort of damage done by his servants and ensure that no more damage will come from them or any of their [kin]. If a misdeed happens, the aforementioned master-baker shall answer by life and limb if he has no other property.

7. **Of villeins and bondage:** Further, if a baron or a knight or other gentleman has villeins, after the fashion of the betagh,[31] and it happens that they are born on the land of the said baron or knight or other freeman, and he [the child so born] may not be held to right as his father was before him, and he takes to flight and comes to the city of Dublin, and does what is needful to enable him to be within the city, by leave of the mayor and the commonalty, as a bondsman, and is in bondage a year and a day without claim or challenge of his lord, whoever he may be, his lord shall never be able to have claim. And if the said bondsman wishes to advance himself beyond bondage, that is to say [to be] in franchise, then he can consider whether he will be in the franchise as a citizen or [remain] a bondsman.[32]

8. **Of testimony of a foreigner:** Further, no foreigner shall be witness against a citizen, unless he has no other witness, or unless he has come in a ship, and then one of the ship's company may well be a witness of any covenant that may be made; and if they be not lawful and trustworthy persons, recourse must be had to others who were of the ship's company if they can be found. And if they cannot be found, [the parties] **[p. 242]** shall be put on their own oath, and whoever fails, the amercement shall be half a mark, unless he have pardon from the bailiffs.[33]

9. **Of *fresche force*:**[34] Further, if any citizen hold a piece of land for a year and a day as of fee and of right, without claim, he shall not answer without the

31 Bateson, *Customs*, ii, p. 90 n. 1: *betagh* is an Irish term for villein. According to the *Dictionary of the Irish language* (RIA, Dublin, 1964), *biattach* is used to denote a 'supplier of food, victualler, farmer; of a land-holder or tenant whose duty it was to use his land to provide through the country' (reference was kindly given by the late Prof. Próinsas Ní Chatháin). Gearóid Mac Niocaill describes the *biatach* of the pre-invasion period as 'the typical Irish commoner' ('The origins of the *betagh*', *Irish Jurist*, 1 (1966), 292–8). However, K.W. Nicholls disagrees ('Anglo-French Ireland and after', *Peritia*, 1 (1982), 370–403). He thinks that the 'discussion of the *betagh* has suffered from that curious aberration which sees Gaelic Irish society as static in all its aspects' (p. 379), and argues that 'In Gaelic Fermanagh, at a later period the term *biatach* carried no implication of unfreedom or low status and one might question whether in the thirteenth century it carried any such implication in Gaelic Irish usage' (p. 378). He therefore sees 'no reason to assume that the *betaghs* with whom King John's administrators concerned themselves were anything but substantial pastoral farmers occupying considerable holdings' (p. 380). 32 Bateson, *Customs*, ii, pp 89–90 (Waterford, ch. 7). 33 Ibid., i, p. 168 (Waterford, ch. 8); an amercement is a fine. 34 *Fresche force* ('fresh force'), according to the *Anglo-Norman*

king's writ [or the writ of his justices].[35] And if claim be entered thereto within a year and a day, he shall answer without the king's writ if [at that time] there are lawful bailiffs [of the city].[36]

10. Of goods eloigned: Further, if any beast or chattel be attached within the bounds of the city of Dublin, the bailiffs ought to seize the said chattel into the city's hand, and ought to have 12 pence for their attachment, by way of forfeit. And if there be man or woman who seeks his beasts or chattels, he shall come forward and shall prove the same by skin and hide or by twelve lawful men that the beasts are his, and he shall have them quit. And if he who bought them cannot find his warrant on the day and at the term, he ought to find witnesses that he bought them well and lawfully, and in this case he ought to swear that he knows not what man sold them to him, and that he was never night or day in his company and that he knows not where he can be found; and besides this he shall lose the chattel. And if a man buys anything and cannot do this he is hangable by judgment, by the usage of the city, if he be not of the franchise.[37]

11. [Of summons]: Further, no man or woman [of the city] shall be summoned for the morrow [but shall have longer notice].[38]

12. Of apprentices: Further, every citizen ought to answer for his apprentice's wrongdoing and damage, made by day or by night, and at all times, as he would for his son if he were of age, that is to say, if he can count 12 pence, as is the law of citizens and burgesses.[39] And if the child be not of age as aforesaid [i.e., able to count to twelve] he is not bound to answer for him until he is of age.[40]

13. [p. 243] Of distraint: Further, when a man of the city has taken a distress,[41] no matter what kind of beast it may be, if the distress be in a neighbour's house, he who takes the distress cannot move the distresses outside of the house in which they lie distrained, until the judgment has been given upon them and upon him who is distrained, unless it so happen that the house is not easily guarded, or he in whose keeping the goods have been placed is poor, whereby they might be taken away forcibly before the proper time; in that case he who distrains on the goods and he in whose keeping the goods have been placed ought to come before the bailiffs and say, 'I beg you, master

dictionary, is 'a (threat of) forcible dispossession (recently committed); a writ, action or assise in a borough or other minor court to secure redress for a recent disseisin by force, threats or other violence' (http://www.anglo-norman.net/cgi-bin/form-s1). **35** Addition cancelled according to Mac Niocaill, *Buirgéisí*, i, p. 6, n. 1. **36** Bateson, *Customs*, i, p. 235 (Waterford, ch. 9). **37** Ibid., i, p. 59 (Waterford, ch. 10). **38** Ibid., i, p. 91 (Waterford, ch. 11). The chapter is given a title only in the Waterford version, which also has 'no man or woman *of the city*'. **39** Ibid., i, p. 222 (Waterford, ch. 12). **40** Ibid., i, p. 63 (Waterford, ch. 12). **41** 'Distress', according to *Black's law dictionary*, is 'the taking a personal chattel out of the possession of a wrong-doer into the custody of the party injured, to procure a satisfaction for a wrong committed' (http://thelawdictionary.org).

bailiffs, that the distresses which I have taken may be set in safer keeping, or I shall lose the distresses.' And if this be done without leave, he who does it, whoever he may be, shall be amerced.[42]

14. **[Of attachment of plea]:** Further, if any man or woman ought to have his summons, then it is proper that he who has given gage[43] should be at every hundred [court] and find pledges of this, unless it be [excused] by favour of the bailiffs; and if he make default, he and his pledges shall be amerced.[44]

15. **Of land let at farm:** Further, if a man or woman takes a house or curtilage or garden timbered with trees[45] for a term of years, and the said farmer despoils the house or the curtilage or the garden timbered with trees, without the leave of him who let the land, whoever he is, he shall lose his farm without any denial, unless he be allowed to continue to hold in order to repair the said house, curtilage, or garden.[46]

16. **[Of widowers' rights]:**[47] Further, if a man marries a woman who has sold land and the aforementioned man rents this land and they engender children, and lives with his wife and their children on this land, if his wife and children die before him, he will hold this land all his life as long as he lives on it. **[p. 244]** And if he lives elsewhere, he will hold it for only 40 days, if he has no other benefice.

17. **[Summons; when not necessary]:**[48] Further, no burgess need answer [without] summons within the city of Dublin before the bailiffs, unless he be absconding, or unless it be any man or woman who cannot be distrained, or one who has lost free law.[49]

18. **Proof of tallies and letters:**[50] Further, every citizen can prove his tally by his own hand, that is to say, the tally stands for two compurgators,[51] and himself for the third. And if he have open letters,[52] he who is plaintiff need do no more than show the seal if the defendant denies the debt.[53]

42 Bateson, *Customs*, i, pp 140–1 (Waterford, ch. 13). 43 Gage (Latin *vadium*) is an object or land given by way of security, guaranteeing the meeting of obligation, payment of debt, etc. 44 Bateson, *Customs*, i, p. 99 (Waterford, ch. 14). 45 *mesun ou curtilage, ou gardyn edefie des arbres.* 46 Bateson, *Customs*, i, p. 283 (Waterford, ch. 15). 47 Neither the Dublin nor the Waterford custumal gives a title to this chapter. 48 Ditto. 49 Bateson, *Customs*, i, p. 92 (Waterford, ch. 17); the term used is *fraunche ley*, meaning law-worthiness, the right of legal action in a case (see *Anglo-Norman dictionary*, s.v. 'franc'). 50 A 'tally', according to *Black's law dictionary*, means: 'A stick cut into two parts, on each whereof is marked, with notches or otherwise, what is due between debtor and creditor'. 51 A 'compurgator', according to *Black's law dictionary*, is: 'One of several neighbors of a person accused of a crime, or charged as a defendant in a civil action, who appeared and swore that they believed him on his oath'. 52 *Lettre overte,* according to the *Anglo-Norman dictionary*, is: 'letter patent, open letter delivered by or on behalf of the King (conferring a right or privilege)'. 53 Bateson, *Customs*, i, p. 203 (Waterford, ch. 18).

19. Of amercements laid down: Further, for maligning the mayor the mercy shall be 40 shillings. And he who maligns any of the 24 jurats shall be amerced 20 shillings. And he who maligns any of the citizens, his mercy shall be 10 shillings, that is to say for those who are not barrators [i.e., troublemakers]. And for those who are barrators the mercy shall be 2 shillings and the half remitted. And if they be foreigners they shall have only 20 pence and the half remitted. And if he be a sergeant of the town who is injured, the injured shall have as amends 40 pence if he will take it. And if blood be shed the mercy shall be half a mark. And if the blood of a foreigner be shed, the mercy is only 40 pence.[54]

20. Of amercements [for injury to] mayors, jurats and neighbours: Further, if the mayor be injured in any way the mercy shall be 40 pounds. And if [his] blood be shed the mercy shall be 100 pounds, or [the offender] shall lose his right hand or lie in prison for life. And if any of the 24 jurats be wounded, the mercy shall be 10 pounds. **[p. 245]** And if the blood of any other citizen who is not one of the 24 jurats be shed, the mercy shall be 5 pounds if he [the offender] be foreign. And if he be of the city it shall be done according to the laws and usages of the city. That is to say, if he be mayor 4 pounds, if he be a jurat 40 shillings, and if he be not a jurat 20 shillings as a citizen and neighbour.[55]

21. Of *fresche force*: Further, if a man or woman makes purpresture [i.e., encroachment] on another in the manner of fresh force, he [the disseisee] shall not be bound to purchase the king's writ, unless it be that he suffers the other to keep in seisin for a year and a day.[56] And if he [the disseisor] has seisin for a year and a day, he shall not answer without the king's writ. And if he has not held for a year and a day, he shall answer at once without the king's writ.[57]

22. Of waste *pendente brevi* [pending a writ]: Further, if a man or woman is impleaded of land, and he fears to lose the land, he may carry off anything that is on the land before the view is made, but not after.[58]

23. Of pleas in court Christian:[59] Further, the mayor and commonalty of Dublin ought to send their sergeants to every consistory and every chapter, and forbid those of the court Christian to plead anything touching the king's crown and dignity. And if those of the court Christian do so, King Henry[60] has granted the citizens [the right] to attach the bodies of those who have held such pleas in court Christian contrary to the king's crown and dignity, until

54 Ibid., ii, pp 21–2 (Waterford, ch. 19). 55 Ibid., ii, p. 22 (Waterford, ch. 20). 56 'Seisin', according to *Black's law dictionary*, is 'the completion of the feudal investiture, by which the tenant was admitted into the feud, and performed the rights of homage and fealty'. 57 Bateson, *Customs*, i, p. 235 (Waterford, ch. 21). The Waterford title of this chapter is *De purpresturis* ('Concerning encroachment'). 58 Ibid., i, p. 287 (Waterford, ch. 22). 59 i.e., ecclesiastical courts. 60 The king is not named in the Waterford copy.

they shall have made amends to the aforesaid mayor and bailiffs and commonalty. And he who pleads in this court and can have right in the court of the city shall have by right judgment imprisonment for a year and a day, and shall lose the franchise, as one who goes about to injure the franchise, unless he has favour of the bailiffs.[61]

24. [p. 246] Of pleas outside the liberty: Further, if any man gives work to another man from the city at an exchequer, or chapter, or the archbishop's court, or any other court outside the boundaries and walls of the city, he may be fined 20 shillings, and be sent to gaol, unless he have pardon from the mayor or the bailiffs.

25. Of [lands let at] farm: Further, if a man or woman has let to another a house or piece of land or a garden under cultivation for a term of years, and it chances that he who has leased the same to farm comes forward and enfeoffs[62] another, be it man or woman, within the term aforenamed, the lessee who has the aforenamed land at hire and holds the same, need not leave his farm unless it seems good to him, and if he wishes to keep the aforesaid farm on, he very well may during his term. And if he who has leased the land at farm comes and ousts the farmer within his term, the said farmer may give his gage [to sue], as in a case of *fresche force*, that he has put him out wrongfully from his free farm within his term. 'And [to prove] that this is true I have what is necessary for me.' And by lawful men who were at the [making of the] agreement, if he has them ready, he shall at once proceed. And if he has not got them ready, he may say that he will have them on [such] a day and at [such] a term. And if it chance that the witnesses die within the aforesaid term, the aforesaid bailiffs ought without delay to make inquest by [right of] their office by lawful neighbours. And if it chance that he who leased the land at farm falls into mercy, the amercement shall be 20 shillings without any abatement. And if it chance that he who leased the land at farm wishes to sell or let it, he ought to offer it in the first place **[p. 247]** to the farmer who holds the same, that is to say, if the term of the lease has not elapsed. And he shall say: 'Fair sir, so much is offered for the land which you hold at farm', and then he may name what sum he pleases. The lessee may say, if he wishes to have it, 'What another will give, I will give.' And if he does not wish to have it, he shall keep the land during his term, in spite of the other's money,[63] without any denial.[64]

26. Of bequests in a will [to the religious]: Further, no rent of assize may be given to a house of religion, and this is to say wherefore. If it chance that a man has a house that is free and pays only a pound of cumin or a grain of

61 Bateson, *Customs*, ii, pp 205–6 (Waterford, ch. 23). **62** *Enfeoffer*, according to the *Anglo-Norman dictionary*, is: 'to give fee and seisin of land; to transfer rights to rent, services, etc …'. **63** Bateson, *Customs*, i, p. 313; in n. 4, she suggests 'Or, perhaps, "in the teeth of the other"'. **64** Ibid., i, pp 312–13 (Waterford, ch. 25).

pepper or a rose, and he thinks that he can give half a mark or 10 shillings, and he thinks that even if he has an heir he can give this much of his goods for his soul to a house of religion, for himself, he cannot and shall not do it if he is wise. And the reason why is that if it should chance that the house be burnt, or blown down by the wind, or fall for want of being kept up, and in such case the rent of the worthy man's devise may be in arrears for six or ten years, then the religious themselves can enter the said house for their alms in disherison of the heirs and in disherison of the city. And if every citizen were to do the same, the city might soon be for the greater part in the hands of people of religion, and the reason why is that when houses of religion have once entered [upon property] they give nothing and render nothing and do nothing for the town like the neighbours and others, as in tallages and town customs which belong to the city, whereby the city might incur damage [in paying] the lord's aid. And further, in this way men's heirs may become beggars and the city be deprived of young people to defend the city if war should break out, or other ills occur, which God forbid.[65]

27. [p. 248] Of summons at fairs: Further, there lies no summons at the city fair while it lasts.[66]

28. [Archbishop's fair pleas]: Further, pleas to the archbishop, as at fair time, last only from one day at noon to another day at noon.[67] And if anyone from the city complains there to a bailiff or the archbishop and could obtain justice in the court of the city, he shall be amerced 20 shillings. And if he is unable to pay the fine, he shall be sent to gaol for 40 days, unless he have pardon from the mayor and the commonalty; the reason for this is that he is near to infringing the laws of the city.

29. Of the making of charters: Further, if it chance that the mayor or a citizen buys land in fee to him and his heirs, beware that his charter does not say that he is enfeoffed by homage and service, for if he be enfeoffed by homage and service, wardship and marriage will be due.[68]

30. Of the viewing of the slain and making inquest: Further, if it chance that a man be killed within the metes and bounds of the city, he must not be buried before the coroners have seen him. And when the corpse is viewed, inquest must be made by twelve of the nearest neighbours. And if the inquest says that such a one is guilty and that they know none other guilty but him only, the bailiffs must enquire, as of their office, how and in what way he is guilty, as in defending himself, or in play, or in hate or rage or drunkenness, or

65 Ibid., ii, pp 202–3 (Waterford, ch. 26). **66** Ibid., ii, p. 187 (Waterford, ch. 27). **67** Ibid., ii, p. 187; this chapter belongs only to the Dublin custumal: Bateson explains, n. 1: 'Not in the Waterford MS, there being at Waterford no rival archiepiscopal jurisdiction.' **68** Ibid., ii, pp 83–4 (Waterford, ch. 29).

through ill-will between them, or by the incitement of another, whereby the dead man was further from life and nearer to death, and whether he who is dead might have escaped if he had chosen. Thus in such manner the bailiffs ought to examine the inquest and counsel them to tell the truth. **[p. 249]** And two sergeants ought to keep the inquest, so that no man or woman who is connected with the dead or the living may come to speak to any of the inquest. And when the inquest comes in, thus shall the bailiff[69] say: 'Are you at one?' 'Sir, yes. We tell you by the oath that we have sworn that we know no one guilty if it be not this one.' Or peradventure they shall say that it was the defendant, or they shall say that[70] he was an enemy, or they shall say that if the one had not killed the other, then he would have been killed himself, and the bailiff shall say again to the inquest: 'Go out again, and by the oath that you have sworn[71] do not fail, through love of the citizen or through hate of the foreigner who is dead, to speak the truth, as you desire not to be attainted before the justices.' Then they shall go out again to take counsel, and come in and say, 'So help us God, and by the oath that we have sworn, we know not what more to say than what we have said.' Then the bailiff shall say, 'Sergeant, have him arrested if he be found within your power. And if he be not found within your power, take these letters and deliver them to the sheriff and tell him to do as the letters direct, if he can find the man within his power, and beg him that he do this for us as he would that we should do unto him in like case.'[72]

31. Counsel: Further, he who dwells in the house where the man[73] was killed (if he wishes to save himself and his household, and if they have not themselves done the deed), shall take twelve of his nearest neighbours, or as many as he can get, and say, 'Good neighbours, this mischance has come to me, that a man or woman was killed in my house whilst I was outside, wherefore if it happens later on that the mayor or the bailiffs make any claim against me or any of mine, you can **[p. 250]** bear witness that neither I nor any of mine is guilty or has done any wrong.' And if he does not do so, he is attachable, he and all those who were in the house, unless they have favour of the mayor and bailiffs.[74]

32. Sound counsel: Further, take good care, you and your household, that you trespass not against any of those neighbours whom you called to your house, there where the slaying was done, before the inquest is over. And the reason is this: if it chance that you or any of yours abuse any of those neighbours who were at the inquest, you or he who talked abusively may be taken or charged, wherefore no man or woman ought to talk abusively, but hold his tongue. For no man or woman knows what may happen.[75]

69 The Waterford text reads 'one of the bailiffs'. **70** Waterford omits the phrase 'it was the defendant, or they shall say that'. **71** The Waterford text reads 'made and sworn'. **72** Ibid., i, pp 13–15 (Waterford, ch. 30). **73** The Waterford text adds 'or woman'. **74** Ibid., i, pp 14–15 (Waterford, ch. 31). **75** Ibid., i, pp 14–15 (Waterford, ch. 32). The

33. **Of *miskennyng*:**[76] Further, there is a cause of *miskennyng*, that is to say that it may be a cause of *miskennyng* if perchance it happens that a man sues at the bar and the other party answers him, the respondent might rise, go out, and imparl [i.e., speak] once, twice, and thrice, and at any time while the bailiffs are on the bench. And if you wish to know what *miskennyng* is, I will tell you. If a man has said to the bench something which he ought not to have said, and he perceives that his *counte* is not as good as it ought to be,[77] he who does this can recover his *counte* at any time while the bailiffs are on the bench, but not afterwards.[78]

34. **Of thieves:** Further, if a thief be taken *hand-habend*[79] and *back-berend*,[80] he shall be hanged by the judgment of the *tounderie*,[81] for he shall never be taken to the gaol to await his judgment, unless he be of such birth that the mayor chooses to send him there.[82]

35. **Of clerks not being hanged:** Further, if he who is taken be a clerk, he ought to be **[p. 251]** taken to the prison. And if he be a layman a priest shall be provided to confess him, and then he shall be well and duly hanged, and he who hangs him shall have the felon's best garment or 4 pence.[83]

36. **Of the malice of bailiffs:** Further, if the provost sits in the *tounderie*, and a man or woman comes before him there who perchance does not know the law of the city as he should, and perchance the bailiff through an old hate grows angry with the man who comes before him, and charges him with having said or done something which he never intended, the bailiff cannot put him to the oath unless he chooses, provided he makes no denial; but if he makes denial he shall purge himself with the seventh hand [i.e., with seven compurgators]. And he shall say, 'Sir, you may say your will, as bailiff'. And against a neighbour,[84] he can purge himself with the third hand.[85]

title of the Dublin custumal includes the adjective *sanum*; this is omitted in the Waterford copy. **76** According to the *Anglo-Norman dictionary*, *miskennyng* is 'mispleading, wrong or false plea', and according to *Black's law dictionary*, in Saxon and Old English law it means 'an unjust or irregular summoning to court; to speak unsteadily in court; to vary in one's plea'. **77** According to the *Anglo-Norman dictionary*, *co[u]nte* means 'count, plea, (formal statement of basis of case at beginning of an action)'. **78** Bateson, *Customs*, ii, p. 2 (Waterford, ch. 33). **79** i.e., having stolen goods in his possession. **80** i.e., carrying away stolen goods. **81** Bateson, *Customs*, i, p. 322, explains: 'A court and a lock-up "en la tounderie" are more than once referred to in the Dublin custumal … The court "en la tounderie" is contrasted …[see ch. 60] with the hundred court. The hundred court appears as the court for king's pleas and real actions, and it may be concluded that the court in the "tounderie" was the court in which the less important personal actions were treated, the mayor's daily, weekly, or fortnightly sessions […] The Dublin and Waterford "tounderie" seems, like the Bristol "tundred", to have been a court at the tolsey', the latter meaning the tholsel or guildhall. **82** Bateson, *Customs*, i, p. 53 (Waterford, ch. 34). Waterford adds 'of his grace' after 'mayor'. **83** Ibid., i, pp 53–4 (Waterford, ch. 35). **84** Ibid., ii, p. 8, n. 1, specifies: 'a fellow-burgess, not an officer'. **85** Ibid., ii, pp 7–8 (Waterford, ch. 36).

37. **Of just distraint:** Further, no man shall ever distrain without the bailiff's leave. And if he does so, he is amerced 12 pence.[86]

38. **Of proof of tally:** Further, any citizen can well prove his tally by his own hand without witness and inquiry if he is trustworthy and has never been inculpated of untrue oath.

39. **Of breach of covenant:** Further, if there be any covenant made concerning money or land or merchandise, and one of the parties would withdraw from the covenant, he who does so shall give 20 shillings if the other party will accept the same.[87]

40. **Of God's pennies:**[88] Further, whoever gives God's silver and repents, be he who he may, shall pay 10 shillings.[89]

41. **Of earnest-money:**[90] Further, if a man or woman gives earnest to another and it chance that he or she does not get the goods **[p. 252]** for which earnest has been given, he shall only double the earnest, and the other can ask for no more.[91]

42. **Of distraint in the chamber:** Further, the sergeants of the town ought to take distraints in the hall and never in the chamber.[92] And if the sergeant be taken in the chamber, he may be taken and well beaten, and he can bring no action, unless it be that the man or wife were abusive towards the bailiffs or towards the mayor, or if he or she would not submit, then distress may be taken in hall and chamber and everywhere.[93]

43. **Of slocking:**[94] Further, if a citizen has a servant or a nurse or another valet like a servant, and it happens that his neighbour takes his servant out of his house, he is amerced 10 shillings. But if he or she be not a citizen, the amercement is but 5 shillings.[95]

44. **Of the same:** Further, if it chance that through the lack of a servant or a nurse he who had the servant or nurse, or his son or his daughter, should die for want of the servant, he who enticed away the servant without leave of the

86 Ibid., i, p. 110 (Waterford, ch. 37). 87 Ibid., i, p. 213 (Waterford, ch. 39). 88 'God's penny', according to *Black's law dictionary*, denotes 'money given as evidence of the completion of a bargain', and is associated with 'earnest-money'. 89 Bateson, *Customs*, i, p. 218 (Waterford, ch. 40). She explains (p. 218, n. 5): 'In the first case the buyer repents, in the second the seller, and his fine is the lighter. Earnest and God's penny, both paid by the buyer, differ only in so far as earnest went to the seller, God's penny to a religious establishment'. 90 'Earnest', according to *Black's law dictionary*, is 'the payment of a part of the price of goods sold, or the delivery of part of such goods, for the purpose of binding the contract'. 91 Bateson, *Customs*, i, p. 218 (Waterford, ch. 41). 92 Ibid., i, p. 105, n. 1: 'The room reserved for the use of the master and mistress, the sitting-room and bedroom combined'. 93 Ibid., i, pp 104–5 (Waterford, ch. 42). 94 *slockyng* (enticing a servant from his master): see Bateson, i, p. 322. 95 Ibid., i, p. 216 (Waterford, ch. 43).

master is held bound to answer in life and limb for that he would not warn the master, as one friend would warn another.[96]

45. **Of the same:** Further, if a citizen desires to have the servant of another citizen, he ought to come to the worthy man or the worthy woman and say: 'Sir or madam, your servant or your nurse has offered me their service, but I do not wish to have them without your leave'. And if so be that the worthy man or the worthy woman to whom the servant belongs is willing to give leave, then the servant may go and serve where he or she chooses. And he who will engage the servant or the nurse should take two witnesses of the worthy man or the worthy woman, so that he may not be challenged hereafter concerning his servants.[97]

46. **[p. 253] Delays in the writ of right:**[98] Further, if a man or woman be impleaded concerning land by a writ of the king, and if you want to know what are the delays, they are as those who are in land, six weeks on the one side and six weeks on the other, and six weeks in the king's hand close, and six weeks in the king's hand open. And then he who is tenant of the land shall come forward and replevy his land within the 40 days. And if he does not do so, then there is open default. And if he does so, the land shall be released to him by plevin,[99] binding him or her to come to the next hundred [court] to answer as should be done by the usages of the city. And then afterwards he can ask a [court] day to answer. And after the day to answer you can cast one essoin.[100] And after the essoin comes the view of the land. And after the view of the land, an essoin, and after that essoin comes the vouching to warrant. And after the[101] vouchor, if your warrant be not of age, he need nowise answer until the time when he is of age, or you will do him wrong.[102]

47. **Of latrines:** Further, no man or woman shall have or place their latrine leaving less than two and a half feet between the latrine and their neighbour's land.

48. **Of pigsties:** Further, pigsties will be situated at the same distance from the neighbour's land if he has not the agreement of his neighbour, and even if he has his agreement, they must make sure not to quarrel,[103] whatever should happen.

96 Ibid., i, p. 216 (Waterford, ch. 44). **97** Ibid., i, pp 216–17 (Waterford, ch. 45). The final word is in the singular in the Waterford copy. **98** 'Writ of right', according to *Black's law dictionary*, was 'a writ which lay for one who had the right of property, against another who had the right of possession and the actual occupation'. **99** 'Plevin', according to *Black's law dictionary*, is a term used for a warrant, an assurance or a security. **100** 'Essoin', according to *Black's law dictionary*, is a term used 'to present or offer an excuse for not appearing in court on an appointed day in obedience to a summons'. **101** In the Waterford copy: *vostre* [your]. **102** Bateson, *Customs*, i, pp 254–5 (Waterford, ch. 46). **103** We have opted for the Waterford custumal's use of *estrit* rather than the Dublin custumal's term *escrit*, as the former yields a more plausible interpretation for the context.

49. [Of prises]:[104] Further, no justiciar of the king, no chancellor, no treasurer, no escheator, nor any other minister of the king will take a prise within the city such as of wheat or any other commodity, without the authorization of the mayor and the bailiffs; and if they have the authorization, they will get a sergeant of the town who will remove the goods.

50. [p. 254] Of *Mort d'ancestor*:[105] Further, in the hundred of the city of Dublin, a man may use the writ of right in manner of a *mort d'ancestor* without any complaint on the part of the justices.[106]

51. Of hue and cry: Further, if hue and cry be raised by day or by night, every neighbour who does not come at the cry, as reason demands, shall be amerced half a mark by the law of the city. And he who raises the hue and cry shall be brought to the prison, and shall be replevied out of prison: this unless his life was in danger or his house broken into, or other injury was threatened whereby he was forced to raise the hue and cry, and provided the neighbours roundabout can bear witness for him before the bailiffs. And if he makes hue and cry where there is no need, he shall go to prison, and if he has any friend who will replevy him, he very well may be replevied and then the amercement is 10 shillings. And if he has nothing whereon the 10 shillings can be levied, he shall stay in prison forty days. And if he wishes to remain in the city, he shall find good security that no harm or mischief or hue or cry shall in any way arise again through him or any of his [kin]. And if he cannot do this, he shall leave the city for ever and shall never come back.[107]

52. Of the 'Courtesy of England':[108] Further, if a citizen takes a wife who has land and it happens that they have a child and that the child is perhaps so weakly that it cannot live and the wife so weakly that she dies, yet if the child can be heard to cry so that two men or women[109] can bear witness to the

104 The seizure of goods for the king's use. **105** An assize brought by the rightful heir against a person for wrongfully taking possession of his or her inheritance on the 'death of an ancestor'. **106** Bateson, *Customs*, i, p. 255 (Waterford, ch. 50). She adds, n. 2: 'This appears to be the meaning of a somewhat obscure sentence'. **107** Ibid., i, pp 1–2 (Waterford, ch. 51). **108** Gilbert (in *CARD*, i, p. 227, n. 3) has the following: '"La curtesie d'Engleterre", [or] "jus curialitatis Anglie" [was] a special privilege having the force of law in England and Ireland, under which a freehold might be acquired by the father of issue born alive. Under this privilege, right to profits of tolls at Dublin, paid by ships for "perchage" or the use of buoys, was claimed in 1347–8, in a petition to Edward III, and his Council in England, by John de Grauntsete [for whom, see ibid., pp 112–14 …] The petition, which is in French, stated as follows: "Et le dit Johan et Alice, iadis sa femme, en sa vie estoient seisitz de la custume de perchage en la fraunchese de la citee de Dyvelyn, come de fee et de droit la dite Alice, et la dite Alice morust seisy. Apres qi mort l'avant dit Johan mesme la custume du perchage tient par la curtesie d'Engleterre, la reversion de ycelle regardant a Wauter de Graunsete, lour fitz et heire. De quele custume la dite Alice ses auncestres et lour feffours estoient seisitz peisiblement du temps dont memoire ne court"'. **109** Bateson, *Customs*, ii, p. 113, n. 1, observes that 'The common law required the witnesses

husband that they heard the child cry, in that case the said citizen shall have the land for his life. But if this be not the case, he shall have it only for forty days.[110]

53. **[Of summons]:** Further, there is no man of the city who is in the franchise who ought to be summoned [to an inquest] or make any oath unless he chooses, unless he be summoned for the death of a man or for robbery, larceny, arson, burglary, or other crime which concerns the crown.[111]

54. **[p. 255] [Of putting on inquests]:** Further, as long as married men can be found to be put on inquests a single man ought never to be taken, unless it be of his own free will, or because there are not enough people, or because he knows more than others.[112]

55. **Of alienation made to the Hospitallers:** Further, if a[113] citizen buys a [piece of] land, and it happens that this man be dying and this citizen comes and gives that land to his wife for her life, and it happens that the aforesaid wife sees that their heirs are weak, and she enfeoffs a house of religion as in the name of her husband and under his seal, or by will as in the name of her husband, and it happens that her husband is so ill[114] that he cannot help himself, and this will or feoffment is made whilst he is alive, and the said [house of religion][115] comes forward and takes the house which is enfeoffed or devised by will, while the man lies ill, and this woman comes and takes feoffment of the said house from this house of religion, and sets a sign upon this house as a mark[116] of the Temple or of the Hospital, and it happens that this same man enfeoffs his heir during his life or devises [the land] to him by will, and [when] the aforesaid wife is dead, it happens that the heir of the worthy man from whom the land is held puts in a claim, and the heir of the wife puts in a claim, so that both make claim, then the mayor ought, in the right of his office, to take the house, or the land, or the rent into his hand, and he who claims to have right in the same ought to give the mayor 100 shillings[117] for taking the inquest of the town on which of the two heirs has right. And if the inquest says that the heir of the worthy man has right, and no righter heir

to be men'. **110** Ibid., ii, p. 113 (Waterford, ch. 52). **111** Ibid., ii, p. 58 (Waterford, ch. 53). **112** Ibid., i, p. 48 (Waterford, ch. 54). **113** Gilbert (ed.), *Hist. & mun. docs*, p. 255, mistakenly transcribes the Dublin Chain Book indefinite article *un* as *une*. **114** In the Waterford custumal: 'so weak and ill'. **115** Waterford custumal's *chelle* is *celle femme* in the Dublin custumal. Bateson replaces the phrase by *mesun de religion* as it 'seems required by the sense': see Bateson, *Customs*, ii, p. 203, n. 2. **116** Ibid., ii, p. 204, n. 2, suggests that 'mark' could mean 'cross' and she refers to Stat. Westm. II, ch. 33: 'In as much as tenants set up crosses in prejudice of their lords, to defend themselves by the privileges of Templars and Hospitallers, it is ordained that such lands shall be treated as mortmain.' 'Mortmain', according to *Black's law dictionary*, denotes 'the alienation of lands or tenements to any corporation, sole or aggregate, ecclesiastical or temporal'. **117** Ibid., ii, p. 204, n. 3, remarks that 'the sum is very large, perhaps to be prohibitive'.

is known than he, he ought to be put in his seisin at once, so that no man or woman come [to claim it] within a year and a day. And he who is put in seisin shall give to each of the sergeants who puts him in seisin 4 shillings. And if it happens that the heir of the wife comes afterwards to demand [restitution for] the wrong done to her, he loses free law for ever without recovery, and all the heirs who issue from such heir, unless he will buy double as dear as the other would be willing to give.[118]

56. [p. 256] Of fugitives to the church: Further, if a man or woman has fled to a church because of killing or for larceny or for receiving criminals, and is in the church, the bailiffs[119] ought to send for a sergeant to cause the neighbours to be summoned to watch the church that the thieves do not escape. And then the bailiffs[120] shall come and shall ask those who are in the church if they will come to the peace of the king or if they wish to keep in the church. And if within 40 days they will come out and abjure the king's realm, the bailiffs[121] ought to charge them thus:[122] Form of the oath: 'This hear you, sirs, bailiffs[123], that we (N.) by name, abjure the king's realm, for the killing which we have done, or for the larceny done, or for the receiving we have done' (or for other wrongs which they have done), 'we abjure the realm for the felony which we have done, so that we will never enter here again unless it be by leave of the king or by leave of his ministers.'[124] And as soon as the bailiffs have done this, they shall set their oath and their names and the date in the roll of the town.[125]

57. [Watch and ward]:[126] Further, the bailiffs of the town ought to carry out their office by governing the four quarters of the town so that no larceny or damage or mischief may happen to the city. And this they ought to do four times a year. And if any damage or mischief happens, the bailiffs are bound to answer for all the mischief and damage that is done.[127]

58. Of pigs: Further, no man or woman shall have pigs at large outside their house if they have not the grace of the bailiffs. If they do not have it, the bailiffs will have such animals slaughtered on three occasions a year.

59. Of lepers: Further, one must not permit any leper to enter the city, unless it be the case that a sick man is accompanied by someone healthy, to look for food. **[p. 257]** And if any man gives them lodging, he will be fined half a mark, or imprisoned for forty days, saving the grace of the bailiffs.

118 Ibid., ii, pp 203–4 (Waterford, ch. 55). **119** The Waterford custumal adds *e corouners* ('and coroners'). **120** Waterford: *corouners* ('coroners'). **121** Waterford: *corouners* ('coroners'). **122** Ibid., ii, pp 34–5 (Waterford, ch. 56). **123** The Waterford version changes 'bailiffs' to 'coroners'. It also uses the first person singular pronoun (*joe*) where the Dublin copy uses the plural form (*nous*). **124** The Waterford custumal adds *si dieu etc* ('so [help me] God etc …'). **125** Ibid., ii, pp 34–5 (Waterford, ch. 56). **126** Neither the Dublin nor the Waterford custumal gives a title to this chapter. **127** Ibid., ii, p. 28 (Waterford, ch. 57). Waterford adds *coueroners &* ('coroners and'), in both occurrences in

60. Of pleaders: Further, if a pleader comes before the justices or before the mayor in the hundred of the city, or before the bailiffs in the *tounderie*, and is to plead for a man or for a woman, and it happens that he is disavowed, he shall be sent to prison. And if he has the grace of the bailiffs so that he does not go to prison, he shall give 10 shillings, unless he has grace of the mayor and bailiffs.[128]

61. Of fire: Further, if the house of a man goes up in flames, through fire, and the flames spread beyond the house or to any other place, the fine is 20 shillings, as long as the fire causes no damage to any of the neighbours. Further, should it happen that a fire is caused by a servant who serves a worthy man, let the servant be taken and cast into the fire if he can be caught. And if he cannot be caught, he should be sought by four sergeants in the four quarters of the town. And if he can be found he shall be attached, and then the city shall take an inquest there where the harm was done. And if he be guilty of the arson he shall hang.[129]

62. Of the bringing of rents: Further, if a man or woman ought to bring rent to another, and he will not receive it, as his ancestors were wont to do before him, he who ought to bring the rent should come before the bailiffs and say: 'Sirs, bailiffs, thus [it is]; I hold land of this man, and he will not receive the rent, as his ancestors were wont to do.' The bailiffs shall cause him to be summoned before them and shall demand wherefore he will not receive his rent. And if he says, 'Sir, I will not receive it,' then he who bears the rent ought to pay the rent to the bailiffs and cause it to be enrolled, **[p. 258]** so that the other who will not receive his rent, shall never recover it, unless he shows cause to the bailiffs.[130]

63. [Of oppression of houses]: Further, if it chance that one house lies up against another, and the wall-course of one neighbour is placed where the house on the other side ought to be, the neighbour ought to move his wall-course until such time as his neighbour has put up the frame of (?) his house, without strife or dispute.[131]

64. [Of the apprentice]: Further, if it chance that two foreigners come to the city, and one should become apprentice to the other, and strife should arise between them, and the master should assault his apprentice, the apprentice may make complaint to the bailiffs. And then the master can take a love-day,[132]

this chapter. **128** Bateson, *Customs*, ii, p. 12 (Waterford, ch. 60). **129** Ibid., i, p. 77 (Waterford, ch. 61). **130** Ibid., i, pp 313–14 (Waterford, ch. 62). **131** Bateson, *Customs*, i, pp 249–50 (Waterford, ch. 63); she translates *lit* by 'wall-course' and adds, n. 7: 'Possibly a box-bed in the thickness of the wall might be disturbed by the falling down or the removal of the adjoining house, but *lit* has also the sense *of course* in building.' Bateson (ibid., p. 249, n. 6) adds that the chapter is 'perhaps alluding to the collapse of one house upon another'. **132** *Un jour d'amour*: this, according to *Black's law dictionary*, is (in Old English law) 'the

and if the apprentice will not come, the master can put him in bondage. And if so be that they cannot agree by their love-day, albeit the apprentice makes plaint, the master shall have his summons; and if he will not come he shall be attached [and brought] to the prison. And if the apprentice be a bondman, the master need only find pledges, unless the apprentice be in danger of death.[133]

65. Of loans: Further, if a man or woman of the *uppelaunde* [i.e., rural parts] lends goods to one of the city and cannot recover his debt in due course, he may go to the bailiffs and give some wherewithal to the king's box, either the half or the third part of the debt, or such sum as may be agreed on, and then the bailiffs must pay him without delay.[134]

66. [Of distraint]: Further, if the distress of a villein be taken, he who has taken it is not bound to release it unless it be at the request of his neighbour, and he [the neighbour] must replevy it in such a way that if the debtor does not make satisfaction, he who replevied shall restore the distress if they cannot come to an agreement. And if they cannot come to an agreement he [the creditor] ought to distrain him [the pledge] once, twice, and a third time, and he may keep the distress until he has made agreement, unless some grace be granted (?).[135]

67. Of buying fresh animal-skins: Further, no man or woman shall buy fresh animal-skin or wool within the city unless he be a citizen. And no man or woman must cut cloth for a tavern keeper or sell wine in a jug unless he is in bondage; and if he is in bondage, he will have 40 days to sell his wine and nothing more.

68. [p. 259] Of payment of foreign merchants: Further, if a citizen buys merchandise of a foreigner from a strange land, if it so be that the citizen will not make satisfaction as soon as the merchant is ready to return to his country overseas, the said citizen shall have only three ebbs and three floods as delay. And if the said merchant cannot get his payment within the three ebbs and three floods, the bailiffs shall make payment to the stranger, if he is willing, and they shall recover from the debtor.[136]

69. Note [Of service on inquests]: Further, no man is bound to be on an inquest unless he wishes to be so of his own free will, and especially not by any distress from the mayor or bailiffs, unless it be because of a man's death or other matter which touches the dignity and crown of the king.[137]

70. Of vouching to warrant: Further, if a man or woman enfeoffs another and dies, and the heirs [of the feoffee and the feoffor] come, and the one

day on which any dispute was amicably settled between neighbours'. 133 Bateson, *Customs*, i, pp 228–9 (Waterford, ch. 64). 134 Ibid., i, p. 127 (Waterford, ch. 65). 135 Ibid., i, pp 136–7 (Waterford, ch. 66). 136 Ibid., ii, pp 184–5 (Waterford, ch. 68). 137 Ibid., ii, p. 58 (Waterford, ch. 69).

impleads the other, and perchance one of them has to vouch, and he who is vouched comes forward and says, 'It is wrong that I should have to warrant, and the reason for this is what I hold, I hold by devise of my father or my mother or my brother: then ought the mayor by his office ask him if he has any brothers, or, if the party be a woman, he shall ask her if she has any sisters or brothers, and if they are older. Perchance they will say yes or no. [If yes] he or she shall not answer at all without the elder brother or sister, although the elder may dwell without the city and the younger within the city. Further, if the elder brother has no goods within the city whereby he can [be] distrain[ed] he who sues against him as the warrantor ought to vouch another [brother] to warrant by aid of the court. But if there is only one brother and he dwells within the city, although he holds under a devise, he shall warrant to the other party the deed of his father, mother, or brother, unless there is a more rightful heir, [for] even if the thing had not been devised, it would have descended to this same brother.[138]

71. [p. 260] [Of the response of sisters]: Further, if there are several females and a writ runs against one and not against all, the writ is abatable. And if there is but one sister, she shall answer after her delays, and shall warrant if the other [the vouchor] has charter or word of mouth.[139]

72. [Duty of pledging]:[140] Further, no man or woman shall be pledge for his tenant, who is taken for felony, larceny, or any other misdeed, unless he chooses; and the amercement is 40 shillings, and the half is pardoned if the worthy man mainprises the felon and he escapes.[141] And if the worthy man has become pledge for a felon who escapes, if the worthy man causes him to be sought for and can find him, he shall bring him back to the city, and if he cannot bring him back by his own force, he shall have the town's letters to cause him to be taken in whatever place he may be found, and the worthy man shall be quit of amercement because of his pursuit.[142]

73. Of the taking of a gage: Further, if a gage be taken for a landgable rent due from any house, he who owes the rent shall be amerced for his rent arrears. And furthermore he shall lose his gage forever, unless it be delivered within a fortnight, unless he has favour from the bailiffs.[143]

74. Of bakehouses: Further, if a baker takes a bakehouse, in fee, to him and his heirs, for a certain annual rent, and he who took the bakehouse does not name the vessels which belong to the bakehouse in his covenant, before the charter is sealed, he who sells the bakehouse can recover all the vessels, unless he be gracious.[144]

138 Ibid., i, pp 269–70 (Waterford, ch. 70). 139 Ibid., i, p. 270 (Waterford, ch. 71). 140 Neither custumal gives a title to this chapter. 141 Ibid., i, p. 101 (Waterford, ch. 72). 142 Ibid., i, p. 9 (Waterford, ch. 72, continued). 143 Ibid., i, p. 303 (Waterford, ch. 73). 144 Ibid., i, p. 320 (Waterford, ch. 74). Vessels here means baking bowls, etc.

75. [Of the paying of landgable]: Further, if a man be impleaded concerning land which owes landgable, he can replevy his house for the landgable that he ought to pay within the year and day. And if he does not pay within the year and day he shall lose his land for his [unpaid] landgable, although he has never been impleaded, as if he owed [landgable at the rate of] 20 shillings a year.[145]

76. Of thieves: Further, if a thief be taken *hand-habend* and *back-berend*,[146] he shall be hanged at once, whatever hour of the day it may be, before dinner or after. And if the said thief says that such a one **[p. 261]** was his companion,[147] whoever such a man may be,[148] the bailiffs ought in right of their office to hold an inquest at once, and if he be an honest man he shall be let go, and if he be guilty he shall be dealt with as the court may order.[149]

77. Of farm: Further, if a man or a woman take land or a house for a term[150] so that the land belongs to the woman, and husband and wife let out this land for their sustenance, and then it happens that the husband dies before his wife, and the wife comes forward and enters claim to it after her husband's death, and says that she was in ward to her husband, and what he chose to do she could not oppose, in that case the wife shall recover the land, unless it be that the land was leased at farm as well for her sustenance as for her husband's; and if that be so, then the wife as well as the husband shall warrant the terms.[151]

78. [Of land in frankalmoign]:[152] Further, no land which is given to a house of religion is free alms if it owes anything to the chief lord, for if the land owns rent, it would not be free alms.[153]

79. Note:[154] Further, if a man or woman is impleaded concerning the land which he holds by a royal writ from the chancery, and [the writ] runs in the hundred of the city, he had better take care, whoever he is, that he does not come into the hundred while the delays are [still to run], [after] the writ has been entered, for if he comes while the delays are still to run, he will have to answer at once without any delays.[155]

145 Ibid., i, pp 303–4 (Waterford, ch. 75). **146** See, ch. 34 above. **147** Ibid., i, p. 74, n. 3, explains: 'i.e., if the thief turns approver' (in other words, offers to prove another guilty, informs). **148** Bateson's translation omits this relative clause. **149** Ibid., i, p. 74 (Waterford, ch. 76). **150** Ibid., ii, p. 116, n. 5, comments: 'But the statement points to freehold.' **151** Ibid., ii, p. 116 (Waterford, ch. 77). **152** *Frankalmoin* or *frankalmoigne*, literally meaning 'free pity/mercy' (from Norman-French *fraunch aumoyne*, '(tenure in) free alms'), a feudal tenure by which an ecclesiastical body held land free of military service such as knight service, but sometimes in return for saying prayers and masses for the soul of the grantor. In the twelfth and thirteenth centuries jurisdiction over such tenures belonged to the ecclesiastical courts, and was thus immune from royal jurisdiction. **153** Bateson, *Customs*, ii, pp 201–2 (Waterford, ch. 78). See ibid., n. 4, for other examples of restrictions on alienations of land to religious communities. **154** The Waterford custumal has no chapter title here and the Dublin version merely the word *Nota*. **155** Bateson, *Customs*, i, pp 255–6 (Waterford, ch. 79).

80. [Of deceit]: Further, if a man or woman has let a house at farm to another, and the other thinks to cheat him if he holds it for a year, or two or three years, without paying the rent, and then the other [the lessor] finds out that he is being deceived, and comes before [the court] and demands his rent, and he who holds it comes forward and answers thus: 'I owe you no rent, and I demand the peace of God and the king and the mayor,' and demands judgment as he has held the land for more than year and day, and whether he need answer without the king's writ, and thus a man may be defrauded of his rent: [Wherefore] if any man or woman lets his land in farm to another, [he shall see that][156] he who owes the **[p. 262]** rent shall come before the bailiffs, and he shall bring with him six worthy men, and he shall cause the covenant to be enrolled, so that he who holds the farm cannot deny the rent that is due. And if then perchance he [the lessee] denies in the form aforesaid, then he who let the land at farm can vouch the record of the roll and of the bailiffs, and then the other shall be amerced 20 shillings for his false claim, for he has attempted a fraud tending to disherison.[157]

81. Note [Of inheritance and partition]: Further, if a citizen marries a woman and has children by her, and the wife dies, and he marries another and has children also by her, and the second wife dies, and he marries a third wife by whom he has children, the son of the third wife shall receive the inheritance by the custom of the city.[158]

82. [Rules of inheritance]:[159] Further, if a citizen has daughters by his wife and no sons, the daughters shall divide the inheritance among them. And if he has a son, he shall have the inheritance and the daughters shall have none of it.[160]

83. [Of devises]: Further, every citizen can devise land and rent to his heirs and his kin on his deathbed, within the metes and bounds of the city, except to houses of religion and to such people as cannot aid or succour the city if there be need.[161]

84. [Of land given in frank marriage]: Further, if a citizen gives his daughter land in frank marriage and the daughter dies, the said land will return to the said citizen or to his heirs if she has no heir of her body, and if the land be not given to her husband for his life.[162]

85. [Of selling the inheritance]: Further, if a citizen be enraged against his son, so that he wishes to eloign or sell the inheritance away from the child, the child shall come forward before the matter has been finally settled and forbid

156 Ibid., i, p. 275, n. 2: 'Not in either MS, but the meaning seems to require something to that effect'. **157** Ibid., i, pp 274–5 (Waterford, ch. 80). **158** Ibid., ii, pp 130–1 (Waterford, ch. 81). **159** Neither custumal gives a title to this chapter. **160** Ibid., ii, p. 131 (Waterford, ch. 82). **161** Ibid., ii, p. 95 (Waterford, ch. 83). **162** Ibid., ii, p. 111 (Waterford, ch. 84).

on behalf of the king and the mayor that anyone buy his inheritance. And if anyone then does so, he will lose his money and the child will recover his inheritance.[163]

86. Of pigs found in the streets: Further, there are four days a year when the bailiffs will let it be proclaimed that no man should be so insolent as to have pigs **[p. 263]** at large within the city: first at Candlemas, next on the Feast of Holy Cross, next on the Feast of Saint James, next on the Feast of Saint Dominic. And if any are found, the bailiffs will obtain, from each offender, four pence on the first occasion. And the second time, eight pence from each offender. And, on the third time [the offence is committed], the pigs will be slaughtered wherever they are found.

87. [Of land returning no rent]: Further, if land or rent or house fall vacant, for instance for lack of an heir, the mayor and bailiffs take the property into their own hand.[164] If perchance twenty or forty years after, an heir comes, whether male or female, and claims the said inheritance, and the inquest says that he is the right heir, he shall recover his inheritance. And if it be built upon, he shall pay only the chief rent for the time that it has been in their hands.[165]

88. [Of the claiming of inheritance]: Further, if a citizen and his wife have only one child, who is their heir, and it chance that this same child goes into a foreign land so that the father and the mother know not where the child is, and it chance that they die, and in dying give this inheritance to a house of religion or to another as by devise, the gift or the devise is worth nothing while the heir is absent. But the mayor and the bailiffs ought, as soon as the corpses are out of the door, to put in their sergeant of the town, and take the rent into the town's hand, so that no house of religion enters nor any man or woman. And if it chance that the said heir be dead, the mayor and bailiffs can take inquest whether there is any heir after his death. And if the inquest says that such a one is right heir, he should be put in seisin at once, and he shall give the mayor and the commonalty 20 shillings because they have guarded his right. And if the inquest says that they know no heir for it so far, and the mayor and bailiffs incur costs for maintaining the thing and it chance that the heir does come back from a foreign land, and wishes to claim the inheritance, he ought to bring with him a **[p. 264]** letter sealed by twelve of the most lawful men of the town where he was wont to dwell, to bear witness of what nation he is;[166] then the mayor and bailiffs ought to take inquest whether he is the nearest heir. And if the inquest says that he is the right heir he ought to be put at once in seisin,

163 Ibid., ii, pp 95–6 (Waterford, ch. 85). **164** Ibid., ii, p. 162 (Waterford, ch. 87). **165** Ibid., i, pp 275–6 (Waterford, ch. 87, continued). **166** *de quele nacion il est*; ibid., ii, p. 101, n. 5, adds: 'Perhaps better "what his birth is"'.

saving the costs which the mayor and the bailiffs have incurred, by view of good people.[167]

89. [Of the killing of dogs]: Further, if a man kills his neighbour's dog unless it be in his own defence, the amercement is [20 shillings],[168] and nevertheless he shall be held to answer the owner of the dog for all the damage that may come to him for the want of his dog, unless he have pardon.[169]

90. Of parchment-makers: Further, if a parchment-maker has an apprentice, and is dwelling within the city, and his apprentice dwells with him ten years or twelve, and it happens that the apprentice knows his trade in two or three years, and perchance strife arises between them and the master assaults his apprentice, so that the apprentice wishes no longer to serve him, the master may take a love-day with his apprentice; and by award of good men, if the master be guilty, he shall lose his apprentice by the law of the city. And if perchance the master come not on the day he shall lose his servant. And if the apprentice come not on his day, his master shall have him wherever he may be found, by the letters of the commonalty.[170]

91. [Of catchpole as attorney]: Further, if a foreigner brings a writ against a citizen, and the sergeant[171] of the town undertakes to be attorney for the foreigner against the citizen, he shall lose his staff,[172] and go to prison. For it cannot be that he does not know the counsel of the town, and if he does anything against any of the city, he is perjured. But he can very well be an attorney by leave of the mayor and bailiffs, though not otherwise.[173]

92. [p. 265] Of the *dernehundred*:[174] Further, if a man or a woman brings a writ against any one, and it happens that he who brings the writ makes default, and comes not to the *dernehundred*, while the defendant appears, his writ is no further advanced than it was on the first day; howbeit, his writ shall hold good so that he need not purchase another, but he will have to plead his plea entirely afresh.[175]

93. [Of tenements alienated]: Further, if a man brings a writ against another and the defendant seeks to alienate the land, he can enfeoff another

167 Ibid., ii, pp 100–2 (Waterford, ch. 88). **168** Missing in the Dublin custumal but added in the Waterford one. **169** Ibid., i, p. 81 (Waterford, ch. 89). **170** Ibid., i, p. 229 (Waterford, ch. 90). **171** Ibid., ii, p. 12, the Waterford version uses *cachepol*, 'catchpole' (the latter being synonymous with sergeant, a petty officer of justice, especially a warrant officer who arrests for debt). **172** *sa verge*: the rod symbolizing his office. **173** Ibid., ii, pp 12–13 (Waterford, ch. 91). **174** According to Bateson, *Customs*, i, p. 254, n. 2: 'The derivation of this word, used in many of the boroughs of Ireland, is obscure'. She refers to her *Glossarial Notes*, ibid., p. 321: *dernhundred* 'was the term used in certain Irish boroughs to describe the full assembly of the community'. She adds that 'the earliest known instance of the use is' in this chapter of the Dublin custumal. **175** Ibid., i, p. 254 (Waterford, ch. 92).

before the writ has been entered. And he who has been enfeoffed can enfeoff another, and so from hand to hand until the land is lost completely to the original demandant; but if a man enfeoffs another after the writ has been entered, the feoffment is worthless.[176]

94. **Of millers:** Further, if a miller takes wheat to be ground, he must take a level measure of grain and bring it to the town hall (?)[177] to be properly measured and weighed twice or three times. And if the miller be attainted of robbery of the grain or of the flour to the amount of 4 pence he shall be hanged from the beam in his mill.[178] And if he who owns the flour does not want to pursue the case, the bailiffs must proceed and they will distribute that flour for the love of God, and they will arrest as many as are found in the mill, humble and great, and cast them into prison for forty days. And after the forty days they will leave the city, unless they can find pledges that they will do no damage thereafter. And if any damage is done afterwards, their pledges will be responsible for the damage. And if the damage is so serious to merit hanging, then he will be summarily hanged, unless he has pardon from the mayor and bailiffs. And even if he has such pardon that he is not hanged, the mayor and bailiffs must seize all his possessions.

95. **[p. 266] Of kilns:** Further, any man who wants to have in his house a lime-kiln and an oven, must be sure to have it 2 feet from his neighbour's wall, if the house is big. And if the house is narrow, one foot and a half at least. And if he does not comply, the amercement is two shillings. And if he refuses to make amends after being given notice, the fine is forty shillings. And if the kiln is not covered as it ought to be, the amercement is three shillings.

96. **[Of vouching]:** Further, if a man impleads another within the city, and they plead to the point at which one vouches another to warrant, and perchance the vouchee has no lands or tenements whereby he can warrant, for, while the plea is pending, his land was sold,[179] he who buys it shall lose its possession until the demandant is satisfied. And if the sale be made before the writ is bought, the sale is good enough, if the demandant does not put forward his claim before the land is sold.[180]

97. **Note [Of jurats]:** Further, we citizens who have purchased the franchises of the city of Dublin and are named Sir Gilbert Lyvet, Ralph de la More, Thomas de la Cornere, Robert Pollard, and many other worthy men of the said

176 Ibid., i, p. 288 (Waterford, ch. 93). 177 *a l'ostel*, a phrase that can mean 'home', 'to one's house', though the word *ostel*, while it has multiple meanings ('lodgings', 'inn', 'dwelling-place', 'merchant's house', etc.), can also mean 'town hall'. 178 Bateson, *Customs*, i, p. 74 (Waterford, ch. 94). 179 Ibid., i, p. 270, n. 3, comments: 'This would seem to be the meaning, though we are compelled to suppose that the text is not quite correct'. 180 Ibid., i, p. 270 (Waterford, ch. 96).

city, have ordained on behalf of the king that all the aforementioned franchises must be observed without infringement in anticipation of all those who will be born after our time. That is to say that 24 jurats shall protect the city besides the mayor and the bailiffs. And these 24 are to elect 48 young men. And these 48 are to elect 96, and these 96 must secure the city from harm or damage. And should harm or damage occur in the city through their neglect they will have to answer for their default.

98. [p. 267] Of feasts held for courtesy:[181] Further, if the mayor and the bailiffs and the 24 are invited to a feast, they must bring with them 24 young men from the city to follow them and learn courtly behaviour.[182]

99. [Of the keeping of the seal]: Further, the mayor, the bailiffs and the 24, although they are the keepers of the common seal, must not enfeoff any man or woman with land or tenement without the assent of all the commonalty of the city. Otherwise their action will have no value.

100. Bailiffs' accounts:[183] Further, if the town must be taxed, the 24 will themselves be the first to pay the tax, and then the 48; and after that the 96; after which they will collect the tax from the commonalty. And when they have done that, they will go to the *tunderie* and each of them separately will bring what he has collected. Whereupon the bailiffs must render account in front of the commonalty, and also the collectors of the rent in the same way, that is to say on two dates per year. The first time is at mid-Lent, the second time in the quinzaine of [i.e., fifteen days before] Michaelmas. And if any of them is in arrears, he shall be held in custody by the town until he settles his arrears.

101. [The clerk of the commonalty]:[184] Further, the commonalty will agree who is to be their clerk, and he will receive 5 marks per year and his post will be duly filled.

102. [Of fees]: Further, the bailiffs' fee is [amount erased] per annum.[185] And the mayor's fee [is] 10 pounds per annum. And each sergeant will receive half a mark per annum.

103. [Of the giving of tenements]: Further, if a man or a woman promises to give [land] of his inheritance with a brother or a sister [in marriage?] and he or she enters into seisin by this promise, this seisin is worthless, if he or she be not enfeoffed by charter or with the oral testimony of neighbours. **[p. 268]** And if the tenant takes rent or fee from such a feoffment, the principal can bring a writ against him as in name of *fresche force* [fresh force].[186]

181 *par cortyse.* 182 *curtesie aprendre.* 183 In the Waterford custumal this chapter is entitled: *Tax imposition*. Mac Niocaill in his edition forgot to mention the title of this chapter of the Dublin custumal: *Compotus ballivorum*. 184 Neither custumal gives a title to this chapter. 185 The Waterford custumal specifies officers' fees in more detail. 186 Bateson, *Customs*, i, p. 276 (Waterford, ch. 103).

104. [Appurtenances to be named in the writ]:[187] Further, if a man brings a writ against another and asks for the land and not for the appurtenances, the writ is abatable.[188]

105. [Of feoffment]: Further, if a man enfeoffs his child under age, the feoffment is void if it is a feoffment of inherited land. But if it is of purchased land it is good. And if it so be that the land is of inheritance and he is impleaded, he shall answer to the first writ. And if it be of purchase, he need not answer while he is under age.[189]

106. [Of attorneys]: Further, if a man brings a writ against another, and the demandant makes his attorney after all the delays of the writ are finished, the defendant can ask the attorney: 'Where is your warrant? For whom are you attorney?' And if the attorney has no warrant but vouches the bailiffs to warrant, and the defendant is driven to answer by the bailiffs and by their judgment, the defendant can appeal against this judgment before the king's justices. And if it so be that the attorney has warrant by writ of the king, the defendant shall answer by law, for this is law.[190]

107. [Of the borrowing of money]: Further, if a man of the city borrows money from an outsider[191] to be paid by a certain day, and pays none of that money on the day appointed, and is impleaded and finds pledges for his going into that country[192] where the man dwells who lent him the money, to make him satisfaction, then, if perchance he is killed on the way, or dies suddenly before the day appointed, the pledges are quit forever.[193]

108. [Of answering]: Further, if a man brings a writ against another, he against whom the writ is brought must suffer all the delays of the writ until the view, if it so be that he has enfeoffed his child under age. And if he answers after the view, or casts any essoin before he says that he does not hold it, but that his son or daughter holds it, he shall answer.[194]

109. [p. 269] [Of the forestalling of food]: Further, no house of religion may engage in forestalling[195] to deprive the citizens of merchandise of any kind, or of food, and if they are convicted they will lose what they have.

110. [Of distraint]: Further, if any citizen be distrained by a foreigner, unless he be himself the principal or his pledge, the men of the city shall make his deliverance by a writ from the chancery.[196]

187 Neither custumal gives a title to this chapter. 188 Bateson, *Customs*, i, p. 319 (Waterford, ch. 104). 189 Ibid., ii, p. 96 (Waterford, ch. 105). 190 Ibid., ii, p. 13 (Waterford, ch. 106). 191 *d'un autre estrange*. 192 *pays*. 193 Ibid., i, p. 99 (Waterford, ch. 107). 194 Ibid., i, p. 256 (Waterford, ch. 108). 195 Forestalling, according to *Black's law dictionary*, is 'the act of the buying or contracting for any merchandise or provision on its way to the market, with the intention of selling it again at a higher price; or the dissuading persons from bringing their goods or provisions there'. 196 Ibid., i, p. 118

111. **[Of plevin]:** Further, if a man is the pledge of another and the pledge offers his gage to him to whom the debt is due, he need not take it unless he likes, but the pledge shall keep the gage for himself and must pay the other with his [the pledge's] own money.[197]

112. **[Of injuring one under arrest]:** Further, if a man is attached by the sergeant of the town, to be led to the prison or to the *tounderie* for his trespass, and a man wounds him who is attached after he is in the sergeant's hand or in his ward, he who wounds him shall be ordered to prison, and [to get] out of prison shall find good security to make amends to him whom he wounded, according to the amount of the trespass, and besides this he shall be grievously amerced.[198]

(Waterford, ch. 110). **197** Ibid., i, pp 99–100 (Waterford, ch. 111). **198** Ibid., ii, p. 26 (Waterford, ch. 112).

The archaeology of medieval James's Street, Dublin

ANTOINE GIACOMETTI

INTRODUCTION

For such a significant and long-established thoroughfare, James's Street is not well documented in Dublin's historical records. The earliest map of Dublin, that by John Speed in 1610, crops James's Street entirely. There are no surviving depictions of James's Gate, today synonymous with Guinness's brewery, which formed the outermost defensive point west of the city in the late medieval and early post-medieval periods.

Archaeological investigations along James's Street in 2014–15, however, revealed tantalizing glimpses of a busy urban streetscape during the medieval period. In front of St James's church excavations discovered an exceptionally well-preserved street surface, at least part of which can be dated to the late twelfth century, and which may have formed an extramural market square. Excavations further east along the street identified waste from a roof-tile manufactory that operated during the thirteenth and fourteenth centuries. This tilery appears to have produced most of Dublin's medieval roof-tiles until the fifteenth century, and was situated off a now-gone street called 'Croker's Lane', which extended further west (outside the Bars) than previously thought.

Archaeological investigations at James's Gate found the remains of post-medieval structures. No definitive gate-like remains were identified, but the archaeology suggests that the gate was not fully demolished in the first half of the eighteenth century, despite a documentary reference to that effect (see below). The medieval gate proved archaeologically elusive, but evidence from a ditched watercourse constricting James's Street in the medieval period suggests that there was a bridge at James's Gate. Evidence for the widening of the road and the rerouting of watercourses in the late medieval period may be associated with the construction of masonry structures either side of James's Gate.

BACKGROUND TO THE WORK AND METHODOLOGY

The archaeological work described in this paper (Licence 13E401) was carried out during monitoring of groundworks along James's Street and Thomas Street, Dublin 8, in 2014 and 2015. The works for the scheme (to provide a Quality Bus Network) involved excavations for new services, new pavements, lampposts and an improved bus lane. The majority of the excavations consisted

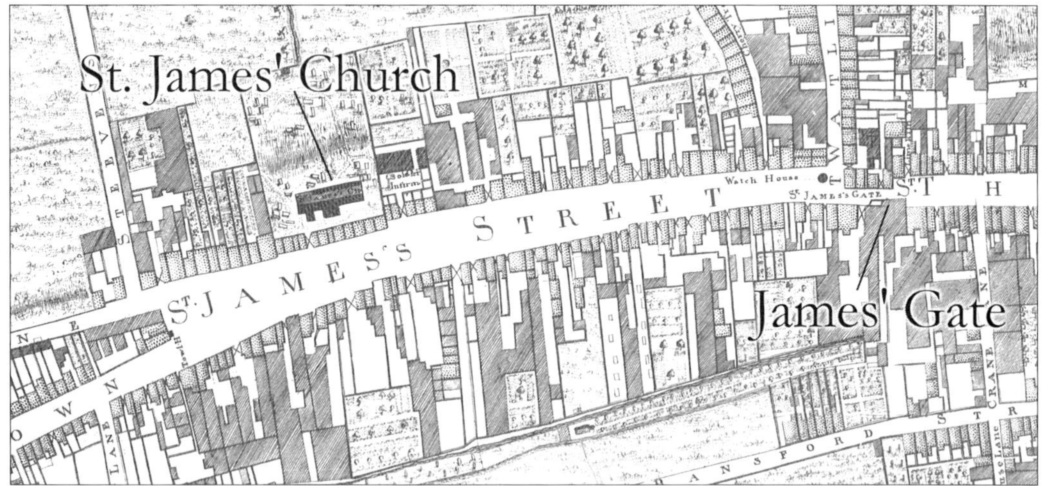

6.1 Rocque's Map of Dublin 1756 showing James's Street

of narrow, shallow trenches cut along the edge of the pavement on either side of the road. Initial work, which took place in 2011 and 2014, catalogued nineteenth-century street furniture along the route: granite kerbs and historic street surfaces (cobbles and setts), bollards, post-boxes, railings, cellar drops and light-wells. Coal cellars, many still in use, were recorded and assessed. Historic street furniture along the route was lifted and replaced, or reused elsewhere.

Archaeological monitoring of sub-surface works was carried out along the eastern half of James's Street (from the junction with Bow Lane to James's Gate and the route of the LUAS red line), the western half of Thomas Street (from James's Gate to the junction with Thomas Court/Bridgefoot Street), and sporadically further east along Thomas Street to the John's Lane junction. Archaeological work was also carried out along parts of Bow Lane, Watling Street and Bridgefoot Street.

The recording of archaeological deposits and features was organized by plot-number as shown on the 1847–8 25-inch-scale Ordnance Survey maps. This recording system was devised in order to best record the archaeological features identified, most of which correlated with the nineteenth-century plots directly. These maps provide individual numbers for every plot and were compiled at a time when the plots along the streets were smaller and more numerous than today, thus allowing for a greater degree of granularity in recording within the James's Street Study Area: plot numbers begin at no. 30 (to the southwest at the Bow Lane junction) and run to 83 at James's Gate, then run from 84 across the road on the northern side of James's Gate to 134 at the junction of James's Street and Steeven's Lane.

MEDIEVAL JAMES'S STREET: HISTORICAL BACKGROUND

It has been suggested that James's Street runs along an ancient road known as the *Slighe Mhór*, part of a pre-Viking road network across Ireland. The axis of this route may have been linked to the postulated settlement of Áth Cliath on the south bank of the Liffey before the arrival of the Vikings (Clarke 1998, 50; Clarke 2002, 2). The focus of the ninth- and tenth-century Viking settlement was further to the east, and by the time Dublin was walled in the eleventh century, James's Street was outside the city (Clarke 1990; 2002, 2–4; Halpin 2005, 100–6; Simpson 2000; Simpson 2005, 59). Following the arrival of the Anglo-Normans, and throughout the medieval period, James's Street was never enclosed by the city walls (Clarke 2002, 7–9), and was considered suburban until the seventeenth century (Elliott 1990, 71).

During the Anglo-Norman period, James's Street and Thomas Street combined were known as 'great street' leading to Kilmainham (Clarke 1998, 50). The first documentary reference to James's Street is in the early thirteenth-century register of St Thomas's abbey (cited in Clarke 2002, 14) and there is a 1584 reference to 'St James's fields ... near the old bridge leading to the mill of Kilmainham' (perhaps Bow Bridge) (McCready 1892, 107). There are also a number of early seventeenth-century references to James's Street (Clarke 2002, 14).

The earliest church on James's Street is St James's church (Church of Ireland) on the north side of the street. Documentary sources record that the church was built in 1185–92 and, according to the register of St Thomas's abbey, was granted to the Augustinian canons some years later (Clarke 2002, 7). The construction of St James's church in the twelfth century probably marks the establishment of the parish boundaries of St James's and St Catherine's by Thomas's abbey. The church was rebuilt in the eighteenth century, and again in the mid-nineteenth century. It lost its spire in 1948, and has recently been converted into a distillery. Two other churches with the same name are also located on James's Street. These are the *c.*eighteenth-century former Roman Catholic chapel at James's Gate (now Bank of Ireland) and the mid-nineteenth-century Catholic church on the south side of the street.

James's Gate is mentioned by documentary sources in 1485 and 1555, and as a tower over a gate in 1599 (Clarke 2002, 22). It is depicted on maps in 1610, 1673 and 1728. The gate formed part of the city defences erected during the Confederate Wars in the mid-seventeenth century, as depicted on the Down Survey map. A reference in the assembly rolls of the city of Dublin from 1733–4 describes James's Gate as a nuisance and requests its removal, the stones to be put to the city's use (*CARD*, v, 126; cited in Thomas 1992, ii, 84). It is generally assumed to have been removed at this point, but it is not obviously gone on Rocque's map of 1756 and McCready has identified a 1786 reference to the gate being widened (McCready 1892, 107). Another important medieval structure on James's Street was the city cistern, which was a large water reservoir supplying drinking water to medieval Dublin (Clarke 1998, 50). A medieval aqueduct, known as the 'high pipe', ran from the cistern at James's Street eastwards into the city (ibid.)

James's Street lies within the zone of archaeological potential for the city of Dublin, and several recorded monuments lie along the route of the groundworks. These are: St James's church and graveyard (DU018–020346); James's Gate (DU018–020001) – which is also a national monument – a bridge to the west of James's Gate (DU018–020233), presumably crossing the watercourse (DU018–020672) running north from the medieval city cistern (DU018–020055); an eighteenth-century smock windmill called St Patrick's Tower (DU018–020323) which was originally part of Roe's Distillery; and the post-Reformation Catholic chapel dating to the 1740s mentioned above (DU018–020494). With the exception of the windmill and cistern, the archaeological programme identified (and preserved) archaeological evidence associated with all of these monuments.

Previous archaeological investigations on James's Street have identified medieval activity. At Nos 30–36 Cryerhall found medieval burgage plots from the mid-thirteenth century and a boundary defining fields that appeared to be in use from the thirteenth to seventeenth centuries (01E1034). A large mid-eighteenth- and nineteenth-century tannery (or leather-making) complex was also excavated to the rear of Nos 42–3. At Nos 141–3 Meenan and Lynch identified a medieval pit truncated by a post-medieval industrial complex (99E144). Monitoring by Kehoe for the Bank of Ireland at 84–7 James's Street identified post-medieval infill raising the level of the street (02E118). Collins' investigations at St James's church (14E0129) identified the remains of the earlier pre-nineteenth-century church building, human remains, and eighteenth-century house remains at Nos 123–5.

GENERAL OVERVIEW OF FINDINGS

209 archaeological features were identified during the works, of which 116 were on James's Street and 93 were on Thomas Street. Leaving aside the Thomas Street features (which included medieval settlement evidence on the southern side of the street near Thomas's abbey), the James's Street features dated to between the twelfth and nineteenth centuries.

One of the key features identified was the patchy remnants of the early eighteenth-century cobbled street, 300mm to 350mm below the present ground level, as this provided a known date with which to interpret other features sealed by it, or cutting it. Other post-medieval street surfaces were identified above and below this, and five limestone-sett former off-street lanes were identified. Twenty-four brick-built coal cellars (of which fourteen were relatively intact) were identified and recorded. Two light-wells or goods drops relating to now demolished (but post-1700) buildings, four brick or masonry drains, and one large brick culvert were documented. Many other wall fragments were identified, often relating to the former façades of Georgian buildings now replaced by the nineteenth-century 'areas' of the Guinness offices to the southeast of James's Street. Building façades and foundations at James's Gate were also found. Much of this archaeological evidence can help date the construction of the historic buildings currently lining the street. Other features recorded included a small truncated section of the late seventeenth-century wooden water pipe system (in front of 106 James's Street), post-medieval ditches, and pits, including a tanning pit in front of 52–3 James's Street.

The remainder of this paper will focus on the medieval features identified on James's Street – a metalled surface, two ditches, a small ditch or pit, a former stream course, and a post-hole – and a number of post-medieval walls and a ditch at James's Gate.

DESCRIPTION OF ARCHAEOLOGICAL FEATURES

Metalled surface

The most surprising archaeological discovery on James's Street was a 'metalled' (meaning cobbled with pebbles) street surface, which survived in good condition as shallow as 250mm below the pavement in front of St James's church. It was formed from small pebbles (*c.*20mm diameter) well-beaten into place, with patchy sections of cobbling (*c.*70mm diameter) that probably indicate repair. At 45–7 James's Street the surface incorporated fragments of red baked clay. At 116–17 James's Street, Dublin-type medieval pottery was crushed into the surface. The longest continuous length of the surface identified was a 31m stretch, exposed in a narrow trench only 200mm in width between 119 and 126 James's Street, below the pavement in front of St James's church. The highest point of the metalled surface was directly in front of the church on the north side of the road, and from here it sloped down to the west, east and south. A slight dip in the surface just west of the existing entrance may mark the medieval entrance to the church, and this is supported by eighteenth-century cartographic sources.

A second section of the metalled surface was exposed further east, in front of the present Guinness Medical Centre (116–17 James's Street). This exposed section, measuring 2m by 1m, had a straight edge along its northern side at an angle (NW–SE) to the present frontage alignment. There was no kerb, but a gritty sub-surface layer directly below the surface continued to the north indicating the metalled surface had not been truncated. This unusual angle may either suggest that the metalled surface was widening just before St

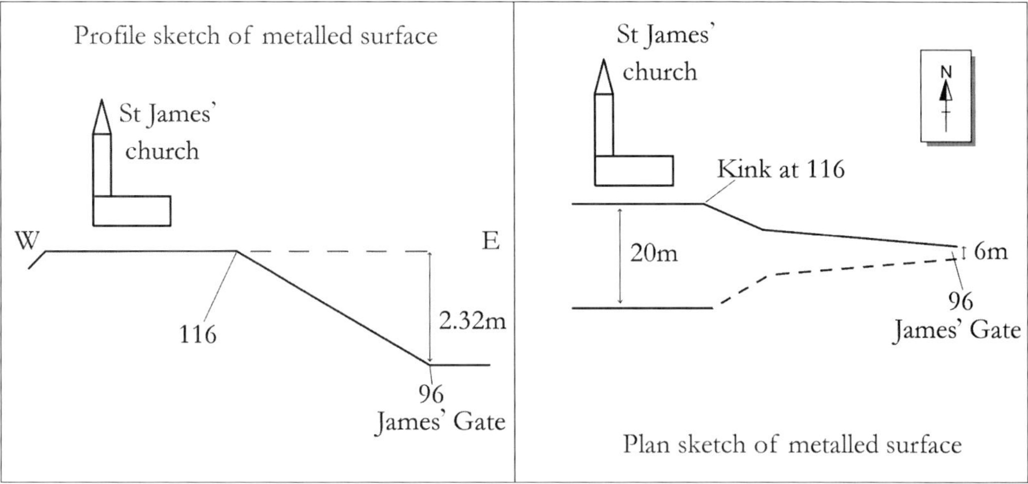

6.2 Sketch plan and profile of metalled surface.

James's church, and/or that the edge of the street was kinked at this point. Further trenches to the east identified the same metalled surface at various points almost as far as James's Gate (no. 96). The surface was also identified on the southern side of James's Street in four locations. The metalled surface was identified both below the pavement and below the existing road. In a number of cases (e.g., at 49–50 James's Street) the metalled surface was deeper where it was identified below the street, suggesting it sloped down from the edges of the street. In two locations the metalled surface was identified in the centre of the modern road. One of these areas was in front of the parochial hall below a traffic island in the middle of the street. Here the metalled surface was at a slightly higher level than at its northern edge, suggesting a slightly raised area in the centre of the road, perhaps dividing Bow Lane and James's Street West.

Assuming all these patches of metalling are from the same surface, the data above can be used to recreate the form and level of the metalled street. The highest point of the surface was directly outside St James's church. It remained relatively level to the east and west of the church, until 116 James's Street. From no. 116, it sloped downwards sharply as it ran eastwards towards James's Gate. Between the highest point outside the church, and the easternmost point at which the surface was identified in 96 James's Street, the surface fell by 2.32m, which is a considerable drop. The width of the metalled street surface showed considerable variation. At the east end of James's Street the metalled surface appeared to span a relatively narrow road (based on the location of a medieval ditch described below), but directly outside the front of St James's church the surface spanned a width of at least 20m. This is equivalent to the modern street of two lanes in each direction separated by a traffic island. It seems extraordinarily wide for a medieval street.

Table 6.1 Location of metalled street surface on James's Street

Plot number	Depth below pavement	OD level
	SOUTH SIDE OF ROAD	
32	650mm	16.350m OD
45–47	850mm	16.074m OD
48–49	850mm	15.835m OD
49–50	970mm	15.432m OD
	CENTRE OF ROAD	
54 (Parochial Hall)	620–700mm	15.660m OD
	NORTH SIDE OF ROAD	
96	540mm	14.550m OD
104	790mm	14.774m OD
105	950–1020mm	14.600m OD
107	850mm	14.579m OD
110	990mm	15.400m OD
116–17	250mm	15.964m OD
119	00mm	16.124m OD
120	500mm	16.358m OD
122 (James's church)	200mm	16.873m OD
124	800mm	16.305m OD

The changes in levels of the metalled surface along James's Street (see table 6.1) suggest three things. First, the medieval topography was bumpier than today. James's church was located on a more prominent hill and the road ran down the hill towards the city of Dublin more steeply than today. Second, the shallowness of the medieval surface at St James's church, where it comes almost up to pavement level and then disappears, must mean it was truncated, probably from levelling during a post-medieval phase of rebuilding of St James's church. Thirdly, the surface is relatively level in front of St James's church, and only starts to slope steeply downhill at the Guinness Medical Centre (no. 116). This point of slope change coincides with a kink in the road and the narrowing of the medieval street from *c.*20m in width outside the church to a narrower typical street width towards James's Gate.

In most of the areas where it was identified, the metalled surface ran below a later cobbled street surface that was dated to the early eighteenth century, on the basis of being cut by the cellars of structures depicted on Rocque's map of

Dublin and early eighteenth-century pottery sealed below it. Between 119 and 126 James's Street the surface was covered by an organic layer containing animal bone, shell, brick fragments, late seventeenth-century pottery and early clay pipe fragments. A similar layer was identified above the metalled surface at 116–17, with inclusions of Saintonge and of post-medieval pottery sherds, and again at 107, with red-brick directly over the surface. Almost everywhere the surface was laid directly on natural subsoil, except at 45–7, 88–95, and 116–17 James's Street. A hand-excavated test-pit through the surface at 116–17 James's Street identified a loose gravel deposit 150mm thick containing animal bone and oyster shell overlying natural subsoil, interpreted as a sub-surface, which extended north past the edge of the metalled surface. At the point where the metalled surface ran over this deposit, thirteenth-century medieval pottery was found crushed into the fabric of the surface and incorporated into the metalling.

This evidence suggests that parts of the metalled surface were in place from at least the late thirteenth or early fourteenth century, and remained in use with repairs and resurfacing until the late seventeenth century. Significantly, no evidence for an earlier surface was identified anywhere along James's Street, and so this surface may represent the earliest formal street surface, or the result of a highly destructive major resurfacing episode in the high medieval period.

Truncated pit or ditch at no. 116

At 116–17 James's Street (outside the Guinness Medical Centre), a small hand-excavated test-pit through the metalled surface uncovered an earlier feature cut into natural subsoil. The feature is likely to be the edge of a ditch, or of a pit extending northwards. Only the edge of the cut feature was exposed. The upper fill of the feature contained a concentrated deposit of medieval pottery sherds, which had been sealed by the metalled surface. Funding by Dublin City Council allowed for detailed analysis by Clare McCutcheon of the pottery from the sealed feature. The assemblage comprised 132 fragments of Dublin-type coarseware jugs, 46 sherds of Dublin-type cooking ware cooking jars, and three sherds of wheel-thrown Dublin-type ware. Most (98.5%) of the pottery sherds were handmade, and McCutcheon concluded that the assemblage as a whole dated to the late twelfth century. She suggested that the three sherds of wheel-thrown ware may mark the introduction of the wheel to Dublin pottery-production at this time.

The infilling of this feature by the late twelfth-century ceramic assemblage may have been directly associated with the construction of the metalled surface. Whether it represents the edge of a ditch or a pit, the stratigraphic sequence indicates the widening of this section of street between 116 and *c.*126 James's Street in the late twelfth century. The late twelfth-century date is significant because it matches the recorded construction date of St James's church, i.e., 1185–92.

Large medieval ditch

The largest of the medieval ditches identified during archaeological works ran along the north side of James's Street to the west of the junction of Watling Street. This ditch was situated in front of nos 88–95 James's Street beneath the pavement and road carriageway. It presumably extended further to the east and west. This ditch was only revealed in certain places and no full section across it was opened during the works; however it appeared to be a minimum of 50m in length, 5m in width and 1.35m in depth. It cut an early natural stream course and may have continued past James's Gate onto the south side of Thomas Street, where a similar medieval ditch was identified. The main upper fill of the ditch contained very large amounts thirteenth- and fourteenth-century pottery, floor tiles, large crested roof tiles, and tile wasters. A sample of the material was analysed by Joanna Wren. Although some medieval tiles were identified, 68% of the assemblage was found to be composed of tile wasters, bricks from kiln walls and substantial amounts of unformed fingered clay that may have been used to form a temporary roof to kilns during firing. All the waste material was from a single ceramic fabric, which closely resembles Dublin fabrics 2 and 3 (DT2 and DT3). The crest forms and decoration used

6.3 Medieval rooftile from ditch.

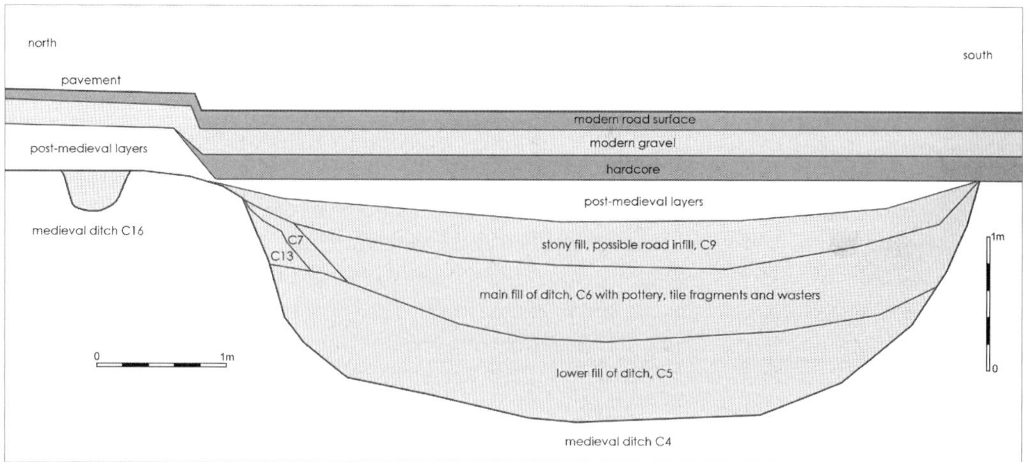

6.4 Profile of large medieval ditch.

on the James's Street tiles were almost identical to those found on tiles in DT2 elsewhere in Dublin (Wren, pers. comm., 2015). ICP analysis to positively identify the tile fabric as DT2 is currently being undertaken.

Above this, distinct layers of packed stones and grit containing broken tile fragments, medieval pottery and some intrusive post-medieval pottery, represented the final backfilling of the ditch and provided a secure sub-surface for the overlying roadway, which appears to have been widened over the top of the ditch. The top of the packed-stone surface sealing the ditch (15.082m OD) outside 93–4 James's Street correlates with the level of the medieval metalled surface described above. Changes in the level of the packed stone over the ditch may indicate the road sloping down to a central open drain. This was also noticed outside St James's church, and along the edge of Thomas Street. A small square-cut post-hole was cut through the backfilled ditch and contained one sherd of medieval pottery. It was located 1740mm in front of 93 James's Street and may mark the location of a signpost or something similar. This was the only feature identified at this level, and is likely to predate the eighteenth century though it cannot be positively dated to the medieval period.

Paleo-channel

A cut feature or natural stream course was identified in front of 89–90 James's Street, 1090mm below ground level (14.190m OD). This had been mostly cut away by the later medieval ditch. From the small amount of the feature exposed, it appeared to run north–south across James's Street and measure at least 3.1m in width and a minimum of 310mm in depth. The sandy fill was sterile and this feature appeared to represent a natural stream course or paleo-channel, later replaced by a formalized ditched watercourse.

Small medieval ditch

A small medieval ditch running east–southeast to west–northwest was identified 600mm (14.50m OD) below the pavement in front of 88–9 James's Street, along the northern side of the street near the junction with Watling Street. It measured 4.5m long (truncated at both ends by later features), 550mm wide and 300mm deep, and was cut into natural subsoil. It contained frequent medieval pottery, oyster and cockle shell, charcoal, roof-slate and animal bone. This may represent a drain or small ditch that defined the northern side of the late medieval James's Street at James's Gate, following the widening of the road represented by the backfilling of the larger ditch.

Post-medieval ditch at James's Gate

On the south side of James's Gate (outside 82 James's Street) a stratigraphic sequence that was different and much deeper than elsewhere was noted during monitoring for a new lamppost. The medieval street surface was not present in this area, and the depth of the stratigraphy indicated that a probably north–south ditch crossed the road at this point, though neither edge was identified. The lowest layers of the ditch contained organic material with frequent redbrick building rubble and two sherds of Dublin-type ware. The brick was very thin, and seemed to be of seventeenth-century date. The base of the ditch (1.6m in depth from the level of the current pavement) was cobbled, but was clearly too deep relative to the medieval street surface to represent a road. The upper fills of the ditch comprised layers and lenses of redeposited boulder clay and organic dumps with demolition building rubble, reaching to the top of the ditch at 400mm below the pavement. The location of this ditch matches the parish boundary between St Catherine's and St James's as shown on nineteenth-century OS maps, which also runs north–south across James's Street.

Masonry remains at James's Gate

One of the key aims of archaeological monitoring at James's Gate was to identify large masonry structures of medieval date extending into the street, which could represent the remains of the former defensive structure. Unfortunately, this turned out to be one of the only areas along James's and Thomas Street where no medieval remains were identified. Archaeological monitoring on the north side of James's Gate identified the walls of standard eighteenth- and nineteenth-century basements, cobbled surfaces of yards and outhouses, and sub-surface industrial and water-management structures, including the remains of a nineteenth-century smithy. The earliest features in this area were related to water management, and all were post-medieval in date.

One of the masonry walls on the north side of the street under the pavement near Watling Street was unusual. It measured 6m in length and 600mm in width, and was truncated to the east and west. In plan it looked similar to the eighteenth- and nineteenth-century basement walls, but unlike these it showed evidence of multiple phases of raising and repair. The foundations of this wall were outset with progressively larger masonry blocks, and reached a similar depth to the eighteenth-century basement walls, but unlike them was not faced or plastered on one side, suggesting this wall was not part of a cellar. No evidence was identified to suggest that the wall was medieval in date, or that is was the foundation of a large gate or tower; but equally the wall did not resemble eighteenth-century domestic architecture. On the south side of James's Gate, just 300mm below the pavement, a small masonry structure extended out under the modern street, surviving over an area *c.*2m by 2m across. Two small low walls and a decayed flagstone floor were recorded. A coin (too eroded to read) was found on the floor. Fragments of red brick below the paved floor indicated a post-medieval date for the structure.

THE ARCHAEOLOGY OF ST JAMES'S MARKET SQUARE

The medieval metalled surface described above appeared to form a relatively flat area on the crest of the hill in front of St James's church, stretching across 20m in width and 120m in length from no. 117 James's Street in the east to Steeven's Gate apartments (*c.*no. 126) in the west. At its western end, James's Street forks, with one branch continuing as James's Street/Mount Brown and the other running down Bow Lane to Kilmainham. Howard Clarke (1998, 50) has suggested that a cross may have marked this junction. Nothing in the modern streetscape explains why the wide flat area narrows and slopes down at its eastern end. However, archaeological evidence for the edge of the surface at an odd alignment may suggest that a former road led northeast at this point.

This is backed up by cartographic sources. A kink in James's Street at nos 116–17 is depicted on the 1848 OS map and on Rocque's 1756 map, correlating with the kink in the metalled surface. Phillip's 1685 map does not show the kink, but he depicts an empty plot next to St James's church which might correspond to it. Brooking's map of 1685 also depicts an empty plot at this location, and denotes some specialized plots situated directly opposite. De Gomme's 1673 map shows the kink, but depicts it further to the west than the later maps. De Gomme also depicts a building directly opposite the kink, which is likely to have been important (as he only marked important buildings). The oldest surviving cartographic depiction of James's Street is the Down Survey barony map of Newcastle from the 1650s. On the Down Survey, James's Street splits at Bow Lane, as it does today, but a second road junction is shown directly east of this. This unnamed second road leads from James's Street north-eastwards and connects with a street which is now gone, but which has been identified as Croker's (or Crocker's) Alley, Lane or Street (and which partially survived in the eighteenth century as Mullinihack). This road appears to connect with James's Street at the same location as the kink on de Gomme's late seventeenth-century map. It is therefore possible that the unusual angle of the northern edge of the metalled surface identified at 116–17 James's Street corresponds with this former road junction of James's Street and Croker's Lane. The wide and level medieval surface in front of St James's church would therefore have formed a junction of four roads, each leading out from one of its corners, with important non-domestic structures on the north (the church) and south (on de Gomme's map) side of the junction.

The assembled evidence for the size and layout of the metalled surface in front of St James's church resembles a 'square' or public assembly space rather than a street. Although there are no documentary records of a public square at this location, there are references to markets held on James's Street. An account of St James's Fair was made by Richard Stanihurst in 1577, who noted that a successful fair was held over six days from St James's Day on June 25 and attracted merchants from England, France and Flanders (cited in Clarke 2002, 27). There is a later reference to the fair in 1640 condemning the practice of the digging up of the street to erect temporary structures for the market (Crawford and Laverty 1988, 32). There are also references to St James's Fair, the 'great mart or fair, being for 'ale only' (Barnaby Rich's *Description of Ireland* (1610); cited in Clarke 2002, 27).

When was this extramural market square constructed? The pottery from within the small truncated feature sealed by the street surface indicates a construction date for at least part of the surface in the late twelfth century. That date matches with the historical 1180s date for the construction of St James's church, suggesting that the construction of the church and the establishment (or at least formalization) of a market square in front of it happened simultaneously. Considering that the parish of St James was almost certainly established by the abbey of St Thomas at this date, this could imply that the abbey also established an extramural market square. Furthermore, the sealed feature may indicate that the establishment, or formalization, of the market square encroached on land which was previously used for other functions. It is possible that the sealed feature represents the edge of a roadside boundary ditch, indicating a localized road-widening for the construction of the new urban space.

THE ARCHAEOLOGY OF THE TILERY ON CROKER'S LANE (OUTSIDE THE BARS)

Further down James's Street, about halfway between St James's church and James's Gate, the large boundary ditch defining the northern edge of the road contained large amount of tile manufacturing waste mixed with thirteenth- and fourteenth-century pottery. The tile waste is almost certainly from a single workshop or tilery situated close to this location, probably on the north side of James's Street. Joanna Wren has noted that all the tile waste has the same fabric, which closely resembles Dublin fabrics 2 and 3 (DT2 and DT3). This finding is significant in terms of the history of tile production in the medieval town. An industry making tiles, finials and louvers in DT2 fabric began production in the early thirteenth century when the practice of employing such elaborate forms of roofing was introduced to Ireland by the Anglo-Normans. It continued in production to the early fourteenth century and possibly later. In the thirteenth and fourteenth centuries, tiles from the DT2 and DT3 kilns accounted for most of the clay building trade in the city. Alan Hayden excavated a kiln making early thirteenth-century pottery and peg tiles from DT1 fabric at Cornmarket (excavations.ie: ref. 1992:055), and Claire Walsh excavated a kiln making late fourteenth- to fifteenth-century floor tiles and peg tiles at St Thomas's abbey in Hanbury Lane (excavations.ie: ref. 1999:206). But until now, the location of the DT2 and DT3 tile manufactory had not been identified.

Clare McCutcheon (2006, 18–27) has assessed the historical evidence for ceramic manufacture and use in medieval Dublin, and has set out the substantial historical evidence for an area of potters outside the west gate of Dublin on Crocker Street/Croker's Lane to the north of Thomas Street (ibid., 21). It is documented from 1190 as *vicus pottorum* but is also known throughout the thirteenth century as *vicus figulorum*. This street was located behind Thomas Street, in Mullinihack, in the suburbs 'outside the town's west gate – presumably because at that location the kilns would not pose a fire threat …' (Murphy and Potterton 2010, 451). Most reconstructions of Croker's Lane have it end to the west at a gate known as Croker's Bars, directly north of James's Gate (e.g., Clarke 2002). However, the kink in the medieval street surface on James's Street suggests it extended further to the west, and Clare McCutcheon also notes that the area of potters appears to have extended west past St Thomas's parish into St James's. For example, McCutcheon notes a reference in 1469 to a messuage granted to Thomas Possewyk, potter, in the suburbs of Dublin, outside the Crocker's Bars in the parish of St James (McCutcheon 2006, 21).

Of course this western extension of the medieval Croker's Lane outside the Bars may not have been called Croker's Lane. But now that we can probably place one of the key tile manufactories of thirteenth- and fourteenth-century Dublin on it (and backing onto James's Street), the name seems appropriate. If indeed a single tilery or tilery-complex just behind James's Street is responsible for producing the majority of roof-tiles from the thirteenth to the early fifteenth century, it would be a very long-lived tilery. Wren has pointed out (2016, pers. comm.) that brickworks run by the same family were in operation from the seventeenth to the nineteenth century in Britain, and so it is conceivable that a similarly long-lived tilery operated in medieval Dublin.

THE ARCHAEOLOGY OF JAMES'S GATE

The archaeological evidence from James's Gate was post-medieval in date. It comprises early modern masonry structures situated either side of James's Gate, constricting the road to a width of *c.*6m across. Some of the structural remains did not resemble residential architecture, and most of the remains correlated with Rocque's eighteenth-century map of this location. No evidence for a medieval defensive structure was found (though it must be emphasized that only small areas were investigated). Rocque's map of 1756 shows a very large building on the southern side of the road (where the main entrance to the Guinness complex is today), jutting slightly out into the road, with an unusual diagonal component that could have formed part of a gate structure (and which approximately correlates to a post-medieval paved structure identified during the monitoring). Intriguingly, the diagonal line shown on Rocque's map matches the line of the parish boundary as shown on the 1850s Ordnance Survey map. That parish boundary was established by the abbey of St Thomas in the late twelfth century, and it is possible that the angled wall depicted on Rocque is set at that unusual angle in order to avoid a defensive ditch associated with James's Gate. This opens the possibility that James's Gate was not completely demolished by the eighteenth century as previously supposed, and that much of its essential character survived into the early modern period as a city block extending into the street that was continually reused and rebuilt. The large non-domestic building on the south side of the gate on Rocque's 1756 map may represent a primarily defensive (or cistern-related) structure, but the remainder of the gate structure survives in the archaeological record as a multi-period jumble of post-medieval water-management features, cellars, walls and smithies.

If this is the gate, when was it built? And why was it built here? The large medieval ditch identified west of the gate may provide some clues. This ditch (which was truncated before it reached James's Gate) indicates that the thirteenth- to fourteenth-century road constricted gradually towards the gate, narrowing to *c.*6m wide. It could be tentatively suggested that the ditch might have turned southwards and crossed the road, then turned eastwards again and ran along the southern side of Thomas Street (where another medieval ditch – perhaps the same one? – was identified). The topographic files of the National Museum (IA/68/53; Reg. 1953:17a–b) record a deep ditch of similar dimensions containing medieval pottery, interpreted as a 'culverted watercourse', running across the road at the gate, supporting this theory.

The ditch defining the northern edge of James's Street would also have defined the boundaries of properties to the north (one of which appears to have been a tilery fronting onto Croker's Lane outside the Bars). Importantly, it must have channelled a medieval watercourse. The location of this ditch does not appear to correspond exactly with the supply to or from the cistern. It

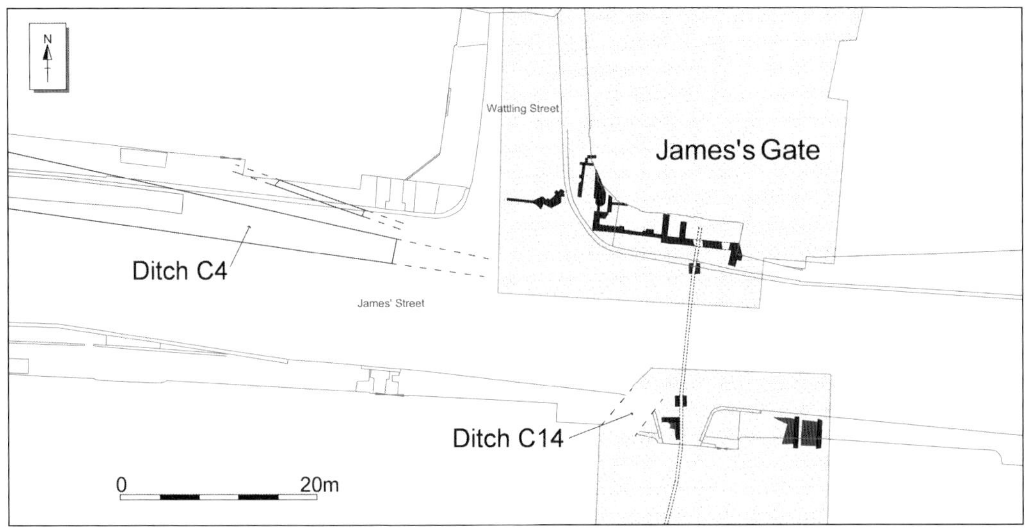

6.5 Plan of James's Gate features.

likely relates to a branch of the medieval Dublin watercourse system (which in this part of Dublin includes the Poddle, Abbey Stream, Glib Stream, Tenter Water and Commons Water), associated with industrial activity such as milling or the tilery, and managed by the abbey of St Thomas. Thus the initial reason for a constriction in the road between James's Street and Thomas Street appears to be due to the route of the watercourse and the bridge crossing it, rather than a masonry gate structure. This crossing point may have been established before the medieval period (as suggested by the discovery of the natural paleo-channel), but it is likely to have been formalized in the late twelfth century when it became the parish boundary between St Catherine's and St James's, probably by St Thomas's abbey.

The ditch/watercourse was infilled by the late medieval period and surfaced with a layer of packed grit at approximately the same level as the medieval street surface. This must represent the rerouting of medieval watercourses – in effect a reclamation of wet ground – between Thomas Street and James's Street, and the widening of James's Street. The exact date this happened cannot be ascertained based on the small scale of the excavations, but the general late medieval date suggested by the ditch stratigraphy correlates with the first documentary references to James's Gate in the fifteenth century, and it seems likely that the reclamation of this ground would have allowed for the construction of additional masonry structures. In the medieval period, James's Gate was essentially the constriction of the street to 6m in width. It was probably associated with some sort of defensive (or cistern-related) structure to the south, but the key element of the gate was the constriction. In the

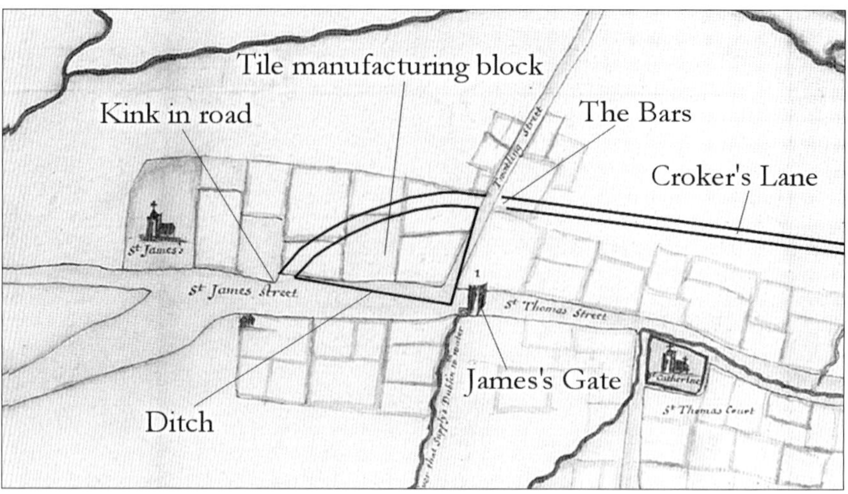

6.6 De Gomme's map of 1728 showing the location of the medieval tilery at Croker's Lane outside the Bars.

thirteenth century this was due to a bridge crossing the watercourse at the parish boundary. By the late medieval period, this constriction was now defined by developed urban blocks (and probably a gate-like structure) either side of a straightened and widened road.

The cobbled post-medieval ditch backfilled with seventeenth-century demolition rubble identified at James's Gate is likely to be the defensive ditch from the 1640s Confederate Wars, rapidly infilled after the conflict. The ditch appears to have run along the medieval parish boundary and former watercourse. The 1650s Down Survey barony map of Newcastle depicts the city defences erected during the war. As Franc Myles (2005) demonstrated at Ardee Street, the defensive lines on that map correspond to large seventeenth-century defensive banks and ditches. James's Gate is not depicted on the Down Survey map but the accompanying text describes the artificial branch of the River Dodder, which was split in two at Ropers Rest, one of which enters the city 'hard by James Gate'. Historical records assembled by Peter Walsh (2005) describe how various people were stationed around the southwest city in 1643–4 during the Confederate Wars. For example, Captain Dillon is at Thomas Court and St Katherine's churchyard, Lord Lambart is on both sides of Francis Street, Sir John Sherlocke is on the southern side of Thomas Street with 46 men, and Lord Brabazon is inside Thomas Court. As part of Lord Kildare's regiment, Sir Adam Loftus, vice-treasurer and treasurer at war for Ireland, is recorded as being stationed on James's Street 'from St James's Gate to the mudd wall, on both sides' (Walsh 2005, 460). A mud wall sounds like an earthen bank, and this reference most likely refers to the earthen defences identified at James's Gate outside no. 82.

CONCLUSION

The archaeological evidence for medieval James's Street relates to what we might call the 'public' sphere – of streets; gates; defensive banks; bridges; and watercourses – rather than the private sphere. Modern concepts of public versus private may not be appropriate in the context of the medieval city. Perhaps it is obvious that little evidence of medieval domestic activity would be found in trenches excavated along the street rather than in individual plots. Nevertheless, the medieval archaeology along James's Street reflects decisions and actions taken at an institutional level rather than a household level. The question of which institutions or municipal authorities could have been involved is an interesting one. The adjacent abbey of St Thomas the Martyr is the most obvious candidate, but a number of ecclesiastical institutions and municipal authorities may have had interests on James's Street and at James's Gate. The archaeology may therefore reflect subversion and competition between institutional powers in the west of Dublin, as well as planned long-term interventions by a single authority.

The archaeological evidence suggests that the establishment of the church and parish of St James's in the late twelfth century, perhaps under the auspices of the abbey of St Thomas, coincided with the construction of an extramural market square. The resurfacing of James's Street, and the formalization of the bridge crossing point into the city at James's Gate, are also likely to have occurred at the same time. A nineteenth-century commission into the five liberties of Dublin, cited by Elliott (1990, 76), notes that two privileges of the Liberty of Thomas Court and Donore were 'a grant of a fair to be held at Donore, and of tolls by a former patent of Elizabeth'. Similar privileges were no doubt secured at an earlier date and it is possible that the abbey of St Thomas had established a tolled bridge on James's Street from the late twelfth century. Additionally, the creation of a formal space for public assembly and trade outside the city's municipal authority could have competed with markets within the walled city, or subverted tolled crossings (such as the bridge at James's Gate, and New Gate) managed by other institutional bodies.

The archaeological evidence for the late medieval (fifteenth-century?) widening and realignment of James's Street, and subsequent construction of a new urban block and gate at James's Gate, required the rerouting of the James's Street watercourses. Documentary sources demonstrate that these medieval watercourses were a significant source of revenue and power for the abbey of St Thomas. They were also a source of dispute between religious institutions and civic authorities, and between competing religious institutions such as St Thomas's abbey and St Sepulchre's (Ronan 1927; Simpson 1997, 24–9). On top of this, many of Dublin's west-suburb industries such as tanning, textile-making and brewing relied heavily on the watercourses. The late medieval rerouting of the James's Street watercourse and construction of James's Gate must have involved numerous institutions and would have had far-reaching consequences beyond the widening of the street.

The tilery on Croker's Lane outside the Bars may have been affected by the rerouting of the James's Street watercourses, or by the political shifts such a rerouting implies. This tilery appears to have produced most of Dublin's tiles in the thirteenth and fourteenth century. During this period tiles were predominantly used on important buildings rather than ordinary houses. No fifteenth-century tile waste was identified on the James's Street archaeological works, and it is likely that this tilery had ceased production at this point, or at least significantly declined. The Bars themselves are reported as ruinous in 1466 (Clarke 2002, 21), just as the first evidence for a structure at James's Gate emerges. This coincides with the shift to a different clay fabric in the manufacture of Dublin's tiles, from DT2 and DT3 in the thirteenth and fourteenth centuries, to DT4 in the late medieval period.

It is tempting to link these archaeological glimpses of medieval James's Street into a single narrative emphasizing planned long-term interventions in the urban fabric of the city by the abbey of St Thomas the Martyr. However, the evidence is more nuanced, and may reflect the competing interests of religious institutions and municipal authorities. The medieval archaeology of James's Street is a manifestation of the flows of institutional power controlling the movement of water and people.

ACKNOWLEDGMENTS

The fieldwork described in this report was carried out by Steven McGlade, Melanie McQuade, Enda Lydon, Peter Kerins and the author, and was funded by Wills Bros and Dublin City Council. Additional funding for ceramic analysis was provided by Dublin City Council Archaeology Department. Ceramic analysis was carried out by Clare McCutcheon, Joanna Wren and Siobhan Scully. ICP analysis of medieval tile waste and seventeenth-century brick is currently ongoing.

BIBLIOGRAPHY

Clarke, H.B. (ed.) 1990 *Medieval Dublin: the living city*. Irish Academic Press, Dublin.

Clarke, H.B. 1998 'Urbs et suburbium: beyond the walls of medieval Dublin'. In C. Manning (ed.), *Dublin and beyond the Pale*. Wordwell in association with Rathmichael Historical Society, Dublin, pp 45–58.

Clarke, H.B. 2002 *Irish Historic Towns Atlas, Dublin Part I, to 1610*. RIA, Dublin.

Crawford, J. and Laverty, D. 1988 *St James's Graveyard, Dublin – history and associations*. St James's Graveyard Project/ Select Vestry of the St Patrick's Cathedral Group of Parishes, Dublin.

Elliott, A.L. 1990 'The abbey of St Thomas the Martyr, near Dublin'. In Clarke 1992, 62–76.

excavations.ie *Database of Irish excavation reports Excavations* (incorporating I. Bennet (ed.), *Excavations: summary accounts of archaeological excavations in Ireland*, 1985–2010, Wordwell: Dublin). Available at https://www.excavations.ie/

Giacometti, A. 2011 *Archaeological desktop assessment, QBN corridor, Thomas and James's Street, Cornmarket and High Street, Dublin 8.* Unpublished report courtesy of Arch-Tech Ltd.

Giacometti, A. and McGlade, S. 2015 *Archaeological Report*: James's and Thomas Street QBC Dublin 8. 13E401. Archaeological report available at www.archaeologyplan.com/projects.

Halpin, A. 2005 'Development phases in Hiberno-Norse Dublin: a tale of two cities'. In S. Duffy (ed.), *Medieval Dublin VI*. Four Courts Press, Dublin, pp 94–113.

McCready, C.T. 1892 *Dublin street names dated and explained*. Carraig Books, Dublin, 1987 reprint.

McCutcheon, C. 2006 *Medieval pottery from Wood Quay, Dublin*. National Museum of Ireland, Dublin.

Murphy, M. and Potterton, M. 2010 *The Dublin region in the Middle Ages: settlement, land-use and economy*. Four Courts Press and the Discovery Programme, Dublin. Medieval Rural Settlement Project.

Myles, F. 2005 *24–26 Ardee Street*. Unpublished final excavation report, Margaret Gowan Ltd.

Ronan, M.V. 1927 'The Poddle River and its branches'. *JRSAI* 57, 39–46.

Simpson. L. 1997 'Historical background to the Patrick Street Excavations'. In C. Walsh, *Archaeological excavations at Patrick, Nicholas and Winetavern Streets, Dublin*. Brandon, Dingle.

Simpson, L. 2000 'Forty years a-digging: a preliminary synthesis of archaeological investigations in medieval Dublin'. In S. Duffy (ed.), *Medieval Dublin I*. Four Courts Press, Dublin, pp 11–68.

Simpson, L. 2005 'Viking warrior burials in Dublin: is this the Longphort?' In S. Duffy (ed.), *Medieval Dublin VI*. Four Courts Press, Dublin, pp 11–62.

Thomas, A. 1992 *The walled towns of Ireland*, 2 vols, Irish Academic Press, Dublin.

Walsh, P. 2005 'Appendix 11: the defences at Ardee Street in the context of the Confederate Wars of the 1640s'. In F. Myles (ed.), *24–26 Ardee Street*, pp 449–94. Unpublished final excavation report, Margaret Gowan Ltd.

'The Mortimer has taken great pains to save and keep the peace': crown, city and community during the Bruce invasion and its aftermath

PAUL DRYBURGH

On 7 October 1320, the mayor and commonalty of Dublin petitioned King Edward II, complaining that 'evil men of the marches near to your said city' were threatening the city and any citizens who wished to ply their trade in its environs. Merchandise was being robbed and hauled off to the fortalices of the Irish and the culprits, they feared, could expect a ready pardon from the authorities.[1] This narrative of lawlessness menacing the heart of government, justice and finance, the local urban and rural economy and mercantile and political elites, the inability of government to combat it effectively, and the criminality of the Gaelic Irish and of those communities of mixed ethnicity on the fringes of English authority is familiar to students of late thirteenth- and early fourteenth-century Dublin and the lordship of Ireland.[2] These, indeed, had been the main concerns debated at the Irish parliament held in Dublin as recently as May of that year.[3] The petitioners also reported rumours, though, that the Scots were massing 'with great power in order to destroy your land of Ireland'. They begged Edward to show them grace, without which 'we could not be relieved even for a single day from the great losses we have suffered due to this war, or maintain your city'.

How much truth lies behind this petition is open to question. The three-year invasion led by Edward, brother of the Scottish king Robert Bruce, Edward's subsequent coronation as king of Ireland in the early summer of 1315 and the struggle to make good his kingship, exacerbated by famine and endemic warfare, had ended abruptly with his death in battle at Faughart on 14 October 1318.[4] As Colm McNamee has shown, the Scots' position in Ulster

1 TNA SC 8/82/4090, apparently incorrectly dated to 1321. The petition is printed and attributed to 1320 in G.O. Sayles (ed.), *Documents on the affairs of Ireland before the king's council*, IMC (Dublin, 1979), pp 105–6, no. 144; Gilbert (ed.), *Hist. & mun. docs*, 391–2. 2 J.F. Lydon (ed.), *Law and disorder in thirteenth-century Ireland: the Dublin parliament of 1297* (Dublin, 1997); R.F. Frame, 'Power and society in the lordship of Ireland, 1272–1377' in idem (ed.), *Ireland and Britain, 1170–1450* (London, 1998), pp 191–220. For the situation in Co. Dublin, see Áine Foley, *The royal manors of medieval Co. Dublin: crown and community* (Dublin, 2010). 3 H.F. Berry (ed.), *Statutes and ordinances and acts of the parliament of Ireland, John–Henry V* (Dublin, 1907), pp 280–90. 4 R.F. Frame, 'The Bruces in Ireland, 1315–18' in idem (ed.), *Ireland and Britain*, pp 71–98; Seán Duffy, 'The Bruce invasion of Ireland: a revised itinerary and chronology' in idem (ed.), *Robert the Bruce's Irish wars: the*

was gravely weakened by this defeat and their command of the North Channel of the Irish Sea was compromised, though never broken, by the activities of John of Athy, the captain charged by the Dublin government with reasserting English naval supremacy.[5] Moreover, in form the petition often acted as a performative, rhetorical device whose wording intended to make the best possible case within legal and discursive parameters. We might therefore view it as a consciously alarmist attempt to persuade the king to dispatch fresh resources to shore up the impecunious lordship.[6] It is all the more intriguing, then, that the citizens end their plea by commending 'the Mortimer', the recently-departed justiciar of Ireland, as he 'has taken great pains to save and keep the peace of your land'.[7]

The 'Mortimer' in question is Roger Mortimer, marcher lord of Wigmore in Herefordshire and of the Irish liberty of Trim in Meath.[8] He had twice acted as chief governor of Ireland during the Bruce invasion, first as the king's lieutenant from late November 1316 to the spring of 1318 and then as justiciar from March 1319 to his departure around eighteen months later. His arrival in Ireland at the head of an army around a thousand strong – at Youghal (Co. Cork) in the first week of April 1317, an event tellingly recorded by the annalist of St Mary's abbey, Dublin[9] – coincided with the slow retreat from Munster back to Ulster of an ailing, hungry Scottish army under King Robert, and the Scottish king's return to Scotland around 22 May 1317.[10]

Only six weeks before Mortimer's landing, hopelessly delayed by the uncertainty of winter sea-passage and difficulties in raising sufficient troops,[11] the Scots had come perilously close to breaching the defences of Dublin, terrorizing the citizens, a more alarming repeat of another near-miss in the

invasions of Ireland, 1306–29 (Stroud, 2002), pp 9–44. For Faughart, see G.O. Sayles, 'The battle of Faughart, 1318' in Duffy (ed.), *Robert the Bruce's Irish wars*, pp 107–18. 5 Colm McNamee, *The wars of the Bruces: Scotland, England and Ireland, 1306–1328* (East Linton, 1997), p. 186. 6 W.M. Ormrod, Gwilym Dodd and Anthony Musson (eds), *Medieval petitions: grace and grievance* (Woodbridge, 2009), pp 9, 135–56. 7 '*le Mortumer se ad moult penee de sauver et garder la pees de vostre terre*'. 8 Ian Mortimer, *The greatest traitor: the life of Sir Roger Mortimer, 1st Earl of March, ruler of England, 1327–1330* (London, 2003); P.R. Dryburgh, 'The career of Roger Mortimer, first earl of March (*c*.1287–1330)' (PhD, Bristol, 2002). 9 *CStM*, ii, p. 355 (7 April). 10 R.F. Frame, 'The campaign against the Scots in Munster, 1317' in idem (ed.), *Ireland and Britain*, pp 99–112; *CStM*, ii, p. 355; John Barbour, *The Bruce*, ed. A.A.M. Duncan (Edinburgh, 1997), p. 594. 11 Six weeks after letters patent of appointment were attested, Mortimer was formally named commander of 150 mounted and 500 foot soldiers: *CPR 1313–17*, pp 563–4; *Parliamentary writs and writs of military summons*, ed. F. Palgrave, 2 vols (London, 1848), II, i, p. 484 (4 January 1317). Sixteen prominent English lords with lands in Ireland were summoned to join the expedition, or to send men, but there is little evidence outside the former justiciar John Wogan that those summoned served: *CCR, 1313–18*, pp 450–51, discussed in Beth Hartland, 'Reasons for leaving: the effect of conflict on English landholding in late thirteenth-century Leinster', *Journal of Medieval History* 32:1 (March 2006), 18–26. Shipping summoned to Haverford for February failed to array until April: *CPR, 1313–17*, pp 574–5, 646.

early months of 1316.[12] But, as I have shown elsewhere, Mortimer's periods in office allowed him to impart and imprint his personal understanding and knowledge of the political and military culture of Ireland and gradually reassert English lordship on behalf of the English crown.[13] From the perspective of 1320, the conflation in the minds of the Dubliners of the preservation of peace and relief from the ravages of war with Mortimer's governance suggests, arguably, a broad recognition of the stability his periods in power brought to Ireland and of the protection he had afforded the city and community. The centre craved stability and strong, experienced leadership to marshal political society in its loyalty to the crown, protect economic activity and restrain and punish the enemies of peace and the rule of law. It also suggests the citizens ardently desired his return, or at the very least an expedition of a similarly well-connected magnate who would inject military and financial resources and prevent the city's repeated vulnerability being fatally exposed should there be a renewed attack from the Scots.

This essay, then, aims to look more closely at the relationship of Dublin and its citizens with a chief governor recruited in England but with deep-rooted local tenurial interests and personal networks and experience. By exploiting a rich surviving source base,[14] it will explore the dissemination of patronage, the employment of force and judicial sanction, and the brokering of compromise in a febrile atmosphere where a Scottish army remained a looming, unpredictable northern presence whose threat remained real for the skittish citizens of Dublin. It will assess the extent of the success of Mortimer and his associates in restoring order and creating harmony both within and between urban and rural communities, native and settler, as the city perhaps faced its greatest challenge throughout the Middle Ages to its place within the English crown's dominions.

MORTIMER AS LIEUTENANT OF IRELAND, NOVEMBER 1316–MAY 1318

Roger Mortimer arrived in Dublin within a fortnight of landing in Co. Cork on 7 April 1317. His first formal act was to convene the Irish Council at Kilmainham on 23 April.[15] Here and in the following months, he paid close

12 Duffy, 'Revised itinerary', pp 23–5, 33–5. 13 P.R. Dryburgh, 'Roger Mortimer's governance of Ireland, 1317–20' in Brendan Smith (ed.), *Ireland and the English world in the Middle Ages: essays in honour of Robin Frame* (London, 2009), pp 89–102. See also A.J. Otway-Ruthven, *A history of medieval Ireland* (London, 1968), pp 233–7; Mortimer, *The greatest traitor*, pp 72–89. 14 Despite the Four Courts bombing of 1922, there survive a memoranda roll and several plea rolls for his administrations together with nineteenth-century Record Commission transcripts of original material, including a justiciary roll: NAI EX 1 (original memoranda roll); KB 1/2 (original justiciary roll), 2/8–12 (calendared justiciary rolls); RC 7/12 (justiciary roll transcript), 8/10–12 (memoranda roll transcripts, 10–14 Edward II). 15 *Jacobi Grace Kilkenniensis Annales Hiberniae*, ed. R. Butler (Dublin,

attention to soothing tensions at the elite levels of Anglo-Irish society and ensuring the community at the heart of the lordship received reassurance of its centrality to the operation of English rule in Ireland. That he was able to attempt this is down to the fact that as lieutenant he literally held the king's place, personifying a monarchy none of whose kings had set foot in Ireland since King John's mission of the 1210s;[16] he was thereby belatedly attempting to bring the community closer to the crown. This was a signal honour previously held only by Piers Gaveston, Edward II's executed favourite, whose mission in 1308–9 had succeeded in subduing much of Leinster.[17] The title recognized not only Mortimer's own place as one of the king's closest courtiers, his place as a senior landholder in Ireland but also the connections he brought to the coordination of English military strategy as Edward II sought to redress the balance in his conflict with the Scots.[18] Mortimer arrived with an enormous fee of £6000, redeemable in the king's wardrobe, not in the Dublin exchequer.[19] This provided him with the financial and military clout to reinforce extraordinary powers to dispense patronage and justice, punish and pardon rebels and criminals, and negotiate with native community leaders on an equal footing, while operating outside the basic military and judicial functions of the justiciar.

The most controversial conciliar debate surrounded Ireland's premier magnate, Richard de Burgh, earl of Ulster. Following a failed ambush on the Scots near Slane in Meath around 15 February 1316 as they headed once more southwards out of Ulster, Earl Richard had fled with his family to the Cistercian abbey of St Mary's in the city. Hearing of the subsequent advance on their city of an army rumoured to be 20,000 men and suspecting collusion between the earl and King Robert Bruce – who also happened to be his son-in-law – the mayor of Dublin, Robert of Nottingham, raised the posse, extricated the earl from the abbey and imprisoned him in Dublin Castle.[20] Despite commands to several Anglo-Irish magnates in March, at the height of the crisis, de Burgh's release had not been secured, and Mortimer came with a royal mandate to liberate him.[21] These events had the capacity to cast long

1842), p. 85. **16** Seán Duffy, 'John and Ireland: the origins of England's Irish problem' in S.D. Church (ed.), *King John: new interpretations* (Woodbridge, 1999), pp 221–45. **17** J.S. Hamilton, *Piers Gaveston, earl of Cornwall: politics and patronage in the age of Edward II* (London, 1988), pp 55–7. On 15 June 1308, Richard de Burgh, earl of Ulster, had been made lieutenant but Edward replaced him with Gaveston on the following day as part of a scheme to offset the shame and financial loss of exile from court: *CPR 1307–13*, p. 83. **18** Dryburgh, 'Roger Mortimer's governance', pp 92–3; McNamee, *Wars of the Bruces*, pp 149–51, 181–4. **19** TNA E 208/2/2, no. 421. **20** *CStM*, ii, pp 298, 299, 352; *Grace*, p. 79. The earl's arrest probably reflects paranoia from the citizens rather than actual guilt on his part; for which, see Duffy, 'Revised itinerary', pp 33–5. **21** *Grace*, p. 81. The recipients were Edmund Butler, Thomas fitz John, earl of Kildare, Richard de Clare, Arnold le Poer and Maurice fitz Thomas. Similarly, letters had been sent at this time to several magnates thanking them for their loyalty and encouraging them to remain loyal: *CCR 1313–18*, pp shadows over trust relationships between the king and the Anglo-Irish magnate community and imperil the Dubliners' status vis-à-vis the crown. Even given the lieutenant's extraordinary authority, the negotiations over the earl's release, first mandated on 8 May,[22] were sufficiently influenced by de Burgh's stormy relationship with other prominent members of the political elite, notably Arnold le Poer, seneschal of Kilkenny, with whom he was embroiled in an interminable land dispute, that it took another two months to secure a safe conduct and release from all pending legal actions against the earl.[23]

In successfully negotiating the earl of Ulster's release, Roger Mortimer walked a tightrope in balancing the broader interests of the lordship against those of the citizens and community of Dublin. Following the failure of the earl's ambush, the Scots descended upon the western suburbs of the city, taking Castleknock.[24] Fearing a full-on assault, the citizens dismantled the Dominican friary of St Saviour's and used the stone to heighten and fortify parts of the city wall nearest the bridge over the Liffey. Houses against the wall were hurriedly pulled down and much of the suburb fired to deny the Scots cover. Total damage was put at £10,000 and penalties were imposed on the citizens.[25] But, by September, Mortimer had created a route by which they could be received back into royal favour and atone for these misdeeds. He attested a pardon in that month for the mayor and community of £600 of old debts 'for good service to the king and their great labours in repairing walls and towers of the city and in the custody of the city'.[26] A six-year reduction in the city's annual farm followed.[27] In December 1317, he secured a further relief of 100 marks of the penalty and ensured actions initiated against them for civic vandalism were prohibited.[28] Perhaps as importantly, on the same day as the pardon for debt, Mortimer attested another pardon for the mayor and bailiffs for taking four pence from each crannock of corn coming into the city before that date without seeking royal licence, with a backdated grant that they could continue to do so until Christmas.[29] The practical fiscal benefit of this measure in famine-ravaged Ireland is difficult to assess, but it symbolized, at least in the short term, a restoration of civic rights and acceptance into royal protection.

Simultaneously, Mortimer also initiated small steps to tackle the devastation and poverty caused by the Bruce invasion in the hinterland of Dublin. On 20 August 1317, he witnessed a licence to the Hospitallers in Ireland to acquire outright their tenants' lands in counties Dublin, Meath and Kildare

464–5 (28 April 1317). **22** NAI RC 8/11, pp 311–12, 519. **23** NAI RC 7/12, pp 399–400; *CIRCLE*, Patent Roll [PR] 11 Edw. II, nos 4, 5, (23 July), 7 (24 July). **24** Duffy, 'Revised itinerary', pp 33–5; *Grace*, p. 78; *CStM*, ii, pp 352–3. **25** NAI RC 8/12, pp 20–6, detail at p. 25. **26** *CIRCLE* PR 11 Edw. II, no. 20; Gilbert (ed.), *Hist. & mun. docs*, p. 404 (8 September 1317). **27** Gilbert (ed.), *Hist. & mun. docs*, pp 392–3. **28** NAI RC 7/12, 175 (10 December 1317). **29** *CIRCLE* PR 11 Edw. II, nos 19–20; Gilbert (ed.), *Hist. & mun. docs*, pp 402–3 (8 September 1317).

'devastated by wars', and enfeoff others with them. This gave the prior and brethren the potential to raise income and more effectively and profitably manage their estates, some of which had come to them only recently with the dissolution of the order of the Knights Templar in 1308.[30] There were also measures gradually introduced to alleviate the suffering of tenants on royal demense manors in Co. Dublin during the lieutenancy: on 28 May 1318, by his bill, Mortimer authorized a pardon of rent in arrears since Easter term 1317 from the tenants of Saggart and Newcastle Lyons, 'so impoverished by the king's Scottish enemies and the men of Ulster that they cannot hold their lands unless grace is done to them'. The exchequer barons were ordered to strike these arrears from the rolls and acquit the king's tenants.[31] This is suggestive of a process of negotiation, inquisition and concession that aimed to relieve some of the worst local consequences of the Scots' invasion.

The fragility of the social and tenurial map of the lordship and more especially within what would in the fifteenth century become the four loyal shires (Dublin, Kildare, Louth and Meath) had been painfully exposed by the Bruce invasion. In the year before Mortimer's expedition – and undoubtedly a prompt for its launch – the lordship of western Meath and the new earldom of Kildare became vacant following the deaths respectively of Theobald de Verdun and John fitz Thomas in July and September 1316.[32] Two major territorial blocs to the west of Dublin had therefore been shorn of magnate leadership. Moreover, certain elements of Anglo-Irish society had, it was rumoured, used the Scots' invasion to fill this vacuum and assert their claim to lands within Mortimer's tenurial sphere of influence in the Irish Midlands.

The landed estates held by the family of Mortimer of Wigmore in Ireland had first constituted Dunamase (Co. Laois), the share of the Marshal inheritance brought to her husband Roger (d.1282) by Matilda de Braose in 1247.[33] But in 1301 the family's Irish interests in Ireland were transformed by the marriage of Roger, the fourteen-year-old heir to the lordship of Wigmore, to Joan, the teenage granddaughter of the former justiciar, Geoffrey de Joinville. This brought him the affluent, settled liberty of Trim in Meath, a prize worth striving to protect;[34] between 1308 and 1314 Joan bore Roger an unknown number of his twelve children in Ireland, a striking commitment to establishing their personal lordship. During this period, Mortimer also

30 *CIRCLE* PR 11 Edw. II, no. 12. They had similar letters in respect of their tenants in counties Cork, Tipperary, Limerick and Louth: ibid., no. 13. For recent research on the Hospitallers in Ireland, see Martin Browne and Colmán Ó Clabaigh (eds), *Soldiers of Christ: the Knights Hospitaller and the Knights Templar in medieval Ireland* (Dublin, 2016), particularly those essays by Helen Nicholson, Margaret Murphy and Colmán Ó Clabaigh. 31 NAI EX 1/2, m. 2d; *CIRCLE* CR 11 Edw. II, no. 10; PR 11 Edw. II, no. 226. 32 Dryburgh, 'Roger Mortimer's governance', p. 92. 33 G.H. Orpen, *Ireland under the Normans, 1169–1333* (rev. ed., Dublin, 2005), pp 319–20. 34 *CCR 1307–13*, p. 15. For Trim see Michael Potterton, *Medieval Trim: history and archaeology* (Dublin, 2005);

stepped confidently into the competitive nature of magnate society in the Irish Midlands, received a blooding in warfare and displayed a capacity for compromise when intervening to broker a peaceful settlement to the de Verdun rebellion in Louth.[35] This, as I have previously shown, acclimatized Mortimer to the troublesome issues and personalities current among the political elite in Ireland.[36] He cannot but have been a regular visitor to Dublin for business and on voyages to and from England and must have become very familiar with the city, its community and its hinterland, accumulating the 'stock of knowledge' Robin Frame believes contributed most to the success of any chief governor.[37] It must therefore have been a terrific shock to Mortimer and the Dubliners when he arrived in full flight in the city following his rout by the Scots in battle at Kells (Co. Meath) on 6 December 1315.[38] Nonetheless, though the citizens panicked, his flight points to his reception and place among the community leaders, and it was upon the judicial and military assistance of local men that Mortimer sought to remove this stain on his reputation and allow him to reset the delicate local tenurial balance in his favour.

The release of the earl of Ulster allowed Mortimer to travel to Trim, to consolidate his personal lordship in a liberty through which the Scots had marched both when intent upon Dublin and when retreating north during that year. As part of this process, he ordered the leaders of the de Lacy family, Hugh and Walter, lord of Rathwire, to return to the king's peace.[39] Relatives of Mortimer's wife, Joan de Joinville, the brothers had been tried in February 1317, but acquitted, of inviting the Bruces to conquer Ireland in 1315 and deserting Mortimer at Kells to guide them through Meath, Kildare and Offaly.[40] They responded by murdering his messenger. But, in a skirmish on 3 June, a posse of local knights defeated Walter beneath the royal standard. A counterattack two days later was repelled and the de Lacys fled, to be outlawed and exiled as traitors on 18 July.[41]

Their exile allowed Mortimer to import some English and other more local clients into estates forfeited by the brothers and their allies.[42] On 6 September in Dublin Mortimer attested a gift to himself of all lands and tenements within the liberty of Trim that pertained to the king by forfeiture.[43] Within the

Dryburgh, 'Career of Roger Mortimer', pp 26–39. **35** For the de Verdun rebellion, see Brendan Smith, *Colonization and conquest in medieval Ireland: the English in Louth, 1170–1330* (Cambridge, 1999), pp 97–105. **36** For more detailed coverage see Dryburgh, 'Roger Mortimer's governance', pp 91–2. **37** R.F. Frame, 'English officials and Irish chiefs in the fourteenth century' in idem (ed.), *Ireland and Britain*, p. 261. **38** *CStM*, ii, p. 348. **39** He was there by 22 May 1317: Duffy, 'Revised itinerary', p. 39. **40** The trial proceedings are printed at *CStM*, ii, pp 407–16; Grace, p. 79. They had also been among those lords thanked by Edward II for their services against the Scots on 28 April 1317: *CCR 1313–18*, pp 464–5. **41** *CStM*, ii, p. 355. **42** *CPR 1313–17*, p. 563. This reveals that an important condition for service as lieutenant was Edward II's promise of the forfeited lands of his tenants who had adhered to the Scots. **43** Herbert Wood, 'The muniments of Edmund de Mortimer, third earl of March, concerning his liberty of Trim', *PRIA*, 40C (1932), next three months, an English client, Hugh Turpilton, received lands and appurtenances in fee at Balylug and Tubbrid within the barony of Kells, forfeited by Walter, son of Walter de Say, similarly outlawed for adherence to the Scots.[44] Rent from Walter's mills in Kells augmented this grant, as did the manor of Martry (Co. Meath) and his forfeited lands in Ulster.[45] Another client from the Welsh March, Richard of Idsall in Shropshire, obtained land in Balrothery (Co. Dublin) in fee to him and his wife.[46] Thomas Hereford was rewarded with lands in fee in Nutstown, Whitestown in the tenement of Ballymadun, and Carpenterstown and Wiltonestoun in Finglas (Co. Dublin), forfeited by John Kermerdin who 'rose in war against the king's banner in the company of Walter and Hugh de Lacy, felons'.[47] These grants significantly increased the stake of those beholden to Roger Mortimer in both Meath and over the border in Dublin. They forged an environment in which Mortimer could exercise his lordship more comfortably and had the intention of preventing the de Lacys once again exercising a hereditary claim to Trim or reasserting themselves in the liberty once Mortimer returned to England. Equally, such grants were meaningful in the wider conflict with the Scots, for men like Turpilton would go on to fight and defeat Edward Bruce at Faughart defending their newly-won estates.

The defeat of Mortimer's personal rivals reinvigorated the Dublin government's militarism. It engaged with problematic communities further afield, and enabled him to secure the capital. On 8 July, the Dublin exchequer disbursed £422 for 'strengthening the peace and putting down the rebellion and insolence of the English and Irish'.[48] After a campaign against Seán Ó Fearghail in Longford,[49] the Irish of Uí Máil in Wicklow were defeated at 'Glynsely' on 6 September.[50] The southern environs of Dublin had long been vulnerable to attack from Wicklow; it was no doubt satisfying that Mortimer received submission of Ó Broin, to be imprisoned at Dublin Castle. This temporarily removed a major power broker and obstacle to peace in Leinster, and demonstrated to the Dubliners and tenants of vulnerable demesne manors – Saggart, Esker and Newcastle Lyons – that their security was being taken seriously when finances allowed.

Success on land dovetailed with success at sea. Around 2 July 1317, a sea battle off the Welsh coast culminated in the arrest, by John of Athy, and

appendix 2, no. VI, p. 333; *CIRCLE* PR 11 Edw. II, no. 214. **44** *CIRCLE* PR 11 Edw. II, nos 151, 155 (1 & 2 December 1317); *CPR 1327–30*, p. 345. **45** *CIRCLE* PR 11 Edw. II, nos 211, 215, 217 (1 March 1318, 1 December 1317, 1 February 1318); PR 13 Edw. II, no. 55 (undated); TNA C 66/170, m. 2. **46** *CIRCLE* PR 11 Edw. II, nos 98 (28 February 1318), 115 (27 March 1318). **47** *CIRCLE* PR 11 Edw. II, no. 34 (23 September 1317). Life grants were made to John Corbaly of tenements in Balysaneth on 6 September 1317, and to John and Laurence fitz Simon near Kells: PR 11 Edw. II, no. 194 (22 March 1318). **48** Philomena Connolly (ed.), *Irish exchequer payments, 1270–1446* (Dublin, 1998), p. 242. **49** *Grace*, p. 91; *CStM*, ii, p. 356. **50** Mortimer received £43 1*s*. 1*d*. for campaigning in subsequent execution of Thomas Dun, the Scottish pirate who had long menaced the coastal communities of the eastern seaboard of Ireland.[51] This was the ripest of the fruits of a collaboration born in the royal household: Athy had joined Edward II's household as a simple knight on 29 March, only a few days before he captained the fleet bearing Mortimer to Ireland.[52] It is evident that the English king and his advisers had come belatedly to the knowledge that the naval dominance on the Irish Sea was a serious strategic advantage to the Scots which they should tackle. Athy was instructed to remain at sea for the defence of Ireland and, no doubt principally, to prevent raiding on Dublin and other coastal towns. Upon his defeat of Thomas Dun, Athy was rewarded on 6 July with the keepership of the Isle of Man.[53] Henceforth, his reassertion of English sea power may have liberated the sea lanes of the North Channel and north Irish Sea for merchants of coastal communities, particularly north of Dublin, to ply their trade more freely and for the Dublin government to transport men and supplies into and out of the lordship.

Two pieces of record evidence document the mutual satisfaction Roger Mortimer and Edward II could share in the appointment of the former as the man to hold the king's place in Ireland during chronic military, political and economic crises. On 17 October 1317, firstly, Baldwin Darcy received £10 in the king's chamber in England for 'bringing the king certain good rumours' about Ireland.[54] The immediate possibility of Scottish conquest had gone, the threat to Dublin been largely removed and some stability restored. Just over six months later, secondly, upon Mortimer's recall to England,[55] Edward II commended Mortimer for having acted 'for the safety of the land and to repel rebels, and many have testified to his good service there'.[56] Edward Bruce had not ventured from Ulster for almost a year and the St Mary's abbey chronicler revealed that an agricultural recovery was underway, reporting the baking of bread following the first good harvest since 1314.[57] King Edward may have received positive testimony on behalf of less wealthy freeholders – those with land worth under £20 a year – who were permitted to offer fines at the Dublin exchequer for their relief rather than voyage to England to perform homage for their lands.[58] This was a boon to the gentry of all areas of Ireland but may well have arisen from requests made by those communities within a relatively short distance of Dublin.

Leinster: Connolly (ed.), *Exchequer payments*, pp 248–9. **51** *Grace*, p. 89. For possible evidence of Dun's surrender to one Geoffrey de Cogery, see TNA PRO 28/136 (Soc. Antiqs. MS 121), p. 57 (8 October 1317). **52** TNA PRO 28/136 (Soc. Antiqs. MS 120), pp 104, 117. **53** *CFR 1307–19*, p. 332. **54** TNA PRO 28/136 (Soc. Antiqs. MS 120), p. 57. **55** Mortimer appears to have left Ireland at the end of May. He witnessed a writ on 28 May, but he was indisputably in Wales sometime in June: NAI RC 8/12, pp 12–13; TNA PRO 28/136 (Soc. Antiqs. MS 121), p. 60. **56** TNA E 159/92, rot. 177. **57** *CStM*, ii, p. 359. **58** NAI RC 7/12, m. 10 (13 October 1317).

Much of this success we might argue, however, had been achieved in the intervening period at a remove from Dublin and stored up controversy for the future. Judicial circuits in southwestern Ireland by Mortimer and the justiciar, Butler, during the winter of 1317–18 actively involved both disciplining and brokering compromise between warring dynastic kin groups within the Anglo-Irish community. Various fines were imposed to secure peace agreements in Cork and Waterford, for example.[59] Pardons, sanctioned by senior magnates, were also issued to leading individuals as part of this process of reconciliation and promotion of loyalty to the English crown.[60] This strategy reflected a more flexible attitude in the Dublin government towards the remoteness of some parts of the Anglo-Irish community from the centre and from personal interaction with royal majesty. It also represented an intervention, albeit transient, into a strategy of longer standing to encourage heads of lineages to discipline their followers, both English and Irish. Endemic warfare in some parts of Ireland had not only drained the financial resources available to the government in tackling criminality but had serious consequences for the wider Irish Sea economy.

We can discern the vocal lobby of the wider community of Dublin behind criticism of the crown's judicial strategy in Ireland at this period. Common petitions of 'the middling folk' and on behalf of 'the community of his [i.e. Edward II's] land of Ireland', submitted in the years 1317–19, railed against pervasive violence and the liberal use of pardons and fines.[61] On 22 October 1317, the mayor and community of Dublin – as they would reiterate in their petition of 7 October 1320, with which this paper began – urged that no felon should be released by any royal minister for damage previously done to the community or county but only by the king himself;[62] victims of robbery and violence were mounting and had little expectation of justice while economic activity suffered.[63] As head of the Dublin government, Roger Mortimer would have been in little doubt of popular opinion and may, as in the case of overtures to the Gaelic Irish community during his period in office, discussed elsewhere,[64] have viewed his vice-regal powers as sufficient warrant to use the levers of patronage as much as military force to try and address social dislocation across multiple communities during the Bruce invasion.

The military situation as 1317 became 1318 displayed starkly the difficulties the government faced and, to an extent, the progress the Mortimer/Butler regime had made both in facing both the worst effects of conflict across parts

59 For specific examples see NAI KB 2/12, m. 2d; RC 7/12, pp 148–51. **60** Discussed in more detail in Dryburgh, 'Roger Mortimer's governance', p. 95. **61** TNA SC 8/177/8820, /218/10873, printed in Sayles (ed.), *Documents on the affairs of Ireland*, nos 136–7, pp 99–101 (undated). **62** TNA SC 8/177/8817, printed in Sayles (ed.), *Documents on the affairs of Ireland*, no. 111, pp 85–6. **63** J.F. Lydon, *The lordship of Ireland in the Middle Ages* (2nd ed., Dublin, 2003), p. 138. **64** Dryburgh, 'Roger Mortimer's governance', pp 96, 98; and, more especially, G.J. Hand, *English law in Ireland, 1275–1324* (Cambridge, 1967), pp 207–9.

of the lordship and in the social engineering that had been attempted. During the autumn of 1317, 200 men under Butler's command were massacred by Donnchadh Ó Cearbhaill.[65] Later, in the month of Mortimer's recall to England, on 10 May 1318, Richard de Clare, lord of Thomond, was ambushed and murdered at Dysart O'Dea.[66] Nevertheless, despite these setbacks, the Scots had been kept in abeyance for over a year and when, finally, in the early autumn of 1318, Edward Bruce moved once more, his army was defeated on 14 October at Faughart (Co. Louth) by levies speedily raised from counties Louth and Meath.[67] As shown above, these were precisely those areas into which Roger Mortimer had extended his personal influence, and, as Seán Duffy perceptively notes, those areas which Bruce repeatedly targeted between 1315 and 1318 when Mortimer, the senior landholder there, was absent from the country.[68] The leader of these levies, John de Bermingham, who had been knighted by Mortimer after the campaign against the de Lacys,[69] had significantly increased his tenurial standing in the county and it was Bruce's misfortune that he met men in the field who had so much more to lose.

MORTIMER AS JUSTICIAR, MAY 1319–SEPTEMBER 1320

Faughart achieved for Edward II what the appointment of Roger Mortimer as his lieutenant almost two years previously had intended: it removed the cancerous influence of a rival royal authority in Ireland and so cemented English rule. It brought royal majesty to disparate groups often physically isolated from and intellectually uninterested in it. It also not only gave the English king a fleeting but important victory and thus a temporary respite in his war with the Scots but it also allowed him to go on the offensive. The Dublin government, in the person of the admiral John of Athy, regained Carrickfergus Castle by 2 December, installing a garrison there some months later.[70] Ulster and some of the towns on the eastern seaboard then more actively participated in a variety of diplomatic and military offensives. Naval diplomats took seductive messages about the benefits of loyalty to the English king into the Western Isles and along the Hebridean coastline of Scotland, areas divided in their loyalty to Bruce's kingship of Scotland.[71] In the summer campaign of 1319 to recover the strategic border town of Berwick, captured by the Scots on 2 April 1318,[72] victuals were to be collected in Ireland for shipping to the English army.[73] This was a sign of agricultural recovery and also of the

65 Bernadette Williams (ed.), *The annals of Ireland by Friar John Clyn* (Dublin, 2007), p. 168. **66** Ibid., p. 170. **67** Sayles, 'Battle of Faughart', pp 107–18. **68** Duffy, 'Revised itinerary', p. 39. **69** Williams (ed.), *Annals of Clyn*, p. 168. **70** *CPR 1317–21*, pp 311, 313. **71** *CCR 1318–23*, p. 127. For more general analysis see Michael Penman, *Robert the Bruce, king of Scots* (Newhaven and London, 2014), passim. **72** Barbour, *The Bruce*, pp 622–6. **73** *CCR 1318–23*, p. 87 (8 June 1319).

fact that those shires closest to Dublin might contribute to the reassertion of English hegemony across the British Isles for the first time since the Bannockburn campaign of 1314.

The job, of course, remained far from complete. The process of stabilizing English rule in Ireland proved patchy and sporadic at best. It had created thorny issues that pricked at the bubble of improved security and social harmony which Mortimer's lieutenancy had blown. Tellingly though, the hiatus in Mortimer governance in Ireland was relatively brief. His return to England in June 2018 thrust him into the tense negotiations between Edward II and his cousin, Thomas of Lancaster, the leader of the baronial opposition.[74] Such was the magnate community's trust in Roger Mortimer and his recent military and administrative achievements that he was elected as one of sixteen councillors without whom Edward II swore to undertake royal business, and then one of four councillors to remain constantly with the king.[75] In the planning of the Berwick campaign in the early months of 1319, Mortimer could argue for a return to Ireland as justiciar on 15 March 1319 as well as lay important groundwork for that mission from this role.[76]

The defeat and death of Edward Bruce removed an immediate military threat to the fragile balance of power across Ireland and permitted further intervention in the seigneurial structure of the Irish Midlands. On the day following his appointment as justiciar, Mortimer was ordered to grant respite to Thomas Hereford and Roger and John Gernon of Meath from the escheats of the king's enemies, due to their service at Faughart, 'that they may be made more ready to render their service in future'.[77] Two months later, Alexander Bicknor, archbishop of Dublin and justiciar of Ireland, attested a grant to the citizens of Dublin that they should not be impleaded outside of their city walls on any plea save those relating to external tenements, as per their charter of liberties.[78] On a grander scale, Mortimer was at court when the victor of Faughart and one of his key advisers during the lieutenancy, John de Bermingham, was elevated to the earldom of Louth on 12 May 1319.[79]

Roger Mortimer returned to Ireland in late May 1319 and left in September 1320. Whether his title reflected a diminution in his status and the powers at his disposal or the de-escalation of the crisis is not easy to determine. His period as justiciar certainly witnessed little change in the programme he had

74 T.F. Tout, *The place of the reign of Edward II in English history* (Manchester, 1914); J. Goronwy Edwards, 'The negotiating of the Treaty of Leake, 1318', *English Historical Review*, 30 (1915), 569–601; Bertie Wilkinson, 'The negotiations preceding the "Treaty" of Leake, August 1318' in R.W. Hunt, W.A. Pantin and R.W. Southern (eds), *Studies in medieval history presented to Frederick Maurice Powicke* (Oxford, 1948), pp 333–53. 75 T.F. Tout, *The political history of England*, iii (London, 1905), p. 270. 76 *CCR 1318–23*, pp 61, 129; *CPR 1317–21*, p. 317. 77 *CIRCLE* PR 13 Edw. II, no. 91 (16 March 1319). Hereford similarly received the lands forfeited by Aymer de Lacy in Portlek by bill of the justiciar: *CIRCLE* PR 13 Edw. II, no. 23 (26 June 1320). 78 *CIRCLE* CR 12 Edw. II, no. 4 (18 May 1319). 79 *CPR 1317–21*, pp 334–5. For discussion of the local impact, see Smith,

led as lieutenant. The scheme to receive Irishmen into English law – meagre though the evidence is – was resumed.[80] In August 1319, more aggressive measures were taken against the Gaelic community by the appointment of two Mortimer retainers Nicholas de Turville, sheriff of Meath, and John fitz Simon, to arrest Irish felons, bring them and their receivers to Dublin Castle and proclaim that no one sell victuals to local chiefs.[81] These measures operated concurrently with further steps to impose a new layer of clients on the shires north and west of Dublin and prop up exhausted communities. On 28 May 1320, for example, Mortimer sent his bill to the Irish chancery to have letters drawn up granting Roger Gernon the castle and manor of Taghobrecok, formerly of Hugh de Lacy, 'for the service and strenuous deeds in the recent conflict at Dundalk [i.e., the battle of Faughart]'.[82] The prior and brethren of the hospital of St John outside the New Gate in Dublin received likewise all deodands adjudged before him or itinerant justices for four years. They were to use them to raise money to rebuild their church and priory buildings 'destroyed by fire and robberies'.[83] Probably most importantly, the government attempted to establish greater rigidity in applying the law in Ireland. Such measures reached their maturation at the Dublin parliament of May 1320.[84]

Parliament, as it had largely done at Kilkenny in 1310 – pointing to the longevity of these issues[85] – recognized that bands of evildoers, retained by men of birth, roamed the country, lodging with and then robbing loyal men. This narrative of billeting and highway robbery owed much to the input of the community of Dublin; it was, as we have seen, prominent in the rhetoric of protest employed at this time by the city fathers. The parliamentary ordinances therefore laid down that the hue and cry would be raised and malefactors pursued and arrested, and heads of lineages were made statutorily responsible for disciplining their kinsmen. The corruption of local officials would be addressed by every county receiving a justice and two knights to hold assizes and inquire into sheriffs' activities. Prise – the arbitrary seizure of goods and victuals by lords from tenants – was to cease.[86] This being said, a conciliar agreement for the relief from rendering the city farm was also made in favour of the citizens of Limerick who 'for various reasons are so impoverished that all the goods of the city are scarcely enough to guard the city against the Irish felons and to repair the walls, which are clearly threatened with ruin'.[87] This highlights a concern for the economy of key strategic centres within the lordship.

Colonization and conquest, p. 113. **80** *CPR 1317–21*, pp 339, 342; *CIRCLE* PR 13 Edw. II, no. 93 (14 June 1320). **81** *CIRCLE* PR 13 Edw. II, no. 19 (28 August 1319). **82** *CIRCLE* PR 13 Edw. II, no. 92. **83** *CIRCLE* PR 13 Edw. II, no. 63 (23 August 1319). This enlarged an earlier like grant of 2 December 1317: PR 11 Edw. II, no. 162. For a further petition concerning the poverty of the order in Ireland, see PR 13 Edw. II, no. 86 (14 September 1319). **84** Dryburgh, 'Roger Mortimer's governance', pp 98–9; Hand, *English law in Ireland*, pp 211–12. **85** Lydon, *The lordship of Ireland*, p. 138. **86** Berry (ed.), *Statutes and ordinances*, pp 280–90. **87** NAI Ex 1/2, m. 33d; *CIRCLE* PR 13 Edw. II, no. 41

In a broader sense, touching perhaps on a perceived lack of depth to the operation of English law in Ireland, the military and judicial statutes of Westminster, Marlborough, Merton, Gloucester and Winchester were to be enforced. Furthermore, the justiciar committed to examining any future English legislation and applying it to Ireland, if expedient. Annual parliaments were ordained. In more personal terms, the formerly exiled earl of Ulster, Richard de Burgh, was granted the right to hold all pleas in his liberty court in Ulster as fully as he did before the Scots' invasion.[88] Given the circumstances in which he had fled Ireland in 1317, essentially in dispute with the mayor and civic community of Dublin, we can only imagine the undocumented tensions that had to be negotiated. Not least, there remained the lingering whiff of suspicion around the earl's loyalty to the English crown and the need to protect the Dubliners from the razor edge of the earl's tongue and violent reassertion of his authority.[89]

The statutes of the Dublin parliament of 1320 reveal a people 'greatly distressed and well-nigh destroyed'. The ensuing summer campaigns led by Roger Mortimer into Munster demonstrated that parliamentary initiative would be very difficult to translate into positive action.[90] Further reinforcement of much that had been statutorily instigated had to be restated in 1324 particularly the responsibility of heads of lineages for the felonious behaviour of their kin.[91] We might posit therefore that the periods of Mortimer administration in Ireland, while temporarily filling a vacuum of royal lordship, did little in the longer term to tackle the weakness of the Dublin government. Increasingly, the centre came to be at the mercy of the periphery as power seeped to magnates with the means to exercise it practically; feuding proliferated, which devastated parts of Ireland and spilled over into English politics.[92]

CONCLUSION

To conclude this survey, we must return to the petition with which we began. That the Dublin civic elite should single out Roger Mortimer in 1320 for his efforts to save and keep the peace reflects, in no small measure, a pervasive view among the mercantile and political elite that Mortimer had been a strong governor during a period of crisis. They even go on to commend his deputy, the new earl of Kildare, for continuing the good work as far as he was able. Mortimer had earned respect for combating the Scots and attempting to

(6 May 1320). **88** *CIRCLE* PR 13 Edw. II, no. 46 (8 May 1320). **89** A pardon of 9 May 1320 to the former mayor and accuser of de Burgh, Robert Nottingham, is possible evidence of this approach: *CIRCLE* PR 13 Edw. II, no. 47. **90** Connolly (ed.), *Exchequer payments*, p. 267 (campaigns against the Barrys and into Slievemargy). **91** Berry (ed.), *Statutes and ordinances*, pp 280–90, 307. **92** R.F. Frame, *English lordship in Ireland, 1318–1361* (Oxford, 1981), pp 166–339.

restore order. By combining military force with darker arts, he reinvigorated, albeit temporarily and patchily, the loyalty and utility of the lordship of Ireland to the English crown. With regard to the Scots' possible dabbling again in Irish affairs, no landing was ultimately attempted, but Robert Bruce may have contemplated exploiting Mortimer's absence from Ireland to bring pressure on multiple fronts, and he would certainly benefit from sowing those seeds of doubt. The Dubliners themselves, who requested that a strong governor be sent, may even have concocted the rumours with Mortimer's reinstatement in mind. Even if not, this contemporary testimony contrasts markedly with communal memory in other parts of Ireland towards the Scots. A Connacht annalist, for instance, reported that the death of Edward Bruce brought 'great joy and comfort to the kingdom in general … for there reigned scarcity of victuals, breach of promises, ill performances of covenants, and the loss of men and women throughout the whole realm'.[93]

Throughout the crisis caused by the Scots' invasion of Ireland, the personal presence and political influence of Roger Mortimer played an important role in securing the city of Dublin and thereby the heart of English government for Edward II. Chief governors in the early fourteenth century spent much effort cultivating that community and those surrounding and supplying it. Few faced a more stressed and dislocated elite than Mortimer, and so it must redound to his credit – whatever the long-term success, or otherwise, of his policies in Ireland – that the civic elite of Dublin saw in him an individual who had taken measures to reassure them and could reassure them in future.

93 AClon, p. 282.

I. Yonge scripsit: self-promotion, professional networking and the Anglo-Irish literary scribe

THERESA O'BYRNE

On a cloudy October afternoon, two men sit in the back of a cart making its way between Trim and Dublin. The older man is overly thin, his pallor suggesting a harvest season spent indoors. The younger man moves with the barely controlled nervous energy of youth. As they are overtaken by a gentle rain, the younger man covers his head, while the older man turns his face up towards the clouds. The year is 1423, and the pair are the Anglo-Irish author and legal scribe James Yonge, and his apprentice, Nicholas Bellewe. Yonge, lately released from ten months of imprisonment in Trim Castle, has been delivered to Bellewe for safe transport to Dublin. Yonge's carefully constructed professional network brought him to this pass, and his professional network will help him rebuild his shattered career and reputation. In turn, Yonge's apprentices, Nicholas Bellewe and Thomas Baghill, will use their master's professional network to build their own careers.

The construction of a professional network of clients, nobles, and colleagues was indispensable for late medieval author-scribes. As scholars such as Derek Pearsall, J.A. Burrow, Kathryn Kerby-Fulton, and many others have demonstrated for the professional scribes of London, these skilled writers often had to scramble in order to bring in a modest income from their clerical skills.[1] Geoffrey Chaucer, who earned his primary living as a public servant rather than as a poet, famously complains to his purse, 'I am sorry now that ye be so light,/For certes ye now make me heavy cheer.'[2] In a similar vein, Thomas Hoccleve, who worked for the office of the Privy Seal, seems to have often been concerned about his uncertain income. For instance, in his 1412 *Regiment of Princes*, he complains,

1 Examples of such studies include J.A. Burrow, 'Hoccleve and the "court"' in Helen Cooney (ed.), *Nation, court and culture: essays on fifteenth-century English poetry* (Dublin, 2001), pp 70–80; Kathryn Kerby-Fulton, 'The clerical proletariat: the underemployed scribe and vocational crisis' *Journal of the Early Book Society*, 17 (2014), 1–35; Derek Pearsall, *Manuscripts and readers in fifteenth-century England: the literary implications of manuscript study* (Cambridge, 1983); Estelle Stubbs and Linne Mooney, *Scribes and the city: London Guildhall clerks and the dissemination of Middle English literature, 1375–1425*. Manuscript Culture in the British Isles (Woodbridge, 2013). 2 'Complaint to his Purse', ll. 3–4, in Larry D. Benson (ed.), *The Riverside Chaucer*, 3rd ed. (Oxford, 1987), p. 656. 3 Thomas Hoccleve, *The regiment of princes*, ed. Charles R. Blyth (Kalamazoo, MN, 1999),

In th'eschequeer, he of his special grace
Hath to me grauntid an annuitee
Of twenti mark whyle I have lyves space.
Mighte I ay payd been of that duetee,
It sholde stonde wel ynow with me;
But paiement is hard to gete adayes,
And that me putte in many foule affrayes.[3]

Hoccleve turned to additional sources for his income, including writing a petition and copying manuscripts.[4] If Hoccleve and Chaucer, so close to the English crown's centre of power, had difficulty maintaining a steady income, it must have been much more difficult for clerks in more far-flung locations to do so. Documentary evidence relating to James Yonge and his circle of students, clients, and acquaintances reveals a complex network of civic offices, parishes, guilds, individual clients, and literary patrons, upon all of whom Yonge and his contemporaries depended for income. Despite this wide range of interconnected income sources, Yonge's circle was surprisingly insular, being geographically focused not just on Dublin, but largely on the walled portion of the tiny colonial city; Yonge's circle was vulnerable to the political vicissitudes plaguing the top tiers of government, both in Ireland and England, and Yonge's client-list in particular exposes some of the cultural tensions present in the Anglo-Irish city.

THE TRAINING OF CLERKS: JAMES YONGE AND HIS STUDENTS

James Yonge was probably born in the 1380s. His family had been in the Dublin area since at least 1300, and his probable father, Edmund Yonge, owned a house above the quays near St Audoen's church at his death in 1417.[5] James became a scribe and notary, a legal clerk given permission to make notarial instruments that authenticated documents and events. He was active in Dublin between 1404 and 1438. The surviving remnants of his career include two literary works: the Hiberno-English translation of the *Secreta Secretorum*, which Yonge calls the *Gouernaunce of Prynces*, and a Latin text he refers to as a *Memoriale*, a record chronicling the journey to St Patrick's Purgatory of the knight Lawrence Rathold, who was a diplomat serving the future Holy Roman Emperor, Sigismund I of Hungary. Yonge also created many legal documents,

ll. 820–26. 4 J.A. Burrow, *Thomas Hoccleve*, Authors of the Middle Ages 4 (Aldershot and Brookfield, Vt., 1994), p. 17. 5 For a discussion of the Yonge family history, see 'Appendix D: the Yonge family, *c.*1300–1600; the Bellewe name; the Baghill family' in Theresa O'Byrne, 'Dublin's Hoccleve: James Yonge, scribe, author, and bureaucrat, and the literary world of late medieval Dublin' (PhD, Notre Dame, IN, 2012), pp 753–71; RIA MS 12.S.22–31, nos. 137, 151 and 144 (26 and 28 Sept. 1415), 141, 150 and 142 (25 and 27 Aug.

of which approximately eighty survive.[6] He trained at least two individuals who became members of his circle: Thomas Baghill, active from 1419 to 1439, and Nicholas Bellewe, whose long career extends from 1423 to 1475.[7]

Like Yonge, Baghill and Bellewe would have got an initial education in an ecclesiastical school such as the one attached to St Patrick's cathedral or the one associated with the parish church of St Audoen from at least the late 1430s.[8] They then served an apprenticeship with Yonge. Much like apprentices in other trades, and much like their contemporaries in London, Baghill and Bellewe probably lived in Yonge's household and learned to imitate his professional skills: how to take notes for a deed, how to cut and lay out parchment, how large and ornate script should be, how to form letters for the best balance of writing speed and legibility, all of the necessary legal knowledge and formulae for various types of documents, and even 'marketing' and 'customer service' – how to find and relate to clients.[9] In return, they owed him their service, and, in the case of Bellewe, the responsibility of safely bringing his master back to Dublin after Yonge was imprisoned for publicly supporting the Butler side in the Talbot–Butler feud. The sole surviving Franchise Roll from the late medieval city of Dublin preserves several apprenticeship arrangements of clerks and notaries. Few Irish names of clerks appear, probably due to a mixture of legal injunctions against those 'of the Irish nation' becoming citizens, the necessity for training in English law, and economic disparities between the Irish and Anglo-Irish communities. Two women, however, are included among the notaries' and clerks' apprentices.[10] While these women appear not to have pursued public careers, and were likely barred from doing so because of their gender, knowledge of the legal clerk's

1417), and 149 and 139 (10 and 12 Jan. 1418). **6** A full list of, editions and translations of select documents may be found in O'Byrne, 'Dublin's Hoccleve', pp 648–71 and 463–559. **7** These associations are based on detailed palaeographical and documentary analysis. A more thorough discussion of the connections between Yonge, Bellewe, and Baghill may be found in O'Byrne, 'Notarial signs and scribal training in the fifteenth century: the case of James Yonge and Thomas Baghill', *Journal of the Early Book Society*, 15 (2012), 305–18, and O'Byrne, 'Manuscript production in Dublin: the scribe of Bodleian e. Museo MS 232 and Longleat MS 29' in Kathryn Kerby-Fulton and John Thompson (eds), *New directions in medieval manuscript studies and reading practices* (Notre Dame, 2014), pp 332–56. **8** RIA MS 12.S.22–31, no. 93 (20 Dec. 1438). **9** Caroline M. Barron, 'The child in medieval London: the legal evidence' in Joel Thomas Rosenthal (ed.), *Essays on medieval childhood: responses to recent debates* (Donington, 2007), 49–50. **10** The father-son apprenticeships include Richard Hyrrell, son of Philip Hyrrell (1470), Richard Boulond, son of John Boulond, William Hacket, apprentice of John Hacket (exact relationship not listed) (1487), and John Bertylmew, son of Peter Bertylmew (Peter Bertholomew was city clerk *c.*1477–93) (1491); non-relative apprenticeships include Patrick White, apprentice of John Boulond (1473), Jenet White, apprentice of Peter Berthylmew, city clerk (1481), John Eliot and Alice Englis, apprentices of Richard Nangle (1483), and John Stanton, apprentice of Thomas Bron (1485): Colm Lennon and James Murray, *The Dublin City Franchise Roll, 1468–1512* (Dublin, 1998), pp 4, 7, 16, 17, 21, 22, 27; Mary Clark, Gráinne Doran and Hugh Fitzpatrick, *Serving the city: the Dublin city managers and town clerks, 1230–2006* (Dublin,

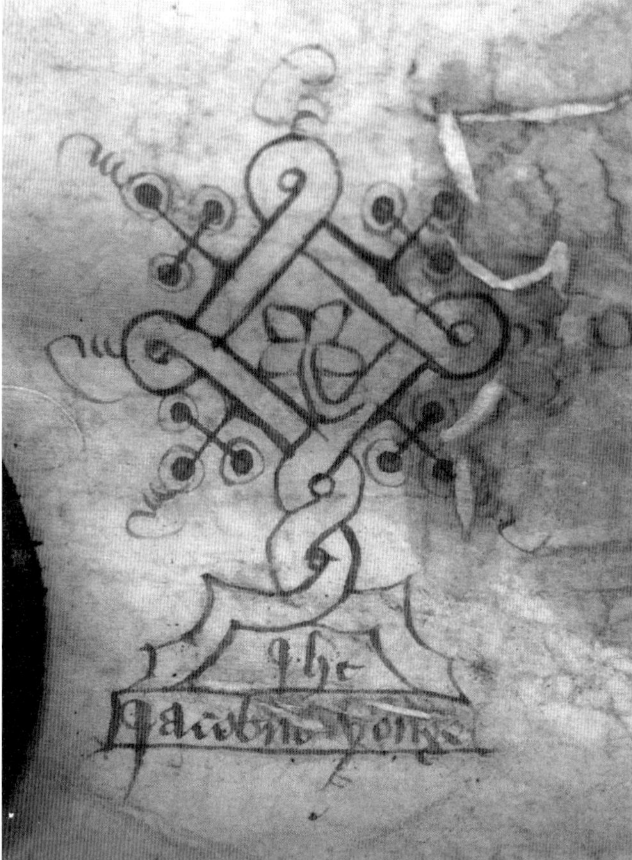

8.1 *Signum manuale* of James Yonge, 1432 (RIA MS 12.S.22–31 no. 343).

trade might have made them great assets in the homes of merchants and landowners.

Yonge's earlier apprentice, Thomas Baghill, became a notary like Yonge, but Baghill's promising career appears to have been cut short in 1439, when his hand, previously common in the extant Dublin records, disappears quite suddenly and completely.[11] There are no literary works or manuscripts ascribed to him. His notarial *signum manuale*, however, provides an important clue for future identification of other Anglo-Irish master-student pairs. Baghill utilized elements of Yonge's *signum manuale* when he created his own specialized symbol for authenticating notarial instruments (figs 8.1–2).[12]

1996), p. 31. **11** The final extant document in his handwriting is Public Record Office of Northern Ireland D430.17, dated 22 July 1439. **12** For a fuller discussion of these marks, their uses, and the implications of their similarity, see Christopher Robert Cheney, *Notaries public in England in the thirteenth and fourteenth centuries* (Oxford, 1972); O'Byrne, 'Notarial signs and scribal training'; eadem, 'Manuscript production in Dublin'.

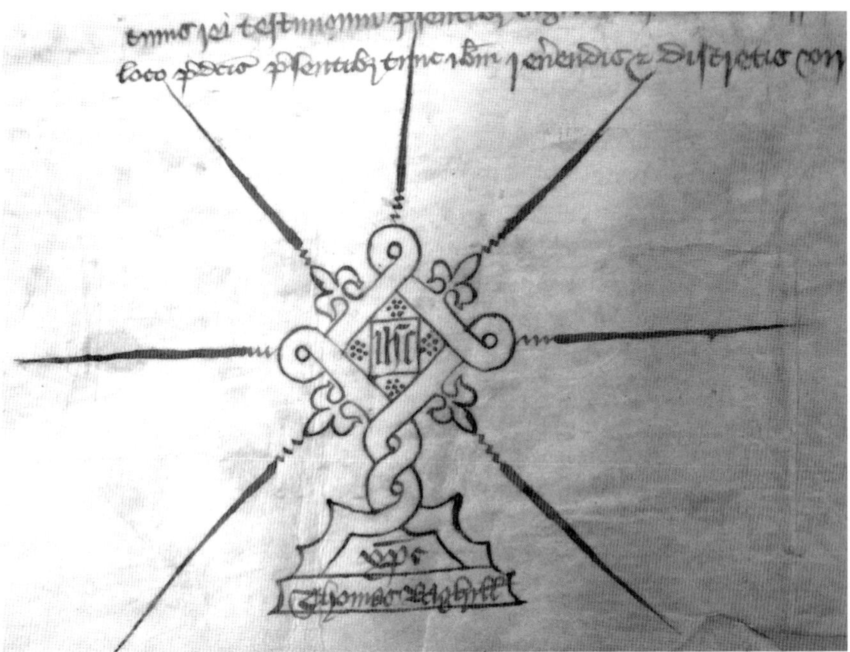

8.2 *Signum manuale* of Yonge's student, Thomas Baghill, 1433 (NAI, 2011/1/141).

Yonge's later apprentice, Nicholas Bellewe, is the more interesting character. Bellewe was not a notary, but he appears to have held the same offices that Yonge and Baghill held in Dublin, and he is the author of at least three literary compositions: a Hiberno-English translation of Edmund Rich's *Speculum Ecclesie*, and works of spiritual advice likely composed for the noblewoman Ismaia FitzWilliam: one known by its first line, *Loue of Kynde and Care*, and one named *The Laddre of Heuyn* by its author. He also translated a work of religious consolation, *O Thou Soul Myn*, from Latin into English.[13] A fourth member of the Yonge circle may have been the rubricator Jon Flemmyn, who contributed to one of the two manuscripts I have attributed to Bellewe, Oxford Bodleian e. Museo MS 232. Little, however, is known of him.[14]

THE YONGE CIRCLE AND ITS CLIENTS

Yonge worked to ensure official employment for Baghill and Bellewe. Along with creating legal documents for private clients in the city, all three scribes worked for the city government in some capacity. They are associated with the

13 See O'Byrne, 'Dublin's Hoccleve', pp 560–647 for editions of these texts. 14 For a fuller discussion of the career of Nicholas Bellewe, see O'Byrne, 'Manuscript production in Dublin' and 'Dublin's Hoccleve', pp 367–99.

8.3a A Drawing of the Seal of the Provostship by H.V. Crawfurth Smith, as it appears in Strickland, 'The ancient official seals of the city of Dublin'.

8.3b A surviving example of the seal, 1459 (RIA MS 12.S.22-31 no. 599).

seal of the provostship of Dublin, a seal used to authenticate documents in cases where the seals of the grantors were not well known. It was employed as a means of authenticating a document through the auspices of the city (fig. 8.3). The seal of the provostship was used in lieu of the city seal, which was kept in the Tholsel, Dublin's city hall, under lock and key. The provostship seal appears to have been somewhat easier for an individual scribe associated with the city to obtain for the purposes of authenticating documents. Despite this, documents with the seal are limited to only a very few individuals among the many scribes working in Dublin in the fourteenth and fifteenth centuries.[15] The city of Dublin had an official clerk, who oversaw the creation and storage of city records; he was assisted by at least two other clerks, and these may have been the individuals who had access to the seal of the provostship.[16] Yonge probably saw to it that his students received preference for the position of assistant to the city clerk when the posts became available.

While Yonge, Baghill, and Bellewe all wrote documents with the seal appended, Bellewe had an even greater role in the governance of Dublin. Probably through his familial connection with Philip Bellewe, who was often the city's treasurer and mayor from 1451 to 1458, Nicholas Bellewe became keeper of the crane and weights in 1456, an office that he held until his death around 1475.[17] Bellewe likely oversaw the maintenance of a cargo crane on the quays and the assessment of duties on goods imported into the city. Perhaps as part of his responsibilities, he produced or transcribed a list of duties to be collected on goods brought into the city, and entered the list into the Dublin Chain Book, a book of laws and regulations chained to the wall or a podium in the Tholsel for every literate citizen to consult at will (fig. 8.4).

Yonge built up a client-list outside of the city offices, a list he shared with his apprentices; these clients included both individual citizens as well as parishes and guilds. The hands of all three scribes are commonly found in the records of the parishes of St John and St Olave on Fishamble Street. Yonge also was one of the main legal scribes used by the powerful guild of St Anne, both as it organized in the late 1420s and as the guild began acquiring properties in the 1430s. When Yonge went into retirement around 1432, Thomas Baghill stepped into the roles abandoned by Yonge. He became the principal scribe for the guild of St Anne, and Baghill also benefitted from Yonge's client-list, executing legal deeds for former Yonge clients, including John Serjeaunt, and John Blakeney, Jr., both prominent Dublin citizens. He also worked for a baker named John Stafford. When Baghill disappeared from the record in 1439, the guild of St Anne appears to have used four or five

15 More information on the history and use of the seal of the provostship can be found in W.G. Strickland, 'The ancient official seals of the city of Dublin' in H.B. Clarke (ed.), *Medieval Dublin: the living city* (Dublin, 1990), pp 163–71, and O'Byrne, 'Dublin's Hoccleve', pp 272–82. 16 Clark et al., (eds), *Serving the city*, 31. 17 *CARD*, i, pp 276–350.

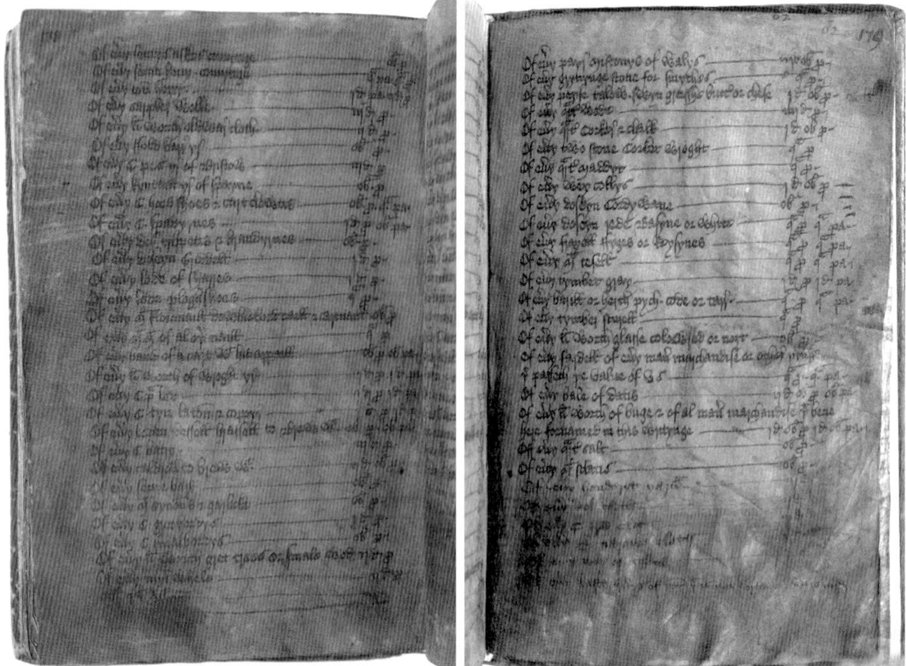

8.4a and **8.4b** The handwriting of Nicholas Bellewe (Dublin City Archives, Chain Book of Dublin, fos. 66v and 67r).

different scribes to create its legal deeds during the 1440s, but beginning in late 1450, Bellewe's hand begins to dominate the extant deeds, often to the exclusion of all others. Bellewe retained his position as the guild's clerk until 1471, when he entered semi-retirement.[18]

As he exited his apprenticeship, Bellewe's initial employment as a personal secretary for the wealthy FitzWilliam family, who owned the manor of Dundrum, south of Dublin, probably also emerged from his master's professional network. In the 1430s and 1440s, Bellewe worked principally for Ismaia FitzWilliam neé Perers, for whom he wrote legal documents, rental records, and a manuscript containing works of religious edification, both his own and those of others, including Chaucer, Rolle, and Hilton.[19] He also occasionally executed documents for Ismaia's husband, William FitzWilliam, and their son, Philip FitzWilliam. Yonge claims in his *Gouernaunce of Prynces* that he was personally acquainted with Ismaia's father, Edward Perers.[20]

18 For a fuller discussion and lists of extant deeds from these collections, see O'Byrne, 'Dublin's Hoccleve', pp 282–375 and 648–96. **19** The legal documents are contained in the Pembroke Estate Papers, NAI, 2011/1, nos. 143 and 147–53; the rental roll is no. 159 in the same collection; the manuscript is Longleat 29. **20** James Yonge, '*Secreta Secretorum*'

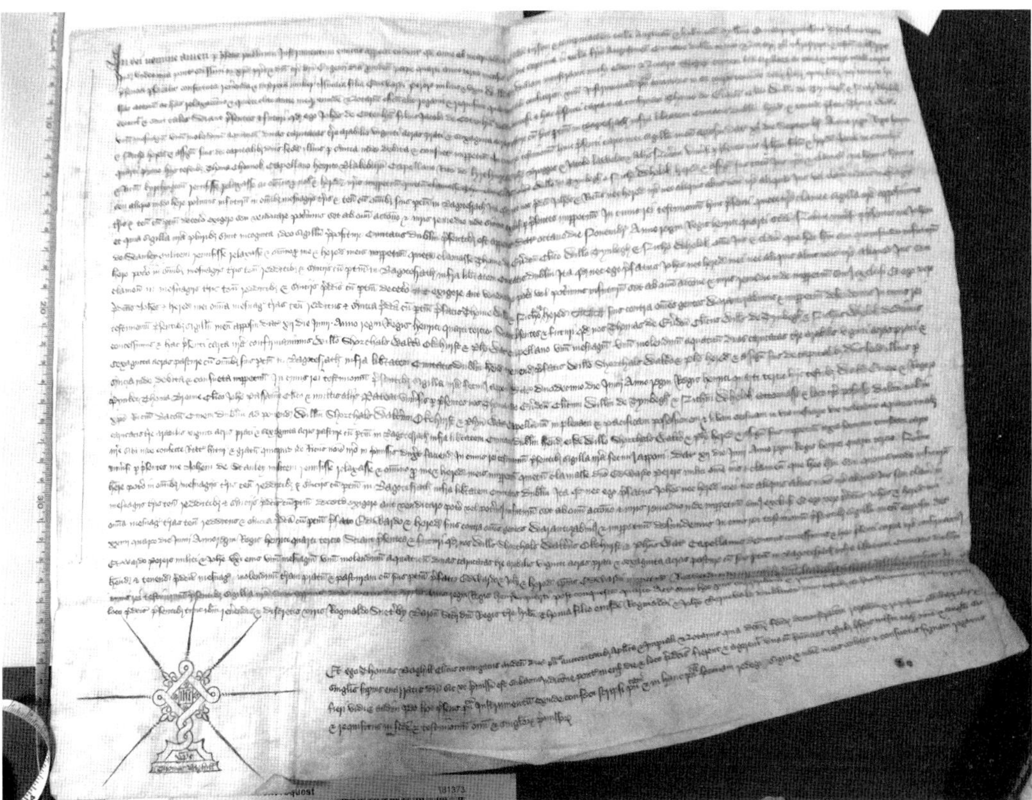

8.5 Document executed for Ismaia Perers, written and notarized by Thomas Baghill, 1433 (NAI, 2011/1/141).

Yonge's acquaintance with Edward Perers, and by extension his daughter, may have originated from a client-list Yonge inherited from his own master, an unnamed scribe who had control of the seal of the provostship, had handwriting similar to Yonge's, and who created several documents for the elder Perers. In turn, Bellewe shared his client-list – or at least his principal client – with Baghill. When Ismaia needed a notary to authenticate some older documents, Baghill filled the role. Bellewe was unable to do so because unlike Yonge and Baghill, he was never credentialed as a notary (fig. 8.5).

All three members of the Yonge circle shared a client in John Stafford, a well-to-do baker.[21] Many of the puzzle pieces are missing, but it appears that a few of the early influential members of the guild of St Anne were bakers, and

in Robert Steele (ed.), *Three prose versions of the* Secreta Secretorum, Early English Text Society Extra Series (London, 1898), p. 129. 21 Deeds for Stafford in Yonge's hand: RIA MS 12.S. 22–31, nos. 551 (1407), 558–60 (1409), 457–8 (1409), 546–7 (1413), 674 (1427), 268 (1427).

Stafford's common association with Yonge and the members of the guild may have facilitated the guild's employment of members of the Yonge circle. Stafford himself had a relationship with the Yonge family and with Yonge's scribal circle that spanned three generations and over forty years. This relationship also included Stafford's receipt of property near the New Gate from John Yonge, James Yonge's presumed uncle, in 1413. These documents were, unsurprisingly, drawn up by James Yonge.[22] Stafford built up an impressive portfolio of properties towards the western end of the medieval city, principally on Cook Street, Francis Street and in the narrow lanes surrounding St Audoen's church. He had a hand in creating the guild of St Anne at St Audoen's in the late 1420s, and he is named in the 1430 founding charter.[23] For his many land transactions, Stafford appears to have shown preference for Yonge when hiring legal scribes. In 1438, Yonge was brought briefly out of retirement, perhaps at Stafford's urging, to execute a will for another baker, Richard Codde, who was a member of St Anne's guild.[24] After Yonge's death *c.*1438 or 1439, Stafford began hiring Baghill to execute land transfer deeds on his behalf.[25] When Stafford himself died in 1451, his widow Johanna turned to Yonge's other student, Nicholas Bellewe, to assist her with the division of Stafford's assets.[26]

While personal connections and word-of-mouth undoubtedly brought Yonge and his apprentices some of their clients, others were perhaps enticed to become initial clients or repeat clients through marketing strategies. Yonge was particularly assiduous about marketing himself to certain clients. He was, however, not as successful as he might have liked. Most transactions requiring legal documents represented one-off work for the scribe, for which he might be employed for only a few hours. The most desired positions for late medieval scribes were those that offered long-term work with guaranteed income. Yonge seems to have particularly desired to become a personal secretary to a wealthy individual or family. Reading between the lines, it seems he might have been somewhat overzealous in some of his attempts to gain such a position, ironically pushing away those he most wanted to serve.

The prominence and wealth of any particular individual client of Yonge's can often be determined by the formality of Yonge's handwriting. A land transaction for a client of middling wealth or influence might be written in a more current hand that was faster to execute (fig. 8.6). For those with more resources, Yonge used more care. His handwriting, while never ornate, becomes more upright and more calligraphic. Yonge was also more likely to sign his name to these documents (fig. 8.7). The tradition of the scribe writing

22 RIA MS 12.S.22–31, nos. 546–7. **23** H.F. Berry, 'History of the religious gild of St Anne, in S. Audoen's church, Dublin, 1430–1740', *PRIA*, 25C (1904), 22–3. **24** RIA MS 12.S.22–31, no. 93. **25** Deeds for Stafford in Baghill's hand: RIA MS 12.S.22–31, nos. 548 (1433), 704 (1433), 662 (1434), 678 (1434). **26** RIA MS 12.S.22–31, nos. 398–400 (1451).

8.6 Yonge's standard script, 1417 (excerpt from TCD MS 1477.77)

his last name at the bottom of a legal deed was a recent innovation from London that was slowly catching on in Dublin. Yonge signs only a small percentage of his extant documents, but the ones he writes more formally are also statistically more likely also to include this mark identifying the scribe's work. In one case, Yonge left an even more blatant advertisement of his skills, a calling card of sorts on the dorse of a lease written on behalf of John Serjeaunt, baron of Castleknock, in 1417. It reads: '*I. Yonge scripsit* (James Yonge wrote this)' (fig. 8.8). I have yet to find a similar signature in the work of any other legal scribe. Was Yonge perhaps engaging too much in hard-sell tactics? Yonge did work on a few occasions for the Serjeaunt family in the first decade of his career, but this 1417 document is the last extant document penned by Yonge for members of this family.[27]

Yonge also promoted himself in his literary works. His earlier work, the 1411 *Memoriale*, contains a colophon that utilizes language from notarial deeds to identify himself as the author of the work and as the authenticator of documents, thereby vouching for the veracity of Laurence Rathold's pilgrim tale of a visionary journey through Saint Patrick's Purgatory.[28] Yonge's 1422

27 O'Byrne, 'Dublin's Hoccleve', pp 315–30. 28 For a fuller analysis of this colophon and its importance, see Theresa O'Byrne, 'Centre or periphery?: the role of Dublin in James Yonge's *Memoriale*' in Kathleen Miller and Crawford Gribben (eds), *Dublin: Renaissance*

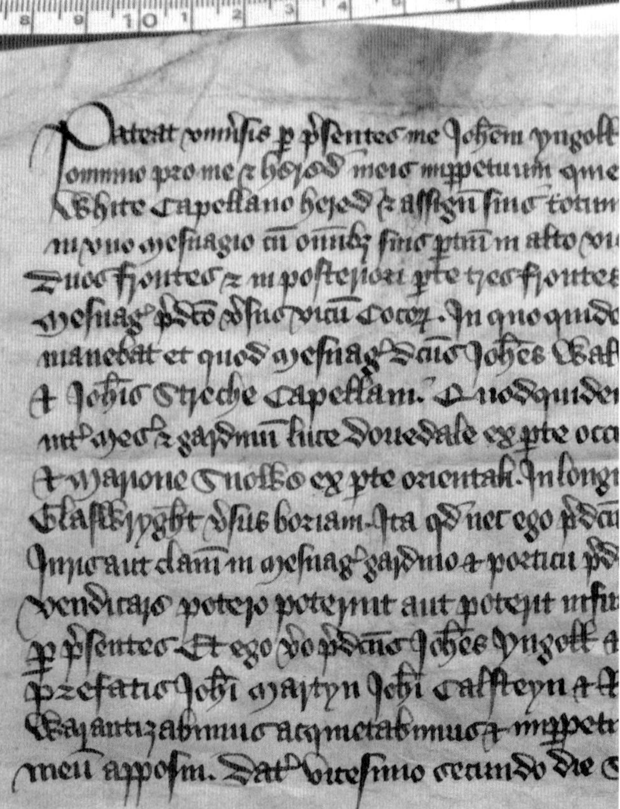

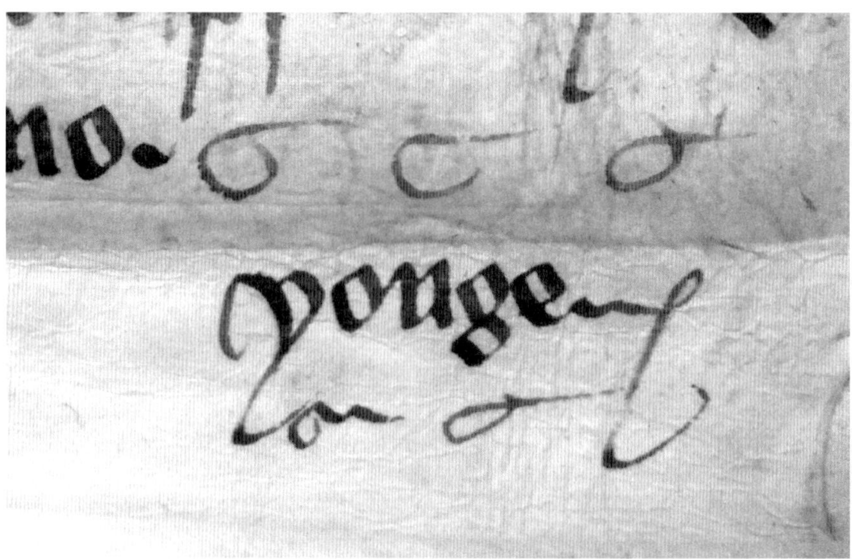

8.7 Yonge's more formal script and signature, 1422 (excerpt from RIA MS 12.S.22–31, no 190).

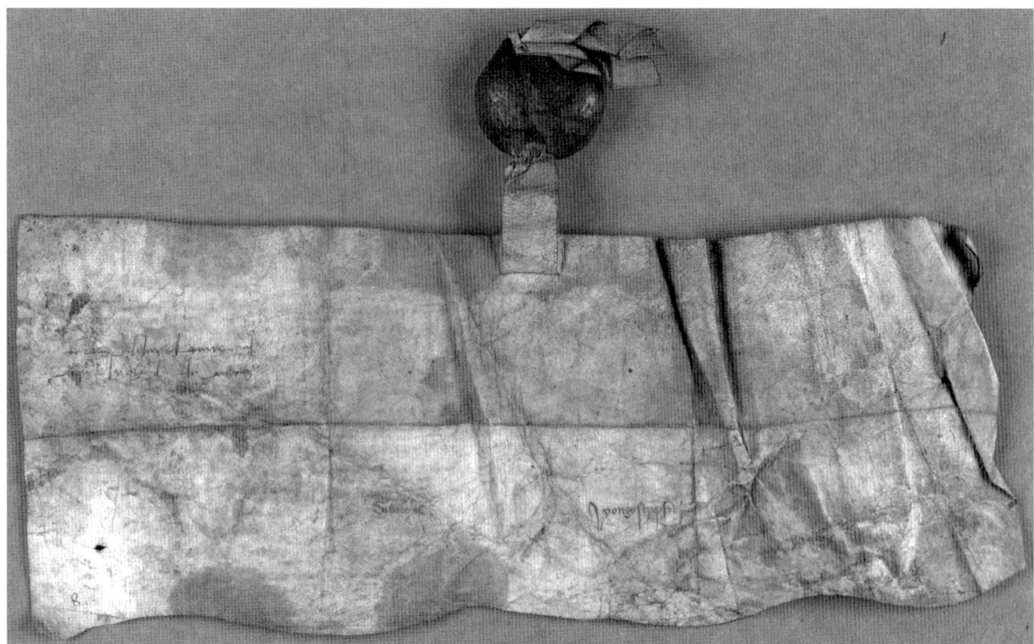

8.8 Deed with Yonge's note attesting that he wrote the document, 1417 (TCD MS 1477.100).

Gouernaunce of Prynces is a heavily interpolated Hiberno-English translation of a Latin text that purports to be a letter from Aristotle offering advice to Alexander. In the title for chapter 50 of his version of the text, Yonge translates 'secretaries' as 'notaries' where pseudo-Aristotle advises the reader,

> Of Notaries:
> To chese the be-houeth, to writte thy Pryuyteis and priuey workys, wyse men of parfite eloquence, and of good mynde. …[a notary should] willyth thy profite and honoure afor al thynges; he sholde be curteyse and Parceuynge in his dedis, And that no man entyr in sygh of thy Preveyteis of wrytynges.[29]
>
> [Of notaries:
> It behoves you to choose wise men of perfect eloquence and good mind to write your secret and confidential works. …(a notary should) desire above all things your profit and honour; he should be courteous and perceptive in his deeds, and (ensure) that no man should enter in sight of your confidential writings.]

city of literature (Manchester, 2017), pp 1–28. Editions of the *Memoriale* include Hippolyte Delehaye (ed.), 'Le Pèlerinage de Laurent de Pasztho au Purgatoire de S. Patrice', *Analecta Bollandiana*, 27 (1908), 35–60, and O'Byrne, 'Dublin's Hoccleve', pp 408–62. **29** Yonge, *Gouernaunce of Prynces*, ed. Steele, p. 212.

And, perhaps most importantly for Yonge, the chapter advises, 'Pay hym well for his Service, so that he hym holde apayed to do the bettyr (Pay him well for his service so that he might think himself satisfied to do better for you)'. Yonge's imagined audience for the *Gouernaunce of Prynces* was broad, including literate citizens of English-controlled Ireland along with the work's patron James Butler, fourth earl of Ormond, and his household. Here, Yonge suggests to his audiences where they might find a notary of the type he describes. Yonge's own name is sprinkled throughout the work, as he takes on the role of an Anglo-Irish Aristotle advising his own Alexander. Yonge hopes his readers will find the precise qualities of a good notary in the person of the author dispensing such wise and profitable advice.[30]

In the *Gouernaunce of Prynces*, Yonge feigns such a close advisory relationship with his literary patron, James Butler, that scholars have long assumed that Yonge was, in fact, Butler's secretary. However, a thorough survey of the extant documents relating to Butler has turned up a paltry few documents penned by Yonge, consisting of three documents relating to Dubliners or lands near Dublin, all written *c.*1430, quite late in the scribe's career.[31] Yonge was, however, fairly close to Butler from 1420 to 1423, when Butler asked the scribe to write the *Gouernaunce of Prynces* for him. To give him time, space, and income to write, Butler awarded Yonge the office of second engrosser of the Irish exchequer – a sinecure, and hence Yonge soon appointed another individual, William Stockenbrick, to carry out the official duties.[32] He himself may have retired to the country outside of Dublin to write. From 1420 to 1424, there is only one extant legal deed in his hand – an unusual hiatus in a career in which multiple documents are extant for most years. During the first two years of this period, Yonge received a steady income from the leper hospital in Palmerstown and from several parcels of land in Saggart; this income was also granted him by Butler in 1420.[33]

Yonge may not however have been aware of his vulnerability to political shifts, not only in Anglo-Ireland, but also in England. The relative ease that Butler's literary patronage brought Yonge was to come to an abrupt end in late 1422. Fast on the heels of the public circulation of Yonge's *Gouernaunce of Prynces*, Butler's own patron, King Henry V, died suddenly at the end of August. The transfer of royal power to Henry VI created an opportunity for Butler's enemy, John Talbot, Lord Furnivall, to take control in Ireland.

30 For a further discussion of this section, see Caiomhe Whelan, 'The notary's tale' in Sparky Booker and Cherie N. Peters (eds), *Tales of medieval Dublin* (Dublin, 2014), pp 119–34. 31 NLI, D.1615 (1428), D.1616–17 (1429), and NAI, 2011/1/140 (1432); see also O'Byrne, 'Dublin's Hoccleve', pp 310–13. 32 *CIRCLE* PR 8 Hen. V, nos. 21–2. I am grateful to Peter Crooks for bringing this record to my attention; see also E.A.E. Matthew, 'The governing of the Lancastrian lordship of Ireland in the time of James Butler, fourth earl of Ormond, *c.*1450–52' (PhD, Durham, 1994), p. 530. 33 *CIRCLE* PR 8 Hen. V, no. 44.

Butler's supporters lost their offices and incomes.[34] Yonge, who had made several veiled criticisms of Talbot and his followers in his *Gouernaunce*, found himself imprisoned '*in ferris et in magna duritia* (in chains and in great hardship)' in Trim Castle, possibly indicating imprisonment in the oubliette underneath the gate house.[35] While Trim, a Talbot centre of power, may have been a convenient place to imprison political enemies like Yonge, Trim also represented for Yonge a place far from the resources and succour that might have been available to him from his Dublin-based support network had he been imprisoned in Dublin. Yonge's distance from Dublin may also have made it more difficult for his social and professional network to advocate for his release, which probably occurred in early 1424, but was not officially recognized until May 1425, just after Butler returned to power.[36]

Yonge's career trajectory was somewhat uneven, marred as it was by his imprisonment in 1423, just as things seemed to be going so well for him. Yonge would, however, manage to rebuild his former career and client-list after his political misstep. The first to embrace him was a regular client and possible friend, John Lytill, who hired Yonge in 1424 to write a document that effectively ended Lytill's long-running and occasionally violent feud with the Burnell family.[37]

By contrast, Yonge's apprentice, Bellewe, started strong and enjoyed a career that seems to have had few of the struggles Yonge experienced. After finishing his apprenticeship, he found, as previously noted, a position in the FitzWilliam household. When Ismaia FitzWilliam died around 1445, he moved on to become a secretary for the Flemyng family in Kilmainham and soon was the scribe for the guild of St Anne after the death of Yonge and the departure or death of Baghill. Using familial contacts, he became, as we saw, keeper of the crane and weights, an office that guaranteed him a dependable stipend to supplement his income from the guild and from private clients. Bellewe was hired to translate and write literary works, as well, and he is responsible for two extant manuscripts, one, Longleat MS 29, for Ismaia Perers and another, Bodleian e. Museo 232, that may have been written under the auspices of the guild of St Anne.[38] What is surprising when examining the careers of Yonge, Bellewe, and Baghill, is that none of them appear to have had many dealings with the offices of the crown. Instead, they worked for the city of Dublin and its citizens. The one exception is Yonge's 1420 appointment as second engrosser to the exchequer, a post largely performed by a replacement.

34 Matthew, 'Lancastrian Lordship of Ireland', pp 111–17, 157–60; Peter Crooks, 'Factions, feuds and noble power in the lordship of Ireland, *c.*1356–1496', *IHS*, 35 (2007), 447–52. 35 *CIRCLE* CR 2 Hen. VI, no. 40. 36 *CIRCLE* PR 3 Hen. VI, no. 45. 37 TCD MS 1477.106b (1424). 38 O'Byrne, 'Manuscript production in Dublin'.

SIGNA MANUALIA AND SCRIBAL CIRCLES IN ANGLO-IRELAND

How does the insularity of Yonge's circle stack up against other scribal circles? Research in this area is yet in its infancy and is hampered by the catastrophic loss of historic documents in the 1922 Four Courts explosion and fire. Nonetheless, there are some scribal groups that can be identified and researched further. In 1427, during the lifetimes of all three of the scribes of the Yonge circle, a small group of scribes in the ambit of the Irish exchequer produced an illustrated and annotated manuscript of the C-Text of Langland's *Piers Plowman*, now known as Bodleian Douce 104. Kathryn Kerby-Fulton and Denise Despres find compelling parallels between the illustrations and annotations of Douce 104 and a single extant image from the *Red Book of the Irish Exchequer*, which was lost in 1922.[39] The scribes and illustrators who created these two manuscripts constitute a group of civil servants brought into association by their work for the crown rather than by a tutelary relationship like the one I posit for Yonge and his protégés.

Indeed, identified master-student scribal pairs are extremely rare. Ian Doyle and Malcolm Parkes posited such a relationship between their scribes D and Δ who wrote manuscripts of Chaucer's *Canterbury tales* and Gower's *Confessio Amantis* in fifteenth-century London, but Yonge and Baghill are the first master-student pair among late medieval Anglophone scribes for which there is compelling evidence of such a relationship.[40] The key to their identification as master and student lies in the similar elements of the notaries' *signa manualia* (figs 8.1 and 8.2). These notarial signs were small images, often incorporating a cross, that identified the work of a particular notary. Each notary created a *signum manuale* that was unique. He would use it without alteration throughout his career. When Thomas Baghill designed his *signum manuale* (fig. 8.2), he borrowed elements of his master's *signum manuale* (fig. 8.1); the outline of the central cross remains the same, while other elements, such as the bar-and-dot design and fleur-de-lis vary between the two notaries' *signa manualia*. This sharing of elements between the marks of master and apprentice was not an isolated case. No such pairs have been found among the marks of English notaries, but an in-depth study of late medieval English notaries' signs has yet to be performed. In English-controlled Ireland, however, at least a few apprentices looked to their masters' marks for inspiration when creating their own. Further research is necessary before this can be declared a standard practice, but it seems to have been not uncommon. The *signa manualia* in

39 Kathryn Kerby-Fulton and Denise Despres, *Iconography and the professional reader: the politics of book production in the Douce Piers Plowman* (Minneapolis, 1999). 40 A.I. Doyle and M.B. Parkes, 'The production of copies of the *Canterbury Tales* and the *Confessio Amantis* in the early fifteenth century' in M.B. Parkes and Andrew G. Watson (eds), *Medieval scribes, manuscripts and libraries: essays presented to N.R. Ker* (London, 1978), pp 163–210, at p. 207; O'Byrne, 'Notarial signs and scribal training'.

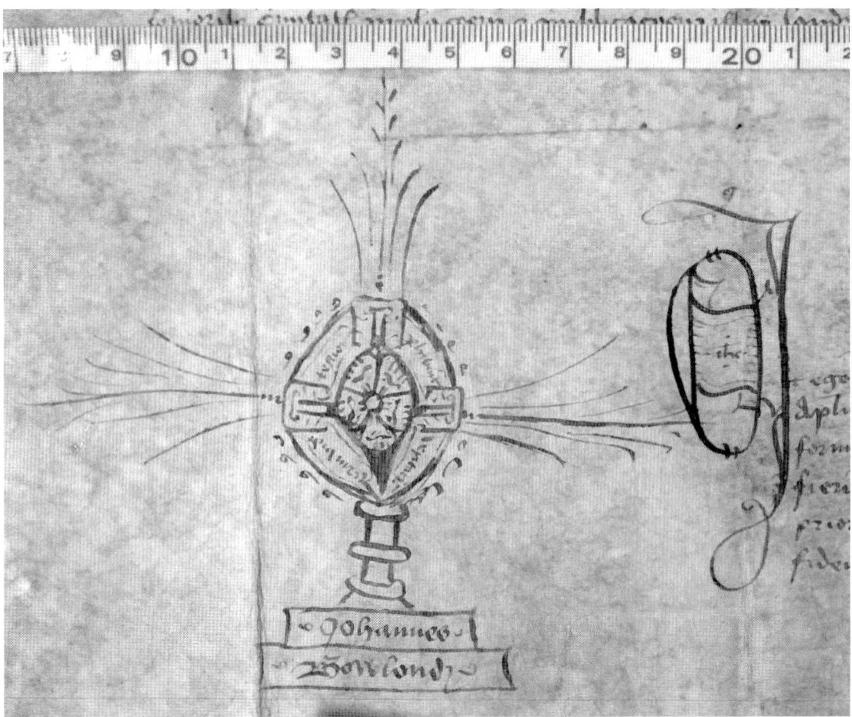

8.9 *Signum manuale* of John Bowlond, 1464 (NAI, 2011/1/191).

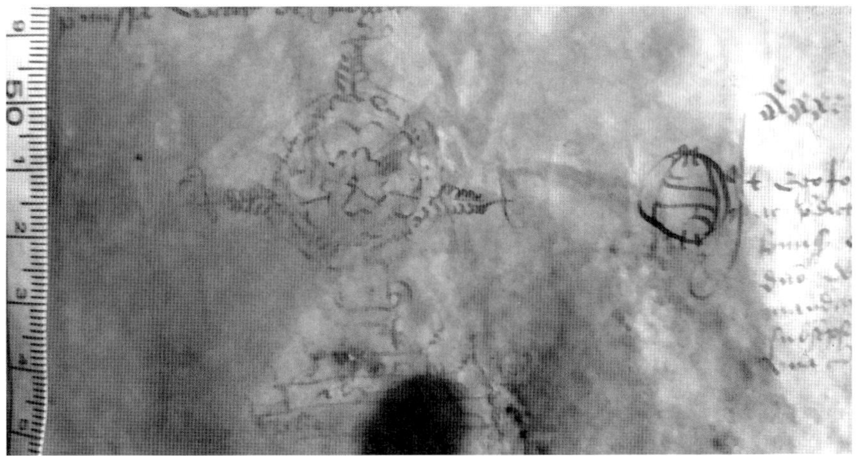

8.10 *Signum manuale* of John Hiland, 1508 (NLI, D.1941).

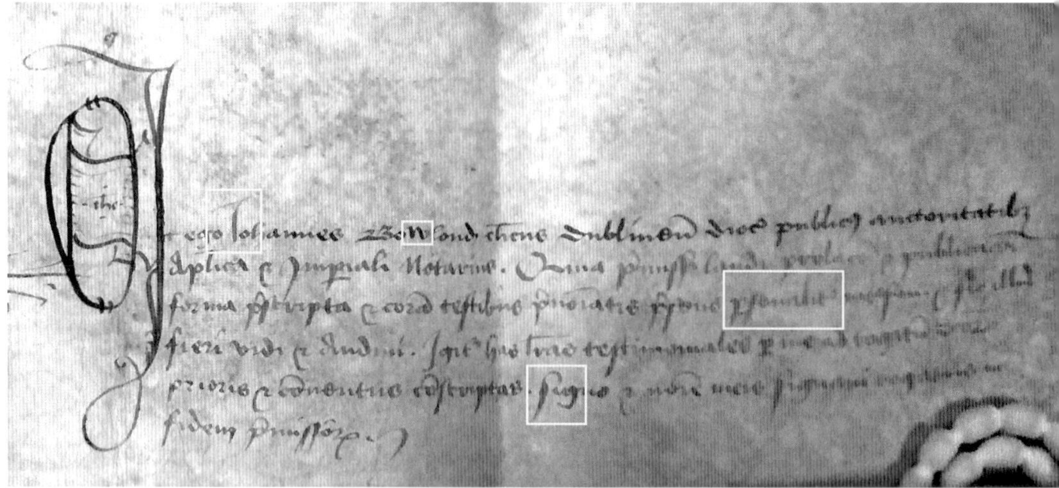

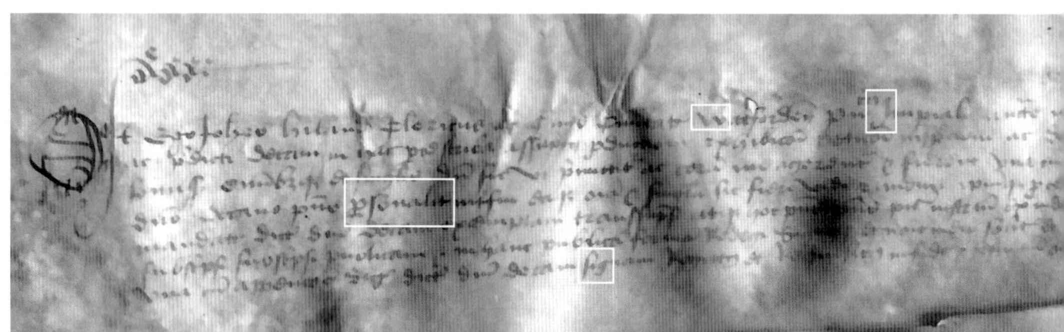

8.11 Comparison of the hands of John Bowlond (National Archives of Ireland, Pembroke Estate Deeds, 2011/1/191, 1464) and John Hiland (National Library of Ireland, D.1941, 1508) with some similar letter forms highlighted by the author.

extant Irish documents reveal two additional possibilities of master-scribe relationships. The first pair might have been acquaintances of members of the Yonge circle, the second pair were removed slightly in space and time from the Yonge circle but, like Yonge, they executed documents for the Butler family.

Based on notarized documents and the lone extant Dublin Franchise Roll, John Bowlond was active in Dublin between 1448 and 1479. His secretary hand appears on two notarial instruments, and he was a witness to a third that was enrolled without his *signum manuale* on the back of the Franchise Roll in 1479.[41] He is also mentioned in 1476 as a founding member of the guild of

41 NAI, 2011/1/166 and 191, Dublin City Archives, Misc. Roll 6, membrane 11d–13d; John Bowlond is also mentioned in deeds of Christ Church, calendared in Hugh J. Lawlor, 'A calendar of the *Liber Niger* and *Liber Albus* of Christ Church, Dublin', *PRIA*, 27 (1908), *Niger* 11 and *Albus* 13, and *CCD*, 298–9, 304, 308, 314–17, 327, 1076.

glovers and skinners, also known as the guild of the Blessed Virgin Mary.[42] That Bowlond would be mentioned on the founding documents of a guild whose primary profession he did not practise is not surprising in light of James Yonge's involvement with the founding papers of the guild of St Anne in the late 1420s as well as the merchant tailors' guild in 1419.[43] It seems that either the ability to draw up the necessary papers, or the scribes' association with the parish churches with which the guilds were associated increased the chances that a scribe would be named in the founding documents.

In addition to his involvement with the merchant tailors' guild, Bowlond took on apprentices in 1473 and 1474, including his son, Richard, according to the Dublin Franchise Roll.[44] One of Bowlond's apprentices does not appear in the surviving Franchise Roll, but the association between John Bowlond and the notary John Hiland, who was active in Waterford in 1508, can be confirmed by comparing the notaries' *signa manualia* (figs 8.9 and 8.10). As with Yonge and Baghill, the marks of John Bowlond and John Hiland bear a striking resemblance to one another. Both notaries use a five-petaled rose encircled by scrolls and formed into a cross by the addition of foliate sprays that emerge from the top and sides. The motto on the scrolls is similar. Bowlond's begins in the lower left quadrant; Hiland's begins in the upper right quadrant. Both quote the first half of John 19:35: '*et qui vidit testimonium perhibuit et verum est eius testimonium* (and he that saw it, hath given testimony, and his testimony is true)'.[45] This is a particularly fitting motto for notaries. A *signum manuale* is always accompanied by a legal formula that identifies the notary and testifies that

> … p*re*sens int*er*fui eaq*ue* om*n*ia & singula sic fieri, vidi, audiui, scripsi, publicaui, & in hanc pu*blicam* formam redegi, signoq*ue* & no*min*e meis solitis & consuetis signaui…
>
> [I was present, and I saw, heard, wrote, made public, and rendered in this public form all and singular thus set down, and I signed it with my usual and customary sign and name …][46]

Bowlond's choice of Bible verse reinforces his role as a witness, recorder, and verifier of legal proceedings.

An initial comparison of the hands of Bowlond and Hiland also reveals parallels in letter formation and patterns of abbreviation that strongly indicate

42 *CIRCLE* PR 16 Edw. IV, no. 3. 43 *CIRCLE* PR 7 Hen. V, no. 67; Mary Clark and Raymond Refaussé, *Directory of historic Dublin guilds* (Dublin, 1993), pp 28–9; H.S. Guinness, 'Dublin trade gilds', *JRSAI*, 12:2 (1922), 145; H.F. Berry, 'The merchant tailors' guild – that of St John the Baptist, Dublin, 1418–1841', *JRSAI*, 8:1 (1918), 19–20. 44 Lennon and Murray (eds), *Dublin City Franchise Roll*, p. 7. 45 *Biblia Sacra: Iuxta vulgatam versionem*, ed. Bonifatius Fischer and Robert Weber, 4th ed. (Stuttgart, 1994); translation from *The Holy Bible, Douay-Rheims Version*, ed. Richard Challoner (Baltimore, MD, 1899). 46 TCD MS 1477, no. 84 (12 November 1411).

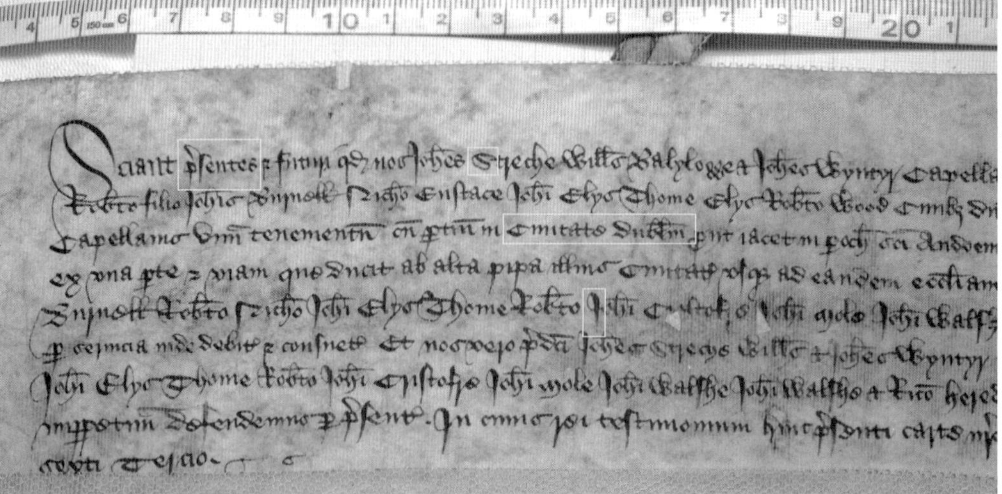

8.12 Comparison of the hands of James Yonge (Royal Irish Academy, 12.S.22–31, no. 562, 1425) and Thomas Baghill (Royal Irish Academy, 12.S.22–31, no. 548, 1433) with some similar letter forms highlighted by the author.

that Hiland learned document preparation from Bowlond (fig. 8.11). These include similar approaches to forming an initial **I**-longa, heavy descenders on long **s**, similar treatment of the **g**, with a heavy back and hook, a heavy, slightly curved descender on the **p** of *per*, and similar approaches to **w**, with a single chamber. In addition, layout and spacing of documents is similar between the two scribes. While such similarities may be chalked up to the conformity required of participants in a pre-print culture of legal record-keeping, close parallels often reflect common training.[47] Such similarities are also present

47 Doyle and Parkes, 'Production of copies of the *Canterbury Tales*'; though a few of their findings have proved controversial, Stubbs and Mooney use a similar approach of palaeographical comparison to draw relationships between London scribes in *Scribes and the city*.

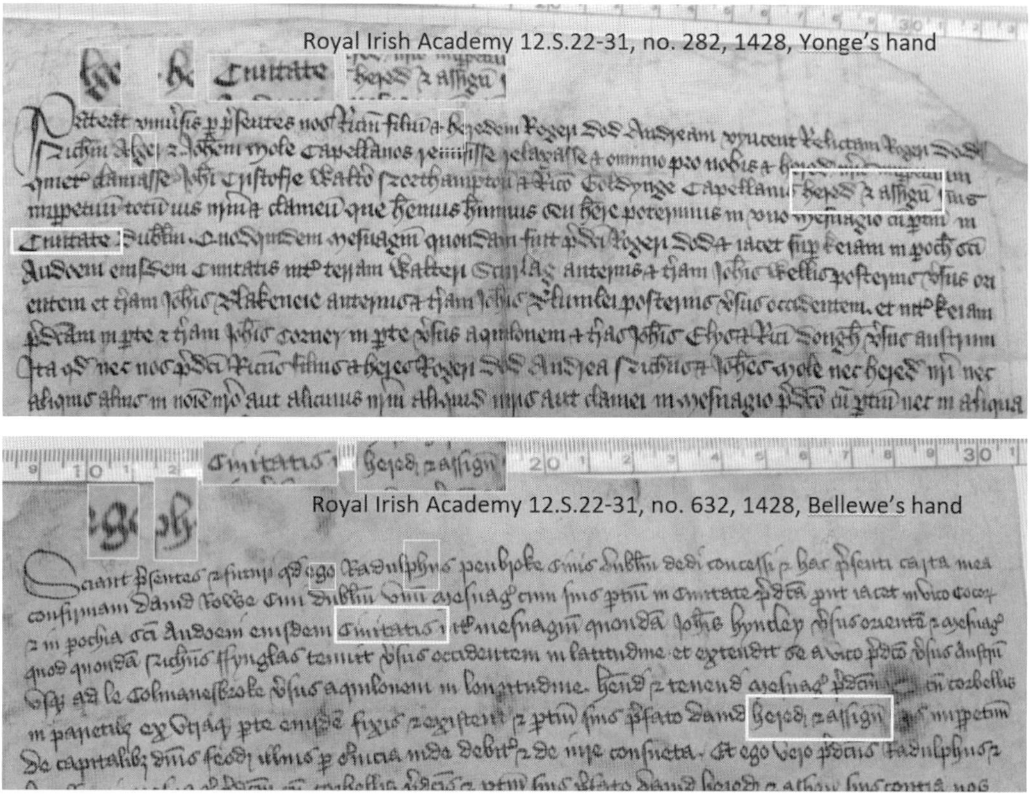

8.13 Comparison of the hands of James Yonge (Royal Irish Academy, 12.S.22–31, no. 282, 1428) and Nicholas Bellewe (Royal Irish Academy, 12.S.22–31, no. 632, 1428) with some similar letter forms highlighted by the author.

between the hands of Yonge and Baghill and Yonge and Bellewe (figs 8.12 and 8.13).[48]

Another master-scribe pair of notaries stands out because of their presumed ethnicity. Most of the scribes and notaries producing legal documents for Anglo-Irish clients have Anglo-Irish names, but John Mohland (*Ó Mothlacháin*?), a notary active in Offaly in the first quarter of the sixteenth century, and his probable student, Patrick Ronan (*Ó Rónáin*), appear to have been Irish. Like Yonge and Baghill and Bowlond and Hiland, the *signa manualia* of Mohland and Ronan share key elements, including the tightly folded interlace and the quatrefoils in the centre of each square void in the central cross (though Mohland appears to have been the better artist) (figs 8.14

48 These are explored in more detail in O'Byrne, 'Dublin's Hoccleve', 'Notarial signs and scribal training', and 'Manuscript production in Dublin'.

and 8.15). The instruments of both men survive in the Butler family deeds, suggesting that they may have been employed on occasion by the Butlers.

The training of ethnically Irish notaries and their subsequent employment by members of the Anglo-Irish population of Ireland underscores the bicultural nature of the Butler family and of the broader community of the Irish marches. Had he survived to see it, however, the Dublin notary Yonge might have been particularly incensed at the competition represented by the employment of ethnically Irish men of letters like Mohland and Ronan. In one of the most oft-quoted passages of his *Gouernaunce of Prynces*, he rails against James Butler's employment of 'rhymers':

> And therefore he is an onwyse man that audyence or Yeftis yewyth to Rymoris othyr any Suche losyngeris, for thay Praysith hare yeueris be thay neuer So vicious. Who-so ham any good yewyth brekyth the statutis of kylkeny, and he is acursid by a xi bisschopis, as the same Statutes makyth mencion.[49]
>
> [And therefore he is an unwise man who gives audience or gifts to rhymers or any other such flatterers, for they praise their givers, no matter how wicked they are. Whoever gives them any goods breaks the Statutes of Kilkenny, and he is cursed by eleven bishops, as the aforesaid Statutes mention.]

To Yonge's audience, the invocation of the Statutes of Kilkenny would have made it very clear which rhymers Yonge specifically meant: Irish poets.[50] The fourth earl ignored this advice, as many in his family did.

As notaries with Irish surnames, Mohland and Ronan are not alone among the notaries working in the Irish marches where Anglo-Irish and Irish cultures came into frequent contact. These include Maurice Cogan of Limerick (whose name may be Anglo-Norman *de Cogan* or Irish *Ó Cuagáin*), John Olonnogan (*Ó Longargáin*) of Armagh, and possibly John Glyssot (if this is Irish *Ó Gliasáin*, Anglic. 'Gleeson') and Walter Kylte (*Ó Caoilte*?) of Meath. Among the notaries thus far identified, only one with an Irish name, John Mulghan (*Ó Maolagáin*?), found employment in the Dublin area (unless John Bowlond was *Ó Beolláin*, Anglic. 'Boland'). John Mulghan was active between 1474 and 1505; most of his documents are associated with Christ Church.[51] He was

49 Yonge, *Gouernaunce of Prynces*, ed. Steele, p. 157 (translation by author). 50 The Statutes of Kilkenny sought, among other things, to regulate intercultural communication between the Anglo-Irish and the Irish. The laws laid out proved unenforceable, but they became a touchstone for those who supported cultural apartheid in Ireland. The portion Yonge refers to is section XV. The full text is available in James Hardiman (ed.), *Tracts relating to Ireland*. Vol. 2 (Dublin, 1841). 51 Lawlor, 'Calendar of the *Liber Niger* and *Liber Albus* of Christ Church, Dublin', *Albus* 47, 59–62; NAI, 2011/1/201.

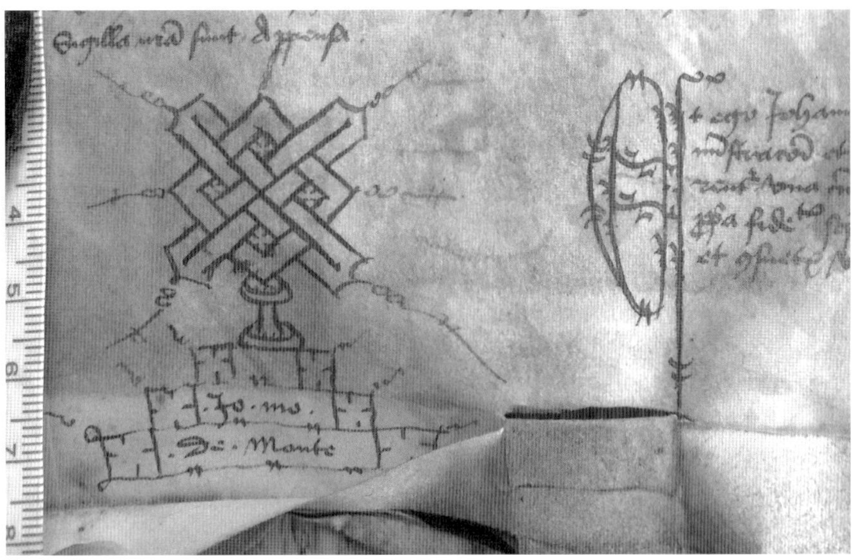

8.14 *Signum manuale* of John Mohland, 1501 (NLI, D.1936).

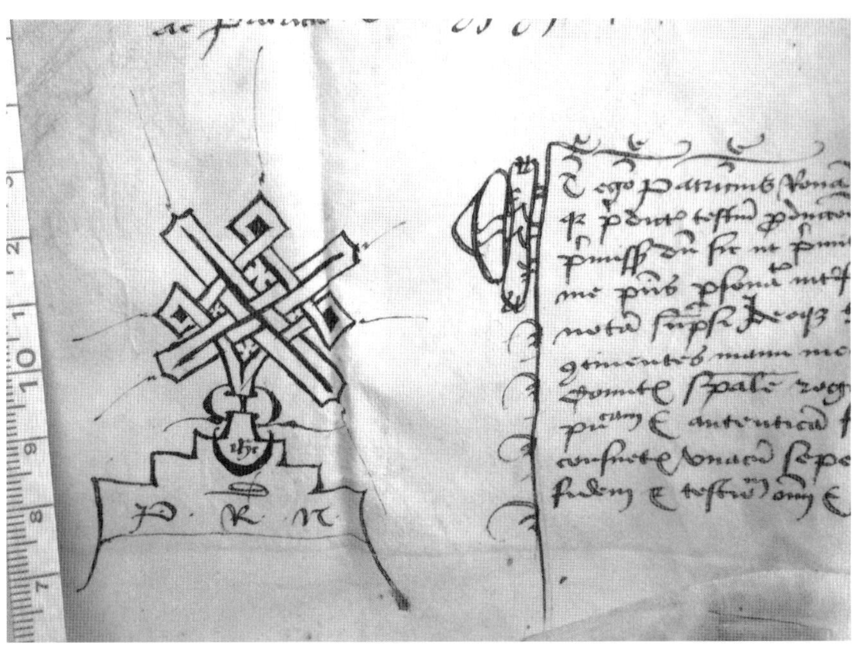

8.15 *Signum manuale* of Patrick Ronan, 1523 (NLI, D.2094).

enrolled as a citizen on the Dublin Franchise Roll in 1474 by petition of his father, James Mulghan.[52] The lattter, his son John, and other members of the Mulghan family were legally treated as English citizens of Dublin. The Mulghans appear to have become Anglicized in the early fifteenth century. In 1407, John Omulghan, possibly the grandfather or great-grandfather of the Dublin notary John Mulghan, paid twenty shillings for a charter of English liberty. Several Mulghans were involved in Dublin civic life during the latter half of the fifteenth century, which indicates that the Mulghan family had adopted the English language and at least some of the Anglo-Irish cultural practices which would have been necessary for regular participation in public life.[53] John Mulghan may well have been steeped in English language and customs. He certainly needed to be familiar with them in order to function first as a clerk, and then as a notary within the Anglo-Irish legal system.

Although there may have been some admixture of English and Irish practices within the daily lives of Dubliners during the late medieval period, as Sparky Booker has convincingly argued, within the realm of English law, rather rigid demarcations between the English and Irish likely persisted, supported by written legal documents executed in the English style and occasionally for an English audience.[54] The Franchise Roll and other documents refer to this distinction by indicating that an individual is 'of Irish blood' or 'of the Irish nation', but such identification may have been made more on the basis of language and culture, rather than ancestry. That is not to say, however, that there weren't individuals who practised bigotry when it came to those who were Irish by culture or by ancestry. James Yonge was among these. Both of his literary works contain strongly anti-Irish sentiments, and Yonge may have refused to work for anyone with an Irish surname. Only one possible Irish name appears among the documents in his hand, and that individual, Walter Molghur (*Ó Maoilchéire*?), is the recipient of property, not the grantor, who would have hired Yonge.[55]

Despite the new connections between notaries briefly explored here, Yonge's circle remains the only well-researched example of several scribal networks that operated in the civic and crown offices of English-controlled Ireland. The interactions of Yonge, Baghill, and Bellewe with one another and with their clients reinforce the piecemeal nature of scribal employment and careers that has been observed among scribes operating in late medieval England, while reflecting some of the political and cultural issues unique to

52 Lennon and Murray (ed.), *Dublin City Franchise Roll*, p. 8. 53 *CIRCLE* PR 9 Hen. IV, no. 65; Patrick and James Mulghan are remembered in the Christ Church book of obits, compiled in the early sixteenth century. Thomas Mulghan was a purchaser of iron and salt for the city in 1469, and he was the constable for Cook Street in 1470: Sparky Booker, 'An English city?: Gaelicization and cultural exchange in late medieval Dublin' in Seán Duffy (ed.), *Medieval Dublin X* (Dublin, 2010), pp 291, 293. 54 Ibid. 55 RIA MS 12.S.22–31, nos. 326–7, 374, 649, and 779 (1435).

English-controlled Ireland. The history of the Yonge circle suggests that many aspects of the Anglo-Irish legal environment, including its political volatility, operated quite similarly to English models. Scribes used their professional networks as a way of gaining and retaining employment. Education through an apprenticeship system gave apprentices access to their masters' professional networks, and in return, masters received labour (and in one instance a ride home from gaol) and clients were assured of specialized services, such as those of a notary, and continuation of that service in the case of their favoured scribe's death. Further investigations, for instance into the master-student relationships of the notaries John Bowlond and John Hiland and the Offaly notaries Patrick Ronan and John Mohland, will, I hope, continue to reveal more details regarding scribes' networking and self-promotion efforts.

The abbey of St Thomas the Martyr and the le Brun family: piety and patronage in Anglo-Norman Dublin[1]

ÁINE FOLEY

INTRODUCTION

The le Brun family were one of the most prominent families to settle in Dublin in the aftermath of the English invasion of Ireland. Though there is no definitive evidence, some members of the family may have done business in the city before the invasion, since commercial links between Dublin and Bristol were firmly established long before the invasion took place,[2] and when Diarmait Mac Murchada was ousted from his kingship of Leinster in 1166 (an event that initiated the invasion) his first port of call was Bristol to seek support.[3] Diarmait stayed with the wealthy Bristol merchant Robert fitz Harding, from whom he received hospitality and financial support, as well as an introduction to Henry II.[4] The city of Dublin was granted to the men of Bristol after the invasion, and the les Brun may have originated from this city. Alternatively, the William le Brun who features prominently in the charters for late twelfth-century Dublin may have come from Cardiff, as a 'Willelmus Brun de Cardiff' is listed in Dublin's Guild Merchant Roll.[5] Cardiff is situated just across the Severn estuary from Bristol and a merchant from here would have undoubtedly had commercial interests with Bristol; indeed, many of the other merchants in the guild roll also originated from Cardiff.[6]

Aside from William, many other les Brun can be found in the Guild Merchant Roll,[7] but caution must be exercised. Le Brun is an extremely common surname; its modern version is 'Brown' and we cannot say that all the les Brun who settled in Ireland after the invasion, particularly those listed in the Guild Merchant Roll, were from the same family. The les Brun featured in many early charters as witnesses, as well as issuing charters in their own right and it is easier to identify people from the same family in this type of document.

1 This essay is based on research conducted by the author on behalf of Dublin City Council on the abbey of St Thomas the Martyr, Dublin. Special thanks are due to Dr Ruth Johnson, the city archaeologist, and Bruce Phillips, the manager of the South Central Area Office. 2 Robin Frame, *Colonial Ireland, 1169–1369* (2nd ed., Dublin, 2012), p. 6. 3 Ibid., p. 8. 4 James Lydon, *The lordship of Ireland in the Middle Ages* (2nd ed., Dublin, 2003), p. 32. 5 Philomena Connolly and Geoffrey Martin (eds), *Dublin Guild Merchant Roll* (Dublin, 1992), p. 13. 6 See ibid., passim. 7 Ibid., 19, 23–4, 30, 33, 39, 41–2, 45, 48–9, 55, 57, 60–1, 63, 69, 71, 73–4, 81, 83, 91–2, 94, 96, 106, 119.

ST THOMAS'S ABBEY

The les Brun can be found in records connected to all of the great ecclesiastical houses in Dublin, including the priory of the Holy Trinity (Christ Church), St Mary's abbey on the northside, the Knights Hospitallers at Kilmainham and the hospital of St John the Baptist just outside the city walls. The ecclesiastical institution that I will focus on in this essay, however, will be the abbey of St Thomas the Martyr, because they feature prominently in the charters of this abbey. Unfortunately, few traces of it remains above ground today, yet it was one of the most important ecclesiastical houses in Ireland and it was also the only royal foundation in Ireland during the medieval period, having been founded by Henry II shortly after the invasion of Ireland. The abbey was extensive, and it stretched from Thomas Street to at least as far as the Coombe.

The location of three mills belonging to the abbey at Harold's Cross suggests that the abbey's precinct stretched further south than the Coombe. Two mills belonging to the abbey known as Double Mills and another mill nearby called Wood Mill were still marked on late eighteenth-century leasehold maps belonging to the earl of Meath. Wood Mill was located on Greenmount Lane, close to the modern-day Grand Canal at Harold's Cross. The estate map also shows fish ponds beside the mills, and there are several references to fish ponds belonging to the abbey from the sixteenth-century inquisition and earlier sources. There was also a mill pond beside Wood Mill and this can also be seen on Rocque's map, which was drawn up shortly before the leasehold maps in the mid-eighteenth century. These maps demonstrate that remnants of the abbey survived well into the modern period, though most have disappeared now, in the suburbanization of Dublin; one rare survival is the Tongue (also known as the Stoneboat) at Kimmage, where the watercourse for the city of Dublin divided off from the abbey's watercourse. The abbey also administered the nearby parishes of St Catherine's and St James's and was clearly a very substantial landholder adjacent to the city of Dublin. Additionally, it held considerable landholdings across Ireland, especially in Meath and southern Leinster.

The church of St Thomas was founded in 1177 by William fitz Audelin, on behalf of Henry II, king of England, in reparation for the death of Thomas Becket, archbishop of Canterbury, who had been canonized four years earlier. St Thomas's abbey was an Augustinian house, and the Augustinians were the most widespread order in Ireland – there were at least 120 Augustinian houses in Ireland during the late medieval period. The abbey of St Thomas followed a version of the Augustinian rule which was established at the abbey of St Victor in Paris, known as the Victorine rule. Wigmore abbey in Herefordshire and St Augustine's in Bristol also followed the same rule, and it is likely that the first canons of St Thomas's came over from Bristol and introduced the rule here.

The abbey was established shortly after the invasion of Ireland and most of its early patrons played a major role in the invasion. Richard fitz Gilbert de Clare (Strongbow) donated lands to the abbey and his sister Basilia was buried within its precincts. The lands she granted to the abbey included territories in the barony of Forth, Co. Carlow.[8] The published register of St Thomas contains several of her charters, and even though she was married to Raymond le Gros, she more often emphasized her familial connections with both her father Gilbert and her brother Richard, and this is the case even in charters she issued in association with her husband.[9] Naturally, it added to the prestige of the abbey to have powerful and well-connected individuals using it as their final resting place. In fact, on occasion they got into disputes with other ecclesiastical houses over the remains of the Anglo-Norman aristocracy. In 1195, Hugh de Lacy's head was buried in St Thomas's abbey and the rest of his remains were buried in Bective abbey in Co. Meath.[10] De Lacy, the lord of Meath, had been slain ten years previously and had originally been laid to rest in Durrow abbey in modern-day Co. Offaly before being moved to St Thomas's and Bective. After a dispute between the institutions, which lasted ten years, de Lacy was disinterred again and his body joined his head in St Thomas's abbey.[11] He was buried in the abbey beside his first wife, Rose of Monmouth, who was a cousin of Strongbow's.

The multiple grants made to the abbey in the immediate aftermath of its establishment made it one of the wealthiest religious houses in Ireland. Because it was a relatively late foundation, most lands granted to it lay outside Co. Dublin. Most of the lands closer to the city had already been granted to older foundations like the priory of the Holy Trinity (Christ Church) and St Mary's abbey. As noted above, the main bulk of the abbey's lands were in Meath and southeast Leinster, mainly because this is where their main benefactors like Hugh de Lacy and Richard de Clare and their various followers held land.[12] John de Courcy, who conquered Ulster, also granted property in his new lordship to the abbey; like other nobles he was keen to be associated with the royal abbey.[13] Walter de Ridelesford, another witness to the foundation charter of St Thomas's, granted the abbey lands in Bray, in modern-day Co. Wicklow.[14] It is also worth noting that other witnesses of fitz Audelin's charter included the ancestors of some of the leading noble families of later medieval Ireland, including the Berminghams, Cogans, Costentins, Poers (or Powers), Clahulls and fitz Geralds, whose power and influence would eventually eclipse that of the major landholders in the immediate post-invasion period.[15]

8 *Reg. St Thomas*, pp 117–18. 9 *Reg. St Thomas*, pp 110–15. 10 Colin Veach, *Lordship in four realms: the Lacy family, 1166–1241* (Manchester, 2014), p. 67. 11 Ibid., p. 264. 12 Ibid., p. 264; *Reg. St Thomas*, p. 349. 13 Ibid., p. 221. 14 Ibid., p. 153. 15 Bodleian Library, MS Rawl. B. 499, fo. 1.

While the new nobility of the Irish colony was among the abbey's most generous patrons, the merchants of the city of Dublin also endowed this foundation, and many of the grants of land within the city and its suburbs came from this class of men and women. Both King Henry II and his son John had close links with the merchant class and the support Henry received from the merchants of Bristol in particular helped him to win his crown. He was so grateful that once he became lord of Ireland he granted his city of Dublin to the men of Bristol, as well as granting them the liberties and customs that they already enjoyed in Bristol.[16] His son John also had many associates among merchants who held lands in Dublin and many of them were generous to the abbey.

John had an interest in Ireland that was virtually unmatched by any other English monarch throughout the medieval period, and this is reflected in the volume of charters issued by both the king himself and his followers to the abbey of St Thomas. No one expected him to inherit the English crown as he had four legitimate older brothers, and his father Henry considered Ireland a suitable acquisition for a younger son. Shortly after William fitz Audelin issued charters to Thomas's abbey in 1177 he was dismissed as keeper of Ireland and Henry replaced him with John, who was ten years old at the time.[17] Did King John have a special devotion to St Thomas? Though his father had once been a personal friend of Becket's, their relationship had soured long before John was born. Moreover, he was only four when Becket died, and therefore it is not possible that he knew him in any sort of personal capacity. John was still very young when his earliest charters to the abbey were issued, and therefore he probably had little direct role in such grants. However, he continued to issue charters into the reign of his brother Richard,[18] and he maintained his interest in the abbey even after he became king, and Ireland was no longer his main focus: for example, after he was crowned king he granted them his tithe of ale which he had by custom out of the taverns of Dublin.[19]

THE LES BRUN IN THE CHARTERS

It is not clear from the charters if the le Brun family owed any of their grants of land in Dublin to King Henry II or his son John, but they do appear as witnesses in some of the charters of his known followers. For example, William le Brun witnessed a charter issued by Strongbow on behalf of Henry II sometime before the latter's death in 1176.[20] It is possible that William le Brun came over to Ireland with Strongbow, because charters were frequently

16 NLI, MS D. 10,032. **17** Ralph V. Turner, *King John: England's evil king?* (Stroud, 2009), p. 37. **18** See, for example, RIA, MS 12 D 38, pp 21–2. **19** Ibid., p. 21. **20** Ibid., p. 23 reverse.

witnessed by the followers and associates of the charter's grantor. As well as being associated with the most important resident noble in Ireland, William appears to have owed at least some of his advancement in Ireland to the church and he has some association with the priory of Holy Trinity. At some point before the death of the archbishop of Dublin Laurence O'Toole in 1180, William le Brun was granted lands in Killester in north Co. Dublin.[21] William le Brun also held lands in Kilmainham, and his son Audoen (sometimes Owen) le Brun assigned these lands to the hospital of St John of Jerusalem at Kilmainham. Audoen le Brun also granted lands in Kilmainham to the citizens of Dublin, but these too eventually passed into the hands of the Hospitallers.[22]

THE MURDER OF WILLIAM LE BRUN

Charters relating to the le Brun family can be dated to before or after William le Brun's death, because it is well documented in the sources. The unfortunate William was murdered in Dublin city sometime in 1199.[23] After his murder, his son Audoen brought an appeal against Warin of London, Richard Gille Michel and Elias fitz Philip for their alleged involvement in this crime.[24] Moreover, Thomas Norreys and Robert of Winchester were also accused of participating in William's murder. William had previously been in conflict with these individuals, who like him were prominent citizens of the city, as they had been bound to keep the peace against him at the county court of Dublin. This case is evidence that there was already a county court operating in Dublin by the late twelfth century.

An unnamed man struck William with a hatchet beside Dublin Castle. He fell into the dyke of the castle and died of his injuries some days later. The men against whom his son took an appeal were charged with aiding and abetting his attacker. As a means of proving their innocence all but one of the accused men agreed to undertake a trial by battle (or trial by combat). This involved two parties – the accuser and the accused – fighting in single combat, the winner to be declared as the one in the right. Since Audoen was a churchman he may have had to nominate someone to fulfil this role, rather than take part in the combat himself. The first criminal trial jury was not introduced into England until around 1220 – and probably later in Ireland – and therefore William le Brun's attackers could not have chosen to be tried by jury.[25] Warin of London had apparently broken his leg during William le Brun's attack and therefore it was decided that he would undergo trial by iron. Ordeal by iron, sometimes

21 *CCD*, pp 123–4, no. 468. 22 *CARD*, i, p. 163. 23 Doris Mary Stenton, *Pleas before the king or his justices, 1198–1212* (London, 1948), i, no. 3169. 24 *CDI, 1171–1251*, nos. 114, 116. 25 Roger DeGroot, 'The early-thirteenth century criminal jury' in J.S. Cockburn and Thomas A. Green (eds), *Twelve good men and true: the criminal trial jury in England,*

called ordeal of fire, required that the accused hold a red-hot iron. If the burn from the hot iron had healed within three days, the accused was deemed innocent. If the wound festered the suspect risked being exiled or executed. Warin appears to have chosen to pay a fine, rather than go through this ordeal, and paid 66 marks, 2 shillings and 3 pence to the crown, as a result of which it seems that he avoided this particular punishment. Richard Gille Michel and Elias fitz Philip also paid the same amount, possibly avoiding their punishment of trial by battle.[26]

Sixty-six marks was a great deal of money at the time and it surely demonstrates that le Brun was an important individual. Incidentally, a Warin of London appears on a witness list on one of Audoen le Brun's charters, in which he granted lands near Kilmainham to the citizens of Dublin.[27] No precise date is provided with this charter, but it is dated to after William le Brun's death. This could be further evidence that Warin was pardoned, though it is a little odd that he shows up as a witness in le Brun's charter. Warin is mentioned in a charter relating to the abbey of St Thomas dating to 1219;[28] if this were the same individual, it would be reasonable to assume Audoen le Brun's charter was of a similar date.[29] Dublin would have been a relatively small city at the time and it would have been impossible for men like Warin and Audoen to completely avoid each other. Also, the fact that Warin had been an accomplice in the murder, rather than the murderer himself, may have made it easier for the le Brun family to tolerate him.

A charter issued by William's daughter Alicia suggests that William was murdered close to his home. The text of the charter is as follows:

> To all the sons of holy mother church to whom the present writing shall come Alicia the wife of Gilbert de Lyvet the daughter of William Browne; Know ye that I by the consent & will of my husband, for the soul of my father William & the soul of my sister Susan & of my brother Owen Brune, & of my lord Gilbert & for my soul with my body, have given to God & to the church of the blessed Thomas the martyr near Dublin & to the canons regular there serving God, all the land & the house in which I have dwelt with the curtilage; namely that house which my father gave to me upon my marriage; so that my above named lord shall hold the above assigned land during the whole of his life of the

1200–1800 (Princeton, 1988), p. 3. **26** *CDI, 1171–1251*, no. 114, Elias fitz Philip is called Philip fitz Elie in this record. **27** *CARD*, i, p. 163. **28** *Reg. St Thomas*, p. 146. **29** The le Brun family were indirectly involved in another murder case almost two centuries later. When an Augustinian monk called Richard Dermot died in mysterious circumstances in 1379 his body was hidden by his fellow monks, and probable murderers, in the well located in the garden of Adam le Brun, a citizen of the city. See F.X. Martin, 'Murder in a Dublin monastery, 1379' in Gearóid Mac Niocaill and Patrick Wallace (eds) *Keimelia: studies in medieval archaeology and history in memory of Tom Delaney* (Galway, 1988), pp 468–98.

> aforesaid house of St Thomas the martyr; rendering thereout yearly to the aforesaid lord half a mark of silver; but after his decease the aforesaid land, with the house and curtilage shall remain to the house of Saint Thomas as is above written, quit and free, in pure & perpetual alms; I have granted also and in pure and perpetual alms to the above named Canons I have given all the land which lies between the land of Henry Tirrell and the land of the said canons which they have of the gift of Samarius the cellarer to wit in the parish of Saint Mary del Dames. And that this my gift and grant in future times may remain ratified established & firm I have corroborated the present writing with the impression of my seal. These being Witnesses my Lord G de Lyvet, Owen Brun, Gilbert Burel, Hugh le Noble, John Vale and others.[30]

Alicia granted the house and land her father had given her on the day she married Gilbert de Lyvet to the abbey of St Thomas. This charter does not specify where the house was located, but in the same charter she granted the abbey land she held in the parish of St Mary del Dame (from which we get Dame Street), which was adjacent to Dublin Castle, where her father was murdered. It is possible the house was located here too. This charter is interesting because Alicia issues it in her own name, not jointly with her husband, which is more common, though she does get his consent and he does witness it, along with her brother Audoen. She mentions her father and brother in the charter, but not her mother Susanna or her sister Hillary, both of whom made grants to the hospital of St John the Baptist.[31] Hillary appears to have survived her sister by several decades, and was her brother Audoen's heir, from which it appears that Audoen was the only son to survive William. Alicia does, however, name another sister called Susan, undoubtedly named after her mother. The charter also mentions that Alicia's plot of land in the parish of St Mary del Dame is adjacent to lands held by Henry Tyrell, who donated lands to the abbey of St Thomas to build the church of St James.

Alicia's husband Gilbert de Lyvet, who served as mayor of Dublin on many occasions, also held parcels of land in the city and its suburbs. In another charter issued after her death, he describes a stone house, with cellars, which he had built on land previously belonging to Thomas the son of Norman (though the location goes unmentioned).[32] Gilbert mentions his second wife Sibilla in this charter; indeed, he mentions both wives and he grants his property here for the health of the souls of his wives, the house being granted to the abbey of St Thomas on the condition that Sibilla can live there for the rest of her life, if she outlived her husband. Clearly, Gilbert was concerned for her physical well-being, as well as that of her soul. In another charter Gilbert

30 RIA, MS 12 D 38, p. 24 (reverse). **31** *Reg. St John*, nos. 30, 32–3. **32** RIA, MS 12 D 38, p. 25.

acquired land to extend his garden;[33] again the charter does not specify where the lands are located, but it does mention that one of the people who gave him land for his extended garden was William de Dun; an examination of other charters establishes that William held several plots of land in Croker's Lane, and nearby areas.[34] William le Brun witnessed one of the charters by which Henry Tyrell granted William de Dun land close to St James's church.[35]

It is clear that the merchants and clergy who settled in Dublin both before and after the invasion were a tightly knit bunch who witnessed each other's charters. William de Dun appears to have been a churchman, being described as a clerk in one charter. He granted out his lands in Croker's Lane to men who were in some sort of trade: for example, William the Carpenter described Dun as his lord in one charter and obtained his permission to grant lands he held in Middle Street, which was opposite Croker's Lane, to Roger the Carpenter. Croker's Lane, sometimes called Potter's Street, is gone now but it was situated between Thomas Street and the Liffey, running parallel to Thomas Street close to St James's church. It is possible that Gilbert's stone house with cellars and extended garden was located here. The Gilbert Lyvet mentioned in a petition dating to around 1278 is presumably a descendant of this Gilbert.[36]

AUDOEN LE BRUN

Like many merchants' sons, Audoen le Brun – as would many les Brun after him, as we shall see – became an administrator within the government of the colony and he acquired the office of chamberlain of the exchequer sometime before 1222. Government offices at the time were dominated by churchmen like Audoen, who also served as clerk to John Comyn, archbishop of Dublin.[37] In 1207, Audoen le Brun was responsible for bringing 1,500 marks of the issues of Ireland over to England.[38] Clearly, he held a position of great trust and the grants of land made to him illustrate how important he was to the Irish administration. Moreover, not only was Audoen le Brun acquiring land, but he was also in a position to grant lands to friends, family and followers. It was in this way that patronage filtered down through the different layers of medieval Dublin society. In 1205, he paid 30 marks – which would have been an enormous sum at the time – for the custody of the land and heir of David Bas.[39] As well as receiving the profits of this land until his ward came of age he also had the right to bestow the marriage of the heir on someone of his own choosing. He could have sold this marriage on to someone else, thereby

33 Ibid., p. 24. 34 Ibid., p. 31. 35 Ibid., p. 26 (reverse). 36 TNA SC 8/258/12896; see also, *CARD*, i, p. 230. 37 *Reg. Alen*, pp 13–14. 38 *CDI, 1171–1251*, no. 357. 39 Ibid., no. 274.

making a profit from the transaction, or married the heir off to one of his own relatives or associates. Accruing land and wealth through marriage was a sure way of enhancing the family's prestige and standing in the community. The source does not say where David Bas's lands were located, but Audoen le Brun acquired several parcels of land across both city and county, including lands that had previously belonged to David Latimer in Artane:[40] Artane is beside Killester, where his father had held lands, and therefore it is likely that Audoen was expanding and amalgamating his father's original grant.

OTHER LES BRUN IN DUBLIN

In 1273, Fromund le Brun, who may have been related to Audoen le Brun, paid over £1,200 of the rent and arrears of the royal manor of Newcastle Lyons into the exchequer.[41] The family was in possession of Brownstown, a grange within this manor, which of course took its name from them. Like Audoen le Brun before him, Fromund had a career in administration. In the mid-thirteenth century, he served as chancellor of Ireland.[42] Fromund le Brun's acquisition of the chancellor's office appears to have been the pinnacle of a long career in the Dublin administration. He served as clerk of the justiciar John fitz Geoffrey in 1248 and he was also at this time described as the pope's chaplain.[43] He did, however, miss out on one of the most important ecclesiastical offices in the country. In 1271, Fromund was elected to the office of archbishop of Dublin by the dean and convent of the Holy Trinity at Christ Church; however he did not have the support of the dean and chapter of St Patrick who decided to choose William de la Corner as their candidate.[44] This double election led to a stalemate and the archbishopric remained vacant for eight years until John de Derlington's investiture.[45] Perhaps in an attempt to assuage the loss of this office, in 1282 the king ordered the justiciar to grant Fromund a prebend or other benefice in his gift.[46]

Other individuals with this surname were involved in the running of the Irish administration. In 1251, for example, another William le Brun served as a baron of the exchequer and in 1255 he was responsible for making an extent of Balscadden – near Balbriggan in north Dublin – which was then part of the king's demesne.[47] Towards the end of the century, Geoffrey le Brun (like Audoen before him) held the office of chamberlain of the exchequer.[48] He was

40 *Reg. Alen*, p. 33. 41 *Rep. DKPRI*, 36, p. 50. 42 *CDI, 1171–1251*, no. 1840; this royal letter mentioning le Brun as chancellor is dated by Sweetman to 1230 but it is undoubtedly of a later date as the subject of the letter – Hugh of Coolock – appears in sources dating to the 1270s. 43 Ibid., no. 2966. 44 *CPL, 1198–1304*, p. 457; *CDI, 1252–84*, no. 913. 45 *CDI, 1252–84*, no. 1545. 46 *CDI, 1293–1301*, no. 1987. 47 *CDI, 1171–1251*, no. 3128; *CDI, 1252–84*, no. 482. 48 H.G. Richardson and G.O. Sayles (eds), *The administration of Ireland, 1172–1377* (IMC, Dublin, 1963), pp 118–19; *CDI, 1285–92*, no. 750; *CDI,*

also clerk of the king's works in Ireland and was responsible for the construction and upkeep of the king's castles here.[49] He held the manor of Lucan and he may have been related to Maurice le Brun, a contemporary of his living on the nearby manor of Ballyfermot.[50]

Nigel le Brun, a knight who was described as the king's valet in the administrative sources, appears to have been a relative of Fromund's and he held the manor of Chapelizod in 1290 and became escheator of Ireland in 1308.[51] He had previously held the position of seneschal of the liberty of Kildare.[52] He also had possession of Balyhaueny, which appears to be Owenstown near modern-day Mount Merrion and it is possible that these lands were called after Audoen le Brun.[53] This property, which was also known as Rabo, corresponds to modern-day Roebuck close to Dundrum. These lands would later pass into the hands of his son Fromund.[54] Nigel's son was clearly named after the older Fromund, which strongly implies that they were related. In 1281–2, Nigel received Fromund's fee for his position as chancellor, confirming this association.[55] When Nigel was granted 160 acres in Balyhaueny in 1306, it was because he did not hold any other lands in the king's demesne at that time.[56] Nigel was subsequently granted extensive royal lands in the Dublin Mountains, including Glencree, in 1308.[57] By 1309–10, he was paying rent of Finnstown and Kissoge on the royal manor of Esker.[58] At around this time William le Brun held lands in Ballydowd, also on the manor of Esker, and it is possible he was related to Nigel.[59] Even though Nigel already held substantial lands, it is clear that acquiring lands on the royal demesne enhanced his social standing within the local community. The status attached to possessing property on the royal demesne cannot be overestimated.

Nevertheless, though he would have actively sought out the grant of these lands they would not have been given to him unless it was also beneficial to the crown. The king rewarded him because he depended on him not only within the lordship of Ireland itself but also in his other dominions. In 1301–2, Nigel received a royal letter requesting aid in the Scottish wars and his enrolment of receipts regarding his pay while in Scotland into the exchequer in 1303–4 confirms that he answered this summons.[60] As well as his service to the crown, Nigel had previously spent time in the service of Richard de Burgh, earl of Ulster.[61] Like several other les Brun before him, Nigel's son, the younger Fromund, was employed in public service and – just like the elder Fromund – held the office of chancellor of Ireland. Once again, the holding of the

1293–1301, no. 98. **49** *CDI, 1285–92*, no. 558. **50** *CDI, 1293–1301*, no. 264; NAI, EX 2/1, p. 10. **51** *CDI, 1285–92*, no. 665; Richardson and Sayles (eds), *Admin. Ire.*, p. 126. **52** *CDI, 1293–1301*, no. 391. **53** *CJRI, 1305–07*, p. 69. **54** *CDI, 1302–07*, no. 319; Francis Elrington Ball, *A history of the county of Dublin*, 6 vols (Dublin, 1902–20), ii, p. 77. **55** Philomena Connolly (ed.), *Irish exchequer payments, 1270–1446* (IMC, Dublin, 1998), p. 66. **56** *CJRI, 1305–07*, pp 213–14. **57** NAI, EX 2/1, p. 295. **58** *Rep. DKPRI*, 39, p. 28. **59** *CJRI, 1305–07*, p. 282. **60** *CDI, 1302–07*, nos. 47, 295. **61** *CDI, 1285–92*, no. 910.

chancellor's office is linked with the possession of lands on the king's demesne. He also had interests in Dublin city because he quitclaimed Buttevant Tower – one of the towers on the city walls – to the mayor and commonalty in 1327.[62] Twenty years later he, or more likely his son, served as sheriff of Dublin – thus marking more than a century and a half of service by this family to royal government in city and county.[63] He was certainly one of the more important people in the county at the time because in an entry in the papal register for 1354 he is called a knight.[64]

The les Brun profited well from their service to royal government. Nigel le Brun, for example, not only held lands on the royal manor of Esker, it seems that he also had lands in Saggart. In 1319, Nigel requested relief of crown rent due to losses incurred from the Bruce invasion and it would not have been surprising if the Scots had attacked the vulnerable manor of Saggart, situated in the foothills of the Dublin mountains. Richard le Brun, who also held lands in Saggart in the early fourteenth century and served as provost in 1313, may have been one of his kinsmen. Robert le Brun was provost of the same manor in 1339–40, and he may have been Richard's son.[65] The further one goes down the social scale the more difficult it is to establish whether all these people were related because the name is very common. However, it is likely that the more prominent les Brun were related, as most held public office and the fact that later les Brun held property called Owenstown (Balyhaueny) suggests that they were related to Audoen le Brun. Undoubtedly, they owed their success within the Irish administration and in acquiring lands around Dublin and elsewhere to these family connections.

CONCLUSION

After the mid-fourteenth century the le Brun family ceased to hold important offices in the Irish administration, though the Thomas Broun who served as a clerk of the crown in the Irish chancery may have been related to the earlier les Brun. The le Brun family remained an important gentry family in south Co. Dublin and continued to hold Roebuck until the mid-fifteenth century when this manor passed into the hands of the Barnewall family through an heiress. According to Ball, the les Brun also owned much of what is now Clonskeagh, which was close to Roebuck, until they died out in the male line.[66]

This family were involved in the administration of the colony almost from its inception and many of them benefitted from grants of land both in Dublin city and county. The first of them to arrive here were merchants, but some joined the church and many of them continued the tradition of holding offices

62 Ibid., pp 115–16. **63** Connolly (ed.), *Exchequer payments*, p. 422; *CPR, 1348–50*, p. 22. **64** *CPL, 1342–62*, p. 526. **65** *Rep. DKPRI*, 47, p. 38. **66** Ball, *Dublin*, ii, p. 77.

within the Irish administration into the fourteenth century. They used their position to acquire lands both for themselves and for family members and associates. Though the main line of the family died out in the mid-fifteenth century, the proliferation of les Brun across Dublin throughout the later medieval period, the relative abundance of this name in contemporary records, and intermarriage with other important gentry families like the Barnewalls, ensured that this family left their mark on Dublin from the late twelfth century up to the end of the medieval period.

Dublin's lost medieval church of St Michael

SHEILA DOOLEY

St Michael's church was a unique place of worship in Hiberno-Norse Dublin. It is believed to have been the private church of Dúnán, Dublin's first bishop, located within his episcopal palace near or close to the site of Christ Church cathedral (Wheeler 1960, 98). Modern research relating St Michael's church has generally featured within a composite analysis of the history of Christ Church cathedral with the possible exception of articles published in the *Irish Builder* in 1891. The Medieval Trust, more popularly known as Dublinia Heritage Centre, undertook new research for a permanent exhibition on St Michael's church in 2014. This paper expands upon this research into the intriguing history of this lost church – from its early foundation to its purported final demolition. It will attempt to consolidate current suggestions regarding the location of the original church and identify the footprint of St Michael's within the current building that houses Dublinia.

The building that houses Dublinia was formerly a nineteenth-century synod hall of the Church of Ireland attached to Christ Church cathedral (fig. 10.1). Prior to the 1870s, the cathedral was in a dilapidated state and had commissioned a great restoration project, including this new synod hall for general meetings. The architect chosen to complete the project was George Edmund Street, an eminent and celebrated English architect who regarded himself as a 'cautious restorer' (Stalley 2000c, 354). While students and associates of Street greatly admired him, others were not so flattering. Thomas Drew, Street's successor as cathedral architect, regarded him as aggressive and unwilling to listen to advice or opinion (Stalley 2000c, 373). Early plans for the construction of the synod hall show that it was initially planned to be part of the nearby St John's church to the north but it was later agreed that this would obscure the vista of the newly redeveloped cathedral (Milne 2000b, 323). Extra funding having been secured, an alternative site was sought. Nearby stood the crumbling St Michael's church and bell-tower, which had been on an inexorable path towards decay for many years. In Street's view, the church was a 'hideous modern structure' not deemed architecturally worthy of conservation (Stalley 2000d, 181; Milne 2000b, 323–4) and so a site for the new synod hall was chosen and with it the demolition of St Michael's medieval church.

10.1 Dublinia Heritage Centre with St Michael's church bell-tower to the west (© Dublinia).

FOUNDATION AND EARLY HISTORY

The dedication of St Michael's church was to the patron saint of mariners and it was referred to by various titles: St Michael and All Angels, St Michael the Archangel, St Michael Within the Walls and St Michael *in Alto* (on the height), the latter indicating its elevated location on the urban townscape. The title St Michael 'Within the Walls' was intended to distinguish it from the other Dublin church dedicated to the same saint, which H.A. Wheeler referred to as the church of St Michael *de Palude* (of the marsh), better known as St Michael le Pole, which was located only a short walk away between Chancery Lane and Ship Street (Wheeler 1960, 97).

Sitriuc Silkenbeard, the Hiberno-Norse king of Dublin, is believed to have been the benefactor of land that accommodated the construction of the episcopal palace between 1028 and 1036 following his return from pilgrimage to Rome (Stalley 2000a, 54; cf. Ó Riain-Raedel in this volume, above). It is possible that he was inspired by the religious experience of his journey and felt compelled to donate a substantial site in affirmation of his faith within the boundary of the town defences (Kinsella 2000, 28–9). This grant of land perhaps contained a church, the site of what became Christ Church cathedral, the episcopal palace (bishop's residence) and a dedicated chapel to St Michael for the bishop's own personal use.

Evidence of the origins of St Michael's is intertwined within the foundation narrative of Christ Church cathedral. The *Liber Niger*, also known as the Black Book of Christ Church, is a medieval register of the priory of Holy Trinity and contains both early (short entries) and late (longer embellished) entries. It states that 'Donatus archiepiscopus [*sic*] primus Dublin fecit capellam sancti Michaelis in placio suo (Donatus [Dúnán], the first archbishop [sic] of Dublin, made a chapel of St Michael in his palace)' (Gwynn 1946, 308). The entry, however, is somewhat problematic as a source for the foundation of St Michael's in the eleventh century since it dates from the fourteenth century, albeit drawing on an earlier source (Gwynn 1946, 308). It errs, of course, in describing Dúnán as an archbishop since there was no archbishop of Dublin until the synod of Kells-Mellifont of 1152 (Kinsella 2000, 31).

The supposed location of the first church of St Michael within Dúnán's palace built sometime after 1028 needs to consider the streetscape of the Hiberno-Norse town during the early eleventh century. At that time the area was tightly packed with inhabitants living in the enclosed Hiberno-Norse settlement surrounded by the defensive earthen bank. High Street, however, accommodated an 'overspill' to the west of the early *dún*, the earliest archaeological levels in this area dating to *c*.1010 (Clarke 2002, 4) and, when the enclosed area extended west of the *dún* in this way, its size was doubled to approximately twelve hectares. The extension coincides with the establishment of Christ Church cathedral and the episcopal palace. Kinsella, in his comprehensive analysis of the cathedral, supports Simms' view that the boundary line of the early *dún* and ditch is retained in features of the earliest levels of Christ Church cathedral's crypt and was once a right-of-way that was subsumed within the development of the cathedral (2009a, 145–8). Historically, this route was conserved up to the early thirteenth century when a grant by King Henry III, dated 19 February 1226, records a request to divert a street under the church of the Holy Trinity (Christ Church) and the prior's chamber into the neighbouring land. A second grant to Archbishop Luke on 23 September 1234 permitted him to enlarge and lengthen Christ Church by closing up the street 'lying near it towards the west' (Kinsella 2009a, 146). The only prerequisite to permitting these changes was that the applicants should create an alternative route and 'carry a road along the neighbouring land of the prior and canons extending to the old street on the other side of that land' to allow entry to the church (Kinsella 2009a, 156).

Evidence of this is thought to survive in visual form in Jonas Blaymire's eighteenth-century drawing of the north side of the cathedral on St John's Lane. A steep stairs extends from an exit point on the north side of Christ Church with what seems to be a ditch-shaped undulation in the foreground. Kinsella suggests that the right-of-way may have exited from the north side near this location and from the crypt (Kinsella 2009a, 144–8). The crypt is considered to be late eleventh century in the earliest sections and the height of this bay may reflect the enclosed and original right-of-way where parishioners once walked. Consisting of five bays, the final bay, the tallest, has been suggested by O'Keeffe to date to Dúnán's bishopric, perhaps constructed under the influence of his Benedictine experience and training in Cologne (O'Keeffe 2017; see also, Ó Riain-Raedel above). Archaeological features were identified during works by Linzi Simpson and Helen Kehoe in 1999. A beaten slate/mortared floor was noted and Kinsella has pointed out architectural evidence of dressed Dundry stone that would have embellished the later twelfth- or early thirteenth-century route-way. An archway still survives on the southern side of the crypt and mirrors another to the north.

The perimeter of the early *dún* and extension of the enclosed settlement allows for the possibility that the bishop's palace may have started on the western side of this right-of-way now perhaps preserved within the fifth bay of the crypt of Christ Church cathedral. The original palace may have extended from this location to the western end of the site of Dublinia, possibly where St Michael's Lane lies to the west of the latter. Dúnán's palace and private chapel may have been of a modest size and design as by 1213 a substantial new episcopal palace had been built at St Sepulchre's in the southern suburbs (O'Donovan 2003, 255). O'Donovan argues that the archbishop of Dublin, John Cumin, who was appointed in 1181, was the instigator of this shift, presumably because his predecessors had not furnished themselves with a sufficiently luxurious palace. Whether the episcopal palace was too small for Cumin we cannot be sure but, with the move to his new and upgraded residence on the site of the modern Kevin Street Garda station, he not only escaped the authority of the city provosts (by moving outside the walls) but provided himself with a palace that may have been more suitable for a royal official of his rank (O'Donovan 2003, 253–5). Whether he lived to see the finished building we cannot be sure for he died in November 1212 and was succeeded by Henry of London in 1213 (ibid., 255).

Before exploring the later medieval history of St Michael's church, there is another curious anomaly from the foundation narratives of Christ Church cathedral that deserves some attention. The earliest dedication refers to a 'chapel of St Michael' followed by a further entry that states 'out of what was left of the money and timber was built the church of St Michael' (Kinsella 2009b, Appendix 4). One entry mentions a chapel, the other a church. Writing about sixty years ago, H.A. Wheeler acknowledges that it is unclear whether St Michael's chapel was a separate building or part of the main foundation, a chapel dedicated to St Michael within the bishop's palace (Wheeler 1960, 98). Kinsella believes that the chapel evolved into a church and that the site of the church, within the archbishop's palace, may still be located within Dublinia. Danielle O'Donovan, in her paper on St Sepulchre's palace, suggested that the original palace was 'located behind the church of St Michael at the southwest angle of Christ Church, probably near the site of the later synod hall' (O'Donovan 2003, 255).

As to what the earliest St Michael's church was constructed of, there is little agreement. The embellished entry in the *Liber Niger* refers to timber as the construction material acquired to build the church of St Michael's. Adrian Empey considered that wood was the preferred material for the earliest Anglo-Norman churches (O'Neill 2002, 10), but Stalley remarks that there was already a tradition of building major Irish churches in stone from the tenth century as identified at Clonmacnois, Glendalough and Clonfert. He also considers the status of the new church and religion within the early *dún* and concludes that it would have demanded a more iconic aesthetic in the form of a dominant stone structure such as those visited by Sitriuc during his pilgrimage to Rome (Stalley 2000a, 54–6). If the earliest cathedral was constructed out of stone, would the earliest chapel also have been constructed of stone?

THE MEDIEVAL CHURCH

The later medieval history of St Michael's is dependent on the history of Church Church cathedral. Archbishop Lorcán Ua Tuathail granted the care of St Michael's to the canons of the Holy Trinity in Christ Church; dated to around 1178 the charter was witnessed by Cenninus, a priest of St Michael's (Wheeler 1960, 98). In 1186, the deeds of Christ Church confirm St Michael's, among many others, as being under the control of Holy Trinity church (*CCD*, no. 6). As mentioned above, a new palace having been erected by 1213, St Michael's was no longer within an episcopal palace, and its status becomes uncertain. It did not become a parish church until 1447 and Wheeler suggested that it continued to function as a dependent church of Christ Church's monastic priory, while it also 'very likely served the spiritual needs of the laity' (Wheeler 1960, 98).

An idea of the activities and professions of parishioners as well as the layout of the church can be retrieved from later records. In 1404, the shoemakers' guild, or guild of the Blessed Virgin Mary, was allowed to found a chantry of one or more chaplains for the daily celebration of mass in the chapel of the Virgin Mary within St Michael's. In 1444 a guild was founded for the daily celebration of mass in the chapel of St Catherine in the church of St Michael. Chantries, a characteristic form of late medieval Christian devotion, were endowed with the intention of providing one or more priests to sing daily mass for the souls of the founders or other specified individuals and it was common for a particular chapel to be allocated for this purpose. Chantries were founded both by private individuals and by corporate bodies such as craft guilds.

By the time Archbishop Richard Talbot officially acknowledged St Michael's as a parish church in 1447 we know of at least one parishioner who attended the church, a merchant land owner named Peter Higley. His final will and testament of 28 October 1476 is preserved in Trinity College Library (Berry 1893, 130–3). The record gives us a glimpse of the variety of goods valued by shop owners and the multi-skilled nature of Higley's business endeavours. In his will he left his wife Millany a third of all the common goods they had acquired together, acknowledging, perhaps unusually, their shared partnership. He bequeathed to his parish church twenty shillings and left the same amount to Christ Church where he requested to be buried in the chapel of St Mary the Virgin. The inventory of his goods includes sixteen weys of salt worth £32, fodder for his sheep, oxen, cows, pigs, calves and cart-horses and vessels of brass, lead and pewter. He states that his shop debts are registered in a book and accumulate to a total £57. The remaining sum is bequeathed to his daughter Agnes and two sons Patrick and Thomas, neither of whom was of legal age at the time of the will. The parochial nature of medieval Dublin is highlighted in the fact that his third son John Higley, one of the attestors of his will, was a brother or canon regular in Holy Trinity (Berry 1898, 130–3).

Tradition had it that oak statues depicting St Michael the Archangel and Lucifer stood over the east window of the eleventh-century church. They remained there until the dissolution of the monasteries between 1536 and 1541 when Henry VIII dissolved the Augustinian priory and canons of Christ Church and established a reformed foundation of secular canons with a dean and chapter in its place. During the archbishopric of George Browne, Henry VIII's appointed archbishop in Dublin in 1536, the statues were taken down and publicly burnt along with precious relics from Christ Church cathedral. The *Irish Builder* reports, somewhat ironically, that Lucifer was saved from the flames and erected over the entrance to a small laneway south of Christ Church popularly known as Hell (Reynell 1891, p79). In 1554, Archbishop Browne erected three permanent prebends (lands yielding stipends to the cathedral) in Christ Church – St Michael's, St Michan's and St John's – and appointed John Corragh the prebendary of St Michael's parish (Wheeler 1960, 98).

10.2 Digital reconstruction of St Michael's church within the medieval city, *c*.AD1550 (by Noho).

The medieval parish of St Michael was almost the smallest in the city, comprising an area of between five and six acres. Of the medieval church (fig. 10.2) we know that the south wall fronted onto High Street and also that the fresh water aqueduct ran just outside this wall on its way to Dublin Castle. Throughout the following centuries the history of St Michael's is recorded as a relentless record of ruination, repairs and rebuilding, in no particular order. Around 1530 William Donowt, citizen and merchant of Dublin and parishioner of St Michael's, bequeathed his body to the tomb of his ancestors in Holy Trinity; as with Peter Higley, he saw fit to leave a yearly sum to be paid to the 'building of the parish church of St Michael in High Street' (*CCD*, no. 419). The clause alludes to a church that was either being redeveloped or in need of it.

In 1667, the south wall was said to be in a ruinous state. In response, St Michael's vestry concluded that workmen should be employed as quickly as possible to build a new south wall where it was 'ready to fall downe' (Reynell 1891, 59). Despite this emergency response, or perhaps due to poor workmanship, 'the whole fabric had to be taken down to the very foundation to be again re-built' in 1676 (ibid.). Reynell suggests that 'the whole of the old eleventh-century buildings were raised to the ground, and a new church and steeple commenced to be erected on the site of the old foundations' (ibid., 60). Reynell also wrote that, during G.E. Street's restoration of Christ Church in the 1870s, the workmen had come across original foundations in the form of 'oak piles driven into peaty soil, a timber framework laid over them' (ibid., 170). He was unable to gain access to this archaeological discovery 'owing to a strike having taken place' among Street's workmen and so 'could not identify

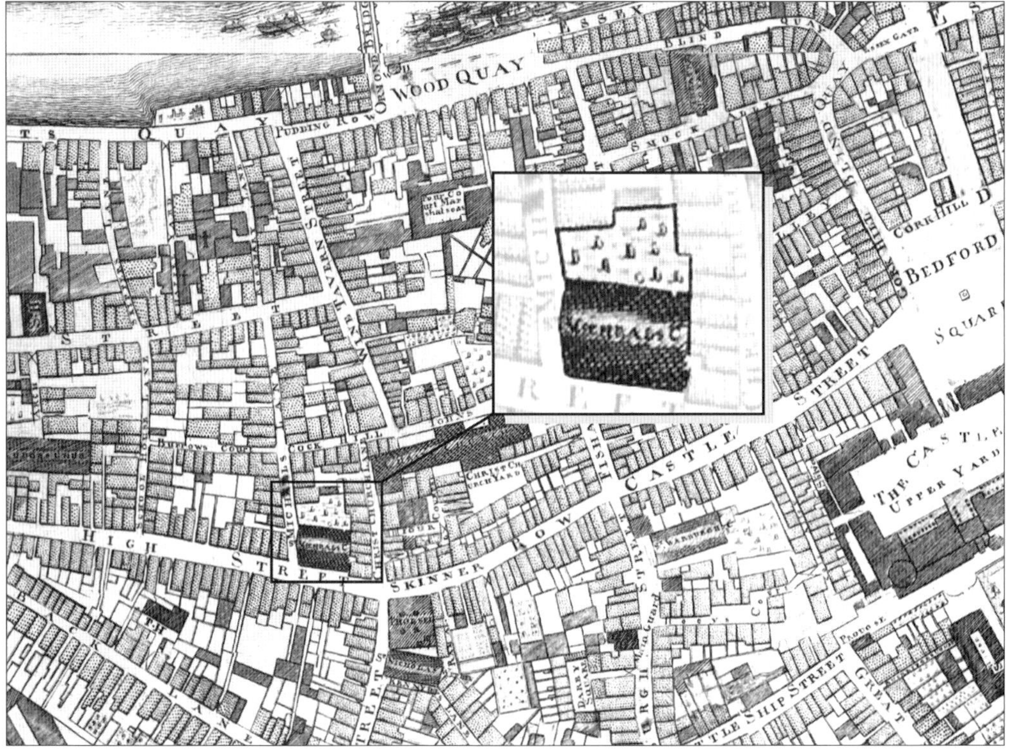

10.3 Close-up of St Michael's church and graveyard from Rocque's map of Dublin, 1756 (Rocque map © RIA).

the age of the timbers'. The author ponders whether these timbers are from the 'eleventh or seventeenth centuries'. In reality, the exposed piles that were identified could have belonged to any number of redevelopment stages before the nineteenth century.

The laying of wooden piles and horizontal timbers, discovered during Street's redevelopment, was a common foundation design used in Dublin in the seventeenth century especially in Temple Bar. Here the land was reclaimed from the river and the ground waterlogged (Simpson and Gowen 2010, 4). Thomas Drew, Street's successor as architect, excavated an area around the cloister of Christ Church and claimed the church to be founded on a peat bog (Stalley 2000a, 54). It is likely that this marshy soil could have been the same organic material that was later discovered during a small excavation in Dublinia in 2008 by Linzi Simpson (09E0331). In the southeast corner of Dublinia's courtyard medieval organic habitation deposits were excavated from a test trench that could be dated to the eleventh and twelfth centuries. It suggested that the area was occupied by post-and-wattle houses within property plots and with associated pits and refuse deposits (Simpson and

Gowen 2010, 2, 9). Six perforated bone pins were recorded in the topographical files of the National Museum of Ireland as having been discovered in 1888 near St Michael's church (www.heritagemaps.ie). During excavation work undertaken by Claire Cotter in 1989 for the current owners of the site, The Medieval Trust, a number of human remains were discovered and left *in situ* underneath the old reception area of Dublinia on the ground level of the current building. These probably relate to the old graveyard of St Michael's church (Simpson and Gowen 2010, 5) (fig. 10.3).

The new seventeenth-century church and steeple took a number of years to complete owing to lack of funds. The steeple was left unroofed until 1694 when further funds were secured and it was raised to eighty-seven feet. Wheeler estimated that, with its south wall fronting on High Street, its length and that of the church from east to west was 74 feet, while the west end of the church, which was 37 feet across from north to south, was on St Michael's Lane (Wheeler 1960, 102). To celebrate the new church a collection of ecclesiastical silverware was commissioned with an engraving of St Michael's church and steeple and was donated by a number of parishioners in 1697 including John North, a bookseller. The engraving is an abstract rendering of perspective but depicts the extent of the south wall with a side entrance and a rear southwest bell-tower (fig. 10.4). Safely stored in the Representative Church Body Library, the silver has lasted longer than the seventeenth-century church.

Less than one hundred years later the situation returned to a crisis point. In 1782, the corporation of carpenters certified that the church was in a 'ruinous state, in danger of falling and ought to be pulled down' (Reynell 1891, 145). In 1786, the city grand jury stated that it needed to be taken down, citing it as a danger and 'common nuisance' (ibid., 163). In later years the parishioners were unsafe and had to be rehoused in St Mary's chapel in Christ Church cathedral. More temporary repairs ensued until 1810 when funds were again secured to begin construction on another, smaller, church. The reduced dimensions of the nineteenth-century church were recorded as fifty-five by twenty-two feet to the east of the seventeenth-century tower which, according to Wheeler, overshadowed the new church (Wheeler 1960, 103). A nineteenth-century writer described the church as 'remarkably diminutive, all tower at one end, and all window at the other' (Godkin 1867, 172). The eastern window facing the cathedral consisted of stained glass, and the tower was described as a dark, heavy, square structure which seemed 'not at all in keeping with the little building with light-coloured walls with which it is connected' (ibid.). In 1815, attendances at St Michael's were such that it was thought to be only one-eighth full at any one time and although it could accommodate about two hundred parishioners, the total Protestant population attending the church was a mere seventy-six parishioners (ibid.).

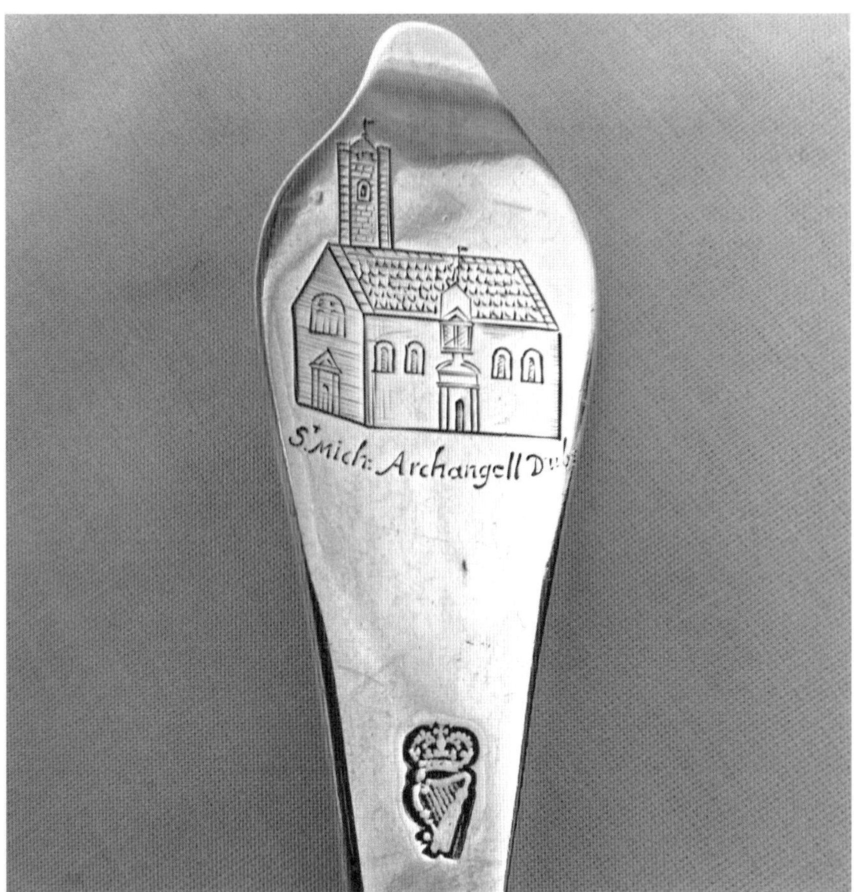

10.4 Close-up of the spoon handle from a collection of silverware depicting St Michael's church, *c*.1697 (© RCB Library).

By the time Street and his workmen came to construct the synod hall they had to contend with this tower and the graveyard. The last recorded interment took place in 1804 and, according to Wheeler, 'bones were reinterred in the crypt of Christ Church in 1877' (Wheeler 1960, 104). At that time parishioners were asked to look out for a new graveyard owing to the current cemetery having reached capacity. No alternative burial ground was sourced and, as a solution, rubbish was occasionally dumped on the graveyard surface to raise the level of the site and to accommodate newly deceased parishioners. The soil under the church itself was found, in 1872, to contain a number of pits completely filled with bones, possibly a clearing out of earlier interments from the medieval graveyard to make room for more burials. It is no wonder then that Street supervised the laying of three thousand tonnes of concrete to support the incoming heavy masonry on ground that had failed to support all previous building attempts (Reynell 1891, 170).

FINDING THE LOST CHURCH

The above review of St Michael's unstable history may incline the reader to think that no visible evidence survives of the earlier church apart from the seventeenth-century bell-tower. A brief visual survey noted evidence of large, possibly medieval, masonry preserved in the lowest standing level of the bell-tower. In the basement level existing in the northern elevation of the site, Simpson noted six to nine round-arched red-bricked crypt spaces visible within the modern building (pers. comm., 2014). Owing to the current use of the building a comprehensive inspection of potentially historic features could not be fulfilled during a heritage assessment in 2009 (Arnold 2009, 21). In more recent times the basement was the home to the caretakers attached to the active synod hall.

In a study of medieval parish churches completed by Michael O'Neill, he noted a consistent wall width of 0.9m. The walls east of the tower, where the footprint of the church would be expected, are between 0.81m and 0.83m in width. A medieval wall is, without a definite rule, roughly 0.8m to 1m in width. It is possible that these walls represent the footprint and possible medieval foundations of the medieval church of St Michael. However, it should be noted that the surrounding south walls around the perimeter on Dublinia's floor plan also have the same thickness as the medieval church wall despite dating to the seventeenth-century.

The existing ground plan of the synod hall contains similarities with earlier maps (Simpson and Gowen 2010, 4). The last church from around 1810 is depicted in detail on the 1864/66 OS map and shows the retained seventeenth-century bell-tower with an adjoining northern structure that may have been a vestry (Arnold 2009, 10). Arnold notes a stairway depicted on the map in the location of this possible vestry and suggests that it descended to provide access to the crypt (ibid., 10). It is equally possible that the stairs may have been an entry point to the bell-tower. A small storeroom on the ground level of Dublinia on the northwest corner of the building contains evidence for a turret stairway that once permitted access up to the bell-tower through a round-arched doorway that still exists in the base of the bell-tower. In the future an archaeological survey might identify a chronology to support this map analysis.

John Rocque's map of Dublin (1756) provides us with a plan of the perimeter of St Michael's church after the seventeenth-century redevelopment and prior to the Wide Streets Commission interventions in the early nineteenth century (fig. 10.3). The church is identified as a block that fronts directly onto High Street unlike the later church, and shows St Michael's at its largest scale. The block depicted by Rocque could be identified as the seventeenth-century church engraved on the collection of ecclesiastical silverware donated to St Michael's (fig. 10.4). In Wheeler's detailed account of the church at this time he noted that the arrangement of the church ran in the normal ecclesiastical manner from east to west but an addition of a 'studded partition' between pillars enclosed the church and shortened the layout at the north and south ends, probably 'to reduce the disproportionate width' (Wheeler 1960, 103).

The inaccuracies of Speed's map are well known but it should be noted that St Michael's is featured as number forty-seven and, like neighbouring churches, contains a western tower. The date of construction of the original bell-tower is likely to be mid-fifteenth to mid-sixteenth century and the first record of a steeple is in 1578 (Leask 1955–60, iii, 41; Clarke 2002, 17). Harold Leask published an important study of Irish churches and monastic buildings in 1955 and concluded that belfry towers belong to the fifteenth and sixteenth centuries. He also noted that these towers were generally located in the middle of churches, except in the Pale where they more often feature to the west, as at St Michael's (Leask 1955–60, iii, 41). Bell-ringing alerted parishioners to a number of varying occurrences – announcing deaths, funerals and changes of time and calendar months.

COMPARATIVE OVERLAY

While medieval churches vary in size, it is helpful to assess these using floorplans and proportional building methodologies. Michael O'Neill and Máirín Ní Mharcaigh undertook surveys of medieval Irish churches in Meath and south Co. Dublin respectively. Both considered size, location, building dimensions, architectural features and morphology in their studies. I shall reference some of these aspects below but, owing to the continual construction and reconstruction of urban archaeological sites, some of the useful indicators laid out by them, in particular windows, window traceries or exposed reused stone, are absent from Dublinia.

O'Neill suggests that the general size and form of medieval churches in the Pale consists of twin-aisled nave churches, with a lower chancel extending east. The general format of the Pale church is a long nave and chancel. Other examples included the original St Werburgh's church on Werburgh Street, southeast of Christ Church cathedral, which was certainly in existence in the late twelfth century. Consisting of a tower, twin-aisled nave and chancel extending east from the north aisle, it is a familiar style 'among the Pale churches, also found at nearby St Audoen's, at St Mary's in Howth and at the [rebuilt] medieval parish church at Lusk' (O'Neill 2012, 132–3).

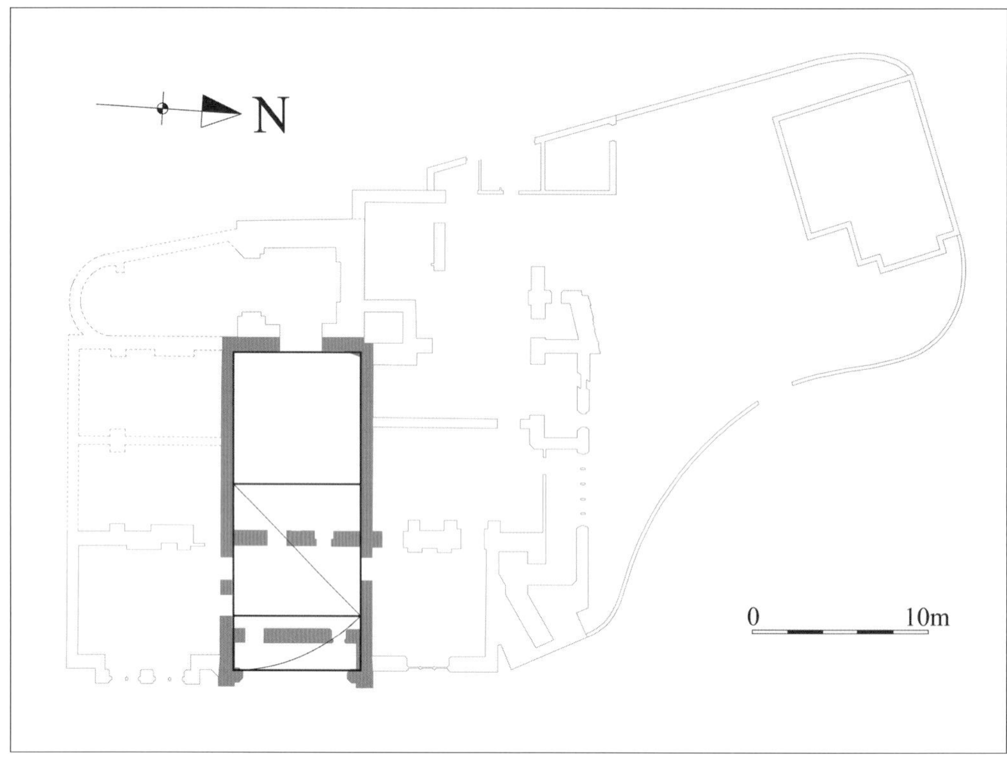

10.5 Root 2 pegging system overlaid onto the floor plan of Dublinia Heritage Centre (drawing by Johnny Ryan).

In O'Neill's study of Meath churches he notes a proportional system that underlies the base dimensions of church chancels and naves (O'Neill 2002, 35). Masons learnt geometrical skills by rote, such as how to produce right-angles using a straight edge square, and worked with complex mathematical equations. They also learnt structural stability, memorizing the proportions for the 'depth and bulk of foundations in relation to the width and height of the building proposed' and considered safety factors that would allow for 'wind-pressure and the thrusts of vaults and roofs and the needed buttresses' (O'Neill 2014, 113). O'Neill highlighted two methods adopted by builders to plan foundations. Both apply to the 'pegging system' of construction, whereby a rope with a peg or anchor at one end is used as a straight line between two points. Figure 10.5 shows the first method called a 'Root 2' rectangle. The outline of a foundation was mapped with a rope pegged in the corners to create a square. Another rope was pulled across the longer diagonal length of the square to create another line which was then shifted along the square edge to extend the foundation plan from a square to a rectangle. The other

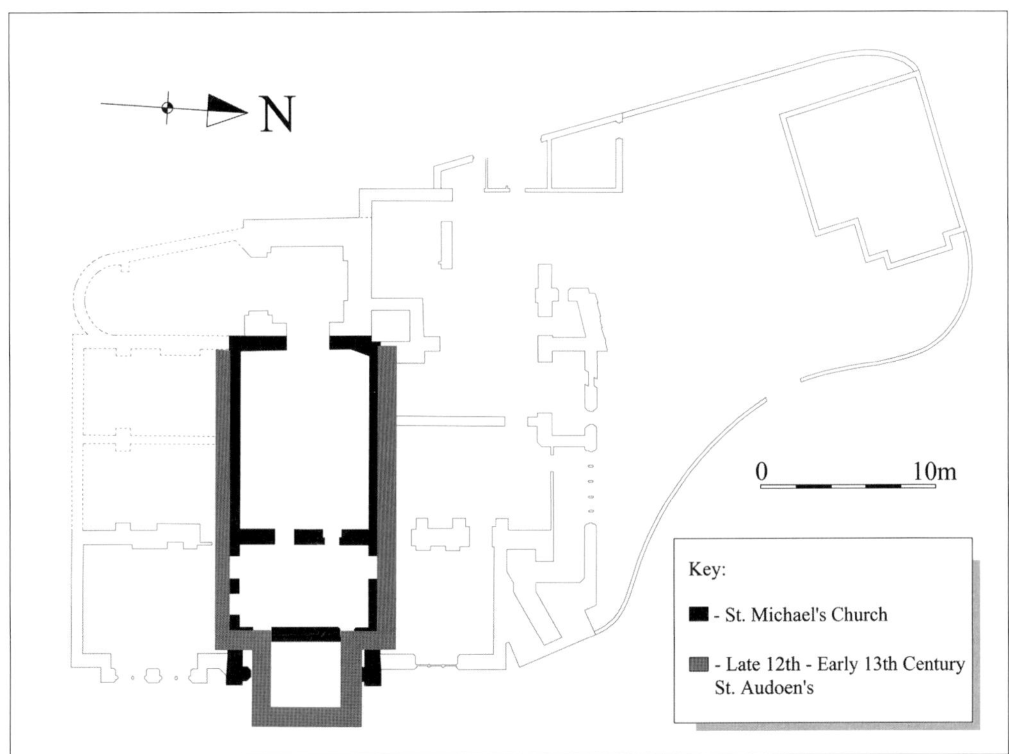

10.6 Overlay of St Audoen's late twelfth-/early thirteenth-century church on the floor plan of Dublinia showing possible footprint of St Michael's church (drawing by Johnny Ryan).

proportional system is the 'Golden Section' rectangle and is similar to the 'Root 2' rectangle except that the diagonal rope measurement is taken from a half-square. He exemplifies this proportional construction method with examples from Killeen, Dunsany and Rathmore churches in Co. Meath. The floorplan of all these churches exhibits a mixture of both the 'Root 2' and the 'Golden Section' measuring systems (O'Neill 2002, 35) incorporating squares, half-squares and rectangles in their measurements.

It is possible to apply the same proportional measurements on a floorplan of Dublinia to identify a preserved medieval nave-and-chancel floorplan. The likely position of the medieval church is east of the tower and here a clear proportional system can be identified with the current floorplan in the background (fig. 10.5). The 'Root 2' method may have been used to build the nave and chancel extending east consisting of a square and rectangle. The internal dimensions of the plan show at an internal measurement of 9.83m for the nave length and 7.35m for the width and the chancel length is 4.55m with a combined internal nave and chancel length of 15.22m.

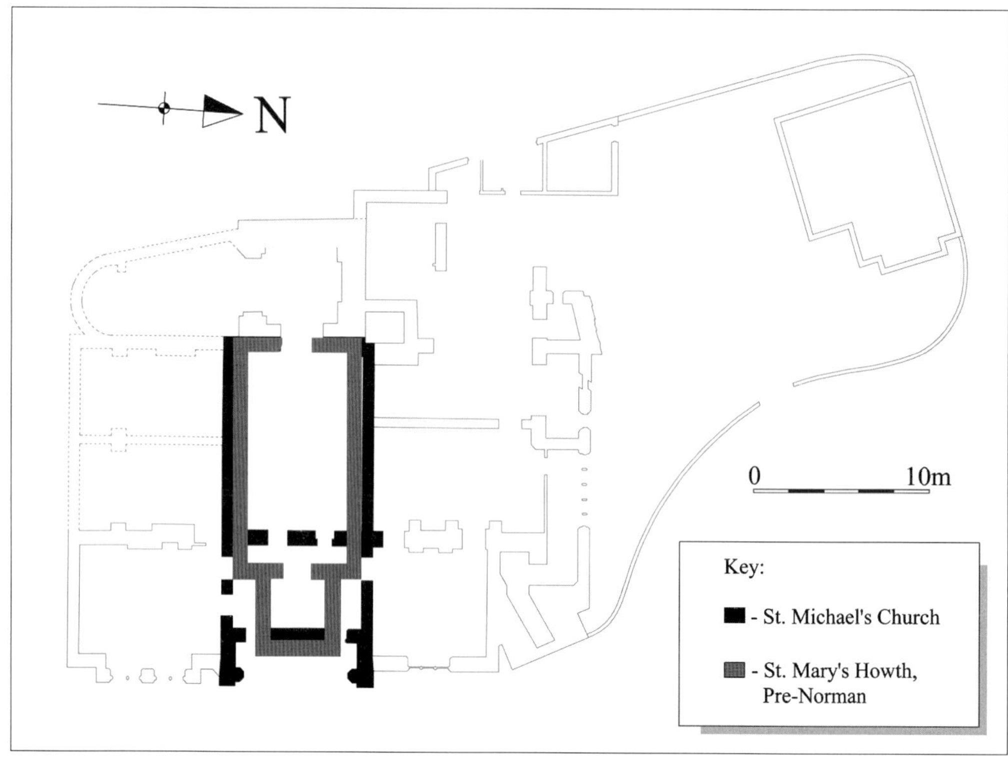

10.7 Overlay of St Mary's church, Howth, on floor plan of Dublinia (drawing by Johnny Ryan).

Similar church plans can be identified in other Pale churches and when superimposed onto the floor plan of Dublinia the east–west nave-and-chancel churches show comparable dimensions. St Audeon's church represents a familiar style of Pale church (O'Neill 2012, 132–3) and Mary MacMahon created a chronology of architectural phases that shows the earliest church building was situated on an east–west axis, similar to St Michael's and was a two-cell structure with contemporary nave and narrower chancel, a plan-form common in Ireland in the twelfth century (MacMahon 2006, 109). The study also highlights the addition of a tower some time from the early fifteenth to the early sixteenth century. The nave measurement is closer to the overall length of St Michael's, reaching *c.*15.5m but the width is *c.*8.0m (fig. 10.6). The narrower chancel is comparable to St Michael's measuring *c.*4.20m sq. (MacMahon 2006, 84–8).

The same process was experimented with the unusual church of St Michael le Pole revealing less comparable results. The church stood only 281m southeast of St Michael's church, just outside the medieval walled town. Based on the report from a pre-development excavation by Margaret Gowen in 1981,

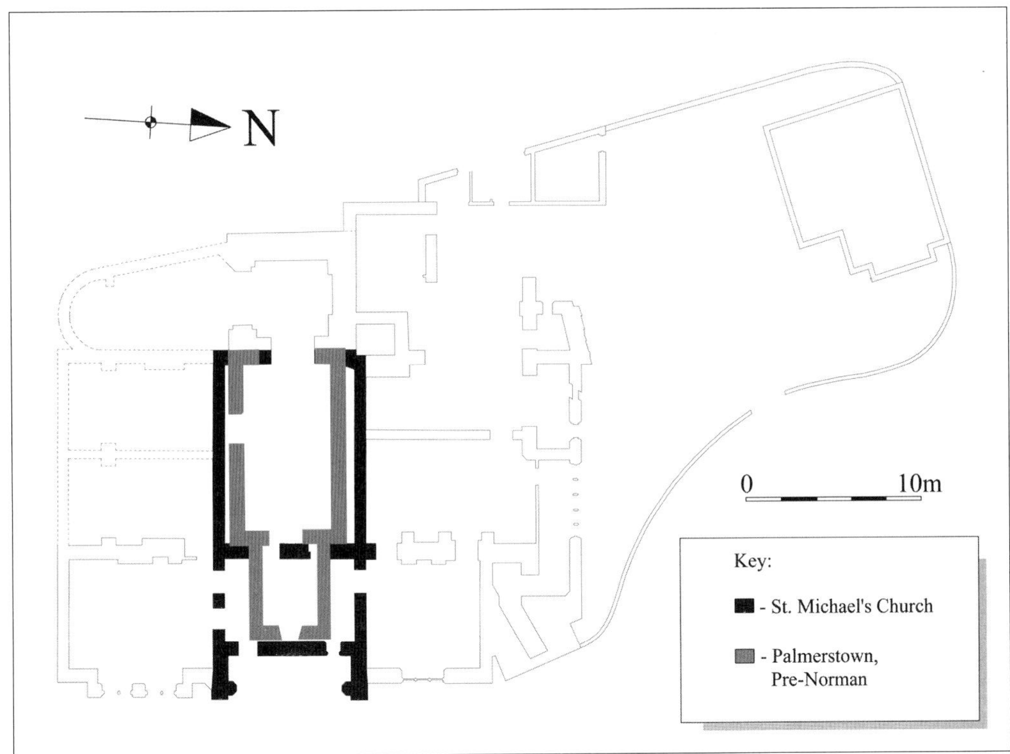

10.8 Overlay of Palmerstown church on floor plan of Dublinia (drawing by Johnny Ryan).

evidence suggests that the church was twelfth-century and includes further evidence of pre-twelfth-century settlement activity (Gowen 2001, 51). Gowen's phase-three exposed the west wall of the twelfth-century church and so it was possible to estimate the overall missing church outline apart from the delineation of nave and chancel. The overall internal dimension is 17.58m with an internal width of 10.63m.

Another church with a studied chronology of architecture is St Mary's in Howth (Cochrane 1896, 10). The church originally existed as a nave and chancel but over time the building was extended and added to, creating a twin-aisled medieval church. The southern aisle pre-dates the other and it is this structure that the nineteenth-century author refers to as 'Saxon' in date (ibid., 3). This pre-Anglo-Norman church has a nave length of 5.67m, smaller than St Michael's, but the total internal length including the chancel reaches 15.87m, similar to St Michael's overall internal length of 15.22m (fig. 10.7).

Ní Mharcaigh's study of medieval parish churches in southwest Dublin is also of use here. She studied the territory which was largely held by the Mac Gilla Mo-Cholmóc dynasty at the time of the Anglo-Norman invasion

(Ní Mharcaigh 1997, 246). The same family is curiously associated with the street name immediately west of St Michael's church, Gilmaholmog Street (*CCD*, no. 87). Ní Mharcaigh's study examines the archaeology of these churches taking into account the size, location, morphology, structural development, dimensions, architectural features and chronology. Her study also mentions the range of churches that show considerable diversity in nave length, width and the size of chancels, yet it allows her to categorize them in terms of single-cell churches and nave-and-chancel churches (ibid., 245). She found ten medieval churches that were on the site of pre-Anglo-Norman ecclesiastical foundations (ibid., 262). One of these churches, Palmerstown, retained archaeological evidence of a pre-Anglo-Norman structure and was the only one to survive before being readapted for use in the Anglo-Norman period (ibid., 250). Originally, this was a single-cell structure with the chancel added early but postdating the nave. This was a nave-and-chancel church with a nave-length closer to St Michael's nave measuring 9.0m long but narrower at 5.0m wide. The chancel length was also similar to St Michael's measuring 4.32m and again the width was narrower at 3.10m (Ní Mharcaigh 1997, 274–5). Whereas St Michael's total nave and chancel measured 15.22m, Palmerstown measured 14.32m (fig. 10.8).

* * *

To conclude, the lost medieval church of St Michael's may not be lost after all, just merely forgotten. This paper has explored the origins of St Michael's church from its foundation perhaps as the first bishop of Dublin's private chapel within the episcopal palace. It has considered the extent of the palace in terms of the extension of the early *dún* and its place within the foundation records of Christ Church cathedral. Whether made of timber or stone we cannot be certain. The post-Anglo-Norman history, although sparse, gives an indication that the church was retained as a dependent chapel for use by the monastic priory attached to Christ Church. St Michael's was not formerly acknowledged as a parish church until 1447 and following the dissolution of the monasteries the church was probably extended to the west with the addition of a bell-tower. The colourful history of St Michael's church has been revealed in part, highlighting a small but active parish intent on saving a church which, from the fifteenth century, was steadily decaying. The following years are heavily itemized in the vestry minutes preserved in the Representative Church Body Library and a detailed review of these, as has been achieved for St Audoen's church minutes, would undoubtedly illuminate the history of the modern parish and serve as a considerable asset to the study of church architecture and the early modern parishes of Dublin.

No other dedicated research has been undertaken on St Michael's since the study published in the *Irish Builder* in 1891 but more is needed to uncover comparative data and possible archaeology that is retained in the walls of the lowest levels of the synod hall. Referring to O'Neill and Ní Mharcaigh's studies of medieval churches within locations of the Pale, the footprint of the former synod hall shows family resemblances to St Mary's Howth, St Audeon's, the pre-Anglo-Norman church at Palmerstown but less so with the church of St Michael le Pole. It is hoped that this study consolidates current theory on the original church of St Michael's and its location with the current building of Dublinia and opens up the possibility that the church of St Michael was always on this site owing to a continuation of worship from the earliest phase – as Ní Mharcaigh states, 'the holding of a particular site is sacred and it continues as a focus for religious rites over many generations' (Ní Mharcaigh 1997, 247).

BIBLIOGRAPHY

Arnold, P. 2009 'Dublinia, former synod hall, Dublin 8, architectural heritage impact assessment'. Unpublished report.

Berry, H.F. (ed.). 1893 *Register of wills and inventories in the diocese of Dublin in the time of archbishops Trequry and Walton*, 1457–1483. Dublin.

Clarke, H. 2002. *Dublin Part I, to 1610*. Irish Historic Towns Atlas, No. 11. RIA. Dublin.

Cochrane, R. 1896 'Notes on the ecclesiastical antiquities in the parish of Howth, county of Dublin'. *JRSAI* 26, 1–21.

Godkin, J. 1867 *Ireland and her churches*. London.

Gowen, M. 2001 'Excavations at the site of the church and tower of St Michael le Pole, Dublin'. In S. Duffy (ed.), *Medieval Dublin II*, 13–52. Dublin.

Gwynn, A. 1946 'Some unpublished texts from the Black Book of Christ Church, Dublin'. *Analecta Hibernica* 16, 281–337.

www.heritagemaps.ie. The Heritage Council. Kilkenny.

Kinsella, S. 2000 'From Hiberno-Norse to Anglo-Norman, *c.*1030–1300'. In K. Milne (ed.), *Christ Church cathedral, Dublin: a history*, 25–52. Dublin.

Kinsella, S. 2009a 'Mapping Christ Church cathedral, Dublin, *c.*1028–1608: an examination of the western cloister'. In J. Bradley, A. Fletcher and A. Simms (eds), *Dublin in the medieval world: studies in honour of Howard B. Clarke*, 143–67. Dublin.

Kinsella, S. 2009b 'An architectural history of Christ Church cathedral, Dublin *c.*1540–1871' (PhD, TCD).

Leask, H.G. 1955–60 *Irish churches and monastic buildings*, 3 vols. Dundalk.

MacMahon, M. 2006 *St Audoen's church, Cornmarket, Dublin: archaeology and architecture*. Dublin.

Milne, K. (ed.). 2000a *Christ Church cathedral, Dublin: a history*. Dublin.

Milne, K. 2000b 'The stripping of assets, 1830–1960'. In K. Milne (ed.), *Christ Church cathedral, Dublin: a history*, 315–38. Dublin.

Ní Mharcaigh, M. 1997 'The medieval parish churches of south-west County Dublin'. *PRIA* 97C, 245–96.

O'Donovan, D. 2003 'English patron, English building? The importance of St Sepulchre's archiepiscopal palace, Dublin'. In S. Duffy (ed.), *Medieval Dublin IV*, 253–78. Dublin.

O'Keeffe, T. 2017 'A cryptic puzzle from medieval Dublin'. *Archaeology Ireland* 31:2 (120), 39–42.

O'Neill, M. 2002 'The medieval parish churches in County Meath'. *JRSAI* 132, 1–56.

O'Neill, M. 2012 'St Werburgh's church'. *Irish Arts Review* 29:4, 132–5.

O'Neill, M. 2014 'The mason's tale'. In S. Booker and C.N. Peters (eds), *Tales of medieval Dublin*, 112–18. Dublin.

Reynell, R.W. 1891 'The history of the church and parish of St Michael the Archangel, Dublin'. *The Irish Builder*, pp 59, 60 (15 Mar.), p. 79 (1 Apr.), p. 145 (1 July), p. 163 (15 July), p. 170 (1 Aug.).

Simpson, L., and Gowen, M. 2010 'Archaeological excavation Dublinia (the former synod hall)'. Unpublished report.

Stalley, R. 2000a 'The construction of the medieval cathedral, *c.*1030–1250'. In K. Milne (ed.), *Christ Church cathedral, Dublin: a history*, 53–74. Dublin.

Stalley, R. 2000b 'The architecture of the cathedral and priory buildings, 1250–1530'. In K. Milne (ed.), *Christ Church cathedral, Dublin: a history*, 95–128. Dublin.

Stalley, R. 2000c 'George Edmund Street and the restoration of the cathedral, 1868–78'. In K. Milne (ed.), *Christ Church cathedral, Dublin: a history*, 353–73. Dublin.

Stalley, R. 2000d *George Edmund Street and the restoration of Christ Church cathedral*. Dublin.

Vestry Book minutes of St Michael's church, Dublin, 1667–1754. Representative Church Body Library, Dublin.

Wheeler, H. A. 1960 'St Michael's parish'. *DHR* 15:4, 97–104.

The Book of Howth's account of the Lambert Simnel conspiracy: an eyewitness account?

RANDOLPH JONES

Browse through any article or book published on the infamous Lambert Simnel conspiracy of the late fifteenth century and you will find passages quoted from the Book of Howth.[1] These are useful in giving details of the conspiracy in Ireland and elsewhere, but its statements are usually accepted at face value. The following essay attempts to shed some light on this problematical source, by examining its origin, as well as the veracity of some of its more interesting passages.

The Book of Howth was compiled between 1569 and 1579 under the direction of Christopher St Lawrence, seventh baron of Howth (*c.*1510–89). He was the grandson of Nicholas (*c.*1466–1526), the Lord Howth mentioned in the Lambert Simnel episode. Rather than a book in the accepted sense, it was very much a 'working document', the purpose of which was to demonstrate the loyalty of the 'Old English' settlers at a time when they were under severe political pressure from the 'New English' in Ireland. The latter, usually Protestants holding official appointments from the crown, tended to lump the Old English together with their Roman Catholic co-religionists, the Gaelic Irish, and treat them as such. The seventh baron chose to demonstrate this loyalty by compiling a history of the English in Ireland from the Anglo-Norman conquest. Although it was produced by different hands in several stages, the bulk was written by a single scribe working between 1569 and 1571. The Book was originally a transcript of several chronicles, providing Howth with a continuous narrative up until the end of the reign of Edward III (d. 1377). Thereafter, his sources failed him, for which purpose he left two folios blank. These were subsequently filled by a rather incongruous account of the siege of Rhodes in 1480. The narrative then resumed from Edward IV's reign with extracts taken from the 'book of Mr Watter Housse's of Dobbore, beside Donsogle, written with his own hand'.[2]

Walter Hussey of Dubber beside Dunsoghly, Co. Dublin, to give his name and residence in modern form, was born between 1447 and 1457. He is first mentioned as the servant of William Howth, allegedly the younger brother of

1 Lambeth Palace Library, MS 632, fols. 114–15; J.S. Brewer and William Bullen (eds), *Calendar of the Carew Manuscripts preserved in the Archiepiscopal Library at Lambeth*, v (London, 1871), pp 188–90. 2 Valerie McGowan-Doyle, *The Book of Howth: Elizabethan conquest and the Old English* (Cork, 2011), pp 39–41, 44, 135–6.

Nicholas the third baron, but probably his uncle, William Howth of Stapolyn (d. 1493). Hussey took part in a successful skirmish with William against Sir James Ormond's men at Kilmainham bridge, in which one of Ormond's brothers and seven of his men were killed. This took place in the summer of 1492, following a heated exchange in the third baron's house at Killester, when Sir James took exception to comments made by Howth in support of Gerald fitzGerald (Gearóid Mór), the eighth earl of Kildare.[3] William Howth died on 11 November 1493.[4] Nevertheless, Hussey remained connected with the St Lawrence family, becoming foster-father to Nicholas' grandson, Richard, who became the sixth baron when his elder brother Edward died in 1549.[5] Richard married Katherine fitzGerald, an illegitimate daughter of Gerald, the ninth earl of Kildare (Gearóid Óg). Hussey was already retained by the ninth earl, receiving a sorrel horse from him in 1513 and a grey one in 1524.[6] When Richard died in 1558, he was succeeded by his younger brother Christopher, the compiler of the 'Book of Howth'.[7]

Hussey also held appointments in the Irish exchequer, where his career spanned sixty years. He is first mentioned as one of the clerks who wrote up the rolls for a subsidy assessment in the summer of 1495.[8] His employment there may have been due to Walter Howth (d. 1503), chief baron of the exchequer, a younger brother of William of Stapolyn.[9] During the Hilary term of 1498, Hussey acted as the attorney for Marion Bernewall, the widow of John de la Felde, when she faced a charge of contempt for not attending the exchequer court on an earlier occasion.[10] On 10 December 1499, he was appointed summonister, the clerk who wrote out the exchequer's summonses and writs. By 1511, he was chief engrosser, the clerk who wrote up the exchequer records in final form.[11] This latter appointment seems to have been renewed with each change of lieutenancy or deputyship of Ireland. Around 1535, Hussey was appointed one of the barons of the exchequer, but he also retained his previous office of chief engrosser for, at Michaelmas 1537, he was paid his salary at the rate of £10 Irish (£6 13*s*. 4*d*. sterling) per annum for the preceding three-and-a-half years.[12] On 26 January 1538, Hussey was reappointed chief engrosser, but he now shared this office with John Ryan. Their joint appointment was renewed on 13 April 1541.[13] During Michaelmas

3 Brewer and Bullen (eds), *Cal. Carew MSS*, v, pp 177, 195. 4 Griffith (ed.), *Cal. inquisitions*, p. 18. 5 Brewer and Bullen (eds), *Cal. Carew MSS*, v, p. 260; Griffith (ed.), *Cal. inquisitions*, pp 123–5. 6 Gearóid MacNiocaill (ed.), *Crown surveys of lands, 1540–41 with the Kildare rental begun in 1518* (Dublin, 1992), pp 320, 328. 7 Griffith (ed.), *Cal. inquisitions*, pp 166–70. 8 Steven G. Ellis, *Reform and revival: English government in Ireland, 1470–1534* (Woodbridge, 1986), p. 97. 9 Francis Elrington Ball, *Howth and its owners being the fifth part of a history of County Dublin* (Dublin, 1917), pp 52, 58–9. 10 BL Add MS 43769, p. 76. 11 Ellis, *Reform and revival*, p. 97. 12 *CPR Ire., Hen. VIII–Eliz.*, pp 14, 15, 29; James Gairdner (ed.), *Letters and papers, foreign and domestic, Henry VIII*, vol. 12, pt 2, June–Dec. 1537 (London, 1891), no. 1310. 13 *CPR Ire., Hen. VIII–Eliz.*, p. 41; 'Appendix X: Calendar of fiants of King Henry VIII' in *Rep. DKPRI*, 7, no. 177.

term of the same year, both men examined the account of Christopher Dowdall, the collector of a subsidy in Co. Louth.[14]

Hussey does not seem to have inherited any property of his own, but on 4 February 1536 William Laundy, the abbot of the Cistercian monastery of St Mary's, Dublin, leased the manor of Dubber, near Dunsoghly, to Walter and his wife Anne. This consisted of a messuage or fortalice, with a dovecot, garden and haggard, 60 acres of arable land, 4 acres of meadow, 34 acres of pasture and a small grove of ash trees covering 2 acres. At the same time, the abbot leased to them a further 10 acres of arable land near the bridge of Finglas, in the parish of 'St Glannoke' (possibly a corruption of St Cainneach), all for seven marks per annum for 31 years, plus the tithes of 8 measures of corn, 8 of barley-malt and 16 of oat-malt. Hussey was still holding these lands in 1540, when he was also renting a messuage and a garden, located near the outer gate of the dissolved abbey, for 3*s*. 4*d*. per annum, as well as two houses in the parish of St Michan's, Dublin, for 4*s*. and 7*s*. per annum respectively.[15] Hussey was favoured with these leases because he had previously acted as attorney of John Burges, the abbot of St Mary's, when he was summoned to appear before the barons of the exchequer in 1518–19. After the death of his predecessor in 1511, Burges was accused of entering the abbey's temporalities without the king's licence. Hussey successfully pleaded an act of the Irish parliament passed in 17 Henry VII (1501–2), which gave St Mary's exemption from seeking such a licence.[16]

Hussey is said to have died on 19 March 1554, when he was either 100 or 107: both ages are mentioned in the Book of Howth, although a document dated 4 May 1537 states that he was then aged only eighty.[17] During the first year of Queen Mary's reign (1553–4), Hussey was replaced as chief engrosser by Ralph Coccrell, who was to hold that office 'in as ample manner as Walter Hussey' did.[18]

* * *

It is clear from Hussey's exchequer appointments that he was literate and able to compose written material. His ability to work well into his old age is borne out by the claim that he 'was as perfect in his wits at his last as he was in his

14 Charles McNeill and A. J. Otway-Ruthven (eds), *Dowdall deeds* (Dublin, 1960), p. 238. 15 *CStM*, ii, pp 43, 53, 56, 58; *Extents Ir. mon. possessions*, pp 1, 2, 6, 8; Griffith (ed.), *Cal. inquisitions*, pp 79, 80, 83. 16 J.B. Leslie (ed.), *O'Morchoe's history of Kilternan and Kilgobbin* (Dublin, 1934), p. 7; details of the same exchequer case can also be found in College of Arms, London, MS Ph 15175, p. 356, but the name of the abbot's attorney is not mentioned therein (Exch. Mem. Roll, 9 & 10 Hen. VIII, m. 19). 17 'Fiants of King Henry VIII', *Rep. DKPRI*, 7, nos. 400, 446; Brewer and Bullen (eds), *Cal. Carew MSS*, v, pp 195, 260; Edmund Curtis (ed.), *Calendar of Ormond deeds*, 6 vols (Dublin, 1932–43), iii, p. 392. 18 *CPR Ire., Hen. VIII–Eliz.*, pp 314, 327; 'Appendix IV: Fiants – Philip and Mary' in *Rep.*

youth.' Unfortunately, the original of Hussey's work is no longer extant. The only copy we have is the one found in the Book of Howth.[19] Hussey's work is said to have commenced with a lengthy, but unique account of the eighth earl of Kildare's victory at Knockdoe in 1504, in which Christopher St Lawrence's grandfather Nicholas was given a prominent part. However, recent scholarship suggests that Hussey's book probably included several earlier episodes involving the same earl, which were placed immediately before the Knockdoe account.[20] This may have been the original extent of Hussey's work, but it seems that a decision was made later to expand it by bringing it up to date and going back as far as the beginning of Edward IV's reign and his 1461 victory at Mortimer's Cross. Hussey says that he took his account of this battle from 'Hale's chronicle', meaning Edward Hall's *The union of the two noble and illuste families of Lancastre and Yorke*.[21] Its inclusion in this narrative of Irish history is rather odd, other than the fact that James Butler, earl of Wiltshire and Ormond, was one of its participants.

Hussey's narrative then jumps to 1468 and the execution of Thomas fitzGerald, the seventh earl of Desmond. Hussey states that this was due to the alleged machinations of Edward IV's queen, Elizabeth Wydeville, who took exception to comments Desmond made about her suitability as the king's consort. She surreptitiously used the king's privy seal to send letters to John Tiptoft, earl of Worcester and deputy lieutenant of Ireland, ordering him to execute Desmond on trumped-up charges. Hussey's account of this episode is very similar to that found in a petition submitted, about 1542, by Desmond's grandson, James fitzGerald, the fourteenth earl – especially the final part which stated that Edward IV was so displeased with Desmond's execution that he recalled Worcester, put him on trial and executed him in turn. This strongly suggests that Hussey had seen a copy of Desmond's petition, probably in his exchequer capacity, for its main purpose was to regain the town (and revenues) of Dungarvan, Co. Waterford, which the earls of Desmond had formerly held, but which were then in the hands of the crown.[22] Hussey also drew on Hall's chronicle for additional information on the alleged execution of two of Desmond's younger sons at Drogheda, to which he added his own information on their sad demise.[23]

At the bottom of the page (fo. 113), brief details were later inserted by a different hand on the burial place of Sir Roland FitzEustace, treasurer of

DKPRI, 9, no. 49. **19** Brewer and Bullen (eds), *Cal. Carew MSS*, v, pp 176–96. **20** McGowan-Doyle, *Book of Howth*, p. 61. **21** *Hall's chronicle; containing the history of England, during the reign of Henry the Fourth, and the succeeding monarchs, to the end of the reign of Henry the Eighth, in which are particularly described the manners and customs of those periods, carefully collated with the editions of 1548 and 1550* (London, 1809), p. 251. **22** Brewer and Bullen (eds), *Cal. Carew MSS*, v, pp cv–cviii. **23** *Hall's chronicle*, p. 286. For an examination of Elizabeth Wydeville's alleged actions, see Peter Crooks, 'The ascent and descent of Desmond under Lancaster and York' in Peter Crooks and Seán Duffy (eds),

Ireland, as well as the lieutenancies or deputyships of Ireland during the 1480s of Richard of Shrewsbury, duke of York, John de la Pole, earl of Lincoln, and Gerald fitzGerald, earl of Kildare. These notices were culled from a manuscript copy of Edmund Campion's 1571 'Histories of Ireland'.[24] Hussey's account of the 1487 Lambert Simnel conspiracy then follows on a new folio (fo. 114), on which more below. The narrative then jumps to 1520–1 and the lieutenancy of Thomas Howard, earl of Surrey. From this point onwards, Hussey's work appears to be an original composition and ends with a brief account of a victory won in 1553 at Carrick Bradagh, near Dundalk, Co. Louth, in which Hussey's foster-son, Richard, the sixth baron, played a part. An attempt was made by Hussey's copyist to extend his narrative beyond Hussey's lifetime, by mentioning the appointment of the earl of Sussex as lord lieutenant of Ireland in 1556, but the work abruptly ends here. Further down on the same page (fo. 120) was written: 'This much from the beginning of Cnocketwo [Knockdoe], that field, to this, was had in a book of Mr Watter Housse's of Dobbore beside Donsogle, written with his own hand; on whose soul God have mercy.' Then, on a new page, a different hand continues the narrative from 1556 onwards.

* * *

Although Hussey may have been an eye-witness to some of the events of the Lambert Simnel conspiracy, the bulk of his account is not an original one. His previous mention of Hall's chronicles should have set alarm bells ringing for previous historians who have quoted from the Book of Howth in their own works. Hall's chronicles were first published in London in 1548 and reprinted two years later. Copies undoubtedly reached Ireland soon afterwards. Hussey does not mention Hall as his source, but a simple comparison shows that his account is a précis of Hall's much longer one. This is perhaps apt for one who had been a 'summonister' or 'summaster' by trade.[25] This is apparent from the similar turns of phrase used in both accounts, some of which Hussey repeats almost word for word – for example, 'elected a scholar called Lambart Symenell, one of gentle nature and pregnant wit, to be the organ … of his feigned enterprise' – as well as the exact order in which the conspiracy's episodes were narrated. Even Hussey's unusual spelling of Lambert's name is the same as Hall's.

The Geraldines and medieval Ireland: the making of a myth (Dublin, 2016), pp 223–6. **24** A.F. Vossen (ed.), *Two bokes of the histories of Ireland compiled by Edmunde Campion Feloe of St John Baptistes College in Oxforde* (Nijmegan, 1963), p. 112. **25** 'The Summaster was the clerk of accounts in great households; also often a literary man, a précis-writer, who abridged or summarized books. Holinshed says, "If the historian be long he is accounted a trifler; if he be short he is taken for a summister".': *T.P.'s Weekly*, 23 March 1929, p. 673. The 'Holinshed' quote can be found in Richard Stanihurst's epistle to Sir Henry Sidney,

As in his account of the execution of Desmond's two sons, Hussey manages to interpolate some additional material of his own. Of the pretender, he states that his adherents in Ireland

> … called him King, then being in Chri[st]church; and for that the throng of people was such that he could not be seen, the child was borne in, and upon Great Darsey of Platan's neck, so that every man might see him.

This is an incident he repeats further down in his account:

> And there in Dublinge in Ireland they proclaimed this child King of England, being borne and sitting upon Darsey's shoulders to be seen of all men, for that Darsey was then the highest.[26]

William Darcy of Platten (*c.*1460–1540) was descended from Sir John Darcy of Knaith, justiciar of Ireland during Edward III's reign. After William's father John died on New Year's Day 1483, he went to London to complete his law studies. He was admitted to Lincoln's Inn on 10 May 1485 and was still there during Trinity term, when he was fined for some unknown misdemeanour. On 8 May 1486, he obtained livery of his father's lands in Rathwire and Kildalkey, Co. Meath, by English letters patent, before returning to Ireland later that same year. He next appeared at the Dublin 'coronation'. Darcy was therefore in England for the events before, during and after Richard III's troubled reign, which may have had something to do with his brief but prominent attachment to a Yorkist pretender. Nevertheless, on 29 July 1488, Darcy gave his homage and fealty to Henry VII before his visiting representative in Dublin, Sir Richard Edgecombe.

Darcy would have been well-known to Hussey. As the sheriff of Meath in 12, 13 and 16 Henry VII (1496–8, 1500–1), he would have presented his accounts in the Dublin exchequer twice a year.[27] He would also have been the recipient of Hussey's writs and summonses. Darcy was appointed receiver-general in 1501 and vice-treasurer of Ireland in 1505. After falling out with the ninth earl of Kildare, he was appointed under-treasurer of Ireland in 1523 during the deputyship of Kildare's rival, Piers Butler, earl of Ossory. He died in 1540, after retiring to a friary in Drogheda, a blind man.[28] Hussey would

for which, see *Holinshed's Chronicles of England, Scotland, and Ireland in six volumes* (London, 1808), vi, p. 273. **26** Brewer and Bullen (eds), *Cal. Carew MSS*, v, p. 188. **27** College of Arms MS Ph 15175, p. 315; *Sixth, seventh, eighth, ninth, and tenth reports from the commissioners … respecting the public records of Ireland* (London, 1819 & 1820), p. 538; John Ross Delafield, *Delafield: the family history* (New York, 1945), i, p. 379. **28** Steven G. Ellis, 'An English gentleman and his community: Sir William Darcy of Platten' in Vincent Carey and Ute Lotz-Heuman (eds), *Taking Sides? Colonial and confessional mentalités in early*

also have known that Darcy's first wife was the aunt of Nicholas St Lawrence, third baron of Howth, and the sister of Robert, the second baron, and William Howth of Stapolyn.[29] In later illustrations, Darcy is usually depicted as an unkempt giant dressed in Irish garb bearing the boy-king on his shoulders, but nothing could be further from the sartorial truth. At the beginning of Henry VIII's reign, Darcy was considered by his son-in-law as one of the few English gentlemen in Meath who had not 'gone native', continuing to 'werithe gowne and dublet' in the English manner.[30]

Hussey's second interpolation is the conduct of 'Sir Nicholas, Lord of Houth' who

> perceiving all this but a mad dance, sent over to the King, and advertised him of all these matters from the beginning to the ending, who was the doers and maintainers of the whole matters in Ireland and Flanders …

a statement he later repeats,

> … which doings, as is aforesaid, was certified the King by the Lord of Houth in Ireland.[31]

Nicholas was *not* the lord of Howth in 1487, for his father Robert was still alive. For some time, Robert had chosen to live in England with his second wife, Joan, also known as Jane Beaufort (d. 1518), one of the daughters of Edmund, duke of Somerset (d. 1455). He married Jane in or before 1478, shortly after the death of his first wife and Nicholas' mother, Alice, daughter and heiress of Nicholas White of Killester, Co. Dublin.[32] Kildare offended Robert when he gave the chancellorship of Ireland to his own brother, Thomas fitzGerald of Lackagh, despite Richard III's English letters patent granting this office to Howth.[33] Due to this snub, as well as his second marriage, Robert's allegiance was very much with Henry VII, his wife's first cousin, once removed.

Although not mentioned in any of the sources, Robert St Lawrence may have fought beside the Tudor monarch at the battle of Stoke Field on 16 June 1487. Exactly one month later, Robert made his rather terse will at Shelton, which seems to have been drafted in a hurry and witnessed by his wife's sister, Eleanor, the countess of Wiltshire and one Richard Brysall.[34] Unfortunately, the will does not state in which county Shelton lay, for there are several places in England with the same name, but there is one in Nottinghamshire only four

modern Ireland (Dublin, 2003), p. 30. **29** John Lodge and Mervyn Archdall, *The peerage of Ireland: or, A genealogical history of the present nobility of that kingdom* (Dublin, 1789), iii, p. 186. **30** Ellis, 'An English gentleman', p. 32. **31** Brewer and Bullen (eds), *Cal. Carew MSS*, v, p. 189. **32** Lodge and Archdall, *Peerage of Ireland*, iii, p. 187. **33** Steven G. Ellis, *Ireland in the age of the Tudors, 1447–1603: English expansion and the end of Gaelic rule* (London, 1998), p. 82. **34** TNA, PROB 11-8-152.

miles southeast of the Stoke battlefield. Robert was apparently still alive on 20 November 1487, when he received an extension of his previous licence to absent himself from Ireland for another year-and-a-half.[35] Nevertheless, Robert must have died soon afterwards, because his will was proved on 11 March 1488. His body was buried in the choir of Blackfriars church, near London's Ludgate, where he was commemorated with a brass memorial.[36] There seems to have been some tension between Robert St Lawrence and his son Nicholas because, after bequeathing his wife Jane a third part of all his lands – the full jointure agreed at the time of their marriage – along with the residue of his goods and chattels not already bequeathed, as well as making her the executrix of his will, Robert prayed that his son 'keep this my will and break it not upon my blessing and [i.e., or] else I give you my curse'. On Robert's death, his lands in Ireland would have been seized by the crown. It was not until 4 March 1490, when Nicholas was 24 years of age, that he was granted Irish letters patent to take livery of both his parents' lands.[37]

Nicholas was not the only person who kept Henry VII informed of events in Ireland. On hearing that a pretender had been crowned, Thomas Botiller, gentleman, travelled to England to inform the Tudor monarch in person. Thomas was encouraged to go there by his brother William, the rector of Kilberry in Co. Meath. Both men were subsequently proclaimed traitors by Kildare and attainted in a parliament held in the name of the pretender king. As a result, William's goods and chattels were seized and his manse or parsonage at Kilberry destroyed, even though he was an absentee from his living 'attending secular courts abroad'. It was not until Kildare had been replaced as lord deputy by Walter Fitzsimon, archbishop of Dublin, that the Botiller brothers petitioned the Irish parliament in 1493 for a pardon, a reversal of their attainder and a return of their property, which was granted.[38] As their surname suggests, the brothers were probably Lancastrian sympathizers and opponents of the Yorkist earl of Kildare. The advowson of Kilberry church was also in the gift of Edmund Botiller, lord of Dunboyne, the head of a cadet branch of the Ormond earls.[39] William Botiller was also probably a marked man: in 1471, while a clerk of the archbishop of Dublin, William publicly excommunicated Sir Roland FitzEustace, Lord Portlester, the

35 *CPR 1485–94*, p. 196; College of Arms MS Ph 15175, p. 302 (letters patent dated 1 March 1486 enrolled on Irish Exchequer Memoranda Roll 2 Hen. VII). 36 Henry Morley (ed.), *A svrvay of London, contayning the originall, antiquity, increase, moderne estate, and description of that citie, written in the Year 1598 by Iohn Stow Citizen of London* (London, 1890), p. 320. 37 College of Arms MS Ph 15175, p. 306 (Exch. Mem. Roll 6 & 7 Hen. VII, m. 13). 38 Philomena Connolly (ed.), *Statute rolls of the Irish parliament, Richard III–Henry VIII* (Dublin, 2002), pp 125–9; Mario Alberto Sughi (ed.), *Registrum Octaviani Alias Liber Niger. The register of Octavian de Palatio, archbishop of Armagh, 1478–1513*, 2 vols (Dublin, 1999), nos. 249, 260, 559. 39 College of Arms MS Ph 15175, p. 297 (Exch. Mem. Roll 1 Hen. VII, m. 15).

treasurer of Ireland and Kildare's father-in-law, for imprisoning William and taking his cattle and cows which 'so scandalized and defamed said Treasurer, in contempt of the King and to [the] damage of the said Treasurer'.[40]

If the Botiller brothers suffered because of their opposition to Kildare's pretender king, it begs the question as to why the same did not happen to Nicholas St Lawrence, especially given his father's close relations with the Tudor regime. It is probably because he openly supported Kildare's cause, either willingly or unwillingly, as did most of the other English magnates in the Irish parliament, both temporal and spiritual. 'Nicholas Sentlarens, lord of Houth' was later pardoned by English letters patent, which were conveyed to him on 21 July 1488, after he swore his oath of allegiance before Henry VII's representative in Dublin, Sir Richard Edgecombe.[41] Another factor may have been the rift between Nicholas and his father, as evinced in the latter's will. In 1487, Nicholas had reached or was on the very cusp of his majority, but Robert continued to hold Nicholas' mother's lands by the 'courtesy of England'.[42] Denial of his mother's substantial inheritance may have pushed a disgruntled Nicholas into the arms of Kildare. Thus, it appears that Nicholas was not so open in his devotion to the Tudor monarch in 1487 as we are led to believe by Hussey's comments, although the retention by the crown of all of Nicholas' lands until 1490, two years after Nicolas' father's death, suggests that Kildare may have felt the need to keep him on a tight leash.

Hussey's account then moves onto his third interpolation: the meeting at Greenwich, where several of the lords from Ireland attended upon Henry VII.[43] They initially conversed at length on Irish matters, resulting in Henry's quip that they would 'crown apes at length'. The visiting lords then took part in a procession in which they were paired with English counterparts. Howth was partnered with one who was very distressed, anxious to know which way the axe faced, which was customarily carried at the head of the king's procession, fearing that there would be some butchery done that day. When Howth asked the reason for his trepidation, he explained that both his father and grandfather had suffered from its effects. Hussey does not mention the name of the English lord in question. As far as I am aware, no one has yet identified him. Although Kingsford's 'Chronicles of London' contains a useful list of 'divers lords, knights and gentlemen … slain in the realm of England since … 1446' – a list which was drawn up in the early years of Henry VII's reign – no obvious candidate stands out apart from Edward, earl of Warwick.[44]

40 College of Arms MS Ph 15175, p. 233 (Exch. Mem. Roll 10 Edw. IV). **41** *CPR 1485–94*, p. 227; Walter Harris (ed.), 'The voyage of Sir Richard Edgecomb into Ireland, in the Year 1488' in *Hibernica: or, some antient pieces relating to Ireland* (Dublin, 1757), pp 36–7. **42** The custom known as the 'courtesy of England' permitted widowers to hold onto the lands held by their deceased wives, for the remainder of their own lives, to the temporary detriment of the deceased wife's heirs, regardless of whether they were the offspring of their marriage or not. **43** Brewer and Bullen (eds), *Cal. Carew MSS*, v, p. 190. **44** Charles

He was the son of George, duke of Clarence, executed for treason committed against his brother Edward IV (albeit drowned in a butt of malmsey), and the grandson of Richard, duke of York, whose head was displayed above one of York's city gates after being killed fighting against Henry VI. Indeed, one could also add his great-grandfather, Richard, earl of Cambridge, who was executed for treason by Henry V in 1415.

Warwick was also the person claimed to have been crowned as 'Edward VI' in Dublin in 1487. Since the commencement of Henry's reign, Warwick had been kept in the Tower of London and was rarely seen in public. His presence at Greenwich was probably a deliberate ploy because later that same day, when the lords from Ireland were attending the king's banquet, they were invited to drink wine served to them by a menial. A gentleman of the court then announced that it was served to them by their former protégé 'King Lambarte Symnell'. The Irish lords refused to accept it, telling the poor servant in effect to go to hell. Nevertheless, Howth did so in an act of bravado 'for the wine's sake and my own sake also'. Why he chose to break ranks with his fellow lords is not clear. These three aspects of the Greenwich meeting suggest that Henry VII orchestrated an astute piece of political theatre to convey a subtle message to his guests: to ensure their future loyalty to him, as well as obtaining confirmation perhaps of which person was the real earl of Warwick. They do not seem to have recognized the terrified lord processing with them but responded positively to the menial serving them wine.

No date is given by Hussey for these events, although the seventeenth-century antiquarian, Sir James Ware, ascribed them to 1489.[45] Ware's history of the reign of Henry VII was based on scrupulous research into governmental and ecclesiastical records then held in Ireland, many of which have since disappeared or been destroyed.[46] Normally, his statements can be relied upon, but not so in this case. Although 'The Herald's Memoir' states that Henry stayed at Greenwich only once in 1489, holding a banquet there on Christmas day, he mentions no other lords present from Ireland, apart from Thomas Butler, earl of Ormond, the queen's chamberlain, who, despite his Irish title, had long made England his home.[47] It is also unlikely that the earl of Kildare was present. He was then deputy lieutenant of Ireland and could not absent himself without appointing a deputy, of which there is no record. He also presided over a parliament held at Trim on 8 January 1490, which would have made his presence at Greenwich on Christmas Day nigh on impossible.[48]

Lethbridge Kingsford (ed.), *Chronicles of London* (Oxford, 1903), pp 276–9. **45** Sir James Ware, 'The annals of Ireland during the reign of King Henry the Seventh' in *The antiquities and history of Ireland, by the Right Honourable Sir James Ware, Kn.*, (Dublin, 1705), p. 15. **46** The evidence can be seen in his notes now stored in the British Library and the Bodleian Library, Oxford. **47** Emma Cavell (ed.), *The herald's memoir, 1486–1490: court ceremony, royal progress and rebellion* (Donnington, 2009), p. 182. **48** S.G. Ellis, 'Parliaments and great councils, 1483–99: addenda et corrigenda', *Analecta Hibernica*, 29

Although Henry called on Kildare to come to England on 28 July 1490, he made his excuses, backed up by a letter from the lords in the Irish parliament dated 4 June 1491.[49] At the end of the same year, 'Perkin Warbeck' made his first appearance in Ireland, arriving on board a Breton merchant's ship. He was first mistaken by the inhabitants of Cork for the 'earl of Warwick', crowned in Dublin in 1487. When he denied this on the gospels, he was asked whether he was Richard III's base-born son, John of Pontefract, which he again denied in a similar manner. He was then taken under the wing of John Atwater, former mayor of Cork, who persuaded him that he was Richard of Shrewsbury, the second son of Edward IV, thought to have been killed in the Tower of London by his uncle Richard III. After word had been sent of his new persona to the courts of France, Flanders and Scotland, Warbeck left Ireland in March 1492 and took residence at the court of Charles VIII, king of France. When Charles made peace with England at the end of 1492, Warbeck moved to the court of Margaret, dowager duchess of Burgundy, at Malines in Flanders. To boost the boy's credentials, it was later claimed that the fitzGerald earls of Desmond and Kildare supported him.[50]

Alarmed at the news of 'Richard's' appearance, Henry VII sent Sir James Ormond and Thomas Garth with a small army to suppress 'his enemies and rebels' in cos. Kilkenny and Tipperary.[51] Henry then decided to replace Kildare as the deputy lieutenant of Ireland in June 1492 with Walter Fitzsimons, archbishop of Dublin. Sir James was also appointed treasurer, in place of Roland FitzEustace, lord of Portlester, Kildare's father-in-law.[52] Matters came to a head in August 1492, when Sir James came to Dublin with an army of native Irish, probably his mother's people the O'Briens, and encamped at Thomascourt Wood.[53] The disturbances mentioned above then followed: Ormond's argument with Nicholas, lord Howth, at Killester, and William Howth's skirmish with Ormond's men at Kilmainham bridge on their way back to Thomascourt. It was then agreed that Kildare and Sir James should meet at St Patrick's cathedral to try and resolve matters peacefully. Following clashes with Ormond's men, the Dublin citizens decided to take matters into their own hands and rushed into the cathedral shooting their arrows, meaning to kill Sir James and his entourage. He took refuge in the chapterhouse, where Kildare eventually persuaded him to come out after assuring him that he would not be harmed. He achieved this by cleaving a hole in the chapterhouse door and placing his hand inside as a gesture of good faith

(1980), p. 107. **49** James Gairdner (ed.), *Letters and papers illustrative of the reigns of Richard III and Henry VII*, 2 vols (London, 1861–3), i, pp 377–9; ii, p. xxxvi. Ware erroneously assigns this letter to the year 1486 in his account of Henry VII's reign in Ireland. **50** Ian Arthurson, *The Perkin Warbeck conspiracy, 1491–1499* (Stroud, 1997), pp 42–4, 46–50. **51** *CPR 1485–94*, p. 367. **52** *CPR 1485–94*, p. 376. **53** Randolph Jones, 'Janico Markys, Dublin, and the coronation of "Edward VI" in 1487' in Seán Duffy (ed.), *Medieval Dublin XIV: Proceedings of the Friends of Medieval Dublin Symposium 2012* (traditionally said to be the origin of the phrase 'to chance one's arm'). Nevertheless, despite temporarily holding the advantage, Kildare had no option but to surrender the deputyship and retire to his own estates. The citizens of Dublin were later excommunicated for their sacrilege in the archbishop's cathedral and the mayor forced to walk barefoot through the city's streets once a year in an act of penance.[54]

Despite Kildare's show of loyalty, rumours continued to persist of his support for Perkin Warbeck. To exculpate himself, he sent messengers to the king, 'with letters and instructions such as I thought should have contented his mind'. To his bewilderment, he later learned that they had been thrown into prison on arrival. On 11 February 1493, Kildare wrote to Thomas Butler, earl of Ormond, the queen's chamberlain, begging him to use his influence with the king. Kildare was able to play a trump card, because Ormond's nephew, Sir James, was then claiming Thomas's Irish earldom for himself. In collusion with the archbishop of Dublin, Sir James was seeking to be legitimized by the Irish parliament and recognized as the heir of his father John, Thomas's elder brother and predecessor as earl.[55] Alarmed, Thomas pressed Kildare's 'urgent entreaty' for a pardon upon the king. This was granted in March and again in June 1493, conditional on Kildare presenting himself before the feast of All Saints (1 November). These pardons also included safe conducts for himself, his entourage of up to eighty persons, as well as his baggage. In addition, he was to send his eldest son beforehand.[56]

After clashes on Oxmantown Green and elsewhere in Dublin in July 1493 between Kildare's men and some of the citizens supporting the archbishop and Sir James, Kildare acknowledged a £1,000 bond to keep the peace, by adhering to various provisions agreed at a council meeting held at Trim on 12 September.[57] The archbishop of Dublin was no longer deputy lieutenant, having been replaced in this office by Robert Preston, Viscount Gormanston.[58] Departing Ireland in November 1493, Kildare presented himself to the king shortly afterwards, for on Twelfth Night 1494, two unnamed members of his retinue were knighted by Henry at a banquet held at Westminster.[59] On 10 March 1494, the king also ordered his treasurer in England to pay Kildare £5 a week, so that he could sustain himself and his retinue from 25 February 1494 onwards. As Kildare later received two payments, one for £40 and another for £20, he appears to have stayed with the king twelve weeks, up until 19 May 1494.[60] During this period, Henry was at Greenwich only twice, 6 and 30

(Dublin, 2015), pp 203–4. **54** Holinshed, *Chronicles*, pp 274–5. **55** Gairdner (ed.), *Letters and papers Rich. III & Hen. VII*, ii, pp 55–6; David B. Quinn (ed.), 'Appendix. Ormond papers, 1480–1535, in the Public Record Office, London, and the British Museum' in Edmund Curtis (ed.), *Calendar of Ormond deeds*, iv, pp 318–19. **56** *CPR 1485–94*, pp 423, 425, 429. **57** Jones, 'Janico Markys', pp 203–4. **58** David B. Quinn, 'The bills and statutes of the Irish parliaments of Henry VII and Henry VIII', *Analecta Hibernica*, 10 (1941), 88–91. **59** Kingsford (ed.), *Chronicles of London*, p. 200. **60** David B. Quinn,

April, between which dates he travelled into Kent, visiting Canterbury and Dover. He is next heard of at Sheen on 1 June. Therefore, the Greenwich banquet mentioned by Hussey probably took place in early May 1494.[61]

The other Irish lords mentioned by Hussey as being present were the earl of 'Wormone' (i.e., Ormond); William Barry lord of Buttevant; Maurice Roche lord of Fermoy; Thomas Birmingham lord of Athenry; James Courcy lord of Kinsale; Robert Preston, Viscount Gormanston; Richard Nugent lord of Delvin; Christopher Fleming lord of Slane; Edmund Plunket lord of Killeen; Nicholas St Lawrence lord of Howth; Christopher Barnwell lord of Trimleston and John Plunket lord of Dunsany. It is interesting that Hussey does not mention the archbishop of Dublin, whereas Ware informs us that Fitzsimons went to England in October 1493 'where he fully informs (sic) the King of the State affairs of Ireland'. Neither does he mention Sir James Ormond, who 'hast[en]ed into England; and in presence of the Kings Council he laid many crimes to the Earl [of Kildare]'s charge'.[62] Sir James may have still been there in March 1494, for William Preston was then acting as his deputy in Ireland as treasurer.[63] Indeed, Sir James may have been the earl of 'Wormone' referred to in the procession above, but in this instance Thomas, the queen's chamberlain, may have been meant. On balance, it seems that Henry VII called over both factions in Ireland but treated with them separately – the anti-Geraldine party first, followed by the Geraldines later.

Apart from Kildare, no evidence has been found to confirm the presence of any of the other lords mentioned by Hussey. As deputy lieutenant, Gormanston attested letters patent in Ireland on 28 November 1493, 20 February, 10 and 12 March, 4 July and 26 September 1494. Although not conclusive, the gap in attesting activity between March and July suggests that Gormanston may have been at Greenwich in early May, although there is no evidence of any deputy being appointed in Ireland to cover his absence in England.[64] A safe conduct was issued to William lord Barry in 6 Henry VII (1490/1), to go to England with a retinue of forty men.[65] The inclusion of lords from the isolated south-eastern counties – Barry, Roche and Courcy – suggests that they were there as the representatives of Maurice 'Bacach' fitzGerald, ninth earl of Desmond. Courcy and Roche co-signed a letter Desmond sent to the king in July 1491 supporting Kildare's decision not to come to England but to remain in Ireland instead.[66] Desmond was an active supporter of Perkin

'Guide to English financial records for Irish history 1461–1558, with illustrative extracts, 1461–1509', *Analecta Hibernica*, 10 (1941), pp 37, 59. **61** Gladys Temperley, *Henry VII* (London, 1917), p. 414; Samuel Bentley (ed.), *Excerpta historica; or, Illustrations of English history* (London, 1831), pp 97-8. **62** Ware, 'Annals', pp 25–6. **63** BL Add MS 4793, fo. 151r. **64** College of Arms MS Ph 15175, p. 310; BL Add MS 4793, fols. 150v, 151r; NAI Ferguson iii, fos. 335, 350. Ellis asserts that Gormanston's son William acted as his deputy between the first two dates, but I have not been able to identify his source: see Ellis, *Reform and revival*, p. 218. **65** Brewer and Bullen (eds), *Cal. Carew MSS*, v, p. 461. **66** Gairdner

Warbeck during his presence in Ireland for the winter of 1491–2, for which he and his brother Thomas received pardons from Henry dated 10 April 1493.[67] Desmond was probably summoned to attend the king in England when Kildare went at the end of the year, but he refused to travel, swearing an oath of allegiance instead on 18 March 1494 at Youghal, before 'Maurice Roche of Cork esquire', Richard Salkeld, Henry's groom of the chamber, and others.[68] Salkeld was hastily sent to Ireland by the king in January 1494, with 'our especial and hasty messages', being paid 20 marks in advance towards his expenses.[69] Barry, Roche and Courcy probably returned to England with him. On 14 May 1494 Kildare signed an indenture with the king at Westminster, in which he promised to make Desmond keep his oath and send him Desmond's son and heir whenever he was called upon to do so.[70] This was to no avail, because Desmond rebelled again before the ink on the document recording his oath of allegiance was dry. When Perkin Warbeck reappeared in Ireland in the summer of 1495, Desmond assisted him in a major attack upon the loyal town of Waterford.[71] Barry, Courcy and Roche joined him in his rebellion against the Tudor monarch, for which they were later pardoned.[72]

Hussey also mentions that the Lord Howth was rewarded with the apparel that the king wore on the day of the Greenwich banquet, as well as £300 in gold, to compensate him for the expenses incurred during his prolonged stay in England. Although a trawl made by Quinn through the English exchequer records of the period revealed the abovementioned payments of £40 and £20 to Kildare, there is no mention whatsoever of Nicholas. The sum Hussey quotes also seems to be rather excessive for one of Howth's rank. This also seems to be a tall tale which probably grew in the telling in the hall of Howth castle.

* * *

In conclusion, what can we say about Hussey's account of the Lambert Simnel conspiracy and its aftermath? Hussey may have been present at the coronation in Dublin of 'Edward VI' but his account of the conspiracy is not an original one but rather is culled from a longer version printed in Hall's chronicles. This indicates that Hussey could not have written it before 1548, when the first edition of Hall's work was published in London. Nevertheless, Hussey took the opportunity to add some local colour by interpolating three episodes which

(ed.), *Letters and papers Rich. III & Henry VII*, i, pp 381–2. **67** *CPR 1485–94*, p. 423. **68** Agnes Conway, *Henry VII's relations with Scotland and Ireland, 1485–1498* (Cambridge, 1932), pp 151–3. **69** Quinn, 'English financial records', pp 58–9. **70** Conway, *Relations*, pp 153–5. **71** Brewer and Bullen (eds), *Cal. Carew MSS*, v, p. 472. **72** Arthurson, *Perkin Warbeck*, p. 105.

he may have witnessed himself, or was subsequently informed about by his patrons, members of the St Lawrence family.

First, the mention of William Darcy carrying the boy-king through the streets of Dublin is curious. It is an episode that clearly captured the writer's imagination, but the reason why Darcy was singled out, when other sources state that 'tall men', including the mayor of Dublin, carried the boy-king in the processions between Christ Church and Dublin Castle, is not stated. Nevertheless, there is little reason to doubt this as a genuine occurrence, for Hussey would have known the man personally, both through his exchequer work and his service with the St Lawrence family, of which Darcy was a member.

Second, Hussey's claim that Nicholas St Lawrence was loyal to the Tudor monarch in 1487, by keeping him informed of events in Ireland, does not ring true. His father's will, written in England within weeks of the Dublin coronation and only a short distance from the Stoke battlefield, suggests there was a major rift between the two men, not only in politics, but also over Nicholas' inheritance of his mother's lands, which his father retained after her death.

And third and finally, Kildare's meeting with King Henry in Greenwich can be placed in early May 1494. Although Lambert Simnel is the underlying theme in Hussey's account, he overlooks the meeting's real purpose, which was to head off any future trouble in Ireland due to the appearance of a new pretender, Perkin Warbeck, who had adopted the persona of Richard of Shrewsbury, duke of York, the second son of Edward IV. Henry achieved this by an astute piece of political theatre, the full meaning of which seems to have gone over Hussey's head. Henry's jocular comment about the Irish lords 'crowning apes at length' was graphically reinforced by presenting both the real and fake earls of Warwick, one of whom had been crowned king in Dublin six years previously. After warning them of the fate of false princes, as well as his inability to reconcile the two opposing factions in Ireland, it comes as no surprise that Henry decided to appoint his own English-born deputy, Sir Edward Poynings, in whose company Kildare returned to Ireland later that year. What happened next is another story, which Hussey failed to record in his remarkable history for some inexplicable reason.

APPENDIX 1[73]

Will of Robert, second baron of Howth (d. 1488)

In Dei Nomine Amen.

I Robert Saint Lawrence Lord of Howth whole of mind blessed be Almighty God make and ordain this my present testament in the parish of Shelton in the

73 Thanks to Heather Falvey of the Richard III Society's Milles Wills Project for her comments on my transcript of the original will, rendered here with modern spellings.

presence of my Lady Wiltshire [...] and Richard Brynsall the 16th day of July the second year of the reign of King Henry VII in the form ensuing.

First, I bequeath my soul to almighty God my redeemer and saviour and to our Lady Saint Mary and all Saints and my body to be buried in the church of the Friar Preachers before Ludgate in London.

Also, I will my wife Dame Jane Beaufort have after my decease the third part of my lands and also all the jointure that I have made to her.

And the residue of all my goods and chattels I have not bequeathed the which I have in Ireland and England I give and bequeath to the foresaid Dame Jane my wife and she thereof to dispose for my soul after her discretion.

Which foresaid Dame Jane my wife I make and ordain executrix of this my present testament and I pray you my son that you keep this my will and break it not upon my blessing. And else I give you my curse.

Given the day and year above said.

(*Source*, TNA, PROB 11-8-152)

APPENDIX 2

Extract taken from the Irish Exchequer Memoranda Roll, 6, 7 Henry VII, m. 13

Memorandum Nicholas de St Laurence gentleman son and heir of Robert de St Laurence knight late lord of Houth deceased produced letters patent and sought them to be enrolled: –

Henry etc., whereas Nicholas de St Laurence gentleman son and heir of Robert de St Laurence knight late lord of Houth deceased petitioned that said Robert was seized in fee of the manor of Houth with all messuages etc., courts, wrecks etc., as also in Stapolyn, Dublin and Clondalkin, Grenoke, Cashel, Donaghmore near Navan, Kells and Balskaddan, Ballibragan, Drogheda, a chief rent out of Sutton and Correston, etc. held of the king *in capite* rendering for Houth 40s. when scutage occurs; that all same came to the king's hands *rone prime seisine*; also that the said Nicholas as son and heir of Alice White deceased daughter and heiress of Nicholas White of Killester Co. Dublin esquire deceased which Alicia died seized of different manors etc., in Kilbarrok, Killester, Skyfabble, Cowloke etc., etc., and held said manor of Kilbarrock of Edward IV by service of two pairs of gloves all which said Alicia's estate said Robert held after her death *in feodo per legem Curtesie Angl*; said Nicholas is now aged 24 as by inspection *corporis sui nobis constat* and prays for possession of all same: the king therefore now grants same 4 March 5th year [Henry VII, i.e., 1490].

(*Source*: College of Arms MS, Ph 15175, pp 306–7)

County Dublin Archaeology GIS: a research resource for medieval Dublin

RUTH JOHNSON

INTRODUCTION

The County Dublin Archaeology Geographical Information System (GIS) hosted at www.heritagemaps.ie provides an accessible web-based archaeological resource.[1] This GIS is a useful resource of relevance to the Friends of Medieval Dublin, the archaeological profession, decision-makers, scholars and the wider public. It contains previously hard to access unpublished archaeological 'grey literature' and information generated through the 3267 archaeological investigations conducted under licence in Co. Dublin prior to and including the year 2012. The GIS resource provides access to copies of all the available archaeological reports for diving, excavation, and geophysical survey to 2012. Along with metadata, it includes copies of the National Museum of Ireland's topographical files for the county, links to the *Excavations* bulletin summaries at www.excavations.ie, and a number of historic and synthetic maps provided by the Royal Irish Academy's Irish Historic Towns Atlas.

BACKGROUND

In 2001, on succeeding Dáire O'Rourke as Dublin City Council's Archaeologist, she outlined to me in a handover conversation an objective to map archaeological information from the investigations carried out in the city to enable research, analysis and better decision-making. In particular, she wished to plot the levels of the archaeological horizons encountered during site investigations, enabling the creation of a 3D contour map of archaeological horizons in Dublin. She asked me to continue logging these archaeological levels from the reports submitted. The logic in synthesizing the archaeological information into a searchable map was clear and I agreed to continue the work.

Our handover coincided with the development of the first local Heritage Plan for Dublin City 2002–6, which was coordinated by the then Heritage

1 This paper is presented on behalf of the project partners and consultant team with the aim of reaching a wide audience of interested public. I am especially grateful to Dublin City Council Heritage Officer Charles Duggan, Siobhan Deery of Courtney Deery Ltd, Rob McLoughlin of Compass Informatics, and archaeologist Padraig Clancy for supporting this

Officer, Donncha Ó Dúlaing. The archaeological working group that informed the new plan included a number of Friends of Medieval Dublin, namely archaeologists Dáire O'Rourke, Linzi Simpson, myself and historians Howard Clarke and Seán Duffy. At this time, GIS in cultural heritage was still relatively new, but the working group, which comprised archaeologists, historians, architectural historians and planners, saw the merit in adopting new technology to create an accessible synthesis of archaeological data for Dublin.

The primary objective agreed by the group for delivery under the heritage plan was 'To compile a systematic, comprehensive and accessible body of relevant information relating to the archaeology of Dublin city'.[2] The targets were to:

a. Investigate existing GIS models relating to archaeology
b. Identify and compile existing information
c. Standardize information in archaeological reports.

And the actions identified were as follows:

a. Set up a group and produce a report identifying sources and current use of GIS information nationally and internationally
b. Compile a list of relevant information, its location, format and accessibility
c. Produce guidance booklet and checklist form: compile a handbook (Dublin-specific) on archaeological reports, content and presentation.

Several important actions that aligned with this objective were delivered under the Heritage Plan. These include (under target b.) the Dublin City Industrial Heritage Survey (DCIHR),[3] and the creation of a dedicated Archaeological Archive in Dublin City Library and Archives at Pearse Street.[4] A guidance book of 'Sources for Archaeologists' working in Dublin city was published under action c. of the Heritage Plan. This provided a summary of the cartographic sources, publications and primary and secondary archives and material available to the archaeological researcher.[5]

article. 2 *Dublin City Heritage Plan 2002–6*, Dublin City Council, 2002. 3 The Dublin City Industrial Heritage Record (DCIHR) was undertaken as an action of the Dublin City Heritage Plan 2002–6 on a phased basis between 2004 and 2009 by consultants Mary McMahon (Archaeologist) and Carrig Conservation. The DCIHR consists of a database containing the information gathered in both the desk-based inventory and the field survey. It consists of digital and hardcopy mapping annotated with each site's unique reference number, spatial extent and survival status. For each of the fieldwork areas the DCIHR contains an historical overview of industrial development, together with a summary of the fieldwork referring to site types found, rate of survival and condition. Of a total of 1218 sites surveyed, 514 sites were found to have some degree of surviving remains, indicating a survival rate of 42% across the entire city area. 4 *Dublin City archaeological archive guidelines*, Dublin City Council (Dublin, 2008). 5 *Dublin City: sources for archaeologists*, ed. Judith Carroll, Dublin City Council (Dublin, 2003).

The aim to investigate existing GIS models relating to archaeology was not progressed as a project under the 2002–6 Heritage Plan. Nevertheless, it remained a goal of the Dublin City Council archaeology business plan and the archaeology team continued to log data, explore potential applications, and analyse critically the information in archaeological reports for future GIS.

In the course of the in-house analysis – work supplemented by many volunteers, Job-Bridge interns and several administrative staff – a range of issues was scoped out. For instance, archaeological reports (particularly the older ones) were not standardized in presenting information, and so we had to hunt through hardcopy reports for it. The use of period terminology was not agreed and standardized (one person's Early Christian is another person's Early Medieval) and so dates had to be reconsidered before they could be entered into a database. This often meant rereading the report in full to be certain about the dating and sometimes speaking to the practitioner to clarify. Maps were at varying scales and quality, often without red-line boundaries showing the subject site, though some even had accurately mapped trench locations. Site addresses did not always conform to the modern Ordnance Survey street maps or to the planning application address. Site levels were frequently expressed as BPGL (Below Present Ground Level) but there was often no record of the Ordnance Datum (OD) for the ground level from which to extrapolate relative depths of material. In the older reports, it was not always clear which OD was used, i.e., the Poolbeg sea level or that of Malin Head (the latter was adopted as the national datum in 1970 and is 2.7 metres above Poolbeg). The Council's records furthermore related only to those sites that were investigated as a planning requirement and this left a gap in the dataset (e.g., where research excavations or pre-planning work had taken place).

It became clear that the collation of archaeological data and presentation in a GIS must be undertaken with the consensus and support of the statutory authorities and with that of the licensees who generated the information, whilst issues around copyright and reproduction would need to be investigated. It was clear that such a complex project would necessitate a multi-agency approach, with a steering group of key stakeholders, extensive consultation with the archaeological profession and the appointment of a consultant team with both archaeological and GIS capabilities. In short, the Heritage Plan was the perfect vehicle for its delivery.

Fast forward to 2012, at which time the Dublin City Heritage Plan review took place, coordinated by the Heritage Officer, Charles Duggan. The plan and the 40 or so archaeological projects delivered by Dublin City Council and partners through Heritage Plan funding from 2002 to 2012 were subject to a review by a team of Dublin City Council archaeologists (Ruth Johnson, Stephen Hickey and Damien Maguire), Charles Duggan and others, including

12.1 Snapshot from the Heritage Map Viewer showing Aungier Street/Ship Street area overlaid on John Rocque's map of Dublin, 1756. When viewed online, in full colour format, excavation licences are immediately visible as stars and topographical files as dots.

planners and architects. An external 'world café'-style consultation process, combined with the Dublin City Council review, confirmed that Archaeological Objective 1 of the 2002 plan was still relevant and of primary importance. Furthermore, in the ensuing ten years, GIS technology had become a more effective and economic method of presenting and accessing cultural heritage data and there had been a shift towards open data in the digital humanities.

At the same time a team from Dublin City Council was looking anew at the Aungier Street area to better understand and manage the historic street, with its complex layers of archaeological and built fabric. The area bounding Aungier Street had long been recognized as being of high archaeological potential, posing unanswered research questions about the early medieval ecclesiastical site of Dubhlinn, the location of the Viking *longphort*, the nature and extent of early medieval and medieval ecclesiastical foundations and the development of a high-status suburb in the late seventeenth century. Discovery of early fabric in buildings such as 9 and 9A Aungier Street coupled with the recognition of early building morphologies by the then Conservation Officer, Nicola Matthews, and others, led to an interest in the area which had suffered decades of dereliction and was now facing considerable development pressure.

So, in 2012 it fell to me to search and map the sixty or so archaeological investigations that had been carried out in this area via a street-by-street search of the online excavations summaries for Dublin.[6] This simplest of mapping tasks – the bread and butter of an archaeological desktop study for planning and Environmental Impact Statement purposes – took me nearly a week to do and necessitated drawing a map of the locations (fig. 12.1). A similar search and reference map can be generated in a matter of minutes using GIS. The time and effort needed to retrieve each of the archaeological reports in full and visiting the topographical files was exponential.

The Aungier Street project thus presented an excellent business case for demonstrating to the planning department the need to develop a GIS for the city's archaeological heritage. Following the Heritage Plan review the archaeology GIS was adopted as a priority project by Dublin City Council. The business case identified project partners and provided a detailed model for phased delivery of a comprehensive dataset utilizing the excavation summaries in www.excavations.ie. The application for funding to the Heritage Council was successful and funding and staff resources came ultimately from the following partners: the Heritage Council, Dublin City Council, Dún Laoghaire Rathdown County Council, Fingal County Council, South Dublin County Council, the National Monuments Service, and the National Museum of Ireland.

The project's delivery was coordinated by Charles Duggan with a steering group comprising subject-matter experts from Dublin City Council, the Heritage Council, the National Monuments Service, the National Museum of Ireland, the publishers Wordwell, the Institute of Archaeologists of Ireland, and the Discovery Programme. The project consultants were Courtney Deery Ltd with Compass Informatics. The consultant project archaeologist's role was to carry out the retrieval from all available sources, recording and review of the

6 See Ruth Johnson, 'Aungier Street's archaeological heritage' and 'Appendix B' in *Aungier Street: revitalising an historic neighbourhood*, Dublin City Council (Dublin, 2013).

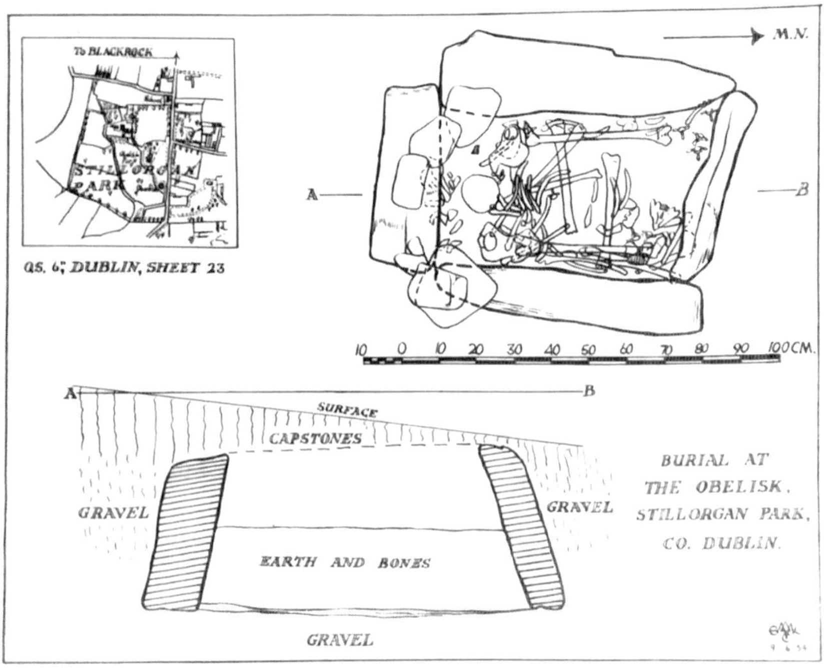

12.2 Sample of content available in National Museum of Ireland topographical file (Stillorgan, Co. Dublin).

licensed archaeological reports. The GIS developer was responsible for the geo-referencing of the reports into the GIS system and the redaction of sensitive information from the reports.

The creation of the County Dublin Archaeology GIS was relatively quick, though not especially easy (the many complexities are logged in the consultant reports). It took place over four years starting in 2012 with a pilot based on the Dublin City historic core. With the assistance of the National Monuments Service, the consultant-team was able to source, copy and map (as a point) all the licensed archaeology reports generated down to and including 2007. At the same time, as a separate exercise the National Museum and Dublin City Council's archaeology team together explored the feasibility of including the National Museum's topographical files in the dataset (fig. 12.2). In Phase 2 (2013) all the available licence reports from the area of Dublin city between the two canals were located and the topographical files for the area were included. In 2014, the project partners and steering group expanded to include all the local authorities in Co. Dublin. In 2015, the licence reports from Dublin city and county (generated down to 2012) and the remaining topographical files for the area were added.[7] After looking for a suitable platform for hosting the GIS from the very outset, the ideal home for it was found on the Heritage Council's Heritage Map Viewer at www.heritagemaps.ie.

On accessing the GIS, one is presented with a layer list under headings with subsets that can be clicked on and off (figs 12.3–7). As of August 2018 the layers in it comprise licensed excavations (National Monuments Service licence excavation sites, dive surveys, geophysical surveys); National Museum of Ireland topographical files; contextual information (Dublin Medieval Core, INSTAR Areas, Dublin City Zone of Archaeological Potential, Dublin city graveyards, Fingal graveyards, Dublin city canals); protected sites (directives, underwater sites); administrative boundaries (e.g., local authority areas); and historical mapping (RIA Medieval Dublin map *c*.840 to *c*.1540, Dublin growth map *c*.1610, Rocque's map of Dublin, *c*.1756).

The topographical files in the National Museum of Ireland relate to approximately sixty years of Museum acquisitions. These are arranged alphabetically by county, and subdivided by townland or by street. Although the topographical files are comprehensive for the period between 1930 and 1990, they do not refer to artefacts acquired by the Museum before or after this time. In total, 923 topographical files exist for Co. Dublin, 716 of which are in Dublin City Council's functional area, 61 in Dún Laoghaire Rathdown, 104 in Fingal and 41 in South Dublin. For the purposes of the GIS, all 923 paper files for Dublin city and county were scanned, reviewed for sensitivity issues (e.g., names and addresses) and geo-referenced onto the GIS systems initially by Dublin City Council archaeology interns as a pilot project and later by the consultants, who were able to develop and apply more effective tools and software based on the pilot study. The inclusion of these files in the project provides a significant and accessible digital archaeological resource.

GAPS AND OPPORTUNITIES

The County Dublin Archaeological GIS has now been tried and tested especially for the city area and it is a tool used daily in Dublin City Council for planning and research, and by professional consultant archaeologists working in the Dublin area. Three years after going live the GIS is now in need of a review, corrections, updates, additions and improvements. Most importantly, this would involve the addition of the licensed reports generated from 2013 onwards. To achieve this at local level would require an action of the relevant Heritage Plan and the commitment of essential staff resources by the National Monuments Service.

7 Unpublished reports by Courtney Deery Ltd and Compass Informatics.

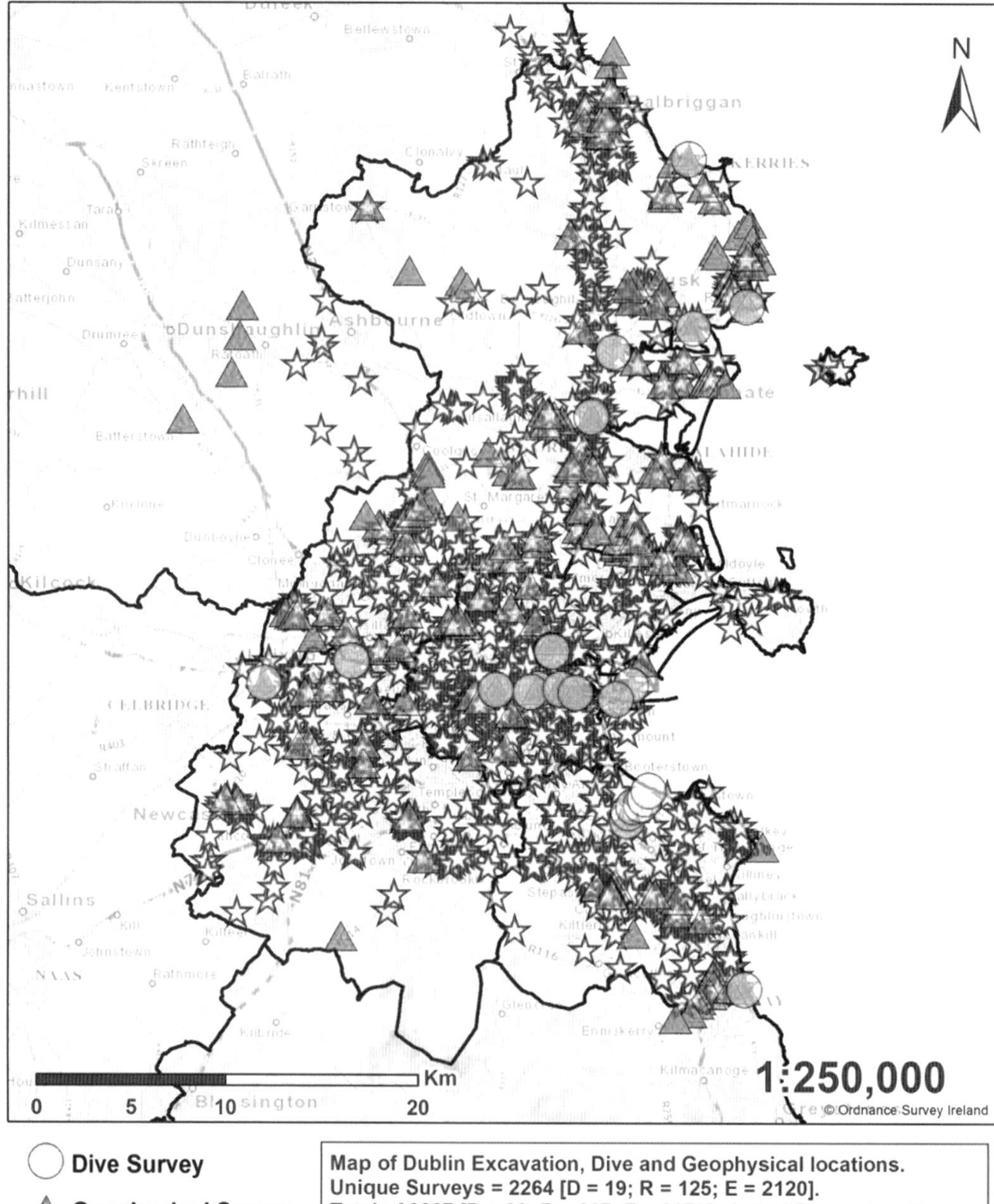

12.3 Excavations, dives, and geophysical surveys for Co. Dublin (these are of course colour-coded and readily distinguishable in the online version).

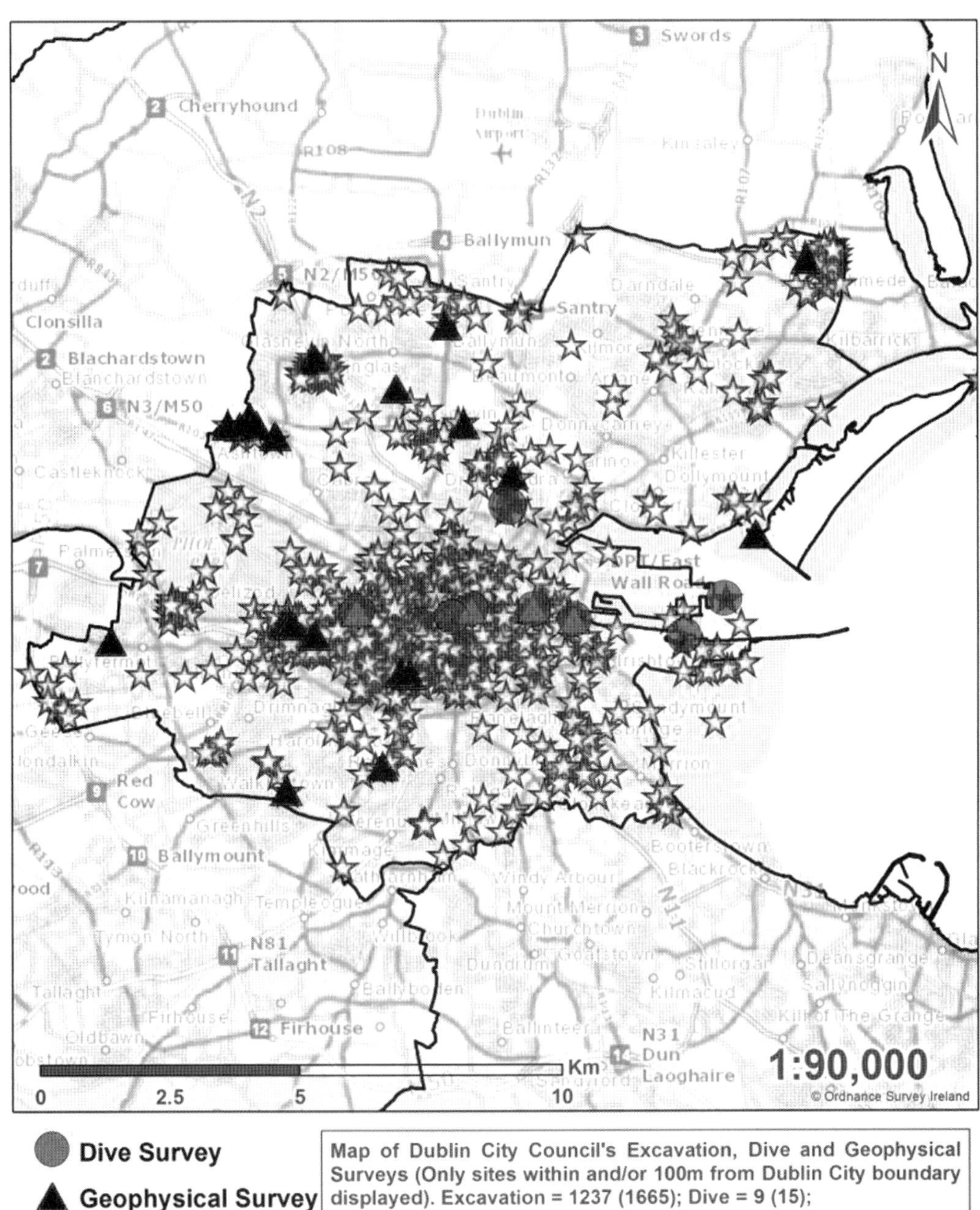
Swords
Cherryhound
R108
N2
Ballymun
N2/M50
Santry
Clonsilla
Blachardstown
N3/M50
Killester
Wall Road
Red Cow
Ballymount
N81
Tallaght
Firhouse
N31
Dun Laoghaire
1:90,000
© Ordnance Survey Ireland
0 2.5 5 10 Km
N
Dive Survey
Geophysical Survey
Excavation Survey
Map of Dublin City Council's Excavation, Dive and Geophysical Surveys (Only sites within and/or 100m from Dublin City boundary displayed). Excavation = 1237 (1665); Dive = 9 (15); Geophysical = 20 (27). Data created by Compass Informatics in conjunction with Courtney Deery Ltd.

12.4 Excavation sites within the Dublin City Council area

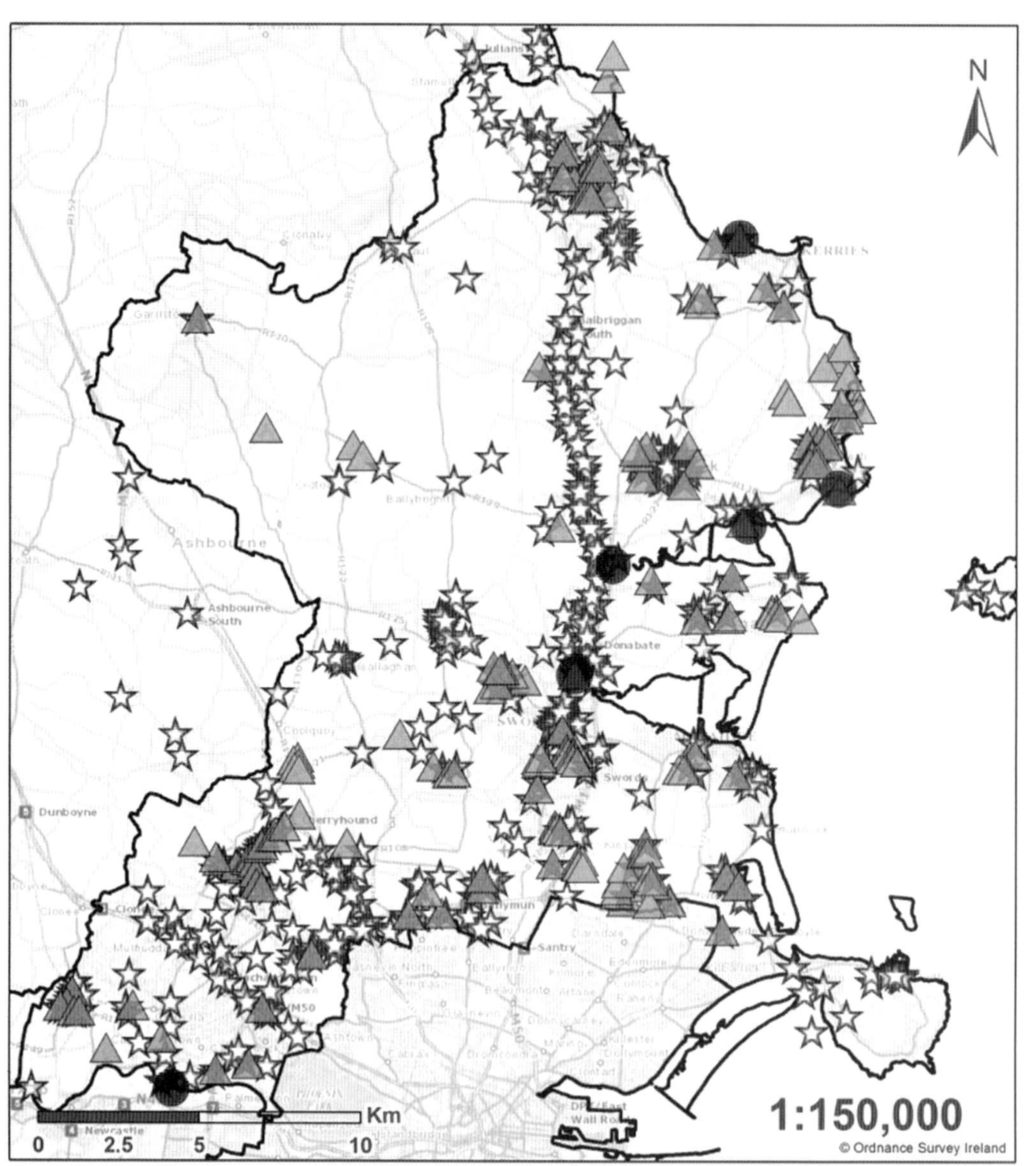

● **Dive Survey**
▲ **Geophysical Survey**
☆ **Excavation Survey**

Map of Fingal County Council's Excavation, Dive and Geophysical Surveys (Additional coastal and Meath sites also displayed). Excavations = 408 (630); Dive = 7 (7); Geophysical = 78 (186). Data created by Compass Informatics in conjunction with Courtney Deery Ltd.

12.5 Excavation sites within the area of Fingal County Council

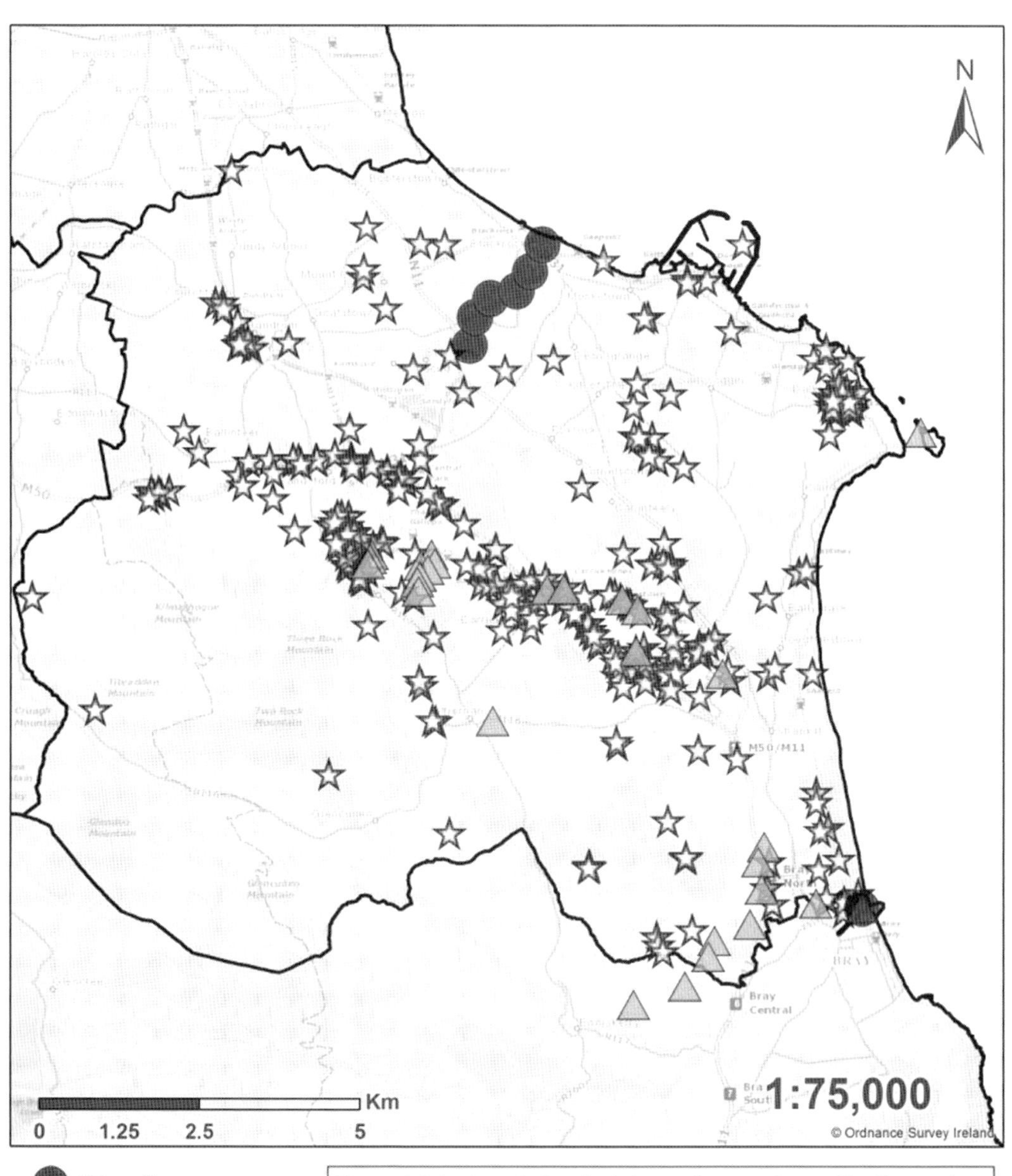

12.6 Excavation sites within the area of Dún Laoghaire Rathdown County Council

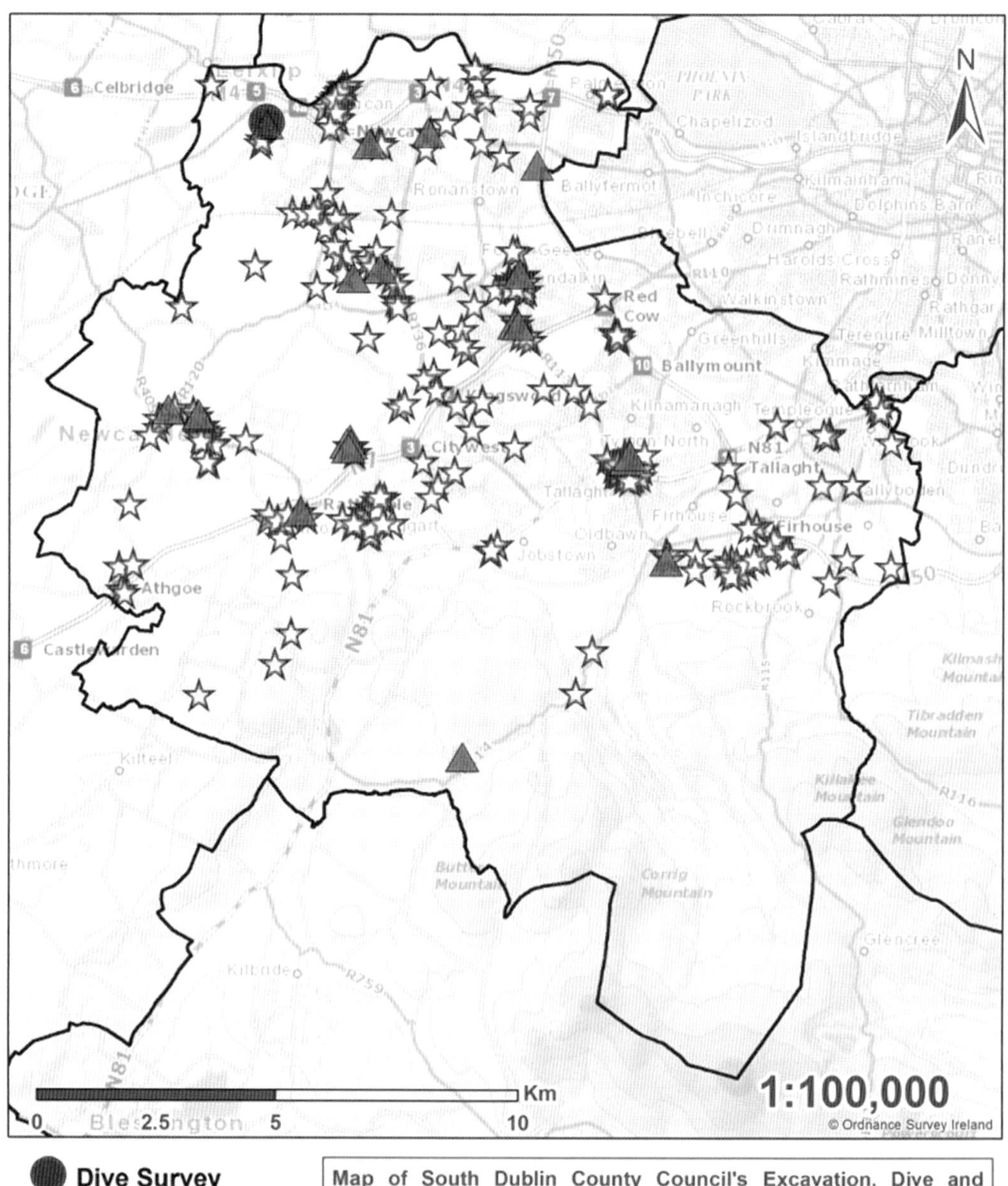

Dive Survey
Geophysical Survey
Excavation Survey

Map of South Dublin County Council's Excavation, Dive and Geophysical Surveys (Only sites within and 100m from South Dublin boundary displayed). Excavations = 220 (291); Dive = 1 (1); Geophysical = 15 (22). Data created by Compass Informatics in conjunction with Courtney Deery Ltd.

12.7 Excavation sites within the area of South Dublin County Council

Users will inevitably find that there are some gaps in the web map, the most obvious of which is around Wood Quay, where the National Museum of Ireland conducted a campaign of ten rescue excavations between 1962 and 1981. Although there are numerous publications for these sites, the stratigraphic reports do not exist.[8] Other gaps include the complex State-run excavations at Dublin Castle (the subject of ongoing post-excavation work by the licensees) and a number of commercial sites where the developer funding for post-excavation work was lost to the recent recession. I am hopeful that any future phase of the GIS will include the excavation summaries for all unreported excavations. Like all data sets, there are also errors and Dublin City Council archaeology team continues to log any errors noted in the current database when using it for planning purposes.

For research and analytical use, the ability to search and interrogate data is of paramount importance. Most archaeological data today is 'born digital', and any reports added to the GIS in the future could be uploaded in a fully searchable format rather than as static scans. The future addition of extant complementary datasets, such as the Industrial Heritage Record (McMahon and Carrig Ltd.) and the Archaeology of 1916 survey data will add significant value to the GIS and Heritage Maps viewer in 2019.

It is important to note that the County Dublin Archaeology GIS on the Heritage Map Viewer is not an online archive. At present there is no long-term infrastructure for digital archives in Ireland although there has been a move in this direction with the establishment of the Digital Repository of Ireland (DRI). Inclusion of the GIS data into the DRI when each report is assigned unique Digital Object Identifiers would be an important step in terms of archiving and referencing digital records in publications. The GIS could be scaled-up for nationwide coverage, and a toolkit for project development was devised by the consultant team and included in the last phase of work. This approach would enable a standardized approach for implementing the project on a county-by-county basis, to form a seamless single national archaeology GIS.

In conclusion, it is hoped that this paper will encourage anyone with an interest in medieval Dublin, whether professional or otherwise, to experiment with and exploit the research possibilities afforded by the County Dublin Archaeology GIS and the overall Heritage Map Viewer. I hope this paper demonstrates how people and organizations with their respective data, skill sets, roles and responsibilities can work together towards a common aim over a protracted period to create a resource that is greater than the sum of its parts. Finally, I hope that I have demonstrated the value of continuing to add

8 I.W. Doyle, David Jennings, Jackie MacDermott, with Dana Challinor and George Lambrick (eds), *Unpublished excavations in the Republic of Ireland, 1930–1997*, Oxford Archaeological Unit for the Heritage Council of Ireland (Kilkenny, 2002).

baseline data to the GIS, of adding new layers and of expanding it into a nationwide project. This could be done either on a county-by-county basis through local heritage plans or as a central government scheme. Access to data is paramount. A national archaeological GIS would unlock the potential of decades of archaeological investigation results and enable it to be utilized in infinite new ways by different audiences.